2021

RURAL REVITALIZATION

世界旅游联盟

旅游助力乡村振兴案例

《2021世界旅游联盟—旅游助力乡村振兴案例》编写组　编

旅游让世界和生活更美好

BETTER TOURISM, BETTER LIFE, BETTER WORLD

中国旅游出版社

世界旅游联盟

前言

世界旅游联盟自成立以来，以“旅游让世界和生活更美好”为宗旨，以“旅游促进和平、旅游促进发展、旅游促进减贫”为使命。2018—2020 年，世界旅游联盟连续三年联合世界银行和中国国际扶贫中心共同发布《世界旅游联盟旅游减贫案例》，并以此为蓝本，拍摄了两季共 8 集旅游减贫案例微纪录《旅游让世界和生活更美好》，获得了业内和社会的广泛关注和高度评价。同时，世界旅游联盟也在旅游减贫理论研究、经验宣传等方面开展了一系列实践活动和国际交流活动，向国际社会展示了旅游减贫事业的重要经验和巨大成就。

2021 年是中国巩固拓展脱贫攻坚成果同乡村振兴有效衔接的起步之年，值此之际，世界旅游联盟联合世界银行和中国国际扶贫中心开启旅游助力乡村振兴新篇章，共同发布《2021 世界旅游联盟——旅游助力乡村振兴案例》。通过世界旅游联盟、文化和旅游部、国家乡村振兴局、各省级文化和旅游部门，会员单位等，多渠道广泛征集相关案例。根据可量化的效果、创新性、可复制性、积极的社会影响、可持续性和提交材料质量等标准，最终确定 50 个典型案例。经文化和旅游部推荐，本书被列入纪念中华人民共和国恢复联合国合法席位 50 周年配套活动之一。

在经济社会发展的历史进程中，加快推进乡村振兴任重而道远，世界旅游联盟将继续发挥国际平台作用，汇集全球会员力量以及世界范围内的合作者，推动国际社会关注旅游助力乡村振兴及相关社会公益事业，为实现“旅游让世界和生活更美好”的宗旨而不断前行。

Preface

Since its establishment, the World Tourism Alliance (WTA) has steadfastly upheld its mission for "Better Tourism, Better Life, Better World" and its vision of "promoting peace, development and poverty alleviation" through tourism. For three consecutive years—from 2018 to 2020—the WTA worked together with the World Bank (WB) and the International Poverty Reduction Center in China (IPRCC) to release the results of the *WTA Best Practices in Poverty Alleviation through Tourism.* A total of eight episodes in a two-series micro-documentary on poverty alleviation through tourism were filmed based on these practices. They were screened internationally and were widely acclaimed and uniformly lauded for their powerful imagery and inspiring message of how tourism can improve the lives of people.

This year marks the start of the consolidation of the results of China's poverty alleviation and rural revitalization programs and their inextricable link. In commemoration of this important milestone and in cooperation with the WB and IPRCC, the WTA is releasing the *WTA Best Practices of Rural Revitalization through Tourism 2021.* Curated from various sources, including WTA's member units, the Ministry of Culture and Tourism of the People's Republic of China, the National Administration for Rural Revitalization and provincial culture and tourism departments, this book is a compilation of 50 cases that have met the criteria of quantifiable results, innovation, reproducibility, positive social impact, sustainability and quality of submitted materials. With the recommendation by the Ministry of Culture and Tourism of the People's Republic of China, this book is one of the supporting activities to commemorate the 50th Anniversary of the Restoration of the Lawful Seat of the People's Republic of China in the United Nations.

Although much progress has been made, rural revitalization is an ongoing process whose social and economic development continues to evolve and expand. As an international platform, the WTA will continue to engage and rally its global members and partners to this important cause. In keeping with its mission, WTA is committed to be a leading voice in advancing rural revitalization and public welfare initiatives for a "Better Tourism, Better Life, Better World."

目录 / Contents

浙江金华市武义县柳城畲族镇梁家山村：
民宿经济助力乡村振兴

Liangjiashan Village, Liucheng She Nationality Town, Wuyi County, Jinhua City, Zhejiang Province:
B&B Economy Boosts Rural Revitalization

摘要

浙江省金华市武义县梁家山村坚持把梁家山村“古村落”非物质文化遗产、山清水秀的原生态资源作为乡村活化的主线，对梁家山村进行原味改造，改善其基础设施，打造从“好看”向“好玩”转变的、吃住娱乐休闲一体化的乡村民宿旅游产业，诠释民宿经济发展新内涵。梁家山村通过充分利用村里的闲置场地，盘活乡村资产，打造特色乡村民宿旅游产业带，实现社会效益和经济效益的双丰收。

挑战与问题

梁家山村位于海拔 600 多米的仙鹤山半山腰，距离县城约 56 公里，距离镇区约 13 公里，其中 5 公里为盘山道路，交通条件差。全村 116 户 402 人，可种植水田面积仅有 265 亩，人均 0.65 亩；山村周边梯田、峡谷、山林等自然资源总面积约 3.2 平方公里，且大部分为梯田，农业产业基本处于停滞状态，几乎无可持续发展的产业，村民靠农耕勉强维持日常生活。梁家山村虽有传统古村落非物质文化遗产，但由于无人加以保护与利用，村庄越来越没落，成为“空心村”。

措施

1. 保留古村风貌。在村庄规划、建筑设计的过程中，坚持把梁家山村“古村落”非物质文化遗产、山清水秀的原生态资源作为乡村活化的主线，对梁家山村进行原味改造。保留黄墙灰瓦的古民居，以及石板路、古栈道、青石台阶等传统村落元素，美化提升房前屋后菜地、瓜棚、鸡舍等“乡愁场景”。坚持以“原生态改造 + 新老混居”模式推进村庄硬件设施的完善提升，保留村庄的原有风貌和基本构造，合理开发利用梁家山村原生态的生产生活设施。

2. 拓展村民增收渠道。一是全面摸排梁家山村的现有资源，凡是可能利用的做到能用尽用。村内所有资源，全部以租赁方式予以受让，让闲置的固定资产“活起来”。目前，全村已有 20 幢闲置泥坯房被改造成了民宿，全村村民每年实现增收 60 万元。二是对梁家山村村民承包田地实行生态耕种，自产自销，打造“本土特产”销售产业。目前该村土特产有金华正宗“两头乌”土猪、农家鸡鸭鹅、手工油豆腐、高山绿茶、山茶油、板栗、番薯粉、咸菜等特色农产品 10 余种。2020 年以来，生态农产品销售额达 40 万元，同比增长 166%。三是积极提供多种就业岗位，且优先考虑本村村民。目前，已推出民宿管家、旅居生活服务

人员、基地农作物种植员等十几个就业岗位，已有 20 余位村民成为民宿员工，每人每月工资收入 3500 ～ 6000 元。

3. 做好民宿文章。牢牢抓住梁家山村“古村落”精髓，在改造精品民宿的过程中，将传统农耕文化、特色古民居、自然山水作为民宿的特色，在尊重自然和保持村落原生态的前提下，进行民宿修缮，整改周边环境，增设游乐项目。在保留古韵的同时，巧妙植入现代元素，使乡村风土人情和民宿文化相得益彰。梁家山村民宿围绕本土风俗与元素，开发出包馄饨、摘果蔬、打麻糍、磨豆腐、竹竿舞、篝火晚会等乡村生活特色体验项目，让民宿成为游客玩耍的“快乐天堂”和当地村民的“快乐老家”。

成效

在脱贫过程中，梁家山村民宿经济产业链逐渐清晰，先后修缮古建筑 45 幢（其中用于民宿开发的有 25 幢），铺设古道石板路 5400 余平方米，农户外“赤膊墙壁”立面改造整治 5106 平方米，总投资 6000 余万元。通过积极实施古民居修复和乡村设施建设，梁家山村被列入第四批“中国传统村落”。村民通过承包农田开发、耕种、禽畜养殖等农副产业，2017—2020 年农产品销售额每年均实现正增长，创收总额突破 140 万元。民宿度假、景区观光、飞拉达攀岩及户外休闲运动等旅游产品，引得全国各地游客慕名而来，2020 年游客达 7 万人次，营业创收约 500 万元。

经验与启示

1. 以租代拆，共守生态。梁家山村自明代后期形成村落，至今已有 400 多年的历史，是武义县“古村落”非物质文化遗产。在保护开发的过程中，以生态理念进行资源整合规划，对古民居实施“以租代拆”，在保留古民居独有的整体外貌的同时，对室内进行修缮。原拆原建的一木一瓦，都深藏百年古居的古雅风韵。

2. 就近取“材”，共同富裕。一个原本偏远的贫困山村，在 2015 年发生了翻天覆地的变化，村里的古民居被用来租赁，就连破旧不堪的牛栏屋也“不放过”。以 30 年为基础的租赁，租用方每年支付约 12 万元的租赁费用。30 年的租金高达 360 万元，而这只是村集体增收项目效益体现的一个方面而已，涉及面更广的，是村民致富。伴随着乡村旅游产业的崛起，村民无须再舍近求远，在“家门口”即可进行就业，尤其是贫困村民，被重点吸纳为企业员工。

3. 多元植入，共享自然。初步形成政府、市场和社会共同参与的多元投入机制，吸引大批社会力量参与到“打通民宿经济发展的最后一公里”工作中。城市人群来此旅居生活，让城市人群与本县的民俗、文化、公益、教育、旅游等方面产生互动，同时以自然农耕为特色，打造绿色生态农业产业，对传统绿色农耕蔬菜、高山有机绿茶、山茶油、板栗进行文化植入，使乡村农业生产重新焕发生机和活力。

下一步计划

整体目标：打造全国乡村旅游重点村、乡村精品民宿产业样板；打造省级优质疗休养基地、研学旅行最佳目的地。

近期目标：加快现代与传统人文特色的融合进程，引进先进技术与现代化理念，以新元素“活化”土特色，弘扬与传承本土人文。加强对秘境梁家山民宿产业旅游项目的运营管理，保护传承古村落非遗文化，用好本地人力资源，吸纳原住村民员工，助其实现“家门口”致富。通过旅游减贫，助力乡村振兴。

Abstract

With the intangible cultural heritage of its “ancient village” and original ecological resources as the primary rural development activation line, the Liangjiashan Village in Wuyi County, Jinhua City, Zhejiang Province has renovated and improved infrastructure by maintaining its original style to develop a rural B&B tourism industry and economy. To this end, it has integrated food, housing, entertainment and leisure with the transformation of “beauty” into “fun.” It has also explored new connotations and interpretations. Idle sites in the village have also been optimized to revitalize rural assets and create a characteristic rural B&B tourism industry for social and economic benefits.

Challenges and Problems

Located at the mid-point of the Xianhe Mountain, the village has an altitude of more than 600 meters. It is about 56 kilometers away from the county and 13 kilometers away from the town, with five kilometers of winding mountain roads and poor traffic conditions. There are 402 people in 116 households in the village. The plantable area of paddy fields is only 265 *mu*, with a per capita area of 0.65 *mu*. Its natural resources—most of which are terraced fields—include canyons and forests around the village that cover an area of about 3.2 square kilometers. The agricultural industry is essentially stagnant as there is almost no commercial enterprise for sustainable development. Villagers scrape for a living by farming. Despite its intangible cultural heritage as a traditional ancient village, the Liangjiashan Village has not been protected and developed, leading to its primitive conditions and "hollow village" designation.

Measures

1. Preserve the style and features of the ancient village. During the village planning and architectural design, the village has renovated and improved infrastructure by maintaining its original style according to its intangible cultural heritage of an "ancient village" and original ecological resources as the primary line of rural activation. It has preserved the elements of traditional villages such as ancient residences with yellow walls and gray tiles, rocky roads, ancient plank roads and bluestone steps for beautification. Also, it has evoked nostalgia in vegetable plots, melon frames and chicken coops in front of and behind the houses.

The model of "original ecological transformation + old and new residences mix" has been followed to improve hardware facilities, maintain the original style and basic structure and utilize the original ecological facilities in production and living.

2. Expand channels to increase the income of villagers. First, the existing resources in the village have been explored for comprehensive utilization. All resources have been transferred through leases to activate idle fixed assets. At present, 20 idle mud houses have been transformed into B&Bs, registering an annual income increase of RMB 600,000 for villagers. **Second,** the ecological farming structure on the contracted fields of villagers has been implemented for self-production and sales and for the development of a sales industry of "local specialties." Currently, there are more than 10 kinds of

special agricultural products such as Jinhua pigs "Liang Tou Wu" (named for the color of its coat which is black at the head and tail), chickens, ducks, geese, handmade oily tofu, mountain green tea, camellia oil, chestnuts, sweet potato starch and pickles. Since 2020, the sales of ecological agricultural products have reached RMB 400,000, with a year-on-year increase of 166%. **Third,** a variety of jobs that prioritize local villagers have been provided. More than a dozen jobs have been introduced, including B&B housekeepers, living service personnel and base crop planters. More than 20 villagers are now engaged in the B&B industry. They have an average monthly salary ranging from RMB 3,500 to 6,000.

3. Develop B&B economy. Ancient village, traditional farming culture, characteristic ancient residences and natural scenery have been protected during the transformation of boutique B&Bs. Renovation of B&Bs, rectification of the surrounding environment and the addition of amusement projects have been conducted as guided by the principle of respecting nature and maintaining the original ecology of the village. Modern elements have been introduced while the village's ancient charm is preserved to ensure that rural customs and the B&B culture complement each other. With local customs and elements at the center, characteristic experiential projects on village life such as wonton making, fruit and vegetable picking, fried glutinous pudding production, tofu grinding, bamboo pole dance and bonfire parties have been interwoven into the B&B cultural structure and development. This has effectively turned B&Bs into a cultural haven for tourists and a joyful home for the locals.

Results

The industrial chain of the B&B economy has become clear in the planning and implementation of poverty alleviation measures. A total of 45 ancient buildings have been repaired, 25 buildings of which have been used for B&B development. More than 5,400 square meters of rocky roads have been paved and 5,106 square meters of bare walls in the facade have been renovated with a total investment of more than RMB 60 million. Through the active restoration of ancient residences and the construction of rural facilities, the village was included in the fourth batch of traditional Chinese villages. Villagers have also achieved a positive annual sales growth from 2017 to 2020, with their total income exceeding RMB 1.4 million. Their income is derived from agricultural and side industries such as the contracting out of farmland, farming and livestock breeding. Tourist products including B&B vacations, scenic sightseeing, Via Ferrata rock climbing, and other outdoor recreational sports have attracted tourists from all over the country. In 2020, the number of tourists reached 70,000, with a revenue of about RMB 5 million.

Experience and Inspirations

1. Replace demolition with rental for ecological protection. The village boasts a history of more than 400 years since its formation in the late Ming Dynasty. It bears the prestige of being designated an intangible cultural heritage of an "ancient village" in Wuyi County. Resources have been integrated and planned based on the ecological concept of protection for development. Instead of being demolished, ancient residences have been rented to preserve their unique overall appearance and perform interior renovation. The village's quaint charm is vividly captured on every detail of these ancient residences.

2. Utilize local resources for common prosperity. Once an impoverished mountain village, the remote Liangjiashan Village underwent earth-shaking changes in 2015. The ancient residences in the village were leased and transformed, including the dilapidated cattle pens. Payment of about RMB 120,000 from a 30-year lease agreement is made every year. Thus, the 30-year rental is as high as RMB 3.6 million. This is only one part of the benefits the village collective income receives. More importantly, poverty-stricken villagers have been recruited as corporate employees. With the rise of the rural tourism industry, villagers no longer need to work outside as they can easily find jobs in their hometown. The successful implementation of its development plan has significantly elevated the villagers' standard of living, moving them out of poverty.

3. Introduce multiple efforts for nature sharing. A diversified investment mechanism involving the government, market and society has been formed to draw social forces in the development of B&Bs. When high-end urban residents come for tourism and to settle down, they can experience the county's folklore, culture, public welfare, education, tourism and many other aspects. At the same time, a green and ecological agricultural industry has been developed based on the principle of natural farming. Local culture has been infused into traditional green vegetables, mountain organic green tea, camellia oil, and chestnut, thereby rejuvenating rural agricultural production.

Next Steps

Overall goals: Create a national rural tourism key village and a model for the rural boutique B&B industry. Develop a high-quality provincial recuperation base and transform the village into the best destination for study tours.

Short-term goals: Boost rural revitalization through tourism by accelerating the fusion of modern and traditional cultural characteristics, introduce advanced technologies and modern concepts, activate local characteristics with new elements and promote and pass on local humanities. Continuous efforts will be made to enhance the operation and management of the B&B industry, protect and preserve the intangible cultural heritage of the ancient village, utilize local human resources and recruit aboriginal villagers for employment. All these are expected to help them eliminate poverty and become prosperous.

福建福州市连江县苔菉镇茭南村：
平流尾地质公园旅游开发助力传统渔业转型

Jiaonan Village, Tailu Town, Lianjiang County, Fuzhou City, Fujian Province:
Tourism Development of Pingliuwei Geopark Helps Transform Traditional Fisheries

摘要

2015 年，福建省福州市连江县茭南村为了保护海洋环境，由村民推荐带头人设立了双贵岛渔业合作社，由村民集资保护性开发平流尾地质公园。2016 年，平流尾旅游开发有限公司正式成立，平流尾地质公园开始接待游客。2019 年，平流尾地质公园获评国家 2A 级旅游景区。短短几年间，茭南村便实现了从名不见经传的偏远小渔村到网红热门景点的飞跃，实现了乡村产业转型升级、全体渔民脱贫致富、“让家乡成为有梦的地方”的梦想。

挑战与问题

福建福州市连江县筊南村所在位置为平流尾地质公园，三面环海，与马祖列岛隔海相望。三面环海、一面环山的地理因素，导致筊南村陆地资源有限，平流尾地质公园的景区扩容发展受到土地问题的制约。筊南村以渔业为主，70% 的村民从事传统海洋捕捞作业工作。当地农副产品生产方式传统落后，产品仍处于初加工、粗加工阶段，产品的附加值低，难以取得较高的经济效益，村民经济收入水平低。随着海洋资源的不断枯竭，渔民面临产业衰退、收入锐减、上岸转型困难等诸多问题和巨大的生存压力。

措施

1. 成立村集体所有企业。由镇政府、村委班子支持引导，召开村民大会：设立独立的、村民联合组织的集体所有企业，该企业由全体村民自愿投资形式组成；明确旅游经营收益依据比例分配，由投资股东与全体村民共同所有。通过村民股东大会，全民公开选举乡村建设领头人和管理团队，带动全体村民发展乡村旅游。

2. 分步发展海洋特色乡村旅游。坚持保护独特的自然海洋景观资源，不盲目开发，发展具有海洋文化特色的乡村旅游。总体规划围绕“沙滩环境整治—平流尾公园建设—古村落保护”，实现筊南村旅游点、线、面的开发。根据乡村实际情况，因地制宜，分步实施。以一期建设平流尾地质公园为起点，分期逐步实施平流尾地质公园建设、村内及沿海沙滩环境整治、古村落石头古厝保护、进村公路建设、村道扩宽等工程，全面改善村民居住环境，打造“千年渔村古镇，自然遗产景观”的旅游名片，实现平流尾地质公园的可持续发展。

3. 挖掘渔村文化。茭南村独具特色的黄岐半岛元宵佳节游海神、五月初五海上赛龙舟等活动，都极具魅力。有效利用独特的渔村文化、闽台两岸乡亲共祈福活动等，进一步挖掘“乡愁文化”，吸引城市游客前来参观、体验，为游客打开了解当地民俗民风的一个窗口，增加游客对当地民俗乡土文化、农耕饮食文化、传统民间手工艺等的认识和了解，加强对民间传统文化的激活、保护、传承和弘扬。

4. 缔结闽台“姐妹村”。茭南村借助与马祖列岛隔海相望、一衣带水、连江“一县两制”的特色，增进同乡情谊，加强连江与台湾省旅游、宗亲、经贸等多方面、多形式的交流合作。茭南村与对岸马祖芹壁村进行互动交流，双方缔结为“姐妹村”，建立长期联系机制，共同举办民俗文化交流活动，共同推进乡村旅游发展。

5. 借力互联网新媒体。茭南村积极借势“互联网 +”时代背景，吸引广大游客、自媒体、网红等通过微信、微博、小红书、抖音等渠道传播茭南村极具特色的沿海景观，平流尾地质公园游客量实现井喷式增长。景区趁势增设各类能吸引年轻人的“打卡点”，如月亮湾、海漂木平台、许愿墙、INS 风桌椅等，打造最美婚纱摄影基地，催生出福州周

边网红“打卡”热门景点。同时，茭南村利用直播、短视频等新型移动互联网推广渠道，让乡村农产品、特色产品快速“进城”，形成乡村旅游“经营、管理、营销一体化”格局。

成效

1. 增加村民收入。平流尾地质公园门票收益直接纳入集体收入所有，按原定分配比例，实现年股权分红、村民集体分红。目前，公司累计收入近 7000 万元，直接带动就业岗位 300 多个，解决了周边 20 多个贫困户的就业问题。同时，乡村旅游开发帮助乡镇 500 多户家庭转型参与旅游农家乐、乡村土特产销售、农村电商发展，帮助乡村解决了部分渔民上岸转型的难题。平流尾旅游开发公司设立老人福利基金，每年为村中 70 岁以上老人缴纳医疗保险等。对贫困低保家庭的帮扶举措，大大减少了村内贫困人口数量。

2. 促进产业升级。从乡村变为景区，平流尾

旅游开发带动了当地各项特色产业发展，如土特产、地方特色小吃、民宿等；并有效利用农村剩余劳动力，实现村民就地就业，引入多条农产品精加工生产线，从原先的农产品粗放式生产模式向精加工、标准化生产演进，造就了乡村新型职业农民。顺应新型互联网潮流，结合旅游互联网等，带动村民积极利用直播、微信、淘宝等线上营销渠道，拓展农副产品销路，促进第一、二、三产业融合发展，产业集群发展，从而增加旅游扶贫总体效益。

3. 提升生态环境水平。茭南村平流尾旅游的整体建设发展，保护了海洋自然资源，使得乡村环境水平显著提升，完善了房屋、道路等基础建设，实现了“村容整洁”“美丽乡村”“幸福家园”目标，使其从昔日名不见经传的偏远小渔村一跃成为网红热门景点。

经验与启示

1. 乡村旅游开发需以人为本。乡村旅游开发的原则是以村民为核心，重视村民的主体性地位，鼓励村民积极参与旅游，共享乡村旅游资源和环境，建立合理的利益导向机制。从制度设计上要保证村民的知情权和话语权，如涉及旅游开发的重大问题时，须组织召开村民代表大会等。采用合理的听证制度和公示制度，有利于增强村民的利益表达能力，调动农民参与乡村旅游发展的积极性。

2. 乡村旅游开发需引智聚才。针对现有农民创业旅游从业群体，建立基层服务人员管理和培训机制，真正培养一批“爱乡村、爱农业、懂技术、会经营”的新型职业农民。政府加大返乡入乡创业政策支持力度，招才引智，优化乡村营商环境。同时，通过规划扶贫、对口帮扶等政策，吸引各行业专家为乡村振兴出谋划策。

下一步计划

一是结合景区独特的地缘区位、滨海风光，继续深耕当地丰富的滨海旅游资源，结合自然景观、民俗风情、石头聚落、海滨沙滩，向集休闲观光旅游、拍照摄影、海钓、科普教育、团建拓展于一体的多功能城郊型度假景区目标发展，打造环马祖澳旅游、福州海滨旅游等精品旅游线路，盘活乡村全域旅游资源。二是建立青年创业中心，鼓励有志青年回乡创业、建设新农村，打造真正意义上的“海上桃花源”。三是进一步提升村民福利，让村民共享旅游开发成果。不断提升老年人福利待遇，完善村民养老医疗基金、扶贫基金、奖学金等机制，鼓励下一代积极上进，实现乡村振兴的“接棒”，实现“让家乡成为有梦的地方”的梦想。

Abstract

To protect its marine environment, the villagers in Jiaonan Village, Lianjiang County, Fuzhou City, Fujian Province established the Shuanggui Island Fishery Cooperative in 2015. To achieve its goal, the villagers raised money for the development and protection of the Pingliuwei Geopark. In 2016, the Pingliuwei Tourism Development Co., Ltd. was created and the geopark was opened to the villagers. In 2019, the geopark was rated as a national 2A-level tourist attraction. In only a few years, the park has become famous for its fishing and beautiful views. This has helped the local villagers rise out of poverty and has transformed their hometown into a beautiful place.

Challenges and Problems

The village is located in an unfavorable location, with the sea surrounding it on three sides and the mountains on the fourth. Because of this, the village has limited land resources and the expansion and development of the Pingliuwei Geopark has been constrained. But the village lies across the sea from Matsu Island of Taiwan Region, so there are a number of people who are willing to visit despite its limited resources. About 70% of the villagers engage in marine fishing. However, their preparation methods are inferior, and they are not focused on making a profit. The low economic values and low income for the villagers puts a great amount of pressure on the village.

Measures

1. Establish collectively-owned village enterprises. There are annual meetings with the villagers that are held regularly by the village leaders and government officials. The goal of these meetings is to inform the villagers that the development is focused on creating independent collectively owned enterprises that are run and established by the villagers. In addition, these meetings inform the villagers of the pay scale and the distribution ratio. Most of the leaders in the village are elected as shareholders and guide the villagers towards the development of rural tourism.

2. Develop rural tourism with marine characteristics step by step. One avenue for the protection of its unique natural marine landscape is to develop the village's marine culture. Development efforts are underway with the goal of the improvement of beaches, the Geopark, and the protection of ancient villages with the overall plan

of developing tourism through the village year-round. Most of these development and improvement projects have been carried out in phases. These include the coastal beaches, protection of old-age stone houses, and the widening of the highways and village roads. All these measures work to improve the living environment of the villagers and develop a tourist brand of a thousand year old fishing village with natural heritage landscapes and a sustainable geopark.

3. Maximize the fishing culture of villages. The village has two great local festivals that are attractive to tourists. They are the Sea God Praying on the Lantern Festival of Huangqi Peninsula and the Dragon Boat Race on the Sea. There is a great local custom that is nostalgic for the villagers and it attracts urban visitors to experience it. This can be a great way for tourists to be informed and understand the local folk culture, agriculture food culture, and traditional handicrafts.

4. Establish a "sister village" relationship between Fujian and Taiwan Region. The village is separated from Taiwan Region by only a strip of water. Because of this, the local customs are multi-form and multi-faceted, resulting in exchanges and cooperation between Lianjiang County and Taiwan Region. The two areas share relatives, economy and engage in trade, leading to a strong connection between them. Also, a recently-created sister village on the opposite bank was established for a long-term exchange mechanism. Together, they will forge a binding folk culture and exchange activities which will promote the development of rural tourism.

5. Utilize new internet media. Social media has helped boost the tourism industry. Social media apps such as Tik Tok, WeChat, and Weibo have all helped in increasing its popularity among the young people who like places such as Moon Bay, Driftwood Platform, and the Wishing Wall. The Geopark has also seen an increase in its number of visitors as a result of social media exposure. The village is also trying to bring more awareness to their agricultural asset by posting videos online of their products, operation, and management.

Results

1. Increase villagers' income. Admission fees are included with the collective income that the villagers receive. Currently, the company has brought in nearly RMB 70 million and has created more than 300 jobs for local villagers from surrounding areas. In addition, rural tourism has helped more than 500 households in the nearby villages with the development of agritainment, local product sales in rural areas, and rural e-commerce. This has solved the problem of some fishermen to switch to

ashore industries. The Pingliuwei Tourism Development Co., Ltd. has created a welfare system for those over 70, which offers sustenance funds and insurance to the elderly, reducing the number of people in poverty.

2. Promote industrial upgrading. The Geopark has helped impoverished villagers find a sustainable way of life. This has been done through the creation of industries featuring local products, local specialty snacks, and B&Bs. There have also been new production systems to replace the old and outdated ones. This results in a new system of efficiency and creates a refined process. Through their internet usage, the villagers are able to reach more people and earn more money as a result. By integrating this into their economy, they are able to rise out of poverty and enjoy more benefits.

3. Improve ecological environment. The Geopark has created many benefits for the village. These include improved infrastructures such as houses and roads and achieved the goals of "a clean and tidy village," "a charming village," and "a blessed homeland," transforming the little-known remote fishing village into an internet-famous tourist attraction.

Experience and Inspirations

1. People-oriented concept for rural tourism development. The developments of projects should be focused on the local villagers as the core for rural tourism.

They should be encouraged to engage in tourism and share their experiences. For example, when an issue arises out of the industry, they should be able to convene and resolve it.

2. Talents required for rural tourism development. Because of the influx of new business operations, there has been an emphasis on creating a skilled workforce. The villagers were trained in management, customer service, and other skills. The government has also offered help by creating polices that help the rural tourism industry. In the meantime, the policies of poverty alleviation through planning and paired assistance have attracted experts from all over to help bring ideas and suggestion for rural revitalization.

route of Central Matsu Island Tourist Area and seaside of Fuzhou City and revitalize the rural all-for-one tourism resources.

A new youth entrepreneurship program that will focus on bringing the youth back to their hometown to help develop the business and encourage active participation in the village will be established.

Finally, there will also be an increase in the welfare system. This will assist the tourism industry as more people would be able to partake in the business. The elderly will be able to take part in pension funds, scholarships and other programs that will help transform their hometown into a dream land.

Next Steps

The unique location of the village and its beautiful coastal scenery has created an outstanding tourism industry. Its natural landscape, folk customs, stone clusters, and coastal beaches, a multi-functional suburban resort area integrating leisure sightseeing, photography, sea fishing, science education, and outdoor training will be developed to create a boutique tourism

青海西宁市大通回族土族自治县朔北藏族乡边麻沟村：

景区先行助力美丽乡村建设

Bianmagou Village, Shuobei Xizang's Ethnic Township, Datong Hui and Tu Autonomous County, Xining City, Qinghai Province:

Scenic Area Development Drives Beautiful Village Construction

摘 要

青海省西宁市大通县边麻沟村在660亩的荒山上种植了50多种花卉，将亩产不到300斤粮食的旱地建成了“花海农庄”，成为集花卉基地、人文景观、餐饮住宿、休闲娱乐及其他配套设施于一体的乡村旅游品牌。边麻沟村花海景区以原生态的山林河谷为依托，打造出自然与人工设计相结合的乡村旅游景区，既保护了生态的原生性，又使村民通过发展旅游业实现了脱贫致富。

挑战与问题

边麻沟村位于青海西宁市大通县朔北藏族乡东部，全村有162户612人，是一个以汉族、藏族、蒙古族、土族为主的多民族聚居村，少数民族412人，占全村总人口的67%。全村平均海拔2800米，年降水量580毫米，辖区总面积3.5平方公里，其中耕地面积1600亩，均为山坡旱地，人均耕地面积2.6亩，农作物以油菜、小麦、土豆为主。

长期以来，由于偏远、高寒，这里饱受霜冻、冰雹、干旱等自然灾害的困扰，在区位条件不佳等因素的影响下，边麻沟村发展迟缓、动力不足。除了年复一年种植油菜、青稞、土豆，没有其他收入来源，村民经济收入普遍较低。2015年，村贫困人口人均纯收入仅为2386.7元。

措施

1. 精确识别贫困户，精准施行扶贫策。边麻沟村依据“先看房，次看粮，再看学生郎，四看技能强不强，五看有没有残疾重病躺在床”的“五看法”准则，精准识别扶贫对象。针对贫困户差异化的致贫原因，进行分类施策。对因病致贫的贫困户，做到医疗保险、大病保险和“健康保”全覆盖；对缺技术的贫困户，结合乡村旅游对其开展旅游接待技能培训，并由县林业部门设立生态公益林管护岗位，解决贫困户就近转移就业问题；对缺资金的贫困户，由县金融部门通过“530”扶贫贷款解决其发展资金问题。精准的扶贫施策，以及养老保险、最低生活保障、教育、医疗、低保兜底等扶贫惠民政策，让全村贫困户在脱贫路上实现了“一个都不掉队”。

2. 靠山吃山建花海，旅游致富保生态。边麻沟村由于受地理环境限制，村里的土地贫瘠，且很多山地已经撂荒，在边麻沟村发展种植、养殖等传统产业无法形成规模，更无法取得良好的经济效益。但是，边麻沟村与大通县国有东峡林场相连，树木葱茏，流水潺潺，属于天然的“青山绿水”，生态资源禀赋优越，具备发展乡村旅游的先决条件。经过反复论证，边麻沟村被确立为“坚持生态保护与经济发展双赢，以生态资源为依托，以美丽乡村建设为平台，以打响特色旅游品牌为主要举措”的试点村。村“两委”班子带领村民着力打造乡村花海，并引导和鼓励村民发展农家乐、乡村民宿、农家种植养殖业，形成完整的产业链，努力走出一条依托生态文明建设助农增收的路子。

3. 改造村容村貌，提升村民幸福感。收入多了，生活好了，村“两委”班子进而带领乡亲们大力整顿和改造村容村貌：改造危旧房，落实农村奖励性住房，改造村落墙体，修建广场，整修村道，建敬老院……如今的边麻沟村，眼前的景象让人欣喜，洁净宽阔的柏油路四通八达，清新亮丽的民居错落有致，恬静优美的农家庭院如诗如画，成为全省唯一的“全国生态文化村”。

4. 积极引入规划设计，辐射带动连片脱贫。在成功打造边麻沟“花海农庄”景区的基础上，2017 年，大通县联系南京大学、东南大学专家团队对窎沟片区的 10 个村，按照“一村一特色、一村一景点”原则进行规划设计，梳理出“一核一带三组团”乡村旅游发展理念，精准定位片区 10 个村的乡村旅游发展思路、主导产业和实现途径，并整合东西部协作、美丽乡村、“厕所革命”、林下产业发展等各类资金，建设窎沟片区乡村旅游扶贫产业园，引领群众增收致富奔小康。2019 年，实现了片区发展向“绿水青山”要“金山银山”的巨大转变。

成效

2015 年，全村贫困人口人均纯收入仅为 2386.7 元；2016 年，边麻沟村退出贫困村之列，全村人均纯收入达到 10925.03 元；2018 年，全村农民人均可支配收入达到 13459.63 元；2020 年，全村农民人均可支配收入达到 14953.6 元。目前，全村农家院已发展到 55 家，家庭宾馆有 15 家，全村近一半农户从事乡村旅游业，为 85 人解决了当地就业问题。边麻沟村已被打造成为集花卉基地、人文景观、餐饮住宿、休闲娱乐于一体的，配套设施建设完善的“花海农庄”乡村旅游品牌。

昔日破落穷困的边麻沟村，如今已成为远近闻名的富裕村，成了全省的乡村振兴试点示范村，并先后获得“全国生态文化村”“2018 年中国美丽休闲乡村”“全国乡村旅游重点村”“民族团结进步示范村”“省级文明村镇”“省级卫生村”“青海省 5 星级乡村文化旅游接待点”“西宁市先进基层党组织”“市级文明村镇”“大通县先进基层党组织”等荣誉称号。

经验与启示

边麻沟村立足于良好的生态资源优势，在绿色转型发展上探索出了一条具有当地特色的新路子，为着力推动“四个转变”在农村基层落地生根、开花结果树立了示范典型。

1. 树立转型观念。面对边麻沟村经济发展落后的现状，大通县深深感到：要想改变落后面貌、让群众过上好日子，必须得转变传统思想观念，转变发展思路和发展模式。2015 年以来，县委、县政府转变思想、明确方向，将边麻沟村发展思路确定为“以良好的生态资源为依托，以加快美丽乡村建设为平台，以打响特色旅游品牌为主要路径，带动全村群众多渠道、多方式增收致富”，积极在边麻沟村生态生产生活良性循环转型发展上动脑筋、谋举措，为转型发展奠定基础。

2. 培养转型人才。大通县高度重视在基层以“能人”带动群众，充分发挥其“领头羊”作用。2014 年，优秀共产党员、致富能手李培东当选为边麻沟村党支部书记，他积极借鉴外地先进的发展经验，最终确定了利用生态旅游资源优势和荒坡土地，全力打造“花海”旅游品牌，带动全村群众就近务工或发展农家乐经济、乡村宾馆、自驾游、牲畜养殖等相关产业的转型发展思路。

3. 明晰转型路径。2015 年以来，大通县积极探索生态文明体制改革、农业供给侧结构性改革、农村土地制度改革，助力“美丽乡村”建设：一是以土地入股形式流转边麻沟村 600 亩村民土地用于“花海”景区建设。这样不但解决了建设用地问题，而且化解了该片耕地长年受冰雹、霜冻灾害影响导致收成不良以至于撂荒的问题。二是将针对贫困户的 14.6 万元产业到户发展资金进行入股，让贫困户真正成为景区的“主人”，激发了群众参与的积极性，保障了项目资金的长期收益。三是积极引导村民参与集体林权制度改革，将村级股份合作组织中的 3800 亩林地以入股方式流转到大众生态农业观光合作社中，这就有效解决了村林业经营主体无场地、林权持有者增收难的问题。

4. 提升转型效益。边麻沟村不断探索实践让农牧民由单一的种植、养殖、生态看护，向生态、生产、生活良性循环模式转变。为了提升“花海”景区的整体竞争力和影响力，县委、县政府对以边麻沟和东至沟村为核心的窎沟片区 10 个村进行了乡村旅游规划设计，实施污水管网、旅游木屋、弱电改造、墙体立面改造等基础设施建设，景区游客中心、餐饮一条街、休闲木屋、游乐场等项目相继建成，实现了从边麻沟这个“点”向窎沟整个“片”的辐射带动。

下一步计划

一是坚持产业兴村，发展壮大村集体经济和种养优势特色产业，增加村集体收益和村民收入。同时，积极联系农业科技部门，做好种植业培训，加强疾病防御等田间管理，确保农业增收。二是按照实际需求有针对性地开展技能培训，特别是农家乐、餐饮、舞蹈等与乡村旅游结合密切的专业，提高村民经营管理和服务水平，打造精品民宿，驱动乡村旅游提质增效，进一步激发乡村内生发展动力。三是继续开展招商引资工作，结合花海旅游优势资源，吸引一批旅游设施投资，推进旅游景点项目提档升级，增强景点的影响力和吸引力。积极探索乡村振兴新业态，拓展村民持续增收致富渠道。四是突出生态环保工作，继续开展绿化造林，补植花草，保护好自然生态，加大人居环境整治力度，紧紧依托田园风光、生态山水等资源，建设美丽乡村风景带，打造优美的生态宜居环境。五是继续加大宣传力度，充分利用微信、客户端等自媒体和新媒体，多渠道扩大宣传，多维度进行报道，持续推动乡村旅游提质增效，进一步提升“花海”景区乡村旅游的知名度，吸引更多的游客来“花海农庄”观光旅游，为村民通过旅游业增收致富提供更多的便利条件。

Abstract

More than 50 types of flowers have been planted on the barren hills of 660 *mu* in Bianmagou Village, Datong County, Xining City, Qinghai Province. This is intended to build the dry land with a yield of less than 300 *jin* of grain into a "Flower Farm," developing the village into a rural tourism brand integrating indigenous flowers, cultural landscapes, catering and accommodation, entertainment, games and other supporting facilities. Relying on the original ecology of mountains, forests and river valleys, the scenic spot in the village has been established into a rural tourist attraction combining natural and artificial designs. This protects its native ecology, and helps villagers shake off poverty and become better-off through tourism development.

Challenges and Problems

Located in the eastern part of Shuobei Xizang's Autonomous Township, Datong County, Xining City, Qinghai Province, with 612 people of 162 households, the Bianmagou is a multi-ethnic village dominated by the Han, Xizang's, Mongolian, and Tu nationalities, with 412 minority people accounting for the 67% of the total. It has an average elevation of 2,800 meters, an annual rainfall of 580 millimeters. Its total area of 3.5 square kilometers include 1,600 *mu* of arable lands, all of which are hillside dry land. It has a per capita arable land area of 2.6 *mu*, with oilseed rape, wheat and potatoes as the village's main plantation.

Plagued by natural disasters such as frost, hail, and drought, and severely restricted due to its poor and remote location with harsh cold climate, the Bianmagou village has been largely undeveloped.

Except for the planting of oilseed rape, highland barley, and potatoes year after year, the villagers have no other source of income and are not motivated to change. In 2015, the per capita net income of the impoverished people was only RMB 2,386.7.

Measures

1. Precise identification of impoverished households for poverty alleviation policies. For the precise identification of key targets for poverty alleviation, the village adopted the criteria for five specific factors: houses, grain, students, skills, and people with disability and serious illness. Since poverty is caused by different factors, categorized policies were implemented among different impoverished households. For those caused by illness, they are provided with medical insurance coverage, critical illness insurance, and "health insurance." For impoverished households lacking technologies, training on tourism reception skills are provided in combination with rural tourism. The county's forestry departments have also established posts of ecological public welfare forest management and protection to facilitate the household's family members nearby employment. Those lacking funds, the county's financial departments are solving the problem on development funds through "530" poverty alleviation loans. Targeted poverty alleviation people-benefiting policies such as endowment insurance, minimum subsistence allowances, education, medical care, and the minimum living standard security system, have ensured that all the impoverished households in the village are lifted out of poverty.

2. Develop a sea of flowers for tourism and ecology development. Limited by geographical environment, the village land is barren. Many mountainous areas are abandoned, so traditional industries such as planting and breeding can neither be developed in a large scale nor yield sound economic benefits. However, with its connection to the state-owned Dongxia Forest Farm in Datong County and its advantageous ecological resources such as lucid waters and lush mountains, the village has the prerequisites for rural tourism development. After repeated demonstrations, the village has been established as a pilot village "in adherence to a win-win situation between ecological protection and economic development, in reliance on ecological resources, with beautiful village construction as a platform, and with distinctive tourism brand marketing as a main measure." Its two committees—the village Party branch and the villagers' autonomous committee—have led the villagers in developing a sea of flowers. Both have guided and encouraged villagers to develop agritainment, rural B&Bs, planting and breeding industry for a complete industrial chain to increase the farmers' income based on the construction of an ecological civilization.

3. Renovate the village appearance for villagers' happiness. With more income and a better life, the two village committees have led the villagers to renovate the village appearance, remodel dilapidated houses, implement such projects as rural incentive housing, village walls renovation, square building, village road improvement, and gerocomium building. Nowadays, the village is a picture of progress, contentment and social satisfaction with its wide, clean wide asphalt roads extended in all directions; neatly scattered bright and comfortable dwellings; and serene, picturesque rural courtyards. All these have contributed to the transformation of Bianmagou into the only "National

Ecological Cultural Village" in the province.

4. Introduce planning and design for contiguous poverty alleviation. The successful creation of the "Flower Farm" scenic area in the village prompted Datong County to contact expert teams in Nanjing University and Southeast University in 2017 for the planning and design of 10 villages in the Diaogou contiguous area. This was done in accordance with the policy of "one feature for one village, one scenic spot for one village." Also, it followed the rural tourism development philosophy of "One Core, One Belt and Three Sectors," which means one core scenic area of rural tourism, one development belt of industrial clusters, three sectors of tourism comprehensive services, characteristic agricultural industries and rural culture experience. The accurate positioning of the rural tourism development ideas, leading industries and realization paths of the 10 villages, along with the integration of various funds on cooperation between east and the west, beautiful village, "toilet revolution" and under-forest industry development for poverty alleviation through rural tourism in the contiguous area, have resulted in the prosperity of the masses due to the increase of their income. In 2019, this contiguous area has substantially changed, gaining invaluable assets from lucid waters and lush mountains.

Results

In 2015, the per capita net income of the impoverished people throughout the village was only RMB 2,386.7; in 2016, the village was lifted out of poverty, with the per capita net income of RMB 10,925.03; in 2018, the per capita disposable income of farmers reached RMB 13,459.63; in 2020, the per capita disposable income of farmers reached RMB 14,953.6. At present, there are 55 farmyards and 15 family hotels in the village, and nearly half of the peasant households are engaged in rural tourism, helping 85 people find jobs locally. All in all, the village has been built into a well-developed rural tourism brand of "Flower Farm" integrating flower bases, cultural landscapes, catering and accommodation, entertainment, games and other supporting facilities.

The village, dilapidated and impoverished in the past, is well-known and prosperous at present, and becomes a pilot demonstration village for rural revitalization in the province. It has successively awarded honorary titles such as "National Ecological Cultural Village," "China's Beautiful Leisure Village in 2018," "National Rural Tourism Key Village," "Ethnic Unity and Progress Demonstration Village," "Provincial Civilized Villages and Towns," "Provincial Health Villages," "Five-star Rural Cultural Tourism Reception Site in Qinghai Province," "Advanced Grassroots Party Organization in Xining City," "Municipal Civilized Villages and Towns," and "Advanced Grassroots Party Organization in Datong County."

Experience and Inspirations

Based on advantageous ecological resources, the village has explored a new path to green transformation and development with local characteristics. It has established a model for the development of "Four Transitions" at the rural grassroots level.

1. Establish transformation concepts. The backward economic development of the village makes Datong County aware that traditional concepts, development ideas and development models must be changed and people's lives must be transformed. Since 2015, the county party committee and county government have changed their mindset. They have gained directional clarity and understanding "in reliance on advantageous ecological resources, with beautiful village construction as a platform, helping villagers increase income and become better-off in multiple channels and with multiple

methods." They have adopted active measures to advance the virtuous cycle in ecology, production and life, laying a foundation for the transformation and development of the village.

2. Recruit and train transformation talents. The Datong County attaches great importance to the leading role of "capable people" in driving the masses at the grassroots level, In 2014, Li Peidong, an outstanding Communist Party member and an acknowledged wealth generation expert was elected as the Party branch secretary of Bianmagou Village. Through the advanced development techniques he has learned and borrowed from his experience in other places, he has developed the tourism brand of "A Sea of Flowers." The concept maximizes advantageous eco-tourism resources and barren lands, and drives the development and transformation on such related industries of the villagers' nearby employment or agritainment economy, rural hotels, self-driving tours, and livestock breeding.

3. Clarify transformation paths. Since 2015, Datong County has been actively exploring reforms in ecological civilization system, agricultural supply-side structure and rural land system to facilitate the construction of "beautiful villages." **First,** the 600 *mu* land belonging to the villagers are transferred through the pooling of land for shares which are used for the construction of "A Sea of Flowers" scenic spot. This effectively solves the construction land problems and avoided such problems as poor harvest and land desolation caused by hail and frost for several years. **Second,** the RMB 146,000 industrial development fund for impoverished households were invested as shares to

turn these households into "masters" of the scenic area, stimulate the enthusiasm of their engagement, and ensure the long-term benefits of project funds. **Third,** villagers are guided to participate in collective forestry reform, and property right system to transfer the 3,800 *mu* of forest land in village-level joint-stock partnership organizations to public ecological agricultural sightseeing cooperatives in the way of equity investment. This solves the no-site problem for business entities in village forestry while increasing the income of forestry property right holders.

4. Improve transformation efficiency. The village has continuously explored and practiced the transformation model from unitary planting, breeding, and ecological care of farmers and herdsmen to a virtuous cycle in ecology, production, and life. To enhance the overall competitiveness and influence of "A Sea of Flowers" scenic spot, the county party committee and county government have carried out rural tourism planning and design for 10 villages in the Diaogou contiguous area with Bianmagou and Dongzhigou villages as the core. They implemented the infrastructure construction of sewage pipe networks, tourism wooden houses, current weak and wall facade reconstruction. Also, they launched tourist centers in scenic areas, catering streets, wooden leisure houses, and playgrounds in succession, effectively driving the Diaogou contiguous area development with the Bianmagou Village as the core.

Next Steps

First, in adherence to the philosophy of rejuvenating the village through industrial development, continuous efforts will be made to expand the village collective economy, nurture advantageous characteristic industries, and increase the income of both the village collective and villagers. Simultaneously, the agricultural science and technology departments will be proactively contacted for planning industry related training and field management in disease prevention will be strengthened for a satisfactory agricultural yield. **Second,** targeted skill training will be carried out in accordance with actual needs, especially in the fields of agritainment, catering, and dancing. They will be closely integrated with rural tourism to improve the management and service level of villagers, build boutique B&Bs, develop high-quality and efficient rural tourism, and further stimulate the endogenous development of the village. **Third,** the work of attracting investment will be carried out, and the investment will be introduced into tourism facilities through the advantageous resources of "A Sea of Flowers" to upgrade tourist attractions, increase their influence and allure. Also, new business forms of rural revitalization will be explored to expand the channels for villagers to increase their income and live more comfortably. **Fourth,** ecological environmental protection will be emphasized to carry out greening and afforestation. Planting of flowers and grasses for natural ecology will be reinforced. Also, the management of human settlements will be intensified, and beautiful rural scenery will be developed centered around such resources as idyllic and ecological landscapes to present a beautiful and ecologically habitable environment. **Fifth,** multi-channel and multi-dimension publicity will be conducted through new media including WeChat, client-side and self-media, to promote the quality and efficiency of rural tourism and enhance the popularity of "A Sea of Flowers" scenic spot to draw more tourists to a "Flower Farm" for sightseeing. This is expected to facilitate the income increase of villagers through tourism development.

山西临汾市乡宁县关王庙乡云丘山村：
云丘山景区农旅融合带村脱贫模式

Mount Yun Village, Guanwangmiao Township, Xiangning County, Linfen City, Shanxi Province:
Integration of Agriculture and Tourism in Mount Yun Scenic Area Drives Rural Poverty Alleviation

摘要

云丘山景区以“企业有利润、村民有利益、村委有效益”的三有定位，成功孕育出了“农旅融合、村企共建”的“云丘模式”，使云丘山村基础设施建设、村容村貌发生了翻天覆地的变化。云丘山景区现已发展成为全国“景区带村”旅游扶贫示范项目，成为山西转型的“排头兵”、世界级旅游目的地。

挑战与问题

山西临汾市乡宁县云丘山村是典型的旅游乡村，因地处云丘山旅游景区而得名。云丘山景区所在乡镇农村原来地域封闭，农民思想保守，农业生产落后，旅游产业发展与美丽乡村发展“两张皮”，无法实现深入融合，不但起不到相互促进的作用，反而相互削弱，阻碍发展。特别是景区规划建设中有需要整村搬迁安置的农民，不仅存在搬迁难问题，而且存在整体搬迁后农业生产难、土地流转农民就业难、增收难的问题。云丘山旅游开发公司是由当地煤炭企业转型而来，面对全新的产业建设，面临人才短缺等难题。

措施

1. 围绕“规划先行”，充分利用各项政策。乡宁县委、县政府出具政策文件，从 2005 年支持云丘山景区开发，乡政府配合，同时积极争取中央、省、市政策的支持，这让景区开发有了底气。专业的设计团队和专家队伍受邀前来规划、建设，服务、规范、质量、品牌、宾客第一、员工第一等意识由此在云丘山村逐步确立起来，并逐渐得到强化。

2. 围绕“文旅融合”，不断壮大旅游产业。云丘山景区围绕非遗文化民俗等丰富的文化遗存，引入科技，强化保护，创新方式，做好展示，彰显儒、释、道三教合一；围绕 9 座国家级传统村落，紧扣民俗背景，恢复原貌格局，培育古村落文旅新业态；选准主题定位，在康家坪古村打造国内一流的民宿；保护每一处生态，封山禁牧，植树造林，开发世界罕见冰洞奇景——云丘山冰洞群。

3. 围绕“农旅融合”，实现村企共赢。云丘山景区建设移民新村 105687 平方米，整村搬迁 16

个自然村561户居民，人居环境大大改善。引导村民自主创业，开办乡村旅馆、农家乐；积极吸纳村民参与景区建设和运营，增加其收入，安排当地建档立卡贫困户在云丘山景区直接就业人数269人，月人均收入2950元；景区建设方面，优先吸收当地村民承包工程，帮其组建工程队；当地农民还组建了上河优质粮食种植专业合作社，进行土地流转，并返聘村民种植有机粮食和有机菜、药、茶等，保护开发翅果油树等农业产业；给建档立卡贫困户担保贷款助其进行畜禽养殖，真正实现了农民收入与农业、旅游产业的有机结合。

成效

云丘山景区先后开发自然景源42处、人文景源77处，历经20年潜心打造，如今已成为国家5A级旅游景区。目前累计投资23.95亿元，年接待游客120余万人次，实现旅游综合收入1.6亿余元。云丘山景区全方位带动乡宁县8个乡镇80多个村中建档立卡贫困户2573户8793人脱贫致富，户均增收22000余元。当地农民彻底转变为产业工人，实现了：人人有班上、家家有轿车，老有所养、老有所依。云丘山景区现已发展成为全国“景区带村”旅游扶贫示范项目，景区已成为山西转型的“排头兵”、世界旅游目的地。

经验与启示

1. 科学规划。景区发展规划与乡村发展规划必须相互融合。围绕“打造国内一流目的地景区”这个目标，依托景区发展的周边乡村实质上和景区的发展紧密相连、唇齿相依，只有目标同向、规划融合、合力共为，才能形成双向驱动，实现共同发展。

2. 保护生态。在开发过程中，景区内的文化遗产得到了很好的保护和挖掘；杜绝了乱砍滥伐，生态面貌焕然一新；人居环境大大改善，成了名副其实的“美丽乡村”。

3. 农旅融合。旅游产业作为朝阳绿色产业，其带动乡村发展、促进农民致富、辐射周边发展的作用极为明显。只有农旅深度融合，彼此才能实现深层次促进和发展。景区发展了，农民收入增加了，生产生活条件改善了，农民得到的实惠越多，景区发展就越会得到更为普遍的支持和拥护，从而形成发展的源泉活力，实现景区发展和乡村振兴的“一箭双雕”。

4. 回馈社会。景区投资 1900 余万元与台湾专家合作建成“元谷希望农场”，为身心障碍者提供技能教育服务。三年多来，先后招收 19 名身心障碍者，目前已有 7 名身心障碍者具有了正常生活和工作的能力，进入社会从业，现在他们不仅能自食其力，还能赚钱养家。

下一步计划

围绕建设国内一流景区和乡村振兴的双向发展目标，在景区发展方面，进一步完善云丘山国家 5A 级旅游景区品牌，重点对环境卫生整治、智慧景区建设、研学旅行等方面进行新改善、大提升，实现景区带动促进和辐射作用的全新飞跃。在乡村振兴方面，坚持将农村人居环境整治与旅游产业发展有机结合起来，重点展示民俗文化挖掘和传承、古村古道古井等古文化、民宿文化；加快推进 22 万头现代化生猪养殖基地，8000 亩有机旱作小麦基地的建设，同时依托特有自然生态资源，全面建成药茶、腌菜、糕点、文创产品、面粉等观光加工生产线和高标准设施蔬菜标准化示范基地，力争早日把云丘山村建设成为全国一流的生态文明建设示范村。云丘山景区重点发展乡村旅游、休闲、度假、康养产业，还要把当地有机旱作农业的“云丘山”品牌发展成特色农业品牌，真正实现景区发展与乡村振兴的深度融合。

Abstract

The Mount Yun Scenic Area has successfully bred the "Yunqiu Model" which features "agricultural and tourism integration, village-enterprise co-construction." It is based on the positioning of "earnings for enterprises, benefits for villagers and profits for village committees." Also, it helps promote massive changes in infrastructure construction and the appearance of the village. The scenic area has developed into a national poverty alleviation demonstration project through tourism characterized by "scenic area driving village development" and has become a pioneer in the transformation of Shanxi Province into a global tourist destination.

Challenges and Problems

The Mount Yun Village in Xiangning County, Linfen City, Shanxi Province, is a typical tourist village. It takes its name from its location in the Mount Yun Scenic Area. The village and town where the scenic area is located are geographically confined. Farmers here are conservative in their ways and thinking while agricultural production is backward. Thus, it is difficult to achieve full integration of tourism industry development and the development of beautiful village. Farmers who need to be relocated and resettled in another village during the planning and construction of the scenic area cannot support themselves.

Their relocation present many challenges. Another difficulty is in agricultural production and employment. Farmers who have transferred their land have seen their income increase. As it transitions from being a local coal company, the Mount Yun Development Company faces talent and labor shortage for the brand-new industrial construction.

Measures

1. Utilize policies with planning at the center. Since 2005, the Xiangning County Party Committee and the county government have cooperated in issuing policy documents to support the development of the Mount Yun Scenic Area. Together they sought support from the central, provincial, and municipal agencies for policies that drive the development of the scenic area. Professional design and expert teams have been built to establish and strengthen the awareness for planning, construction, service, standardization, quality, brand, guest first, and employee first.

2. Develop the tourism industry through cultural and tourism integration. The Mount Yun Scenic Area has captured and displayed the integration of Confucianism, Buddhism and Taoism. They have done this by focusing on rich cultural relics such as intangible cultural folk customs, the introduction of technologies with emphasis on protection, innovative methods and an outstanding image. Moreover, based on the surrounding nine national traditional villages and their folk customs, it has restored the original pattern to cultivate new business systems of cultural tourism in the ancient village. Additionally, the correct theme positioning has been selected to develop a national first-class B&Bs in the Kangjiaping Ancient Village. More importantly, great efforts have been made to protect ecology, close mountains to ban grazing, plant trees and develop the Mount Yun Ice Cave Group.

3. Achieve a win-win situation between villages and enterprises through cultural and tourism integration. A new resettlement village of 105,687 square meters has been built in the scenic area. Meanwhile, the relocation of 561 residents from 16 natural villages has improved the settlement. Villagers have been guided to start their own businesses to operate rural hotels and agritainment. They have been encouraged to get involved in the construction and operation of the scenic area to increase their income. As a result, 269 people from archived impoverished households found jobs at the scenic area, with an average monthly income of RMB 2,950. Contract projects of local villagers have been prioritized in the construction of the scenic area to form an engineering team. Furthermore, local farmers have organized the Shanghe Quality Food Growing Professional Cooperative to transfer villagers' land and recruited them to grow organic food, organic vegetables, herbal teas, etc., thus protecting and developing agricultural industries such as Elaeagnus

mollis. Also, guaranteed loans have been provided to archived impoverished households for livestock and poultry breeding to achieve the organic integration of farmers' agricultural income and tourism industries.

Results

After a 20-year effort, 42 natural scenic and 77 humanistic sites have been successively developed which helped transform the scenic area into a national 5A-level tourist attraction. Currently, the scenic area has registered an accumulated investment of RMB 2.395 billion. Its annual tourists' reception has exceeded 1.2 million, with a comprehensive tourism income of more than RMB 160 million. It has helped 8,793 people from 2,573 archived impoverished households in more than 80 villages from eight towns in Xiangning County move out of poverty and elevate their standard of living. The average household income has increased by more than RMB 22,000. Local farmers have also fully shifted and have become industrial workers, ensuring jobs for each person, cars for each household, care and support for the elderly. As a result, the scenic area has now developed into a national poverty alleviation demonstration project through tourism characterized by "scenic area development driving village development." It has become a pioneer in the transformation of Shanxi Province into a global tourist destination.

Experience and Inspiration

1. Scientific planning. The scenic area planning development must be integrated with rural development planning. With the goal of building a domestic first-class scenic spot, the surrounding villages on the scenic area development are closely intertwined and interdependent. Only through the same goal can integrated planning and joint efforts drive each other for common development.

2. Ecological protection. Concrete measures should be made to protect and optimize the cultural heritage in the scenic area, eliminate deforestation for a renewed

ecological environment and improve human settlements for transformation into a beautiful village.

3. Agricultural and tourism integration. Tourism is a rising green industry that radiates peripheral development. Through the years, it has played a prominent role in driving rural development by helping farmers improve their household income. Only through the in-depth integration of agriculture and tourism can the mutual in-depth promotion and development be achieved. With the development of the scenic area, farmers can receive more benefits such as income increase and better conditions for production and living. In turn, they will be in a position to offer more support for the scenic spot development, thereby forming a driving force for rural revitalization.

4. Contribution to society. A total of more than RMB 19 million has been invested into the scenic area for the building of the "Yuangu Hope Farm" in cooperation with professors from Taiwan Region. The goal is to provide educational services for the physically and mentally handicapped. Over the past three years, 19 people with physical and mental disabilities have been recruited. Currently, seven of them lead normal lives and work to support themselves and their families.

Next Steps

With the dual goals of building a domestic first-class scenic area and achieving rural revitalization, the national 5A-level tourist attraction brand of the Mount Yun will be further enhanced. The improvement and upgrade of environmental sanitation is a priority. Also, the focus will be on the establishment of a smart scenic area and research tour that are expected to drive the radiating effects of development. The improvement of rural human settlements and the development of the tourism industry will be organically integrated. Also, the display of folk culture and its legacy, ancient culture and the construction of B&Bs in ancient villages, roads and wells will be highlighted. Construction of modern pig breeding bases of 220,000 heads and organic dry-land wheat bases of 8,000 *mu* will be accelerated. Sightseeing processing production lines such as medicinal tea, pickles, pastries, cultural and creative and artisanal products, flour and high-standard facilities for vegetable standardization bases will be built based on unique natural biological resources. Efforts will be made to get an early start in transforming the Mount Yun Village into a national first-class demonstration village for ecological construction. Overall, the Mount Yun Scenic Area will showcase rural tourism development, leisure, vacation and healthcare industries. It will advance organic dry-land farming as Mount Yun's characteristic agricultural brand. All these will achieve the full integration of scenic area development and rural revitalization.

华侨城：
智慧赋能，以全域旅游推动海南三亚市天涯区马岭社区发展

Overseas Chinese Town Holdings Company:
Promote Maling Community in Tianya District, Sanya City, Hainan Province through All-for-one Tourism with Wisdom Empowerment

摘要

海南省三亚市天涯区天涯镇马岭社区是一个有着近400年历史的滨海渔村，其集体经济发展滞后，基础设施落后，产业基础薄弱。华侨城集团为该社区提供智力和资本支撑，使马岭社区通过龙头企业带动、集体经济组织、专业机构参与以及公共平台支撑的多元化发展模式，在社区打造华侨城全域旅游总部基地，为社区打造亮丽名片，获取“千万级游客”引流渠道。

挑战与问题

海南三亚市天涯区天涯镇马岭社区是一个有着近400年历史的滨海渔村，占地面积约2平方公里，总户数1358户，总人口6064人，曾经存在集体经济发展滞后、基础设施落后、社区环境脏乱差现象突出、产业基础薄弱、人口结构老龄化等问题。社区居民的主要收入依靠传统的近海捕捞。近年来，因近海渔业资源枯竭，世代渔民亟须转产就业。

措施

1. 政企共建，打造东西文化交融的特色小镇。华侨城出资近500万元提供社区产业策划及社区规划方案，天涯区政府出资4.39亿元在马岭社区完成了立面改造工程。马岭社区现拥有中国唯一的“黄、黑、青、白、红”五龙社区主题街区，社区留存着传统的舞龙、赛龙舟渔风文化；具有中国传统的淳朴民风、友善邻里的社区气质。如今的马岭社区，“海”“天”蓝白呼应，面朝大海，四季花开，一个地中海风情小镇已然初步成型。再加上整洁的社区环境及淳朴闲适的渔风民俗，游客顷刻间仿佛置身于异国他乡。这里被称为中国版的“圣托里尼”，是三亚市知名的网红度假文旅小镇。

2. 社企联动，开展社区治理。华侨城联合三亚市生态环境局和马岭社区，深入开展社区治理工作，创建“无废社区”和“三亚市生态环境保护宣传教育基地”，启动社区治理百日攻坚行动，结合文明城市的创建，大力开展沙滩净化、卫生整治等工作，极大地改善了小镇的人居环境和精神风貌。

3. 文化赋能，重塑传统文化价值。文化自信与乡土文化方面，以当地的“五龙”文化为精髓，成立“五龙”文化协会、海南五龙洋产业发展有限公司，探索重现端午龙舟赛等传统民俗活动；结合时尚元素，包装、设计符合本地“五龙”文化的IP，并运用新媒体广泛推广，使其文化精髓在新时代焕发出强大的生命力和经济价值。以生态文化为乡镇建设的价值引领，加强生态文明建设，积极倡导绿色生产和生活方式。将文化创意作为乡镇振兴的重要动能，深入挖掘当地的生态道德、生活习俗等文化资源，加快乡镇生态振兴。以文化供给为社区人才赋能，开展“轮值镇长”事件营销活动，为小镇的产业兴旺奠定“智慧”基础。

4. 全域旅游，逐步实现产业振兴。始终尊重地域发展的文化脉络和乡村生存的自然法则，以“党建共建为引领、社区治理为抓手、产业振兴为根本”为发展理念，以“智慧撬动、智慧输出、平台化运营”为经营思路，马岭社区坚定龙头企业带动、集体经济组织、专业机构参与以及公共平台支撑的多元化发展模式，在社区打造华侨城全域旅游总部基地，为社区打造亮丽名片，获取“千万级游客”引流渠道。将社区治理与产业兴旺相结合，鼓励村民以废弃或闲置民房参与入股，活化利用废弃或闲置民房、“半拉子工地”等，引入婚尚旅拍产业，打造婚尚旅拍全产业链；建立天涯创客基地，为创客提供一站式孵化平台；创办运营桨板俱乐部，发展休闲渔业；创办天涯区旅游协会整合旅游行业资源，绘制社区智能景区导览地图，为游客提供全方位休闲度假、生活服务平台，促进当地农民增产增收。

成效

马岭社区以“产业同创、运营同创、资本同创、文化同创”的合作模式，带动逾6000万元社会资本投资马岭社区。经过社区美化、亮化、绿化、艺术化、产业化改造升级，马岭社区2020年迎来游客井喷式增长，接待游客量约18万人次。2021年第一季度，酒店、民宿入住率同比2019年第一季度增幅57%，游客结构持续优化，主力客群由50后、60后转向90后及00后，客单价同比提高120%。

马岭社区通过社企合作，以租赁村民闲置房屋、宣传引投租赁、聘用村民职工等渠道，带动村民创收累计约1640万元；引导返乡就业创业村民120人；使实现了在家门口“吃旅游饭”（从事经营活动）的马岭村民增加了50户；村民年人均收入从2018年的3.8万元增长至2020年的约4.8万元。

2020年，马岭社区获评安仁论坛第二届“小镇美学榜样”，并荣获第六届中国文旅产业巅峰大会暨首届中国文旅夜游经济峰会“金峰奖”（最佳文旅目的地振兴示范奖）、中国文旅行业振兴发展大会“2020中国最具人气文旅目的地奖”。

经验与启示

1. 发展模式是乡村振兴的成败关键。马岭社区以“党建共建为引领、社区治理为抓手、产业振兴为根本”为发展理念，以“智慧撬动、智慧输出、平台化运营”为经营思路，坚定龙头企业带动、集体经济组织、居民和专业机构参与及公共平台支撑的多元化运营模式，用好外力、激发内力，形成龙头带动、群众拥护、专业赋能干事创业的合力作用。

2. 集体经济是乡村振兴的核心动力。乡村中集体经济是把人力、物力、财力凝聚起来的有效载体，有了集体经济集中人力、物力、财力资源的整体优势，才能通过产业振兴的核心动力最终实现乡村振兴的伟大目标。

3. 融合发展是乡村振兴的必由之路。全域旅游对乡村振兴影响深远、带动力强，其强大的市场优势、新兴的产业活力、强劲的造血功能、巨大的带动作用，成为撬动地方经济发展、推进乡村振兴的支柱性产业项目和新引擎。随着全域旅游的发展，通过搭建各类平台、整合社会资源、融合乡村一、二、三产业，优化营商环境，引入“人才、资本、智力、流量”，实现社区“宜业、宜居、宜乐、宜游”功能落地，实现生产者受益、投资者获利、游客满意的服务体验，让乡村振兴有了精准的方向，形成文化与产业振兴的闭环。

下一步计划

1. 深化“三变”改革。资源变资产、村民变股东、资金变股金，壮大集体经济，构建良好的全域旅游产业链生态。做强主题民宿、做好特色美食，形成三亚滨海民宿集群优势；发展海上休闲体育运动及休闲渔业、婚尚旅拍产业及文创乡创产业，引导当地居民转产就业，提高整体收入。

2. 提升社区治理。完善社区净化、绿化、美化、亮化、艺术化、产业化，探索社区步行街化，打造面朝大海、四季花开、干净整洁、文明时尚的滨海度假风情小镇。

3. 完善公共配套设施。解决社区停车难、如厕难、公共文化场所匮乏等公共配套设施问题，推动马岭社区及周边的公共停车场、街区公共厕所及文化活动广场的建设。

4. 推动产业转型升级。以“产业、文化、资本、运营”同创的合作模式，在社区创办 100 个社群聚落部，带动 1000 个社区共创项目落地以实现产业转型升级，实现人人有事干、户户有产业，铺就以“文化 + 旅游 + 城镇化”为基本模式的乡村振兴之路。

5. 打造文旅小镇。拟充分利用天涯海角西侧的 23 亩码头用地，将该区域打造成集停车、游客服务、文化演艺中心、跨境电商、精品酒店等功能于一体的游客服务中心。打造集休闲渔业、观光游览、渔事体验、“五龙舟”赛事等于一体的滨海特色旅游产业群，形成独具特色、具有高附加值的综合文旅小镇。

Abstract

Maling Community, Tianya Town, Tianya District, Sanya City, Hainan Province, a coastal fishing village with a history of nearly 400 years, lags behind in collective economy, infrastructure and industrial foundation. Through the support and capital infusion from the Overseas Chinese Town Holdings Company (OCT Group), and the diversified development model with "leading enterprises, collective economy organizing, professional institutions engagement and public platform support," the Maling Community has built an OCT Group headquarters for all-for-one tourism, highlighting its captivating charm to attract "tens of millions of tourists."

Challenges and Problems

Maling Community, Tianya Town, Tianya District, Sanya City, Hainan Province, a coastal fishing village with a history of nearly 400 years, covers an area of about 2 square kilometers, with a total of 6,064 people and 1,358 households. Lagged collective economic development, backward infrastructure, disorderly community environment, weak industrial foundations and an aging population are among some of the problems the community faces. Residents rely on traditional offshore fishing for their main income. In recent years, however, it has become urgent for fishermen to find another source for their livelihoods due to the depletion of offshore fishery resources.

Measures

1. Co-construction of government and enterprises for an East-West culturally integrated town model. The OCT Group has invested nearly RMB 5 million for a comprehensive industry and community planning programs. The Tianya District Government has also invested RMB 439 million to complete the facade renovation project of the Maling Community. Five dragon-themed (yellow, black, blue, white, red) community block features the traditional dragon dance and dragon boat racing. Residents are sincere, simple and friendly and have maintained the traditional Chinese folk customs. The blue sea and white clouds complement each other, leading to a cozy feeling of "flowers bloom in all seasons when facing the sea." A Mediterranean-style small town has taken shape. With its tidy environment and simple fishing customs, being here makes visitors feel they're in a foreign land. The Maling Community,

an internet-famous resort town in Sanya, is known as the "Santorini" of China.

2. Enterprise cooperation for community governance. In cooperation with Sanya City Ecological Environment Bureau and Maling Community, the OCT Group carries out in-depth community governance work, develops "No-waste Community" and "Sanya Ecological Environmental Protection Publicity and Education Base." It has also initiated the hundred-day action plan for community governance. In addition to beach cleaning, sanitation control has been smoothly conducted according to the civilized city concept, which aims to dramatically improve the living environment and outlook of the town.

3. Culture empowerment for reshaping of traditional cultural values. The "Five Dragons" Cultural Association and Hainan Wulongyang Industrial Development Co., Ltd., with the local "Five Dragons" culture as the centerpiece, are established to reproduce traditional folk activities such as the Dragon Boat Race at the Dragon Boat Festival. Also, the IP, in compliance with local "Five Dragons" culture is fashionably designed and promoted extensively through new media. This enables its cultural essence and economic vitality value to shine through in the new era. A strong ecological culture guides the construction of towns and promote its development and advocacy of green production and lifestyle. Cultural creativity facilitates revitalization and serves as an important driving force for local resources, including ecology, ethics, lifestyle and customs. Moreover, an abundant cultural supply empowers community talents to launch a rotating "town mayor" marketing program to provide leadership for industrial prosperity.

4. All-for-one tourism for industrial revitalization. In the context of rural living, the development concept of "party building and co-construction as the guide, community governance as the means, and industrial revitalization as the foundation," and the business idea of "intelligence leveraging, wisdom output, platform operation," as well as the diversified development model characterized with "leading enterprises driving, collective economy organizing, professional institutions engagement, and public platform support," the Maling Community is building an all-for-one tourism OCT Group headquarters to promote its brand image to attract "tens of millions of tourists." The combination of community governance and industrial prosperity inspires villagers to transform abandoned or unused houses and semi-finished construction sites into businesses. The wedding photography industry is developed. Tianya Creator Base is established to provide a one-stop incubation platform for creators. Paddle board clubs are established to develop leisure fishery. Moreover, the Tianya District Tourism Association is created to integrate tourism industry resources and guide maps for scenic spots in the community, providing tourists a reliable all-round services platform while simultaneously promoting enhanced

productivity and income to local farmers.

Results

With the cooperation model of "industry co-creation, operation co-creation, capital co-creation, and cultural co-creation," the Maling Community attracts the social capital of more than 60 million in investment. After its beautification, greening, ratification and upgrade, the Maling Community experienced a growth spurt in 2020, receiving about 180,000 tourists. In the first quarter of 2021, the occupancy rate of hotels and B&Bs registered a year-on-year increase of 57% compared to 2019. The main customers have shifted from the post 50s and 60s to the post 90s and 00s, with the year-on-year increase of 120% in the customer unit price.

Through cooperation with social enterprises, the Maling Community has helped villagers generate a total income of approximately RMB 16.4 million by renting idle houses, promoting investment and leasing, and hiring villagers as employees. One hundred twenty (120) villagers have returned to their hometowns for employment and entrepreneurship. The number of villagers engaged in tourism-related businesses in the community has increased by 50 households, while the average annual income of villagers increased from RMB 38,000 in 2018 to about RMB 48,000 in 2020.

In 2020, the Maling Community won the Second "Model of Town Esthetics" at Anren Forum, the "Golden Peak Award" at the 6th China Cultural Tourism Industry Davost Conference & the First China Cultural Tourism Night Tourism Economy Summit (The Best Cultural Tourism Destination Revitalization Demonstration Award), and "The Most Popular Cultural Tourism Destination Award in China 2020" at the China Cultural Tourism Industry Revitalization and Development Forum.

Experience and Inspirations

1. The development model determines the success of rural revitalization. The Maling Community adheres to the development concept of "party building and co-construction as the guide, community governance as the means, and industrial revitalization as the foundation," and the business concept of "intelligence leveraging, wisdom output, platform operation," as well as the diversified development model characterized with "enterprise-driven, collective economy organizing, residents and professional institutions engagement, and public platform support." Altogether they entice external support and stimulate internal forces, resulting in a combined development model that generates popular support and professional empowerment.

2. The collective economy represents the core driving force for rural revitalization. The rural collective economy can forge together human, material and financial resources. Their overall advantages can be showcased to achieve the great goal of rural revitalization through the core driving force of industrial revitalization.

3. Integrated development is the only path to rural revitalization. All-for-one tourism can exert a profound impact on rural revitalization. Its strong market advantages, industrial vitality, powerful renovation function and immense driving force are pillars and new engines for leveraging local economic development. With the development of all-for-one tourism, the community function of "working, living, entertaining and traveling" can be achieved by building various platforms, integrating social resources, combining rural primary, secondary and tertiary industries, optimizing business environment, introducing "talents, capital, intelligence and flow." With this, producers and investors can benefit immensely and tourists are assured of a satisfactory service experience.

Next Steps

1. Broaden the application of the "three changes." The "three changes" refer to turning resources into assets, villagers into shareholders, and capital into equity, to develop the collective economy and build a healthy all-for-one tourism industry chain. Themed B&Bs and specialties should be highlighted to maximize the advantage of Sanya's coastal B&B clusters. Marine leisure sports and recreational fisheries, wedding photography, cultural and creative industries must be developed. Local residents must be guided to shift to relevant jobs for more income.

2. Enhance community governance. The focus should be on community gentrification, greening, beautification and industrialization. Deployment of pedestrian streets and the creation of a cozy, clean and civilized coastal resort town must be explored.

3. Construction of public facilities. Parking problems, lack of toilets and public cultural places should be addressed. Through proper channels, the community should compel the government to build public parking lots, public toilets and cultural squares in and around the community.

4. Promote industrial transformation and enhancement. With the "industry, culture, capital and operation" co-creation model, 100 community clusters have been established, and 1,000 community co-creation projects were launched for industrial transformation and upgrade. People have their own business and there is an industry for every household for their livelihoods, paving the way to rural revitalization based on the "culture + tourism + urbanization" model.

5. Build a cultural tourism town. Plan for the full use of the 23 *mu* of land on the west side of The Remotest Corners of the Globe to build a multi-function tourist service center that integrates parking, cultural and performance centers, cross-border e-commerce and boutique hotels. A coastal tourism industry cluster featuring leisure fishery, sightseeing, fishing experience and "Five Dragon Boat Race" are going to be developed to create a unique, high-added value cultural tourism town.

甘肃：
乡村旅游助力脱贫攻坚

Gansu Province:
Rural Tourism Facilitates Poverty Alleviation

摘要

近年来，甘肃省把发展乡村旅游作为打赢扶贫脱贫攻坚战、实施乡村振兴战略的重要任务，大力实施旅游富民工程，积极推进旅游扶贫项目建设，积极培育乡村旅游产业，促进贫困群众脱贫致富。全省乡村旅游呈现出快速发展的强劲态势，有效发挥了旅游就业和收入“双提高”、产业和生态“双促进”、物质和精神“双脱贫”的积极作用。2016 年以来，累计扶持贫困地区 702 个村开展乡村旅游，发展农家乐 9306 户，创建乡村旅游示范村 310 个，培育乡村旅游合作社 301 个；截至 2020 年年底，全省旅游专业村累计达 1270 个，农家乐累计达 21500 户。通过文化旅游，累计带动 59.2 万人实现脱贫。通过坚持不懈的努力，乡村旅游已经成为该省农民增收致富的有效手段，旅游扶贫已经成为甘肃脱贫攻坚的重要力量。

挑战与问题

甘肃是全国打赢脱贫攻坚战最困难的省份，全省建档立卡贫困人口552万人，建档立卡贫困村6220个。86个县、市、区中，有58个县列入国家六盘山、秦巴山和藏区“三大片区”，还有17个县属于省定“插花型”贫困县。2017年，甘南州、临夏州和天祝县共17个县被整体列入国家重点支持的“三区三州”范围，是全省的贫中之贫、困中之困、坚中之坚、难中之难。据统计，全省70%文化旅游资源集中在贫困地区，但由于受到交通不便、基础设施不足等条件的制约，旅游开发滞后，影响了贫困地区的发展。

措施

1. 强化政策扶持。省委、省政府先后召开全省旅游产业发展大会、全省乡村旅游和旅游扶贫大会，研究出台了《关于加快建设旅游强省的意见》《关于加快乡村旅游发展的意见》。文化和旅游部门配套制订了《甘肃省乡村旅游助推脱贫攻坚实施方案》《甘肃省推动乡村旅游提质升级行动方案》等一系列政策措施，为乡村旅游优质发展提供政策保障。

2. 加大项目资金投入。围绕产业扶贫重大任务，严格落实中央和省里各类资金向“三区三州”深度贫困地区倾斜的要求，加大文化旅游扶贫财政性投入，形成文化旅游多元化投入机制。甘肃省制订了《2018—2020年脱贫攻坚财政资金安排计划》，统筹安排3亿元旅游专项资金，并整合资金11.8亿元扶持贫困地区发展乡村旅游。甘肃实施乡村旅游规划公益扶贫行动，为列入“三区三州”的临夏州、甘南州、天祝县编制50个贫困村乡村

旅游发展规划，并全力组织实施。

3. 推进乡村旅游提质升级。深入推进乡村旅游提质升级行动，全省筛选确定了 268 个乡村旅游示范村集中建设，打造示范标杆。政府以公开招标的方式，委托高校、旅行社和媒体组成第三方督查评估和咨询服务组，对乡村旅游示范村进行了绩效评估，对项目建设、业态培育、产品开发、运营管理给予技术指导和咨询服务。在《甘肃日报》开辟专版专栏，西北师大、兰州文理学院和旅游智库以旅游扶贫和乡村旅游为主题分别组织专家撰稿，对全省乡村旅游发展进行集中指导；由旅行社组队对乡村旅游示范村和扶贫重点村进行产品线路开发设计，策划推出乡村旅游精品产品 126 个、线路 60 条。

4. 推动乡村旅游多元开发。积极探索乡村旅游发展的产品布局模式，全省基本形成了景区带动型、城镇辐射型、通道景观型、产业依托型、乡村休闲型、创意主导型 6 种旅游扶贫模式。全省培育具有典型引领作用的中国乡村旅游模范村 27 个，创建全国休闲农业与乡村旅游示范县 8 个，培育“双带双加”旅游扶贫先进典型 12 个，32 个村被国家发改委、文化和旅游部评定为“全国乡村旅游重点村”。

5. 加强乡村旅游培训。政府制定了《甘肃省乡村旅游建设指引》，为全省特别是贫困地区推进旅游专业村及农家乐建设提供了技术指导和支持。将扶贫与扶志、扶智相结合，先后对 500 多个专

业旅游村、1 万多名乡村干部和农家乐业主进行了集中培训，组织 300 多名旅游扶贫重点村村干部参加全国乡村旅游扶贫重点村干部培训班，实现了深度贫困地区乡村旅游培训全覆盖。

成效

甘肃致力于生态优先、绿色发展，着力推动产品创新、基础提升、品牌创建，成功打造全国乡村旅游重点村 32 个、省级乡村旅游示范村 310 个、田园综合体 10 个、乡村旅游精品线路 60 条，乡村旅游富裕乡民、提升乡貌、留住乡愁、文明乡风的作用不断显现。近五年，甘肃乡村旅游接待人数和综合收入年均增幅保持在 25% 以上。2016 年以来，累计扶持贫困地区 702 个村开展乡村旅游，发展农家乐 9306 户；截至 2020 年年底，全省旅游专业村累计 1270 个，农家乐累计达 21500 户。通过文化旅游，累计带动 59.2 万人实现脱贫，全省乡村旅游扶贫脱贫贡献度达到 26.9%，增加收入贡献度达到 29.4%，解决就业贡献度达到 27%。

经验与启示

1. 带动村民参与。在发展乡村旅游的过程中，通过吸纳当地农民参与乡村旅游的经营与管理，增加群众就业机会。村游客服务中心和乡村宾馆为村民提供保洁、保安、服务等就业岗位，村内油坊、磨坊、豆腐坊、手工挂面坊等各种作坊在采购原材料、招聘务工人员时，优先带动村内及周边的农户和贫困户就业，扶贫效果十分明显。陇南市康县花桥村近年来通过发展乡村旅游带动全村整体脱贫，经调查，开办农家乐和农家客栈，月收入 2 万余元，年收入 20 万元左右。另外，定期从贫困户手中购买土鸡、土鸡蛋、山野菜等原材料，聘请贫困户为服务员，可以带动 20 多户贫困户共同发展，每人年务工收入 1.5 万～ 2 万元。

2. 推进基础建设。通过旅游扶贫，将美丽乡村与专业旅游村建设结合，整合各级政府在交通基础设施建设、农村危房改造、农村环境综合整治、生态搬迁、游牧民定居、传统村落及民居保护等方面投入的项目资金，集中实施水、电、路、通信等旅游基础设施建设项目，加强对民居、厕所、环卫等设施的改造，促进了垃圾净化、村容绿化、环境美化，改善了农村发展环境和村容村貌。

3. 盘活农业资源。随着全省乡村旅游的快速发展和旅游扶贫工作的深入推进，贫困地区通过发展观光农业、农家乐接待、土特产品种植与加工，促使传统农业向现代农业转变、单一农业向多元产业转变、粗放经济向效益经济转变，大大提高了农业效益和农村经济发展水平。

4. 弘扬乡村文化。通过发展乡村旅游，使乡

村蕴含的生态美景、田园风光、民俗风情的价值得以体现和开发，使乡村特有的传统工艺、文物古迹、节庆文化、农耕文化得到传承和发扬，真正实现了“望得见山，看得见水，记得住乡愁”。随着乡村旅游发展，当地农民群众越发深刻地认识到乡村生态环境的巨大价值，感受到乡村传统文化的巨大魅力，增强了保护生态环境、弘扬民俗文化的积极性和自觉性，进而推动实现乡村旅游开发和环境保护的双赢。

下一步计划

下一步，甘肃将以乡村振兴战略为机遇，以发展乡村旅游为抓手，以农为本，以质取胜，因地制宜，加强文化旅游产业融合，全面开启甘肃乡村旅游高质量发展新篇章。

1. 构建乡村旅游品牌体系。坚持以品牌引领乡村旅游发展，大力实施乡村特色旅游镇（村）、农家乐、精品民宿、农家旅馆、农家餐馆等品牌创建工程，推动乡村旅游点创建国家A级旅游景区和旅游度假区以及现代农业庄园，重点培育一批资源优势明显、产业基础扎实、发展势头旺盛、示范能力较强的乡村旅游示范县，打造3～5个具有国内一流水平的精品民宿集聚带。

2. 推进陇原乡村文化振兴。将乡土文化作为乡村旅游的内核和核心吸引力，将以非遗艺术为主题的乡土文化作为卖点，促进乡土文化资本向经济资本转化，推动当地农民生产经营方式转变，实现对乡村传统文化价值的重新认识、活化及再利用，建立起乡村民俗文化遗产保护传承的产业链条。

3. 推动乡村旅游消费升级。突出消费升级，加快培育乡村旅游优质产品，真正把农业作为旅游消费的载体，增加乡村旅游的附加值。加强农村农业产品创意设计，积极开发农业观光、休闲度假、健康疗养、民俗演艺、农事节庆、文化遗产和非物质文化遗产等特色鲜明的乡村旅游产品。

4. 激活乡村旅游大市场。把乡村旅游作为重中之重来包装推介。借助“丰收了 · 游甘肃”冬春文化旅游惠民活动，做亮以丰收为主题、以农民为贵宾、以文旅惠民为初衷的推广营销品牌，让甘肃赢得更多的农民“朋友圈”。

5. 打造优质乡村旅游生力军。实施乡村旅游“四大”人才培养工程：开展领导干部研修工程、从业人员培训工程、乡村旅游创客工程、乡村旅游智力扶贫工程，为乡村旅游和旅游扶贫提供智力支撑。

Abstract

By recognizing rural tourism development as an important tool in winning the battle against poverty and implementing the rural revitalization strategy, the Gansu Province has enriched people, created poverty-alleviation projects and cultivated rural industries The rapid development of provincial rural tourism has played a positive role in increasing job opportunities and people's income. Also, it has promoted both industrial and ecological developments and facilitated poverty relief in both material and spirit. Since 2016, a total of 702 villages in poverty-stricken areas have been supported for rural tourism development. It has developed 9,306 sites for agritainment and nurtured 301 rural tourism cooperatives. At the end of 2020, 1,270 professional tourism villages and 21,500 sites for agritainment throughout the province had been built. A total of 592,000 people have been lifted out of poverty through cultural tourism. Rural tourism has become an effective means for farmers to increase their income and alleviate their poverty.

Challenges and Problems

Winning the tough battle against poverty is especially difficult for Gansu Province. In all regions across China, it has 5.52 million archived impoverished people and 6,220 archived poverty-stricken villages. The Liupan Mountain, Qinling-Daba Mountains and Xizang's region are listed on the "Three Major Contiguous Poverty-Stricken Areas." Among 86 districts, counties and cities, 58 counties are on this list. Seventeen counties are provincially-categorized as non-continuously poverty stricken. In 2017, a total of 17 counties, including Gannan Xizang's Autonomous Prefecture, Linxia Hui Autonomous Prefecture and Tianzhu Xizang's Autonomous County were identified as the most impoverished areas in Gansu Province. They were included in the "Three Regions and Three Prefectures" (severely impoverished areas on the state level. Three Regions refer to the Xizang Autonomous Region, the Xizang's areas of Qinghai, Sichuan, Gansu, and Yunnan provinces, as well as Hetian, Aksu, Kashi, Kizilsu Kyrgyz in the south of Xinjiang Autonomous Region. Three Prefectures refer to Liangshan Prefecture in Sichuan Province, Nujiang Prefecture in Yunnan Province and Linxia Prefecture in Gansu Province supported by the state.) According to statistics, 70% of the cultural tourism resources in the province are concentrated in the poverty-stricken areas. However, tourism development is lagging behind due to inconvenient transportation and insufficient infrastructure.

Measures

1. Strengthen policy support. The Provincial Party Committee and the Provincial Government have successively held the Provincial Tourism Industry Development Conference and the Provincial Rural Tourism and Poverty Alleviation through Tourism Conference and released the *Opinions on Accelerating the Construction of a Province with a Strong Tourism Industry* and the *Opinions on Accelerating the Development of Rural Tourism*. Cultural tourism related departments have also formulated policy measures such as the *Implementation Plan for Poverty Alleviation through Rural Tourism in Gansu Province* and the *Action Plan for Quality Promotion and Upgrade of Rural Tourism in Gansu Province* to provide policy support for the high-quality development of rural tourism.

2. Increase project capital. Focused on the major tasks of poverty alleviation through industrial development, and in adherence to the strict implementation of national and provincial requirements of putting more funds to the severely impoverished areas on the list of "Three Regions and Three Prefectures," cultural tourism funding for the alleviation of poverty and the development of a diversified investment mechanism has been increased.

The Gansu Province has formulated the *Financial Funding Arrangement Plan for Poverty Alleviation 2018 — 2020* to allocate special tourism funds of RMB 300 million and integrate RMB 1.18 billion for rural tourism development. It has also implemented fifty public welfare poverty alleviation programs for the impoverished villages of Linxia Hui Autonomous Prefecture, Gannan

Xizang's Autonomous Prefecture, and Tianzhu Xizang's Autonomous County, all of which are included in the "Three Regions and Three Prefectures."

3. Promote the quality and upgrading of rural tourism. To promote the quality and upgrading of rural tourism, the province has created a model benchmark for a centralized construction after screening and identifying 268 rural tourism demonstration villages. The government has commissioned colleges and universities, travel agencies and the media to form a third-party inspection, evaluation and a consulting service team through public bidding. Together they have to evaluate the performance of demonstration villages, provide technical guidance and consultation services on construction projects, business incubation, product development and performance management. A special column has also been created in *Gansu Daily*. Also, experts have been organized by Northwest Normal University, Lanzhou University of Arts and Science and Tourism Think Tank to write articles on tourism-driven poverty alleviation programs and provide concentrated guidance on rural tourism development in the province. Travel agencies have also developed product routes for poverty alleviation demonstration and key villages. The launch of 126 boutique products and 60 rural tourism routes have been planned.

4. Promote the diversified development of rural tourism. Based on a proactive blueprint of rural tourism development, six poverty alleviation models in the province have been created around scenic area-centered, town-radiated, channel landscape-oriented, industry-based, rural leisure-styled, and creativity-led prototype. The province has nurtured 27 rural tourism model villages China, created eight national demonstration counties in leisure agriculture and cultivated 12 advanced models of poverty alleviation through tourism featuring "scenic area development driving village development, talents driving households" and "companies + peasant households, cooperatives + peasant households." 32 villages have been rated rural tourism national key villages by the National Development and Reform Commission and the Ministry of Culture and Tourism.

5. Reinforce training on rural tourism. The government has formulated the *Guidelines for the Construction of Rural Tourism in Gansu Province* to provide technical guidance and support for the province, especially for poverty-stricken areas. It aims to promote the construction of professional tourism villages and agritainment. Recognizing that poverty alleviation requires a change of attitude and educational support, the government has conducted successive intensive training for more than 500 professional tourist villages and 10,000-plus rural officials and agritainment owners, It has also organized more than 300 rural officials from key villages developing tourism for poverty alleviation to receive training in this matter.

Results

The Gansu Province is committed to ecological priority, green development, product innovation, foundation improvement and brand building. To this end, it has developed 32 national key villages in rural tourism, 310 provincial rural tourism demonstration villages, 10 pastoral complexes and 60 boutique routes of rural tourism—all of which present the positive effects of rural tourism in enriching villagers, a new look for the villages while evoking nostalgia and developing civilized

customs. In the past five years, the average annual growth rate of the number of rural tourists and comprehensive income in the province have remained above 25%. Since 2016, a total of 702 villages in poverty-stricken areas have received substantial support for rural tourism development. To date, it has developed 9,306 sites for agritainment. At the end of 2020, 1,270 professional tourism villages and 21,500 sites for agritainment had been built throughout the province. In fact, cultural tourism has helped lift 592,000 people out of poverty, contributing to 26.9 to its poverty relief goal, 29.4% in income increase and 27% in the employment.

Experience and Inspirations

1. Motivate local villagers to get involved. Job opportunities for villagers can be increased by attracting local farmers to engage in the operation and management of rural tourism. Tourist service centers and hotels offer villagers employment opportunities in cleaning, security and services. Job recruitment and the purchase of raw materials in oil and tofu, mills, hand-made noodle and other workshops will be prioritized for peasant and poor households in the village and surrounding areas. In recent years, Huaqiao Village, Kang County, Longnan City have been lifted out of poverty through rural tourism development. Studies have shown agritainment and rural inns have been operating in the village, generating a monthly income of more than RMB 20,000 and an annual income of about RMB 200,000. The government has regularly purchased raw materials — native chickens and eggs, and wild vegetables from impoverished households, promoting the common development of more than 20 impoverished households with an annual per capita income of about RMB 15,000 to 20,000.

2. Advance infrastructure construction. Poverty alleviation through tourism can help with the merging of beautiful village construction and professional tourist village, integrate government project funds in transportation infrastructure construction, rural dilapidated house reconstruction, rural environmental improvement, ecological relocation, settlement of nomads, traditional villages and residence protection. Also, it can implement the construction of tourism infrastructure such as water, electricity, roads, and communications, thereby reinforcing the renovation of residences, toilets, environmental sanitation and other facilities.

More importantly, poverty alleviation through tourism is the impetus that can move local communities toward the fulfillment of its goal of zero garbage, greener villages and beautified environment.

3. Revitalize agricultural resources. With the rapid development of rural tourism in the province and the in-depth advancement of poverty alleviation through tourism, the development of sightseeing agriculture, agritainment, and planting and processing of native products in poverty-stricken areas have transformed traditional agriculture to modern agriculture, unitary agriculture to multiple industries, and extensive economy to efficient economy, which has greatly improved the agricultural benefits and the level of rural economic development.

4. Promote rural culture. The development of rural tourism can help reflect and develop rural ecological beauty, idyllic sceneries, and value of folk customs,

and inherit and promote unique traditional crafts, cultural relics, festival culture, and farming culture, thus developing the village into a "wonderland with lucid waters, lush mountains and nostalgia." With the development of rural tourism, local farmers can understand well the great value of rural ecological environment, experience the great charm of rural traditional culture, and have more extensive enthusiasm and consciousness of the ecological environment protection and folk culture promotion, hereby achieving a win-win situation between rural tourism development and environmental protection.

Next Steps

The Gansu Province will start a new chapter in the high-quality development of rural tourism by taking the rural revitalization strategy as an opportunity. With the agriculture-oriented principle at the center of its quality development, it will adapt measures based on local conditions to reinforce the integration of culture and tourism industries.

1. Build a rural tourism brand system. In adherence to a brand-led rural tourism development, brand building projects with rural characteristic tourist towns (villages), agritainment, boutique B&Bs, rural hotels, rural restaurants will be implemented. A-level tourist attractions, tourist resorts and modern agriculture farms in rural tourist spots will be established and promoted. Rural tourism demonstration counties with resource advantages, solid industrial foundations will be nurtured. Robust development momentum will be maintained and 3-5 domestic first-class boutique B&B cluster will be created.

2. Promote the revitalization of rural culture. Local culture is front and center of rural tourism. With the intangible heritage art as a selling point, the conversion of local cultural capital into economic capital will be promoted, along with the transformation of the production and management systems of the local farmers. This will pave the path to the renewal and repurposing of traditional rural cultural values through the establishment of an industrial chain for the protection and preservation of the folk cultural heritage.

3. Boost the consumption upgrading of rural tourism. The consumption upgrade will be highlighted for high-quality rural tourism products. Agriculture will be regarded as the carrier of tourism consumption to increase the added value of rural tourism. Strengthening the creative design of rural agricultural products is an absolute necessity. To this end, rural tourism products with distinctive characteristics, such as agricultural sightseeing, leisure and vacation, health and recuperation, folk performances, farming festivals, cultural heritage and intangible cultural heritage will be developed.

4. Revitalize rural tourism market. Rural tourism is prioritized for publicity. With the help of the "A Good Harvest, A Tour in Gansu" winter and spring cultural tourism activities, the marketing theme of good harvest will be further developed. Positioning farmers as VIPs and cultural tourism development for the people as the main intent will be enhanced to attract more farmer tourists into Gansu Province.

5. Develop talent resources for high-quality rural tourism. The four major talent training projects for rural tourism will be implemented. Training projects in cadre, practitioner, creator/maker and the poverty alleviation projects will be reinforced educational support and brainstormed ideas for poverty alleviation through tourism.

爱彼迎：

安徽黄山市黟县碧阳镇碧山村
普惠旅游模式下乡村度假产品的打造

Airbnb:

Rural Tourism Product Building under the Inclusive Tourism Model of Bishan Village in Biyang Town, Yi County, Huangshan City, Anhui Province

摘 要

“远村有近邻”乡村游主题活动，由爱彼迎携手黄山市文化和旅游局及中国古迹遗址保护协会，共同宣传黄山旅游目的地，推广本地特色精品民宿和旅游深度体验。活动从 2021 年 4 月中旬开始，通过选拔幸运游客前往黟县碧山村进行古镇乡村生活体验，宣传乡村旅游主题，鼓励当地民宿产业发展，同时致力于保护传统文化和乡村文化的原真性。通过宣传、保护和发展黄山地区的优秀历史文化，更好地增强乡村文化自信，促进乡村文化的传播，助力乡村振兴。爱彼迎倡导普惠旅游和可持续旅游的发展模式，此次活动也是全球“Airbnb Only On”（爱彼迎独家）系列创意活动宣传经验在中国的成功落地，有利于进一步助力乡村原真性文化旅游产品的深度开发。

挑战与问题

安徽省黄山市黟县碧山村是徽州著名古村落。村内有宋代私家园林“培筠园”遗址、明代私塾“耕读园”、清代古塔“云门塔”，保存完好的明清时期古民居和祠堂尚有 100 多座。随着中国乡村旅游的蓬勃发展和“美丽乡村”建设的不断推进，乡村文化在乡村旅游中的重要地位日益凸显，但是现实中缺少乡村文化的原真性和独特性，不足以支撑起乡村文化度假和体验性旅游活动。徽州民宿是黄山山水和古徽州建筑的结合，它既是黄山乡村振兴新的增长点，也是文旅融合的新平台。但由于对乡村古镇以及乡村传统文化和“徽州民宿”品牌的传播力度不够，在开发上资源分配不均，周边乡村旅游还存在开发空间，民宿品牌有必要进一步深化推广。

措施

1. 打造乡村遗产酒店。爱彼迎与中国古迹保护协会共同推广以“猪栏酒吧”特色民宿为代表的“乡村遗产酒店”古民居客栈以及周边旅游资源，在保护的基础上，通过旅游开发，让这些优秀文化活起来并传承下去。村中民宿原为清末民初时所建、历时超百年的传统徽派建筑，原本几近废弃的老宅在猪栏民宿的保护改造下重获新生；民宿在经营过程中注重对徽州乡土文化的继承和传承，收集当地村民的老家具、老物件作为室内装饰。同时，通过改良当地美食作为民宿的餐饮，采购当地村民自种自产的农副产品，带动了当地农业发展。

2. 活化乡村非遗文化。爱彼迎和黄山文旅局有效挖掘丰富的乡村旅游资源，将其包装成独特的旅游产品，一同打造真实的深度文化体验。例如，和当地村民一同守护传统手工艺，与非遗传承人共同体验非遗千张酥的制作；打造沉浸式旅游体验，感受人与人之间的真实联结和不一样的乡村旅游。

3. 造势古村古镇推广。爱彼迎通过自有资源、主流媒体和社交媒体宣传乡村旅游，传播乡村传统文化。以碧山村的示范为例，2021 年 4 月携手知名脱口秀演员李雪琴推出“远村有近邻”品质乡村游活动，目前已通过全社交平台进行了矩阵式传播，包括朋友圈广告、视频号、抖音、小红书、垂直类旅游平台马蜂窝等，引起了市场的高度关注。

4. 提升乡村民宿品质。爱彼迎通过自有平台和爱彼迎房东学院等渠道，对政府推荐的徽州精品民宿进行上线支持和经营指导，为徽州民宿主人提供系统化、专业化的培训，以此促进徽州民宿业的发展。

成效

爱彼迎和黄山文旅局携手推出的体验官招募活动，吸引来自各大城市的逾 3700 人报名，活动总曝光量超过 1 亿人次。在 5 月 19 日“中国旅游日”，邀请主流媒体前往黄山进行深度体验和报道，持续为活动造势，人民网、光明网、新华网、环球网、《中国日报》和中国新闻网，门户媒体搜狐、网易、新浪、腾讯和凤凰商业，旅游媒体 TTG 中国以及地方媒体的报道，总量超过 300 篇。爱彼迎联合黄山文旅局成功打造了普惠旅游模式下的乡村度假产品，不仅展现出黄山地区的特色历史文化，而且吸引了更多青年群体的关注和体验、自主传播，在保护传统文化和乡村文化的原真性的同时，增强了乡村文化的自信，促进了乡村文化的传播。

经验与启示

1. 积极与各方专业权威力量联合。爱彼迎与黄山市文化和旅游局、中国古迹遗址保护协会建立了长期友好合作关系；同时汇集了政府力量、专家学者力量与行业资深从业者力量，最大限度地整合了文旅产业资源，发力挖掘与保护当地原真历史文化遗产，系统规划黄山地区民宿产业布局等众多领域，以便实现综合效益最大化。

2. 创新线上线下同步营销模式。爱彼迎“远村有近邻”碧山村项目的线下行程设置与宣传点均

侧重于文化体验，对村庄和村民进行积极的组织和动员，在设置上最大限度地保护了传统文化的原真性。线下体验确保了黄山特色文化可以最大限度地被感知与接收；线上则以现代化多媒体平台为主要宣发出口，扩大了可触达的人群广泛度，持续增加受众对黄山非物质文化遗产的兴趣度与关注度。

3. 轻设计与介入，重传承与活化。在本项目中，侧重对传统历史文化的挖掘、传承、活化，而不是一味地将产品设计、建筑与线路标准化，以期吸收更多当地村民参与到文旅产业中来，真正保留与活化当地的传统文化。

下一步计划

爱彼迎将联动安徽黄山、四川丹巴、江西虹关村、浙江西邬古村四个乡村遗产酒店及所在村落，进一步扩大线上营销的规模与效果。未来，以黄山碧山村作为示范，在广大乡村地区进一步推广普惠旅游模式下的乡村度假产品，以期在保护传统文化的同时，去探索具有原真性的乡村文化旅游产品，助力各个地区的乡村旅游和民宿产业发展，倡导普惠旅游与可持续旅游的发展模式。

Abstract

Organized by Airbnb, together with the Huangshan Municipal Bureau of Culture and Tourism and Chinese National Committee for the International Council on Monuments and Sites (ICOMOS China), the "Near Neighbors from Villages Afar" project was created to promote the tourist destination of Mount Huang, local characteristic boutique B&Bs and an in-depth tourism experience. Implemented in mid-April 2021, it was aimed at enhancing the publicity for rural tourism through a selection process whereby lucky tourists would be chosen to experience rural life in Bishan Village, Yi County. Also, it was designed to drive the development of the local B&B industry and protect the authenticity of traditional and rural culture. The publicity, protection and development of the Huangshan area's rich historical culture would enhance the local people's confidence and spread the rural culture, driving rural revitalization. As Airbnb advocated the development model of inclusive and sustainable tourism, the project also represented the successful launch of the global "Airbnb Only On" promotional campaign in China, facilitating the development of authentic cultural tourism products in rural areas.

Challenges and Problems

The Bishan Village in Yi County, Huangshan City, Anhui Province, is a famous ancient village in Huizhou. It is home to the relic site of "Peiyun Garden," a private garden in the Song Dynasty; "Gengdu Academy," a private school in the Ming Dynasty; and "Yunmen Pagoda," an old pagoda in the Qing Dynasty, including more than 100 well-preserved old residences and ancestral halls in the Ming and Qing dynasties. With the continuous advancement of the construction of "beautiful villages," rural culture is playing an increasingly prominent role in the vigorous development China's rural tourism. However, its lack of authenticity and uniqueness in reality cannot support the activities of vacation and experiential tourism.

However, Huizhou's B&Bs, a combination of Mount Huang landscape and ancient Huizhou architecture, have become the new driving force for rural revitalization and the new platform for the integration of culture and tourism. Nevertheless, the publicity on traditional culture of ancient towns and villages and the "Huizhou B&Bs" brand has proven to be insufficient. The distribution of resources is unequal in terms of development. There is definitely room for the development and further promotion of the surrounding rural tourism and the B&B brands.

Measures

1. Develop rural heritage hotels. Airbnb, in alliance with the ICOMOS China, have promoted ancient residences & inns of "Rural Heritage Hotels" represented by the characteristic B&Bs of "Zhulan Jiuba" (name of rural inns) and surrounding tourism resources. It aims to develop and revitalize tourism through the preservation and protection of the native culture. The B&Bs were originally traditional Huizhou architecture, spanning more than a hundred years from the late Qing Dynasty to the early Republic of China. Nearly-abandoned old houses were revitalized after protection and reconstruction, with Huizhou's native culture emphasized throughout their construction. Old furniture and objects owned by local villagers were also collected and used as interior decoration for the B&Bs. The enhancement of local delicacies for catering at the B&Bs and the purchase of agricultural and ancillary products grown and produced by local villagers have boosted the development of local agriculture.

2. Revitalize rural intangible cultural heritage. Airbnb and Huangshan Municipal Bureau of Culture and Tourism have utilized abundant rural tourism resources and packaged them into unique tourism products for an authentic and in-depth cultural experience. They have protected traditional handicrafts with the local villagers and developed the intangible cultural heritage experience of "Qian Zhang Su" (a kind of crispy snack made of black sesame powder) to create an immersive travel experience. This promotes real interpersonal connections

and distinctive rural tourism.

3. Heighten the publicity for old villages and towns. Airbnb has promoted rural tourism and disseminated traditional rural culture through its own resources, mainstream and social media. With Bishan Village as an example, the "Near Neighbors from Villages Afar" program was launched in April 2021 through the cooperation with well-known talk show actress Li Xueqin. This was extensively promoted on all social platforms, including ads in Moments, video accounts, Tik Tok, Xiaohongshu, and mafengwo.com, a vertical tourism platform, generating attention.

4. Improve the quality of rural B&Bs. Airbnb provided online support and management guidance to government-recommended Huizhou boutique B&Bs through its own platform and the Airbnb Host Academy (AHA). It offered systematic and professional training for Huizhou B&B owners, which facilitated the Huizhou B&B industry development.

Results

Recruitment for experienced officers that were jointly launched by Airbnb and Huangshan Municipal Bureau of Culture and Tourism attracted more than 3,700 applicants from different cities, with the information campaign for it reaching more than 100 million people. During the China Tourism Day on May 19, mainstream media, namely people.cn, gmw.cn, xinhuanet.com, huanqiu.com, China Daily and chinanews.com, and the portal media of Sohu, NetEase, Sina, Tencent and Ifeng Business, were invited to Huangshan City for an in-depth experience. Their coverage of the event further increased publicity. *TTG China* and the local media produced more than 300 reports.

Rural tourism products under the inclusive tourism model developed by Airbnb and Huangshan Municipal Bureau of Culture and Tourism manifest the characteristic historical culture of the city. They have drawn the interest of young people, allowing them to gain experience and voluntarily protect traditional and rural culture.

Experience and Inspirations

1. Work cooperatively and collaboratively with industry professionals and authorities. Airbnb established a long-term friendly cooperative relationship with Huangshan Municipal Bureau of Culture and Tourism and ICOMOS China, along with local governments, experts, scholars, and senior industry practitioners to maximize the integration of cultural tourism industry resources, explore and protect the authenticity of local

historical and cultural heritage and formulate a systematic planning for the B&B industry in the city.

2. Innovate synchronous online & offline marketing model. For the offline model, the project focused on cultural experiences in creating itineraries. Publicity was used to mobilize villagers to protect the authenticity of their traditional culture and ensure the maximum manifestation of the characteristic Huangshan heritage.

As for the online model, modern multi-media platforms were leveraged as a publicity vehicle to expand audience reach, enhance their interest in Huangshan's intangible cultural heritage.

3. Emphasize legacy and revitalization, instead of design and intervention. More importance was attached to the utilization, legacy and revitalization of traditional historical culture, instead of standardized design of products, buildings and routes. By doing this, more local villagers were enticed to engage in cultural tourism industry, retain and revitalize local traditional culture.

Next Steps

Airbnb, in collaboration with four rural heritage hotels of Huangshan City in Anhui Province, Danba County in Sichuan Province, Hongguan Village in Jiangxi Province, and Duiwugu Village in Zhejiang Province, and the villages where the hotels are located, will expand the scale of the impact and influence of online marketing. In the future, Bishan Village will be taken as a model to further promote rural tourism products under the inclusive tourism model in vast rural areas.

To boost rural tourism development and the B&B industry in various regions and advocate for inclusive and sustainable tourism, the authenticity of rural cultural tourism products and traditional culture must be protected.

湖北黄冈市英山县孔家坊乡新铺村：
神峰山庄助力乡村振兴

Xinpu Village, Kongjiafang Township, Yingshan County, Huanggang City, Hubei Province:
Shenfeng Mountain Villa Facilitates Rural Revitalization

摘 要

2013 年以来，湖北先稌坛生态农业有限公司累计投资 4.481 亿元打造国家 3A 级旅游景区——神峰山庄。山庄以“千里挺进大别山生态循环农业体验游”为纽带，以“新文化 + 新农业 + 新健康”复合经营为导向，形成生态农业产业融合式发展的神峰模式。通过三产融合、村企联姻、群众加盟等新方式，构建以英山县为中心、辐射全国 14 个省市的 4 亿元扶贫产品产销网络。突出“扶志、扶智”，为大别山国家连片特困地区培养了 1 万余名新型职业农民和 400 位职业经理人。公司直接安排就业 3456 人，对接帮扶贫困户 1304 户 3921 人，年均为贫困对象直接增收 3.2 亿元，带动英山县及周边 7 万农民增收脱贫，为大别山 3 省 19 县精准扶贫与乡村振兴树立了全新样板。

挑战与问题

湖北省黄冈市英山县是国家级重点贫困县、湖北省深度贫困县，总人口 40.6 万人。2014 年建档立卡贫困户 3.7 万户 10.49 万人，贫困发生率 30.78%。其中，除 9418 户（约占 24%）属无劳、弱劳户需要实行低保兜底外，其余 76% 的贫困户需要通过产业带动才能实现脱贫。老百姓要脱贫，缺的不是力气，而是观念、信心和勇气。减贫之难，难在农产品难卖、卖不出好价。农村不缺种养人才，缺的是营销人才和龙头企业带动。

措施

新一轮精准扶贫工作启动以后，位于英山县的神峰山庄通过搭建产业大平台、开发城市大市场、力促乡村人发展，走出了 条三产融合助力乡村振兴的成功之路。

1. 搭建产业大平台。神峰山庄主体产业园区总面积 7500 亩，建设有神峰山庄旅游度假村、先农食品科技园、先农酱菜厂、物流配送中心、神峰·森林海温泉小镇等。拥有 40 个果蔬家庭农场，涉及英山、罗田 7 个乡镇 36 个村，流转土地 6850 亩，对接贫困户 1304 个 3921 人，形成环神峰山 24 公里休闲农业观光带。

2. 开发城市大市场。神峰山庄推进供给侧改革，构建线上线下全网营销体系，即“7X 高维度交易入口 + 总部基地 + 互联网 + 实体店面 + 会议模式 + 视频购物 + 商超模式 + 会员系统”，打造生

态农业“私人订制”商业4.0版。先后在武汉、合肥、九江、黄石、鄂州、南昌、安庆、黄州8个城市开设“黑禧猪神峰山庄农乐园”直营店102家。依托15万忠诚会员，“私人订制”与物流配送无缝衔接，打通了服务市民“最后一公里”，每天向都市农乐园配送30吨果蔬、100头猪、1000只鸡及其他农特产品。

3. 力促乡村大发展。神峰山庄完善“四个一”扶贫机制：培养一个新员工脱贫一个农户，山庄员工经过培训变身“九大员”（服务员、演员、导游员、市场营销员、社会体育指导员、游泳救生员、农业技术员、业余通讯员、义务卫生员）；定点一个养殖户致富一个家庭，实施户户“十头猪、千只鸡”养殖计划；发展一批专业小康村，36个美丽乡村应运而生。同时，为土地流转后的农民提供生活（每亩每年付250千克稻谷）、收入（农场每人每天60～70元，山庄月工资3000元，都市农乐园月工资5000～10000元）、增收（养鸡）、致富（养猪）“四重保障”。村集体每年得到10万元左右提成奖。

成效

神峰山庄三产融合项目的实施，给贫困山区农村带来了全新的经济发展方式，取得了明显的成效。神峰山庄游客接待量正以约10万人次/年的速度递增，2020年接待游客50万人次，综合收入4亿元。山庄系统解决了农民土地流转、新型职业农民等问题，富了农民的口袋，并且增加了村集

体的收益。山庄推行“大别山粮草肉油全程可控”理念，通过“猪—沼—菜”生态循环，种植不用化肥、农药，养殖不用含激素、抗生素的饲料，带来了生态修复效应。一个个“环境美、产业美、精神美、生态美”的美丽乡村呼之欲出，“生态、绿色、文明、宜居、宜业、宜游”的乡村振兴蓝图变为现实。

经验与启示

实践证明，实施三产融合，有利因素较多：一是群众有期盼，在龙头企业的带动下，由于发展的是生态农业，科技含量门槛低，农民参与的积极性高。二是政府有支持，符合国家产业政策，在路桥建设、节水灌溉、沼气能源、设施农业、数字农业、绿色通道、贷款贴息、旅游厕所、员工培训等方面有项目支持。三是市民有需求，在乡村旅游、候鸟式养老、居家肉蛋菜供应等方面发展空间大。

神峰山庄通过三产融合助力乡村振兴的成功经验主要有：

1. 思路决定出路。“绿水青山就是金山银山”，依托农村广阔天地，打造连接城乡的产业融合大平台，走生态循环农业之路，是实现乡村振兴的必然选择。通过农旅融合，神峰山庄系统解决了游客怎么引进、游客怎么留住、怎样带动当地经济发展这三个制约旅游发展的难题，创造了“旅游无淡季、天天游客满”的奇迹。

2. 理念决定高度。“大别山粮草肉油全程可控”“农医同根、食药同源”等新理念，顺应了市场需求，开启了绿色标准化生产新风尚，开创了大片区乡村振兴新局面。

3. 模式决定效益。神峰山庄发动群众，依靠群众所开启的“新文化 + 新农业 + 新健康”复合经营模式，为系统解决农业、农村、农民问题，实现大区域乡村振兴提供了最佳方案。

下一步计划

下一步，神峰山庄要继续推进产业升级，巩固脱贫成果，衔接乡村振兴：一是科学规划，建设现代农业科技产业园。在继续完善数字农业监管中心、直播带货中心、数字剧院的基础上，科学编制《英山县现代农业科技产业园建设规划》，重点打造智慧农业物流园、现代化育苗工厂、现代化育雏工厂。二是精心运营，打造休闲度假康养示范区。投资 3.5 亿元建设的神峰 · 森林海温泉小镇开启“21 天养生营”康养新业态，实现候鸟式养老的长短期互补，新增周边村 1000 个低收入人口就业岗位。三是扶志扶智，培养现代农业生力军。与黄冈市城投集团联手开办湖北乡村振兴商学院，年培养乡村振兴带头人 4 万人。计划 5 年内在全国复制 10 个神峰山庄，实现“全国连锁、员工过万人、年综合收入过 40 亿元”的目标，让神峰模式遍地开花，让中国好农业惠及更多的农民。

Abstract

Since 2013, the Hubei Xiannongtan Ecological Agriculture Co., Ltd. has invested RMB 448.1 million to build the national 3A-level tourist attraction, Shenfeng Mountain Villa. The villa is linked to the "Ecological Cycle Agricultural Experience Tour of Leaping into Ta-pieh Mountains from Thousand Miles away" and it is guided by the compound operation of "new culture + new agriculture + new health."

The mountain villa has formed a distinctive Shenfeng model featuring the integrated development of the ecological agriculture industry. A production and sales network of poverty alleviation products of RMB 400 million has been established with Yingshan County as the core, covering 14 provinces and cities across the country. With "a change of attitude and the support of education" at the core, more than 10,000 new-type professional farmers and 400 professional managers have been trained for the contiguous and severely stricken poverty areas of Ta-pieh Mountains. As a result, the company has employed 3,456 people and provided paired assistance to 3,921 people in 1,304 impoverished households, with an annual income increase of RMB 320 million. It has helped 70,000 farmers in the county and surrounding areas increase their income, eliminate poverty and set a brand-new model for targeted poverty alleviation and rural revitalization in 19 counties of three provinces.

Challenges and Problems

Yingshan County, Huanggang City, Hubei Province, is a national poverty-stricken county. With a population of 406,000, it is also identified as a severely impoverished county in the province. In 2014, there were 104,900 people in 37,000 archived impoverished households, 30.78% of whom were living in poverty. 76% of impoverished people can only be lifted out of poverty through industrial development. What the people lack, however, is not strength, but concepts, confidence and courage. The difficulty lies in the selling of agricultural products for which they are unable to charge a premium price. While there is no shortage of farming and breeding talents in rural areas, there is a shortage of marketing talents and leading enterprises that can play a leading role.

Measures

After the launch of a new round of targeted poverty alleviation, Shenfeng Mountain Villa in Yingshan County embarked on a successful road to rural revitalization based on the integration of the primary, secondary, and tertiary industries in building industrial platforms, developing urban markets and promoting rural development.

1. Build industrial platforms. With a total area of 7,500 *mu* of the main industrial park, the mountain villa includes Shenfeng Mountain Villa Tourist Resort, Xiannong Food Science and Technology Park, Xiannong Pickle Factory, Logistics Distribution Center, and Shenfeng-Senlinhai Hot Spring Town. There are 40 fruit and vegetable family farms, involving 36 villages in seven towns of Yingshan County and Luotian County. The mountain villa covers an area of 6,850 *mu* of transferred land, with 3,921 people in 1,304 impoverished households engaging in business, forming a 24-kilometer leisure agricultural sightseeing belt around Shenfeng Mountain.

2. Develop urban market. The Shenfeng Mountain Villa has promoted supply-side reforms. They have also built an online and offline inbound network marketing system called the "7X high-dimensional trading portal + headquarters base + internet + physical store + conference mode + video shopping + supermarket model + membership system." Its goal is to create "private customization" commercial version 4.0 of ecological agriculture. A total of 102 directly operated stores of "Hei Xi Zhu Shenfeng Mountain Villa Agricultural Park" have been operated in eight cities—Wuhan, Hefei, Jiujiang, Huangshi, Ezhou, Nanchang, Anqing, and Huangzhou. Relying on their 150,000 loyal members and the seamless connection of "private customization" and logistics distribution, the "last kilometer" of serving citizens was opened. This has delivered a massive 30 tons of fruits and vegetables, 100 pigs, 1,000 chickens and other special agricultural products to urban agricultural parks on a daily basis.

3. Promote rural development. The mountain villa has done well in alleviating poverty. It has trained new employees to lift peasant households out of poverty, developing them into waiters, actors, tour guides, marketers, social sports instructors, swimming lifeguards, agricultural technicians, amateur correspondents and voluntary health workers. It has also made farmers prosperous by implementing the "ten pigs and a thousand chickens" breeding plan for each household. It developed a batch of professional villages to improve their living standard, thus displaying 36 beautiful villages. It has supported them with an annual 250 kg of rice per *mu*, income of RMB 60–70 per person per day in the farm, RMB 3,000 monthly salary in the mountain villa and RMB 5,000–10,000 monthly salary in the urban agricultural park. Also, it has increased income from chicken and pig raising which has been provided to farmers whose land have been transferred. The village collective is also awarded an annual commission of about RMB 100,000.

Results

The implementation of the three industries' integration project of Shenfeng Mountain Villa has brought about a new economic development method to poverty-stricken mountainous villages. So far, it has achieved great results. Tourism to the mountain villa increased by about 100,000 people annually and in 2020 it received 500,000 tourists, with a comprehensive revenue of RMB 400 million. The mountain villa system has solved the problems of farmers' land transfer and new-type professional farmers, helped them become better-off, and increased the village collective income. The concept of "full-process control on grain, grass, meat and oil of Ta-pieh Mountains," through the "pig-methane-vegetable" ecological cycle and owing to the methods of chemical-free fertilizers and pesticides for planting and hormone-free feed and natural, organic antibiotics for breeding, the mountain villa has restored the ecology. Therefore, beautiful villages featuring "natural environment, booming industry, rich culture, and beautiful ecology" are emerging, thus achieving rural revitalization with "ecological, green, ethical, livable, workable, and travel-friendly" features.

Experience and Inspirations

Several factors favor the implementation of the three industries' integration. **First,** there are high expectations. Driven by leading enterprises and low requirements for science and technology in the development of ecological agriculture, farmers are highly motivated to participate.

Second, the government's strong support. In line with national industrial policies, support for road and bridge construction, water-saving irrigation, biogas energy, facility agriculture, digital agriculture, green channels, subsidized loans, tourist toilets and employee training should be provided. **Third,** citizens have demands. There is room for rural tourism development in conjunction with the migratory bird-style, elderly care and household meat, eggs, and vegetables supply. The successful experience of the mountain villa in driving rural revitalization through the three industries' integration is listed as follows.

1. Attitude and mindset determine the outcome. Lucid waters and lush mountains are invaluable assets. A platform that connects urban and rural areas should be created based upon the vast resources of rural areas. The decision to follow an agricultural path and ecological cycle inevitably leads to rural revitalization. Through the integration of agriculture and tourism, the mountain villa system solves the three major problems restricting tourism development: how to attract tourists, how to retain tourists and how to drive local economic development.

2. Ideas determine the breadth and depth of rural revitalization. New concepts that "agriculture and medicine share the same root, and food and drugs share the same origin" conform to market demands and have led to the development of a new trend in green and standardized production and a new pattern for large-scale rural revitalization.

3. Models determine benefits. The "new culture + new agriculture + new health" cooperation framework initiated by the mountain villa based on the support from villagers has provided the best plan for the systematic resolution of agricultural problems, rural areas, farmers and large scale rural revitalization.

Next Steps

For the next steps, Shenfeng Mountain Villa will promote industrial upgrading and consolidate the poverty alleviation results for rural revitalization. **First,** scientific planning will be made to build modern agricultural science and technology industrial parks. Based on the continuous perfection of the digital agriculture supervision center, livestream marketing center and digital theater, the *Construction Plan on Modern Agricultural Science and Technology Industrial Parks in Yingshan County* should be compiled in a scientific manner and focused on the building of smart agricultural logistics parks, modern seedling factories, and modern breeding factories. **Second,** a demonstration area for leisure, vacation and healthcare will be developed and operated with high efficiency. With an investment of RMB 350 million, the Shenfeng-Senlinhai Hot Spring Town has initiated a new wellness model of "a 21-day health preservation camp" which complements the long and short-term elderly health care for migratory bird style. This will create job opportunities for 1,000 low-income people in surrounding villages. **Third,** a shift in attitude and educational support will be pursued to train the new force of modern agriculture. Hubei Rural Revitalization Business College has been co-founded with Huanggang Urban Construction Investment Group, training 40,000 people for rural revitalization annually. It is planned to replicate 10 Shenfeng Mountain Villas across the country within five years to achieve the goal of a national chain, with more than 10,000 employees and an annual comprehensive income of over RMB 4 billion. Thus, the Shenfeng model is expected to be developed all over the country to benefit more farmers.

中青旅：
山水酒店新化宾馆提质升级助力乡村脱贫

CYTS:
Upgrade on Xinhua Hotel of Shanshui Hotel Facilitates Rural Poverty Alleviation

摘要

湖南省娄底市新化县是中华始祖蚩尤故里，属国家级贫困县。中青旅积极发挥自身文旅综合优势，导入文旅产业扶贫体系，助力地方产业发展，于 2019 年 9 月主推中青旅旗下山水酒店集团与新化县正式签署协议，投资 1590 万元升级改造新化宾馆，将新化宾馆成功升级改造为文旅扶贫标杆，使国有旧物业焕发新气象、创造新价值，为新化县当地旅游事业的发展注入了新的活力，有力地带动了当地文旅产业的发展，以点带面，助推新化县实现脱贫摘帽。

挑战与问题

湖南省娄底市新化县是中华始祖蚩尤故里，属国家级贫困县。新化县虽然周边有各类风景名胜及深厚的历史文化底蕴，但交通不便，自身产业经济基础薄弱、商贸活动活力不足，商旅住宿需求缺乏稳定的支撑；旅游资源开发利用率低，游客少，导致酒店旅游客源也不足，新化县区内酒店整体价格水平较低，投资回报较差。新化宾馆组建于 1958 年，是隶属于县委、县政府的一家二星级旅游涉外饭店，位于县城老区中心位置，交通拥堵、基础设施陈旧、配套不完善；城区规划也在一定程度上影响着项目定向消费，故而酒店经济效益十分受限。新化县贫困户普遍就业困难，现代服务意识和技能都严重不足，旅游服务专业人才十分短缺。

措施

新化县是中国光大集团的对口帮扶单位，中青旅作为光大集团大旅游战略核心平台，积极发挥自身文旅综合优势，导入文旅产业扶贫体系，助力地方产业发展，投资 1590 万元升级改造新化宾馆，通过着手改善新化当地旅游市场环境，有力带动当地文旅产业的发展，以点带面助推新化县实现脱贫摘帽。

1. 项目前期深度调研、认真设计、严谨决策。中青旅山水酒店集团抽调最资深的投资运营团队考察新化宾馆物业和当地旅游市场，结合前期专业市场调研和工程勘察实情“量身定制”改造方案，并多次召开投资决策会议进行严谨认真的评估分析，出具项目可行性具体改造规划、经营定位和投资分析报告，项目团队在与各方沟通接洽中所展现出的专业性和责任感，赢得了新化宾馆业主方的高度认可。

2. 克服疫情挑战按时完工，多项举措切实助力扶贫。2020 年暴发新冠肺炎疫情。为帮助新化县在疫情防控期间打赢脱贫攻坚战，中青旅山水酒店集团克服各种困难积极复工复产，举集团之力多方调集人员、资金、物资，全力保障新化宾馆改造工程的质量与进度。为了符合国家节能减排要求，减少有害污染物的排放，中青旅山水酒店集团除更新改造大堂及客房的酒店环境外，还主动完善新化宾馆配套设施，更换老旧锅炉及空调机组，并对电力进行增容，实质性地提升了新化宾馆固定资产的物业价值，将兼顾“里子”和“面子”的合作实惠带给新化宾馆业主方。首期投入 1590 余万元的新化宾馆改造项目，于 2020 年 9 月下旬胜利竣工，通过专业改造，新化宾馆无论是酒店内外环境还是人员服务水准都焕然一新，赢得当地政府各级领导和新老客人的一致好评。中青旅山水酒店项目团队多次就营销方案、客流导入与光大集团设在新化的企业扶贫小组进行沟通，同时在酒店大堂特别开设扶贫展销专区，助力新化县特色农副产品流通升级，通过持续加大消费扶贫力度，帮助当地贫困群众增收脱贫。

3. 争取当地政府支持，同舟共济共渡难关。新化宾馆改造项目在筹建期恰逢新冠肺炎疫情暴发，项目施工进度、资金周转均受到不同程度的影响，这给中青旅山水酒店集团带来了一定的运营压力。在项目组负责人的积极争取下，新化县委、县政府给予了新化宾馆改造项目巨大的支持，当地政府主动纾困解难，按照相关政策特批延长 4 个月免租期，大大缓解了项目筹建期间宾馆的经营压力。

成效

1. 完善旅游配套设施。改造后的新化宾馆，以中青旅山水时尚酒店 · 新化迎宾路店的全新形象，于 2020 年 9 月底正式开业。全新的简约中式设计风格经典时尚，首期推出的 113 间全新客房配套齐全、温馨舒适，专业贴心的全新服务有口皆碑，成为当地旅游住宿服务市场的一大亮点。酒店焕新开业有力提升了当地的酒店服务水平，为商务接待和旅游市场的发展提供了有力的配套支持。

2. 助力乡村就业脱贫。酒店 20% 的员工来自当地贫困户。项目的落地，切实为新化百姓创造了更多的就业机会和收入，充分彰显出中青旅文旅产业体系助力新化脱贫攻坚的企业责任与情怀。

3. 带动乡村旅游经济。中青旅集团和山水酒店集团投入 1590 余万元全面改造酒店。带动旅游消费经济，设立扶贫产品展销专区推销新化产品，助力消费扶贫。在产业扶贫方面，研究部署政企协同与文旅开发，以点带面导入文旅产业投资、开发和运营，通过旅游产业链全面带动乡村振兴。

经验与启示

1. 使命驱动，创新支持，致力共赢。项目前期，面对当地薄弱的经济基础及商旅住宿需求，中青旅山水酒店集团以承担社会责任为重，认真、严谨、负责地对项目进行调研和方案设计，并积极与当地政府沟通项目痛点、难点和需求，牢记扶贫使命，确保项目既满足扶贫的民生需求，又符合可持续运营的商业规则。通过一系列专业、负责、创新的设计和沟通，保障了项目的圆满顺利落地，实现多方持续共赢。

2. 发挥优势，以点带面，授人以渔。在新化宾馆的改造过程中，中青旅山水酒店集团充分发挥自身专业优势，立足集团成熟的管理培训体系，从当地贫困户家庭中招募酒店员工，为他们提供专业的酒店技能培训，使其成为酒店专业服务团队的一员，从“授人以鱼”的输血式慈善扶贫升级到“授人以渔”的造血式产业扶贫。通过酒店连锁集团服务体系的本地化落地，树立了新化酒店服务标杆，既满足了企业的经营用工需求，又提升了当地旅游从业者的服务意识和技能水平，以点带面推动当地文旅产业经济发展。

3. 同心协助，产融结合，高效运作。项目前期筹建过程中有效借助了光大集团的产融扶贫优势，在光大金融体系内为本项目争取到宝贵的贷款支持，使项目前期因疫情造成的资金紧张困难得到有效解决，在规定时间内高质量完成任务，高效助力新化县同步脱贫摘帽。

4. 政企联动，连接客户，焕发活力。扶贫是一项需要政府、社会、企业共同努力奋斗的事业，在项目运营中，各方力量需要积极联动，共同为达成项目目标保驾护航。酒店开业后积极邀请政府机关单位、相关企业客户前来考察、交流，获得新化县各级领导和各企业客户的一致好评，并被授牌成为新化县党政机关会议住宿定点场所。通过项目改造和运营再次焕发出市场新气象的新化酒店，正不断创造新价值，成功实现国有老旧物业的市场重生，并成为当地产业扶贫及乡村振兴的亮眼名片。

下一步计划

一是立足酒店运营，做好政府单位及社会企业住宿、会议接待工作。充分利用酒店展销平台挖掘新化县土特产品，跨界携手各方开发网红爆款，以期在给游客带来惊喜体验的同时，为群众提供更多的就业机会和商机，帮助当地百姓共奔小康。二是实施酒店二期改造，对酒店停车场、会议室等继续进行升级改造，全面提升住宿、会议、餐饮等一站式服务品质。三是依托中青旅产业振兴、人才振兴、文化振兴的三大路径，以旅游产业发展为抓手，借力当地政府的政策支持及优势资源创新旅游产品，开发“旅游＋住宿”“旅游＋特色美食”“旅游＋扶贫产品”等受市场欢迎的全新项目，助力地方政府打造新化旅游新名片，把游客与消费引进来，同步推进企业社会责任的履行与旅游业务的拓展开发。四是积极对接光大集团的当地企业，酒店充分发挥自身的优势和价值，与兄弟单位加强合作，积极创新业务产品，形成新的业务体系，携手共同提振当地经济，为乡村振兴贡献光大力量。

Abstract

Xinhua County in Hunan Province, a national poverty-stricken county, is the hometown of Chi You, the ancestor of China. The China Youth Travel Service (CYTS) has leveraged its cultural tourism advantages and introduced a poverty alleviation program to promote local industrial development. In September 2019, Shanshui Hotel Group, a subsidiary of CYTS, signed an agreement with Xinhua County to invest RMB 15.9 million for the upgrade and renovation of Xinhua Hotel. The successful renovation has become the benchmark for cultural tourism, allowing villagers to realize that old state-owned properties can sport a new look and create new value. This project has also boosted other tourism development efforts and helped lift the county out of poverty.

Challenges and Problems

Xinhua County is the hometown of Chi You, China's ancestor. Although it is poverty-stricken, it boasts beautiful scenic spots, ancient historical heritage and a long cultural tradition. The village, however, has not been properly developed and lacks the necessary economic foundation and critical infrastructure such as transportation services and decent roads to travel. Thus, businesses within the village have not generated a profit. This has led to a low number of tourists, resulting in regional hotels not making

a profit. Founded in 1958, Xinhua Hotel, affiliated with the county Party committee and county government, is a two-star hotel catering to overseas tourists. Located at the center of the old county, it has long been plagued by traffic jams, outdated infrastructure and inadequate supporting facilities.

Measures

The county is supported by China Everbright Group. As the core platform of China Everbright Group's grand tourism strategy, CYTS maximized its cultural tourism advantages and introduced a poverty alleviation system to drive the local industrial development. They have invested RMB 15.9 million into upgrading and renovating Xinhua Hotel which is expected to improve local tourism.

1. Adhere to in-depth research, careful design, and rigorous decision-making in the early stage of the project. CYTS has selected an investment group that will formulate a plan for upgrading the Xinhua Hotel. This renovation plan will be based upon previous professional market research and engineering surveys. This team has held multiple meetings that focus on rigorous decision-making process and will seek to analyze the plan thoroughly. It has demonstrated its professionalism and sense of responsibility as it has produced a series of reports that encompass project feasibility, concrete, measurable transformation and business position.

2. Overcome epidemic challenges for on-time project completion and implement various for poverty alleviation measures. In 2020, COVID-19 broke out across the country which made CYTS rethink their business operation. To help the country win the tough battle against poverty, CYTS mobilized personnel, utilized funds and acquired materials to guarantee the progress and the quality of the renovation. To meet the national requirements on energy conservation and emission reduction and the emission reduction of harmful pollutants, the Group has updated the hotel environment in the lobby and guest rooms. It also improved the hotel's supporting facilities, replaced old boilers and air-conditioning units and increased electrical capacity. This resulted to an increase in the property value of Xinhua Hotel's fixed assets, which benefits the owners and the tourists. The first phase of the renovation project was an investment of more than RMB 15.9 million and it was completed in September 2020. The renovation project has resulted in the Hotel taking on a new look, pleasing the government officials. The CYTS Shanshui Hotel project team has had frequent exchanges with the Xinhua-based corporate poverty alleviation team of China Everbright Group on marketing plan, passenger flow and poverty alleviation strategy. Also, an exhibit that outlines its poverty alleviation strategy has been placed in the hotel lobby for guests to notice and help bring awareness to the issue.

3. Win local government's support to surmount difficulties with all-in-one mind. COVID-19 has negatively affected the projects construction. A certain degree of operational pressure has been placed on

CYTS Shanshu Hotel Group and other properties. The government has taken steps to help the group through their renovation project. The local government has taken the initiative to relieve the difficulties that COVID-19 caused by extending a four-month rent-free period. This has helped ease the operating pressure during the preparatory period of the project.

Results

1. Improve tourism supporting facilities. The renovated Xinhua Hotel will be officially opened at the end of September 2020 in the name of CYTS Shanshui Trends Hotel — Xinhua Yingbin Road Branch. It provided 113 new well-equpped rooms with comfortable, professional, and reliable services. It also featured a simple Chinese design and will be the spotlight for local tourists. The opening of the hotel has improved the local hotel service and has been given strong support from the local government.

2. Create more jobs for rural poverty alleviation. A total of 20% of the hotel employees are from local impoverished households. The implementation of the project has created more job opportunities and income for people of the county, demonstrating the corporate responsibility and feelings of the CYTS cultural tourism industry system in lifting the county out of poverty.

3. Drive rural tourism economy. CYTS Group and Shanshui Hotel Group invested more than RMB 15.9 million to renovate the hotel. A special exhibition area for poverty alleviation products was set up to drive local tourism consumption economy. It is important to keep many avenues open when it comes to poverty alleviation as there are many different ways to coordinate this effort. Poverty alleviation requires industrial development and government-enterprise efforts that will facilitate tourism based rural revitalization in all aspects.

Experience and Inspirations

1. Achieve a win-win situation supported by innovation and driven by the mission. The early stages of the project was faced with weak local economic foundations and a low travel demand. This has prompted the CYTS Shanshui Hotel Group to focus on social responsibility and to conduct research into the project's design. It has also communicated with local government officials to ensure the project meets proper standards for poverty alleviation as well as checking to see if the business adheres to rules of business operations. By being responsible, innovative and ensuring smooth implementation of plans, it has been able to ensure a win-

win agreement for all parties.

2. Leverage advantages to teach people the way. When Xinhua Hotel was under construction, CYTS Shanshui Hotel Group, based on the Group's highly developed management training system, leveraged its professional advantages to recruit hotel staff from local poor families. Once these members were trained, they would be able to serve on the hotel's professional service team. This model of localized hotel chains has created a new benchmark in the county which shows that the business needs of enterprises are met. It has also enhanced the awareness and skill level of local tourism professionals.

3. Make concerted efforts to integrate industry and finance with efficiency. The pre-project phase was a heavy financial burden, so China Everbright Group was tapped to secure valuable loan support for the projects. These funds were important as they were able to ensure that the pandemic did not affect the completion date.

4. Government-enterprise coordination for customer contacting and rejuvenation. Poverty alleviation is a cause that requires joint efforts of the government, society and other enterprises. During the project operation, all parties need to work together to ensure that objectives are met. After opening, the hotel invited customers from government agencies and related enterprises to inspect and exchange views. Such efforts won unanimous praise from the county leaders at all levels, various enterprises and guests. The hotel was licensed as the designated place for conference and accommodation of Xinhua County Party and government agencies. It has created a new value through the market rebirth of state-owned properties.

Next Steps

First, hotel operations will allow government agencies

and enterprises to come together for accommodation and conference receptions. The hotel exhibition platform should be used to bring attention to the importance of poverty alleviation and should work to develop Internet famous products. More business opportunities will be made available to the local villagers,which will improve their standard of living. **Second,** infrastructure will be updated: parking lots, meeting rooms and other areas. This will improve the quality of accommodation, conferences and catering. **Third,** by relying on the three paths laid out by CYTS, emphasis will be placed on several areas from industrial revitalization, talent revitalization, and cultural revitalization. Local support for government policies, resource oriented tourism products and new programs will be developed. Some of these include "tourism + accommodation," "tourism + characteristic delicacies," and "tourism + poverty alleviation products." Also, efforts will be made to boost awareness, including business cards to promote and boost popularity. **Fourth,** local enterprises of the Everbright Group will be proactively involved. The hotel will give full play to its own advantages and values for more cooperation with associate organizations, innovate business products for a new business system and jointly boost the local economy to contribute to rural revitalization.

江西龙南市临塘乡东坑村虔心小镇：
“虔”心“虔”意助力乡村扶贫

Ch’an Town, Dongkeng Village, Lintang Township, Longnan City, Jiangxi Province:
Ch’an Model for Rural Poverty Alleviation with Piousness

摘要

江西省龙南市临塘乡东坑村虔心小镇，是一个以生态农业为基础，以“虔”文化为主题，融合当地丰富的山、水、茶、竹等优质资源，集自然风景、客家民俗、虔茶文化于一体的现代生态旅游示范基地，被评为国家 4A 级旅游景区、省 5A 级乡村旅游点。近年来，虔心小镇依托“休闲度假旅游板块 + 有机虔茶基地板块 + 虔山飞鸡农业板块 + 毛竹林生态林业板块”，带动周边贫困户深度参与生态旅游产业，走出了一条旅游助力乡村脱贫的新路。

挑战与问题

虔心小镇位于江西省龙南市临塘乡东坑村，在农业产业发展方面，虔心小镇以有机茶、赣南油茶、竹林飞鸡、中草药种植、水果种植等为基础。但是当地的农业技术人员稀缺，农村留守的多为年龄超过 50 岁的老年人，产业发展规模和质量受限。虔心小镇未来规划是在现有茶旅融合特色小镇的基础上，升级成为高端康养旅居度假目的地，但作为民营企业，其在项目用地、政策扶持、金融政策等方面受到一定限制，导致项目进展受限。

措施

1. 景点建设 + 项目扶贫。统筹安排景点建设项目，以虔心小镇旅游景区景点建设带动贫困村环境整治提升。在道路整治方面，龙南市政府投入 6800 多万元建设了长 8.2 公里的旅游公路，改善了虔心小镇的交通；在村容整治方面，虔心小镇投入 600 多万元对彭屋、老村等 11 个村庄实施了村容整治项目，既提升了景区周边环境水平，又改善了村民的居住环境；在供水方面，启动了投资 230 万元的东坑村农饮水工程，让村民都喝上了干净水，不仅保障了水质安全，而且实现了景区和村庄一体化供水。

2. 劳务用工 + 就业扶贫。虔心小镇在开发建设、运营服务的过程中，优先吸纳贫困户进入景区务工就业，并向贫困户提供茶叶采摘、茶叶加工、山鸡饲养、石斛种植、林业护理等多种就业岗位。现已吸收固定员工 600 ～ 800 人，其中贫困户 300 多人，每人每月平均工资已逾 3000 元；在每年春、秋采茶季，聘请雇用大量临时工，间接带动的就业人数达 3000 人，每人每天的采茶收入可以达到 200 元。另外，景区建设施工方面也吸纳了大量东坑村以及周边村落的劳动力，每人每日可

获得 80～120 元的酬劳。景区的发展建设，不仅带动了东坑村和临塘乡的村民就业，而且提高了整个龙南市的阶段性就业率。虔心小镇为当地的贫困户提供了“家门口”的就业岗位，增加了当地贫困户的工资收入，根本性地改善了村民的生活水平。

3. 旅游产品 + 产业扶贫。主要采用三种方式：一是倒包返租型。虔心小镇不仅主攻旅游项目，还开发特色生态农业项目，如“虔山飞鸡”和“有机虔茶”。通过“公司 + 农户”的模式辐射带动贫困户，帮助他们增收增产，昔日的贫困户，如今年人均收入有 5 万～6 万元。二是自我发展型。采取“企业 + 基地 + 农户”的产业化经营模式，动员当地农户跟进发展优质油茶产业、土窑鸡产业、竹筒酒产业、石斛产业，并与农户签订收购协议，增加农户家庭的经营性收入。而且，在农产品销售方面，采用“电商 + 互联网 + 基地 + 农户”的模式，将油茶、山鸡、虔茶、竹筒酒等农副产品销往北京、上海、深圳等地。三是基地共建型。鼓励农户将山场、耕地、低产油茶林、闲置土坯房等资产资源折价入股，明确低保福利，再根据盈利情况分红，目前已吸收贫困户入股资金 290 万元。这样一来，既保证了企业不断做大做强，又能对贫困户生活水平的提高起到立竿见影的作用。

4. 旅游企业 + 社会扶贫。虔心小镇带头参与捐资助学、健康基金、健康义诊等系列扶贫活动。在教育扶贫方面，虔心小镇捐资 114.74 万元新建了临塘学校教学楼，捐资 100 万元筹建了龙南中学电子图书室，不仅完善了学校教育设施，丰富了学校的图书资源，而且大大改善了孩子们的读书环境。在健康扶贫方面，针对因病致残或者没有劳动力的建档立卡贫困户，虔心小镇按照每年每户 1000 元的标准发放医疗基金小册子，村民在龙南县的中医院看病时，用小册子中的金额抵扣医药费即可。目前，享受该健康基金的贫困户已达 500 户，整个临塘乡基本上都已覆盖到。虔心小镇在做好旅游发展的同时，也在积极履行旅游企业的社会责任。

5. 遗产保护 + 文化扶贫。虔心小镇通过旅游项目开发，在有效利用文化旅游资源的同时，对非物质文化遗产的保护也做了大量工作。一方面，通过非遗中心建设，部分珍贵文物得以保存；另一方面，当这些非物质文化遗产与经济“挂钩”，对非物质文化遗产的保护，便逐渐从政府行为转变为群众自主行为。虔城手工艺世代相传，有着上百年的历史及完整的工艺流程，往往是采用天然材料，运用具有地方特色的工艺品种和技艺，加工茶、油、布、陶及特种工艺。虔心小镇在向游客展示这些手工艺的同时，也推动了这些非物质文化遗产的传承与发展。斗茶表演、客家山歌等传统文化也在此生动演绎。虔心小镇每年在虔茶开园这天都会举办一次复古的祭茶仪式，通过还原宋代茶礼，展现中国茶文化的丰富文化内涵。通过遗产保护开发，虔心小镇不仅带动了一批贫困户作为传承人直接就业、创业，而且极大增强了村民的文化认同感和自豪感，提升了群众的文化自信。

成效

在虔心小镇的辐射影响下，该镇所在地域的经济生活水平有了极大提高：居住土坯房人数大量减少，新增混凝土住房明显增多；农业生产方式有了质的飞跃，从传统的铁犁牛耕转变为现代化机械生产；农民衣食住行方面也有了明显改善。围绕虔心小镇旅游发展农家乐、生态采摘等经营模式逐渐兴起，据不完全统计：虔心小镇观光餐饮年收入在 100 万元左右，农业特色产品年销售收入约 300 万元，其他收入正以每年 10 万元的增量逐年增加。

经验与启示

脱贫攻坚能否与乡村振兴有效衔接，关键在于是否有产业支撑。虔心小镇从发展之初就找准了自己的发展定位：一定要有既独具特色又能因地制宜的产业基础。依托十万亩林地资源，虔心小镇大力发展有机茶、纯放养竹林鸡、油茶、脐橙、蔬菜、笋干等产业项目，紧密围绕这些特色农产品，从种植、加工、销售等环节着手，加强与贫困户的利益联结，塑造地方特产品牌形象，走产业化、规模化、品牌化道路，形成从生产端到销售端的全链条产业发展模式。在农业特色产业支撑的基础上，虔心小镇建设六大农业产业基地，做大做强产业升级，提高脱贫保障能力，增添乡村振兴活力。

1. 六大基地打造第二家园。依托“国家 4A 级旅游景区”“国家森林康养示范基地”“全国首批乡村旅游重点村”等“名片”带来的流量，虔心小镇以现有万亩有机茶园，百草园中草药基地，猕猴桃、冰橘基地，油茶基地等农业产业资源为基础，升级规划建设了“六大基地”，即：生态茶园与制茶基地，葡萄庄园与酒庄基地，生态农耕、蔬菜基地，百果采摘基地，中草药基因库，森林康养基地；同时，瞄准大湾区客户，推行“第二家园计

划”，即：通过“一亩田林”的认领方式，客户可成为虔心小镇极具荣誉感的“庄园主”，与贫困户深度帮扶，开启候鸟式旅居度假的新生活方式，把虔心小镇变身为粤港澳大湾区的“第二家园”。

2. 合作机制保障扶贫效应。针对贫困户存在缺资金、缺技术、缺市场的实际情况，虔心小镇采取“企业 + 基地 + 合作社 + 农户”的方式实现有针对性的帮扶，构建可容纳、联结机制可操作、带动扶贫有效应、贫困户融入有途径、收益有保障、扶贫产业有看点的整体格局，强化“造血”功能。

3. 线上线下创新发展模式。探索传统产业与“互联网 +”相结合的线上线下联动方式，带动周边发展，走出一条农业创新发展的新路子。在线下，打造以虔心小镇为中心的产业圈。虔心小镇已是国家 4A 级旅游景区，已注册有“虔茶”“格物之源”两个品牌；从 2020 年起，虔心小镇还将投资 60 亿元注入乐启生生态健康产业项目，建设八大中心和六大基地，此举必将带动周边温泉、民宿、餐饮业的发展，给贫困户增收和乡村发展带来新的动力。在线上，以“虔心小镇”线上商城为中心，探索“基地引领”抱团发展模式，除销售自产的高山茶油、蛋、蜂蜜、冬笋等产品，还可整合本地特产脐橙、大米、大豆等生态农产品，帮助农户打开销路，增强脱贫可持续性。

下一步计划

围绕虔心小镇“瞄准珠三角，对接粤港澳，打造粤港澳大湾区第二家园”的发展定位，完善建设六大农业产业基地，做大做强产业升级，提高脱贫保障能力，增添乡村振兴活力。针对湾区客户，推出“一亩田林”私人订制庄园计划，涵盖：1 份稻田、1 份蔬菜、1 份茶园、20 株果树（葡萄、猕猴桃、冰橘、柿子等）、若干种中草药等。客户认领后，虔心小镇向其颁发“庄园主”田林证书，并通过二维码对其订购的农作物进行溯源识别，客户日常通过手机终端便可实时查看田林种植管理情况。订制后的田林由虔心小镇统一代管，虔心小镇再发包给当地贫困户种植管理，由此搭建客户与贫困户之间的交流平台，贫困户成为客户的“田林管家”，提供“管家式服务”，通过建立微信群，实时将田林情况拍照、拍视频传输给客户，邀请他们一起参与劳作、打理，丰收时一起采摘果实。通过互动，让每位客户不但有亲近田林的惬意感，更有支持贫困户脱贫致富的社会荣誉感。

Abstract

Ch'an Town, Dongkeng Village, Lintang Township, Longnan City, Jiangxi Province, is a small town that is rooted in ecologic agriculture and has a "pious" culture. It is known for its lucid waters, lush mountains and abundant bamboos. Also, it is a modern ecological tourism demonstration base, a national 4A-level tourist attraction and a provincial 5A-level tourist attraction, which integrates natural scenery, Hakka customs, and Ch'an Culture. In recent years, the village has taken the tourism model to facilitate rural poverty alleviation. This was done through the "leisure and vacation tourism + organic Ch'an tea bases + Qianshan chicken-raising agriculture + ecological phyllostachys pubescens forest."

Challenge and Problems

Ch'an Town develops agriculture based mainly on organic tea, Gannan oil-tea camellia, chickens, and Chinese herbal medicine cultivation. However, finding people who are skilled in agriculture is rare as most skilled workers are over 50 years old. This limits the amount the village can produce, turning it into a low-scale industry. The town plans to develop high-end holiday destinations for healthcare and recreation on the foundation of the tea and tourism industry. Private enterprises are, however, restrained in terms of project land use, policy support and financial policies, resulting in the project's thwarted progress.

Measures

1. Scenic spots construction + poverty alleviation through projects. The goal of the construction project is to upgrade the scenic spots in the town and improve the environment in poverty-stricken villages. The Longnan municipal government invested more than RMB 68 million in the construction of 8.2 kilometers of tourist roads to make the town more easily accessible. It invested more than RMB 6 million to renovate 11 villages, including the Pengwu and Lao villages, which improved the surrounding environment of the scenic spot while enhancing the living environment of villagers. The Dongkeng Village Agricultural Drinking Water Project, with an investment of RMB 2.3 million, was launched to help villagers gain access to safe drinking water, ensuring water safety and integrated water supply for scenic spots and villages.

2. Labor employment + poverty alleviation through employment. During the development, construction, and operation, the town gave employment priority to impoverished households. These villagers main line of work are tea picking, tea processing, pheasant breeding, dendrobium planting and forestry governance. This program has provided jobs for 600 to 800 people. Out of these, 300 are from impoverished households. In addition, the workers are making a monthly salary of RMB 3,000. Furthermore, during the annual picking season in spring and autumn, the village hires more than 3,000 temporary workers who can earn up to RMB 200 per day. Villagers from surrounding towns have also been picked up to work. These people come from Dongkeng Village, Lintang Township, and Longnan City. The town has offered many jobs to people living in impoverished households, raised their income, and improved their standard of living.

3. Tourism products + poverty alleviation through industries. There are three main methods that this project relies on. The first is the leaseback method. The "companies + peasant households" model was taken to increase the income and output of impoverished households, with the annual average income of RMB 50,000 to 60,000. The second method is the self-development model. The industry management model of "enterprises + bases + peasant households" was adopted to mobilize local peasant households to develop high-quality camellia industry, clay chicken industry, bamboo wine industry, and dendrobium industry. In addition, purchase agreements were made with peasant households that will seek to increase their income. The peasants agreed to a contract where sales of agricultural products, the model of "e-commerce + internet + bases + peasant households" would be adopted to sell agricultural and sideline products such as camellia, pheasant, Ch'an Tea, and bamboo wine to Beijing, Shanghai, Shenzhen cities and other places. The third model is the base co-construction. Peasant households were encouraged to convert mountain farms, arable land, low-yielding camellia forests, idle adobe houses and other asset resources into discounted shares to clarify subsistence allowance and obtain profit-based dividends. Currently, the funds of RMB 2.9 million from impoverished households are absorbed. This measure can facilitate the vigorous development of enterprises and also improve the living standards of impoverished households immediately.

4. Tourism enterprises + poverty alleviation through social support. The village took the initiative

to relieve poverty in their village. This included such measures as school donations, health funds and free doctor visits. School donations were aimed at giving students more opportunities to learn. The total donation was around RMB 1,147,000 for building a new school in Lintang and RMB 1,000,000 to build an electronic library at Longnan Middle School. The town is also focused on medicine as they donated RMB 1,000 per household for free of charge doctor visits and visits to the Longan Traditional Chinese Medicine Hospital. The number of impoverished households is currently 500, most of whom have access to these funds. This makes the town actively engaged in their local people's social welfare that affect its tourism development.

5. Heritage protection + poverty alleviation through culture. The town has focused on protecting the intangible cultural heritage projects while continuing the development of the village. Some cultural relics have been preserved through the construction of cultural heritage centers, with some of these preserved through government actions and private people taking the relics to their own homes. The Qiancheng (an alternative name of Ganzhou City, Jiangxi Province) handicraft has been handed down from generation to generation, along with its century-old history and technological process. It uses natural materials and applies craft varieties and techniques with local characteristics to process tea, oil, cloth, pottery and special crafts, which is inherited and developed through the tourists display in Ch'an Town. Traditional cultures such as tea appreciation performance and Hakka folk songs are also performed here. Every year on the opening day of the Ch'an Tea Garden, the town holds a vintage tea ceremony to showcase the rich cultural connotation of Chinese tea culture by restoring the tea rituals of the Song Dynasty. Through heritage protection and development, a group of impoverished households are encouraged to serve as inheritors for employment and entrepreneurship, which has enhanced cultural pride and sense of identity for the villagers, as well as cultural self-confidence of the masses.

Results

The quality of life and economy have been greatly improved as a result of the poverty alleviation projects in Ch'an Town. Many villagers have migrated from old adobe homes and have moved into concrete residences. This signifies their qualitative change from the traditional iron plough and cattle to modern machinery production. They have also enjoyed higher quality clothing, housing and food standards. The business models of the town's agritainment and ecological development is centered on rural tourism. According to incomplete statistics, the annual income of sightseeing and catering in the town reaches to about RMB 1 million, while the annual sales revenue of agricultural specialty products is about RMB 3 million. Other income increases year by year with an annual increment of RMB 100,000.

Experience and Inspirations

Industrial support is needed to effectively link poverty alleviation and rural revitalization. Starting from its early days, Ch'an Town has oriented its development towards

a distinctive industrial foundation that adapts to local conditions. Relying on 100,000 *mu* of forest resources, it has developed industrial projects such as organic tea, pure free-range chickens raised in bamboo forests, oil-tea camellia, navel orange, vegetables, and dried bamboo shoots. The village, however, must strengthen its cooperation with impoverished households, create brand images of local specialties and embark on a path forward to industrialization, economy of scale and branding. Supported by agricultural characteristic industries, the town is able to build six agricultural industrial bases for industrial upgrading, support against poverty and an invigorated rural revitalization program.

1. Build a second home through six bases. The village has been granted many honors such as the 4A-level tourist attraction, the national eco-healthcare demonstration base, and the first batch of key rural tourism villages in China. It has also tapped into their agricultural and industrial resources that include organic tea gardens 10,000 *mu*, Baicaoyuan Chinese Herbal Medicine Base, as well as certain fruits. The town has worked to upgrade the "Six Major Bases" of its native ecology. These bases are as follows: the ecological tea gardens and tea production, the base of vineyard and winery, the base of ecological farming and vegetables, the base of fruit picking, Chinese herbal medicine gene pool, and the base of forest healthcare. It has also implemented the "Second Home Plan" through the adoption of the "one mu of farmland and woodland" scheme whereby a customer can become an honorary manor owner of the town. It has also started a brand-new migratory-bird program that enables deeply impoverished households in

the Guangdong-Hong Kong-Macao Greater Bay Area to move to the village and make it their second home.

2. Support poverty alleviation through cooperation mechanism. It is difficult for impoverished households to become self-reliant. Therefore, the town has adopted the model of "enterprises + bases + cooperatives + peasant households" to achieve targeted assistance. It has built an operable cooperation mechanism, in which poverty alleviation is effective, impoverished households are integrated, income is guaranteed, and with the poverty alleviation industry stressing the importance of self-reliance and improvement.

3. Innovate development models online and offline. The area surrounding the village has not been developed enough to include internet services. Thus, the village has adopted the model of internet online and offline linkage modes to drive the development of its surrounding areas and blaze a new path forward for agricultural innovation. In the offline area, it has built an industrial circle centered on the town. As a national 4A-level tourist attraction in Jiangxi Province, Ch'an Town has registered two brands of "Ch'an Tea" and "Prime of Nature." Starting from 2020, the town also invested RMB 6 billion into LuckSun ecological health industry project by building eight centers and six bases, promoting the development of surrounding hot springs, B&Bs, and catering industries; increasing the income of poor households, and advancing rural development. For online development, the town is focused Ch'an Town's mall and has explored the concept of "making joint efforts for development under the guidance of bases." In addition to selling home-grown alpine, tea oil, camellia, eggs, honey, winter bamboo shoots and other products, it has integrated ecological

agricultural products including local navel oranges, rice, soybeans, expanding sales channels for farmers and driving poverty alleviation.

Next Steps

There will be a development targeting the Pearl River Delta that connect Guangdong, Hong Kong and Macao. It will build the home of Guangdong-Hong Kong-Macao Greater Bay Area. Ch'an Town will improve the construction of six major agricultural industrial bases, strengthen industrial upgrading, provide strong support for poverty alleviation, and increase the vitality of rural revitalization. For customers in the Great Bay Area, a privately tailored manor plan of "one mu of farmland and woodland" will be launched. It will cover one piece of rice field, one piece of vegetable, one piece of tea garden, 20 fruit trees (grape, kiwi fruit, ice orange, persimmon, etc.), several kinds of Chinese herbal medicine and others. After the recognition, the town will issue a farmland and woodland certificate exclusively for clients. The source of their crops is traceable through a QR code. The client can view daily the planting management in real time through the mobile terminal. The customized woodland and farmland will be managed by the town, which in turn contracts them to local poor households for planting and management. The town will also work as a bridge to build a communication platform between clients and poor households. The goal is for the latter to become the former's "farmland and woodland housekeepers." The establishment of a WeChat group, photos and videos of the farmland and woodland will be sent to the clients during harvest so they can pick fruits at the same time. Through the interactions with impoverished households, each client can have a sense of accomplishment and enjoy the scenery of farmland and woodland.

北京房山区周口店镇黄山店村：
精品民宿带动村集体经济发展

Huangshandian Village, Zhoukoudian Town, Fangshan District, Beijing Municipality :
Boutique B&Bs Drive Development of Village Collective Economy

摘 要

黄山店村坚持“绿水青山就是金山银山”的发展理念，依托生态资源和历史文化资源优势，采取高端民宿品牌和景点品牌两相结合打造的方式，将住宿和景点观赏同民俗风情、特色餐饮、农业生产活动结合起来，将农村乡土气息与现代都市生活融合起来，形成了以坡峰岭景区为核心，以特色精品民宿为支撑，集亲子、康养、休闲、度假为一体的全域旅游产业格局。

挑战与问题

北京房山区周口店镇黄山店村下辖 3 个自然村，有 352 户 1004 人，是 2012 年“7 · 21”特大暴雨及洪涝灾害的重灾区。黄山店村在旅游脱贫过程中面临着诸多问题：一是客流季节性明显；二是基础设施不完善，甚至没有停车场等硬件配套设施；三是产业链单一，购物、餐饮、文化娱乐活动设施和配套的文化活动缺乏规划和开发，可供游客消费的场所和活动严重不足，且改造工作量和资金量需求巨大。

措施

1. 利用灾后重建，回收闲置农宅。借由房山区对自然灾害易发点民居实施搬迁的契机，村集体在对搬迁腾退的农宅院落进行评估作价后，将其回收为集体资产。同时，为了维护村民的切身利益，村集体组成经济合作社，为配合搬迁并符合集体经济组织成员身份的村民配发产业股，让村民享受集体资产经营带来的利润分成。

2. 融合旅游资源，打造精品民宿。黄山店村依托独特的自然景观，曾陆续推介坡峰岭景区和快活林、醉石林景点，成功举办过八届红叶节、三届黄栌花节，吸引了络绎不绝的游客。村集体与专业公司合作，统一规划、集中开发老街区，因地制宜、分批分期对原农宅进行民宿改建，同时在改建时尽量做到就地取材，既节约成本，又自然地保留了本土原有的文化特色。统一规划，集中改造、管理和运营，打造精品民宿，使其与坡峰岭、快活林等景区实现景点联动，进一步统筹域内旅游资源、配套发展，全力构筑一座原生村落生态系统。

3. 引入专业团队，实现合作共赢。为了更精准对接市场、适应市场，黄山店村引入远方网合作运营民宿。按照“保底 + 分红”的模式，集体负责基础设施建设，远方网负责运营管理，集体资产所有权不变，获益部分双方以 5 : 5 的比例进行分成，村集体享有每年每个房间 100 元的保底收益。每年，村集体可获得收益约 450 万元，而远方网可获得净利润约 100 万元，双方实现共赢。

4. 提供专业服务，带动周边经济。积极修建停车场、旅游公厕，不断完善基础配套设施，景区开通摆渡车接送游客进入景区，减少道路拥堵现象，为游客做好服务。聘请专业公司对村民进行民宿管理服务等培训，为每个宅院都配备了“管家”，让农家特色与现代生活方式相融合，充分满足了现代都市人对居住舒适度的需求。精品民宿不仅吸纳了大量周边村庄劳动力，还在一定程度上带动了周

边餐饮增收，促进了本地区商业服务业以及农副产品的生产、加工和销售。

5. 探索新兴业态，主动打开市场。2018 年以来，为适应精品民宿市场日趋激烈的竞争态势，满足游客对特色化、品质化旅游产品和服务的需求，黄山店村又先后引进了烘焙、餐饮、芳香理疗等新型民宿业态，使农村乡土气息与现代都市生活实现了多元融合，打造出更高品质的慢生活空间，为精品民宿带来新动能。

成效

黄山店已经利用旧宅分期改造建成了 40 多个精品民宿院落，精心打造了“姥姥家”“黄栌花开”“桃叶谷”“云上石屋”4 个精品民宿品牌。春节、红叶节、黄栌花节等节日期间，民宿全部被游客提前预订，全年入住率近 60%，民宿总收入 2700 万元，绿色可持续发展的道路越走越宽。黄山店村先后获得“全国文明村镇”“中国最美休闲乡村”“全国生态文化村”“房山区五星级民俗村”等荣誉称号。

经验与启示

1. 要保护绿水青山，才能获得金山银山。金山银山固然重要，但绿水青山是人民幸福生活的重要内容，是金钱所不能代替的，我们必须把握好“守住绿水青山”与“获得金山银山”之间的关系。黄山店村摒弃了以往“吃传统资源饭”的老路，通过发展生态旅游，实现了生态修复、村民增收和村集体资产的增值，这充分证明：蓝天白云、青山绿水是长远发展的最大本钱，生态优势可以变成经济优势、发展优势，源源不断地带来财富。绿水青山就是金山银山，只有保住绿水青山，经济才能实现可持续发展。

2. 要坚持“干”字当头，才能抢抓发展机遇。2008 年，随着北京奥运会的到来，黄山店村果断清退低端产业，探索转型发展的新路子，抓住绿色

发展机遇，逐步开发满山的黄栌和红叶资源，建成坡峰岭景区，实现了“旅游强村富民”。2012 年“7 · 21”特大暴雨后，作为重灾区的黄山店村在上级政府和相关部门的大力支持帮助下，利用村里闲置集体资产发展精品民宿，实现了产业升级、效益倍增，真正进入了可持续发展的轨道。实践证明，只有真干、实干、巧干才能抓住机遇，在危机中育新机，于变局中开新局。

下一步计划

1. 继续改造闲置农宅。目前，黄山店村仅完成了约 10% 的闲置农宅改造工程。为逐步扩大接待能力，将对后续的约 300 套农宅进行有序改造，今年计划打造 15 套小院作为精品民宿，满足广大游客的需求。

2. 进一步拓宽消费产业链。黄山店村的民宿，除游客住宿费用外，对产业链上游客购买力、消费力的延伸能力仍然较弱。我们会不断补充其他业态来为民宿做配套服务，例如建亲子乐园研学基地、非遗博物馆等，以满足游客日益增长的消费需求，提供更优质、更全面的景区服务，从而保证客流黏性。

3. 进一步开发配套文娱活动。结合景区现有的文化娱乐设施以及“春赏百花、夏避酷暑、秋观红叶、冬亲冰雪”的宣传定位，群策群力开展更有黄山店村风俗风貌的配套文化活动，如戏水、垂钓、学做农活、学做农家饭、篝火晚会等，从而吸引更多的游人参与，丰富景区的观赏性、娱乐性和趣味性。

Abstract

Huangshandian Village has developed both high-end B&B brands and scenic spots by relying upon their ecological resources. Lucid waters and lush mountains are invaluable assets to the region so developing this is important. Because of its natural beauty, its scenic spots are integrated with the history and culture of the village, along with the integration of folk customs and agricultural production. Overall, the village offers an all-in-one tourism pattern that integrates parent-child campaigns, recuperation, leisure, and vacation as a whole. This pattern is exclusive to the Pofeng Ridge Scenic Area as it is the core attraction.

Challenges and Problems

The village is made up of 1,004 people from 352 households. During the rainstorm disaster on July 21, 2012, the village was hit very hard. Using tourism for poverty alleviation presents three difficulties. **First,** the passenger traffic varies by season. **Second,** the village infrastructure of the village is not ready to sustain a good number of tourists. **Third,** there has been a lack of planning and development for shopping, entertainment, and other venues for the tourists to use. The shortage of such venues could lead to a higher demand for renovations and funds. However, the supply chain must first be improved.

Measures

1. Recycle idle farm residences through post-disaster reconstruction. It is possible to turn at-risk villages into collective assets by taking advantage of the villagers who live in areas prone to natural disasters. This process would involve the relocation of farmhouses and yards. At the same time, by protecting the villagers the collective village is turned into an economic cooperative where industrial shares are distributed among the villagers who are willing to relocate. In this way, the villagers can share in the profits brought by the collective assets.

2. Integrate tourism resources for boutique B&Bs. The village sits on a unique natural landscape that features the Pofeng Ridge Scenic Area, Kuaihuo Forst, and Zuishi Forest. Because of this natural beauty, the village has hosted the Red Leaf Festival and the Cotinus Coggyria Scop Flower Festivals. The village collective has worked alongside professional developers for unified planning and centralized development. Their goal is to

refurbish original farm residences into B&Bs in batches and phases. A major goal of this project is to ensure that local materials are being utilized in the building of this project, which will save costs, retain original cultural characteristics of the village, and keep the folk culture alive. By keeping a unified plan with centralized transformation, the management and operation of the project is much more likely to succeed. Furthermore, this is an attempt to link scenic areas such as the Pofeng Ridge and Kuaihuo Forest. Hopefully, this will lead to the development of supporting facilities in the region and the creation of a native village ecosystem.

3. Introduce professional teams for win-win cooperation. The village has partnered with likefar.com. This site will ensure that the villagers who are participating in the collective village program receive a minimum guarantee plus dividends for their cooperation. It mandates that both parties agree to a guaranteed income for the villagers. Further more, both parties share in the profits by a 5:5 ratio. In addition, the goal of likefar.com is to provide for infrastructure construction, operation, and management of the collective. Using the model can result in the collective bringing in a profit of about RMB 4.5 million for the village and RMB 1 million for likefar.com, making this a win-win partnership.

4. Offer professional services for development of surrounding economy. Most of the villagers who cooperate in the project have been trained in skills that are important to the well-being of the tourists. For example, professional companies have been hired to train the villagers on B&B management, housekeeping, and storekeepers. One important thing to note is that while the villagers have been trained by professionals, they are encouraged to maintain their cultural heritage or village characteristics. Besides the training, parking lots and public toilets have all been added to increase the overall comfort of the villagers. One major part of the collective skill building is the Boutique B&B as it absorbs a great number of villagers into the labor force.

5. Explore emerging business forms for market opening up. To keep up with the boutique B&B competition in the surrounding areas, the collective village has been focused on expanding their existing business models. This is done by creating baking boutiques, catering, and aromatherapy business. By expanding these models, the village is able to create a higher quality of life for the villagers which will help drive the development of all boutiques.

Results

The village has worked to repurpose old residences into more than 40 boutiques B&B courtyards. This process was done in phases and meticulously created to be in line with the culture of the village. Some of these

new boutiques are named: Grandma's House, Cotinus Coggyria Scop Flower Blosssom, Taoye Valley, and Yunshang Stone House. During the holidays, these boutiques generate a large number of guests, which leads to enormous profits. The annual occupancy rate is nearly 60%. The total income of these boutiques is RMB 27 million. One of the most important goals for the village is to make it green and sustainable. This can only be done if more tourists visit it. Because of these profits, the village was able to earn a number of different awards, including the National Civilized Village Award, China's Most Beautiful Leisure Village, National Ecological Cultural Village, and Five Star Folk Village in Fangshan District.

Experience and Inspirations

1. Certain assets of the village must be protected, which mostly include lucid waters and lush mountains. While most people can live without beautiful mountains, most people cannot live without lucid waters. The protection of the water in the village is a top priority for the managers of the village. This village has abandoned the previous model of using traditional resources for ecological restoration by focusing on its natural beauty and cultivating an appreciation for its collective assets. The eco-tourism model the village is built on relies on appreciating the lucid waters, lush mountains and its ecological foundations. This model has resulted in an increase of the villagers' income and their collective assets. However, this change cannot be realized until the appreciation of the natural resources is fully understood.

2. The collective efforts toward progress can only be achieved through hard work. Following the Beijing Olympics in 2008, many villages saw the cleanup and

exploitation of their resources. The new transformations and developments were aimed at changing the existing resources into green development. This process was done in the Cotinus Coggyria Scop and red Leves and the Pofeng Ridge Scenic Area. The tourism that this process created has been a great help to the villagers because they can enjoy more income. In addition, after the extraordinary rainstorm on July 21, 2012, the village came together to build B&Bs. This was done with support from high level government officials as well as private developers. The new B&Bs came together to form a sustainable development aimed at achieving industrial level upgrade and exploitation of natural resources. These two efforts prove that opportunities can only be seized through hard work, continuous efforts, and ingenious ideas.

Next Steps

1. Continue to renovate idle rural residences. So far, the village has completed only 10% of the renovation projects. There are still 300 farm residences and 15 small courtyards that will need to be renovated in an orderly manner. The goal is to complete this in time for the 2021 tourist demand.

2. Further broaden the consumption industrial chain. In addition to the accommodation revenue, the tourists' purchasing and consumption power relative to the industry chain remains weak. Because of this, other forms of business must be supplemented to provide service for the B&Bs. These new business could be parent-child park, cultural heritage museum, and other services that seek to increase the flow of tourists into the area.

3. Further develop supporting cultural and entertainment activities. The village weather will play a major role in determining how many tourists the village will draw. For example, the red leaves are only visible in autumn and not in summer. The ice and snow in winter cannot be enjoyed at any other time of the year. Because of this, the village must work to develop new systems that are available year-round. These could be venues such as entertainment and cultural facilities and other similar ones. Additionally, local customs such as water playing, fishing, farm work and bonfire parties should all be available for the tourists to engage while they're in the village.

广东惠州市博罗县横河镇河肚村禾肚里稻田民宿田园综合体：
“禾肚里民宿 +”模式助力乡村振兴

Heduli Paddy B&Bs Pastoral Complex in Hedu Village, Henghe Town, Boluo County, Huizhou City, Guangdong Province:
“Heduli B&Bs +” Model Facilitates Rural Revitalization

摘 要

广东省惠州市禾肚里稻田民宿田园综合体因地制宜提出把“农耕主题”作为禾肚里核心，全面激活了农村闲置物业，使“农房变客房”，将 31 间风格迥异的农耕主题客房及 3 栋独栋田舍镶嵌于稻田间或山坡上，再加上一站式餐厅、多维度办公，“禾肚里民宿”成为珠三角最美民宿。同时，禾肚里开展“春耕秋收”等稻田农耕体验、传统手艺现场教学活动，打造了中小学生研学体验基地、房车露营体验基地等，不断深化“民宿 +”模式，三产融合、联动发展，实现农民增收、促进农业发展、助力乡村振兴，走出了独特的“禾肚里模式”。

挑战与问题

禾肚里稻田民宿田园综合体文旅项目，坐落于广东省惠州市博罗县横河镇河肚村，距离国家5A级旅游景区罗浮山18公里，总投入约3000万元人民币。禾肚里稻田民宿田园综合体项目的建设主要面临两个问题：一是民宿客栈的选址一般交通要相对便利，比较靠近客源市场。而河肚村位置较偏，距离高速路口、机场、车站等均有一定路程，在区位上并没有很好的地理优势。二是民宿客栈一般还是依托于景区景点、古城古镇、美丽乡村等旅游目的地而存在，虽然也有“为了一个客栈，到一个地方”的情况，但是如果没有好的旅游资源作为依托，要单打独斗发展起民宿是很困难的。即便是去和河肚村距离最近的罗浮山景区，也需要驱车前往，所以无法借助景区资源进行有效引流。同时，当地并没有独特的自然景观和旅游资源可以利用。

措施

1. 打造农耕文化主题内涵。采用创意农耕主题，在稻田上抒写文章，打造“田园牧歌”这样一幅自然的乡村民宿图景。

2. 玩转乡村文化主题社群。通过与各教育机构、社区学校、公益团体、大型研学机构合作共享，让禾肚里不仅有可供休闲的乡村建筑，而且成为乡村产业的载体和展示乡村文化的窗口。

3. 打造乡村民宿主人文化。一般以“情怀”二字为主导的民宿主人都有一些共同的特质：他们有自己独特的生活品位和兴趣爱好，有丰富的人生阅历，且富有亲和力等。他们乐于分享自己起起伏伏的人生经历，喜欢亲自下厨、亲自当导游带领客人玩，就像老朋友一样，欢迎远道而来的客人。民

宿很大程度上也是他们自身气质的展现，民宿主人的爱好、品位、生活理念，本身就是一个民宿最好的品牌文化。本项目创始人郑春桃女士具有丰富的创业故事和乡村情怀，其对山乡的顾念和对农耕文化的深刻思考，有助于本项目主题的弘扬。

4. 打造精品民宿产品体系。禾肚里的改造设计，除了外在的整体形象让人惊艳，每一个细节都经得起手机镜头的考验，并且有独特的品位，与周边环境协调，能表现出闲适乡野生活，营造出一定的文化氛围。同时，充分利用周边的空地，打造小巧精致的菜园、花园，或者利用室内空间打造书吧、清吧、餐厅、生活交流空间、手工作坊、露天天台等，提供多样化的体验，营造真正的休闲生活空间。

成效

禾肚里稻田民宿田园综合体 31 间风格迥异的农耕主题客房及 3 栋独栋田舍镶嵌于稻田间或山坡上，再加上一站式餐厅、多维度办公，其特色引起强烈市场反响，目前已经接待各类游客逾 20 万人次，被誉为“珠三角最美民宿”；2016 年，入选“中国最美民宿”；2017 年，获评首批全国民宿产业发展示范单位；2018 年，成为广东省全域旅游示范点和中国扶贫基金会合作运营商；2019 年，入选国家乡村发展典型案例和广东省休闲农业与乡村旅游示范点。

经验与启示

1. 精准定位，创意设计。禾肚里创始人曾先后走访考察国内外同类型民宿或酒店，并与当地民宿主交流，在情怀中沉淀思考，找准经营定位，找

准盈利方向；因地制宜提出把“农耕主题”作为禾肚里核心，客房以 24 节气串联，把亲子旅游作为重要业务板块，并搭配本地农特产品与稻田文创产品，实现盈利多样化。在设计上发挥创意，把学校宿舍变成农耕主题客房，把操场变成内部观景栈道，把稻田变成亲子游乐园和乡村漫步道，并充分结合乡野乐趣，开辟了农业科普观光园、陶艺吧、房车露营基地、亲子采摘园等配套娱乐设施，打造出一幅自然的田园牧歌乡村民宿图景。

2. 民宿学院，品牌输出。禾肚里利用人才优势，开办民宿学院，联合高校、农民企业家、农户，开展民宿人才培训班，培养大量的民宿经营管理人才及服务人员。民宿目前是乡村旅游扶贫的重要支撑点和发力点，禾肚里积极响应号召，助推旅游扶贫，于 2018 年 9 月成功竞选湖南凤凰古城拉毫村项目，成为中国扶贫基金会合作运营商，正式走出广东省投入全国精准扶贫行列。

3. 资本先行，全域旅游。民宿在某种程度上属于重资产投入，回报周期较长，禾肚里正在与多方资本接洽，在禾肚里品牌外输的道路上，让资本成为民宿发展的“助力棒”。禾肚里积极顺应旅游产业发展趋势发展全域旅游，在修炼“内功”的同时，有选择性地“外拓”和“输出”，全面激活了农村闲置物业，让“农房变客房”；通过开展“春耕秋收”等稻田农耕体验、传统手艺现场教学（陶艺制作、编稻草人等）等体验活动，打造了中小学生研学体验基地；同时，民宿配套较全面的服务功能，实现手机端服务，有效提升区域旅游的接待能力。

下一步计划

未来，禾肚里将一如既往地深化“民宿 +”模式，进一步带动三产融合、联动发展，实现农民增收、促进农业发展、助力乡村振兴。一是立足农村，继续开发打造新的乡村旅游特色民宿项目，与乡村、村民一起达成共建、共生、共享、共治的和谐业态；二是在梅州大埔打造以养生为主题的中草药产业园，结合产业实体，开展文化传播并打造主题旅游；三是推动以中草药研学为主题的研学活动，让中小学生走出校门，有学习，有实践，更加亲近大自然、了解大自然、熟悉大自然；四是大力推动发展乡村振兴培训学院，与高校合作，设计与时俱进的课堂教程，分享、传播禾肚里经验，为地方培养更多有技术、懂政策、善干事的领导干部和村民代表。

Abstract

In keeping with the farming theme of the village, Heduli Paddy B&Bs pastoral Complex in Huizhou City, Guangdong Province has revitalized rural idle properties for the transformation of rural homes into guest rooms. So far 31 homes with different styles have been renovated and rebuilt in ways that incorporate the local customs. Some homes have been built in great locations such as on a hillside or on the river. There have also been developments into the city's educational programs. For example, spring plowing and autumn harvesting have been added as educational programs that can help develop knowledge of the local customs. So far traditional craftsmen have helped in research experiences and the integration of various projects.

Challenge and Problems

The Heduli Paddy B&B pastoral complex is a cultural tourism project. It is located near Hedu Village, Henghe Town, Boluo County, Huizhou City, Guangdong Province. The area has a total investment of RMB 30 million. Two construction projects are currently underway. One of the problems here is the remoteness of the village to other villages despite the B&Bs excellent transportation. It lacks basic amenities such as gas stations or airports. Another issue is that people do not want to visit a tourist spot without scenic views. While the B&B has great services, scenic beauty is direly lacking here. One would have to drive up to the nearby Mountain Luofu Scenic Area in the absence of unique natural landscapes and tourism resources in local areas.

Measures

1. Develop farming with cultural connotations. Creative farming themes have been adopted to give off a scent of charm and a natural feel for the B&Bs has been developed.

2. Create rural culture-themed communities. Huduli has developed a rural architecture for leisure and is a carrier of rural industries. This has been done through cooperation and co-sharing with various educational institutions, community schools, and public welfare organizations.

3. Strengthen the culture of rural B&B owners. B&Bs are known for their relaxing and comforting environment. Many of them share unique sentiments, different hobbies, and a strong affinity for new experiences. More importantly, their owners are pleased

to share their homes to those who are looking for a place to stay and treat them like old friends. Overall, B&Bs are a manifestation of the owners' temperament, hobbies, and life philosophies. Ms. Zheng Chuntao is the founder of this project. She cherishes abundant entrepreneurial stories and rural feelings. In addition, she cares for the mountain village and facilitates the promotion of a themed project.

4. Establish a boutique B&Bs product system. The stunning scenery of the village can withstand the test of the mobile lends of tourists who are keeping an eye on unique landscape. A design in harmony with its surrounding landscape creates distinct cultural connotations. Surrounding open spaces have been fully utilized to create small and exquisite vegetable farms and gardens. Indoor spaces have been configured into book bars, public bars, restaurants, exchange spaces, manual workshops, outdoor rooftops, etc., thus providing diversified experiences and unique leisure spaces.

Results

All of the 31 farm-themed guest rooms have different styles while independent farmhouses have all been built on the hillside. The addition of restaurants and multi-use office areas have received an influx of visitors, resulting in a strong market response. More than 200,000 tourists have visited the pastoral complex. It has been known as the "most beautiful B&B in the Pearl River Delta." In 2016 it was named the most beautiful B&B in China and in 2017 it was awarded the first batch of national demonstration units of B&B industry development. In 2018 it became a demonstration site of all for one tourism and the cooperative operator of China Foundation for Poverty Alleviation (CFPA). And finally in 2019, it was listed as a typical example of national rural development

and demonstration site of a leisure agriculture and rural tourism in Guangdong Province.

Experience and Inspirations

1. Precise positioning and creative design. The founder of the B&B has done researches into other villages and derived inspirations from them. He has exchanged ideas with many other owners. According to local conditions and with farming as the theme and core of Heduli, the guest rooms are interconnected by 24 solar terms. The parent-child travel is considered an important business segment, local agricultural products and paddy-related cultural and creative products are combined to generate diversified profits. Creative design ideas are implemented to turn school dormitories into farm-themed guest rooms, playgrounds into internal viewing planks, and paddies into parent-child amusement parks and rural walkways. These are all done to develop and support entertainment facilities such as agricultural land, sightseeing parks, and gardens.

2. B&B college and brand output. The B&B college will train and instruct workers on the best management methods of running a B&B. In addition, the colleges are tasked to deliver training to all who undergo this program so they can be valuable personnels for their villages. While B&Bs are important for tourism and leisure, they are also important to facilitate poverty alleviation. In September 2018 the village won a campaign project of Lahao Village that was focused on poverty alleviation.

3. Capital-driven all-for-one tourism. A large investment is required for this project to be successful. Multiple sources of capital are drawn to this. Hopefully, it will boost the Heduli brand and the development of B&Bs. All-for-one tourism has been developed in compliance with the development trend of the tourism industry. The project has selectively expanded its external marketing while enhancing its internal functions, fully revitalizing rural idle properties by transforming rural houses into guest rooms. Activities such as "spring plowing and autumn harvesting" paddy farming experience and on-site teaching of traditional craftsmanship have helped develop research experience bases for primary and elementary school students. At the same time, the comprehensive supporting service functions of B&Bs can be remotely realized through mobile phones, effectively enhancing the reception capacity for regional tourism.

Next Steps

In the future, the B&Bs model will be more integrated with three more industries for an interactive development. Overall, the farmers' income will increase over time and the land will be revitalized. **First,** new characteristic B&B projects of rural tourism will be developed based on rural conditions, to develop a harmonious business model featuring co-construction, co-sharing, and co-governance with villages and local villagers. **Second,** a Chinese herbal medicine industrial park with a health preservation theme will be built in Dabu County, Meizhou City, to carry out cultural dissemination and promote tourism in combination with industrial entities. **Third,** research activities with a Chinese herbal medicine theme will be promoted to help primary and elementary school students learn outside their classrooms and bring them closer to nature for familiarity and better understanding of the natural world. **Fourth,** the development of training colleges on rural revitalization will be advanced, and courses keeping pace with the times will be designed with colleges and universities to share and spread the Heduli experience. More leading cadres and village representatives with more skills, knowledge of policies and who are eager to learn will be trained.

上海青浦区朱家角镇张马村：
农旅融合打造田园张马，产业联动助力乡村振兴

Zhangma Village, Zhujiajiao Town, Qingpu District, Shanghai Municipality:
Agricultural and Tourism Integration for Idyllic Sceneries, Industrial Linkage for Rural Revitalization

摘 要

张马村以美丽乡村为基础，以全域旅游理念为引领，大力实施乡村振兴战略。通过以项目聚焦强筋骨、以产业文化促提升，深入挖掘本地乡村特色、村落游览和民宿产业等，将乡村田园作为一个大景区进行打造，推进农村三产联动，加快农业生产转型、产业结构调整，培育、发展农村新业态、新动能，逐步实现农业增效、农民增收、农村可持续性发展。2019 年 10 月，张马村被评为国家 4A 级旅游景区，全年接待游客约 50 万人次，成为全国最美休闲乡村。

挑战与问题

张马村位于上海市青浦区朱家角镇最南端，是上海母亲河黄浦江的水系源头。张马地势低洼地难种，以种植茭白、水稻为主，只有农业，村级经济基础薄弱、落后。20 世纪 90 年代，民营资本企业逐渐入驻张马村，先后建立了太阳岛、寻梦源、农情园、蓝莓园等，村内农事旅游格局初见端倪。但由于农村基础设施建设相对薄弱且缺乏统筹考虑，多个园区之间未形成交通串联，道路通行不便。同时，各园区拥有独立的管理机构，张马村村委会作为属地化管理单位，综合协调难度较大。长期以来，张马村虽有优良的生态资源和丰富的历史文化底蕴，但一直没有得到很好的挖掘，产业发展滞缓。

措施

1. 规划引领，统筹产业布局。根据“发展农事旅游”这一产业定位，张马村先后规划、编制了《张马村庄规划》《张马地区美丽乡村旅游发展总体规划》《4A 级景区创建提升规划》，通过“多规合一”统筹村庄建设。结合张马村独特的生态、文化优势（泖河、唐代泖塔）和产业基础，整合各条线资源，着力完善寻梦源、蓝莓园、农情园、生态园等，以创建国家 4A 级景区为目标，积极推进和深化“大美丽乡村”建设，推动乡村振兴工作。

2. 公司运作，完善基础设施。2017 年，张马村与三家镇管单位共同成立了上海张马旅游发展有限公司，借助民间资本，大力优化、整合资源，集中打造田园综合体示范区。2019 年，在已有基础上成立上海朱家角实业发展有限公司，统筹推进张马村的乡村振兴建设和景区管理。全面启动张马游客接待中心、停车场、张马景区微信公众号等，并落实了对连接“四园一岛”核心区域的沿线标识标牌、景观步道、A 级厕所等软硬件设施的建设。

3. 整合资源，加强产业融合。紧抓“旅游＋农业”“旅游＋教育”，张马村以“游学张马、寻梦田园”为策划思路，以农事旅游为切入点，重点打造乡村旅游产业，将寻梦源、农情园、蓝莓园、生态园、太阳岛这“四园一岛”农事旅游点串连成线，构建生态旅游产业格局，丰富农业的非生产功能，提高农业全产业链收益，做活乡村“美丽经济”。

4. 村企联合，助推产业一体化。张马村村委会与上海朱家角实业发展有限公司联结协作、相互配合，通过搭建载体、凝聚力量，进一步推进张马旅游、农业产业的发展壮大。在景区范围内，划清村与公司的管理边界与职能，对标景区管理标准，强化了环境卫生、生态管控、公共服务、旅游咨询等服务功能。在农业生产中，创新形成张马鲜米产品“产、供、销”一体化模式，由村级合作社负责生产、存储、包装，实业公司负责宣传、推广、销售，进一步增强了村集体自身的“造血”功能。

成效

随着4A级景区创建和乡村振兴建设，张马驶入了加速发展的“快车道”。建设整合村实际现状，因地制宜，全面完善基础设施配套，优化了村庄整体公共服务配套设施建设，全面提升了人居环境质量，切实增强了村民的获得感、幸福感和安全感。张马村村民通过“四园一岛”各景点实现了再就业，包括136人全职（每人每月3000元）、142人兼职（每人每天120元），实现岗位适配，增加了工资性收入；通过开设农家乐、杂货店以及建立合作社，不断增加村民的经营性收入。同时，发展乡村民宿，将农民闲置房屋规范流转到张马村村民委员会平台，现有40余栋民宿以每栋30000元/年（每年环比增长3%）的租金价格进行出租。张马村民宿发展还与木船俱乐部及新型零售等品牌业态布局相结合，带动当地就业人数逾30人，吸引了部分大学生、乡村青年回乡创业。

经验与启示

1. 稳住农业基本盘，守好“三农”基础。张马村以“美丽乡村”“乡村振兴示范村”的深化建设为抓手，科学把握乡村振兴阶段性的特征，统筹推进乡村产业导入和发展。根据村实际情况“固根基、扬优势、补短板、强弱项”，对农村基础配套、公共服务设施做进一步完善，推动农村人居环境整治工作，抓牢农业生态底线，不断寻求产业培育与发展的突破，着力激发农业农村的动力、活力和潜力。

2. 优化营商环境，抓好顶层设计。首先，提供“好配套”。进一步做好产业引入的前期规划和调研，持续优化农村产业空间布局，完善基础保障，做好建设用地的指标调配，为农业招商做好基础保障。其次，出台“好政策”。完善农业招商政策，研究制定农产业引入的优惠政策。借助周边优

势，探索村企联动协同发展模式。

3. 抓好产业导向，助推农村发展。基于张马优良的资源禀赋，通过总体规划布局，张马村集田园观光休闲、乡村社会实践、自然文化教育、家庭亲子教育、户外拓展运动、健康养生度假等功能于一体，通过美丽乡村开放式景区的创新发展模式，以乡村振兴建设促进旅游区开发，以旅游区建设带动区域乡村人文、环境、经济的可持续发展，打造美丽乡村旅游休闲新天地。

下一步计划

一是根据《(旅游景区质量等级的划分与评定）国家标准评定细则》的要求，进一步查漏补缺，切实加强 A 级景区质量管理，提升专业化服务水平。持续开展各景点监督引导工作，不断强化旅游景区的 A 级意识、服务意识、安全意识和创新意识，在运营质量提升、品牌形象打造等方面下功夫，进一步督促各景点健全完善规章制度，努力提升管理和服务水平，以高质量、高标准的要求，持续推进张马景区运营、管理等工作。二是推进研学产品开发和推广。结合近几年开发设计的旅游线路和学农实践活动成果，整合张马景区（农情园、南绿舟学农基地等）学农资源，形成可推广的学农实践活动方案。三是加快业态产业发展。推动游船线路运营，以月潭江与莫家村江“两江”为主要游船线路，依托新建的游船码头，实现游客中心、寻梦源、民宿的相互串联与衔接，形成一幅“小河之舟赏田园，江南之韵醉张马”的优美画卷。四是坚持走出去，发挥主动性。围绕现代农业、乡村旅游、生态康养等领域，以“走出去”宣传推介、网络招商等形式，建立农业招商项目库，挖掘“接地气”的好项目，引入有实力的企业，加快推进张马村产业导入。

Abstract

With all-for-one tourism as its guide, the Zhangma Village has implemented rural revitalization strategies, explored local rural characteristics, village tour and the B&B industry. It has done this by enhancing industrial cultural projects and establishing the countryside as a scenic area. Also, it has promoted the linkage of the primary, secondary and tertiary industries in rural areas. This was achieved through the accelerated transformation of agricultural production, adjustment of industrial structures and development of new rural business models for increased agricultural efficiency. As a result, the farmers' income has grown along with its sustainable rural development. In October 2019, the village was designated a national 4A-level tourist attraction, with an annual reception of about 500,000 tourists. It has become a most beautiful national leisure village.

Challenges and Problems

Located at the southernmost tip of Zhujiajiao Town in Qingpu District, Shanghai Municipality, the village points to the Huangpu River, the city's mother river. Due to its low lying location, developing a plantation industry here is difficult. The village economy is consequently weak and backward as it only relies on agricultural development. In the 1990s, private enterprises gradually settled here and successively established Sun Island, Dreamland, Agricultural Style Garden, Blueberry Garden, etc. They displayed the emerging pattern of rural tourism. However, due to its undeveloped infrastructure and lack of overall planning, there is no available means to access its multiple parks. Contributing to this inconvenience is the fact that each park is managed by independent management agencies. This setup makes it difficult for the village committee to conduct comprehensive coordination for a localized management unit. For a long time, despite the village's abundant ecological resources and centuries-old culture it has not been developed, leading to its lagging development.

Measures

1. Planning should play the leading role for a coordinated industrial layout. Based on the industry positioning of rural tourism development, the village has planned and prepared the *Zhangma Village Planning, Master Plan for Tourism Development of Beautiful Villages in Zhangma Region* and *Plan on Creation and Improvement of 4A-level tourist attraction.* The goal is to carry out a coordinated construction of the village through multiple planning phases. In combination with the unique ecology, cultural advantages (Mao River and Mao Pagoda of the Tang Dynasty) and its industrial foundation, it has integrated various resources to improve the Dreamland, Blueberry Garden, Agricultural Style Garden, and Ecological Garden, etc. It has also strengthened the construction of "beautiful villages" to create a 4A-level tourist attraction for the advancement of rural revitalization.

2. Conduct enterprise operation for improved infrastructure. In 2017, the village, in cooperation with three town management units, established the Shanghai Zhangma Tourism Development Co., Ltd. This venture optimized and integrated resources with the help of private capital and with the goal of making a concentrated effort to build a pastoral complex demonstration area. In 2019, Shanghai Zhujiajiao Industrial Development Co., Ltd. was established to advance the construction of rural revitalization and the management of the scenic area in the village. Concerted efforts have been made to open WeChat public accounts for the tourist reception center, the parking lot and the scenic area. Also, the construction of software and hardware facilities such as signages, landscape trails and A-level toilets along the core areas connecting the four gardens and one island have been launched.

3. Consolidate resources for enhanced industrial integration. The village is focused on "tourism + agriculture" and "tourism + education" with "enjoying study tours in Zhangma Village, seeking dreams in idyllic scenery." By taking rural tourism as the starting point, the village has highlighted the building of the rural tourism industry and connected the "four gardens and one island" tourist attractions. These four are named Dreamland, Agricultural Style Garden, Blueberry Garden, Ecological Garden, and Sun Island. The hope is to build an ecological tourism industrial pattern. All these have enriched the non-production functions of agriculture, increased the income of the full industry chain of agriculture, thus advancing the economic development of villages.

4. Establish village-enterprise alliances for industrial integration. Based on the coordinated cooperation and carrier building with Shanghai Zhujiajiao Industrial Development Co., Ltd., the village committee has further boosted the development of tourism and agricultural industries. Within the scope of the scenic area, it has clarified the management boundaries and functions of the village. The company evaluated the management standards of the scenic area and also strengthened the service functions of environmental sanitation, ecological control, public services and tourism consultation. During the agricultural production, a new integrated model of "production, supply, and marketing" of fresh rice products in the village has been developed. This model stipulates that the village cooperative is responsible for production, storage and packaging, while the industrial company is responsible for publicity, promotion and sales. This setup has further clarified the role of the village collective in fostering self-reliance and working toward an upgrade.

Results

With the establishment of the 4A-level tourist attraction and the construction of rural revitalization, the village has developed rapidly. Measures to improve infrastructure, optimize the construction of public service and improve the quality of human settlements have been adjusted. As a result, the villagers are enriched as their sense of security and feelings of happiness are fulfilled.

Local farmers have been reemployed at the four gardens and one island, including 136 full-time staff (RMB 3,000 per month) and 142 part-time staff (RMB 120 per day) — achieving job adaptation and increased income. Their operating income through agritainment, grocery stores and the establishment of cooperatives have likewise increased. Idle houses of farmers are transferred to villagers' committee platform and more than 40 B&Bs are rented at an annual charge of RMB 30,000 (a year-on-year growth rate of 3%). The B&B development in the village was also combined with the business structures of brands such as the wooden boat clubs and new retail. This has helped more than 30 people find local jobs and attract some college students and rural youth to return to their hometown for employment in business startups.

Experience and Inspirations

1. Maintain the foundation of "agriculture, rural areas and farmers" for development. The village has mastered the phased characteristics of rural revitalization and made overall plans to advance the introduction and development of rural industries based on an in-depth construction of "beautiful villages" and "demonstration villages for rural revitalization." Continuous efforts should be made to solidify foundations, promote advantages and make up for shortcomings to achieve more progress. Specifically, energy should be devoted to perfect rural infrastructure and public service facilities, improve rural human settlements and make breakthroughs in industrial cultivation and development based on the bottom line of agricultural ecology to tap into the potential of agriculture and rural areas.

2. Optimize the business environment for a sound top-level design. First, supportive planning and policies should be offered. Preliminary planning and investigation are essential to optimize the spatial layout of rural industries. They are necessary in obtaining more support and for a reasonable allocation of land indicators for construction. Also, it ensures the basic guarantee of agricultural investment. **Second,** favorable policies should be issued. Policies for agricultural investment should be improved and preferential policies for the introduction of agricultural industries should likewise be formulated. The advantages of the surrounding areas should be leveraged for the coordinated development of villages and enterprises.

3. Clarify industrial orientation for rural development. Based on its abundant resources, overall planning and layout, the village has integrated many new developments that include pastoral tourism, rural social practice, natural cultural education, parent-child education, outdoor sports, health and vacations and other functions as a whole. It has adopted the innovative development model of building beautiful villages into open scenic areas as rural revitalization can accelerate the development of tourist areas. In turn, the construction of tourist areas can drive the sustainable development of regional rural culture, environment and economy—creating a beautiful destination for rural tourism and leisure.

Next Steps

First, more work needs to be done to further check the omitted items for remedy, strengthen the quality management of A-level tourist attraction and improve the level of professional services. This should be done according to the requirements of the *National Standard Evaluation Rules for Quality Grade Evaluation and Classification of Tourist Attractions.* Continuous efforts will be made to carry out the supervision and guidance of various tourist attractions to increase A-level awareness as well as service and safety. Awareness of innovation

in tourist attractions must be equally enhanced. Quality improvement and brand building must also be emphasized along with the supervision in the perfection of rules and regulations in tourist attractions and improvement of the level of management and services. All these will go a long way toward topnotch operation and management of the scenic area. **Second,** the development of research products will be promoted. Based on the tourism routes that have been developed and designed in recent years and the results of agricultural practice, the resources of the scenic area (Agricultural Style Garden, Nanlvzhou Agricultural Base, etc.) will be integrated to create an agricultural program that can be popularized. **Third,** the industrial development of various businesses will be accelerated. It is essential to promote the operation of cruise routes and connect the tourist center, Dreamland, and B&Bs based on the main cruise routes of Yuetan River and Mojiacun River and the newly-built cruise wharf. All together they will showcase the invaluable concept of "appreciating idyllic scenery in a small boat, immersed in the charm of Zhangma with Jiangnan style." **Fourth,** the principle of going global will be followed for more initiative. Centered on modern agriculture, rural tourism, ecological healthcare and other fields, great efforts will be made to establish a database of agricultural investment projects through ways such as "go global" publicity and online investment promotions. Well-adapted projects must also be explored, and powerful enterprises should be introduced to accelerate the village's industrial development.

浙江旅游职业学院：
服务乡村振兴战略　助力万村景区建设

Tourism College of Zhejiang:
Serve the Rural Revitalization Strategy for Construction of Ten Thousand Scenic Villages

摘要

浙江旅游职业学院自 2017 年 5 月启动“师生助力全省万村景区建设”项目，坚持以人为本、以质取胜，开展精准帮扶，助力帮扶村庄乡村旅游体验更精致、公共设施更精良、生态环境更精美、游客服务更精心、运营管理更精细。五年来，对浙江省内 11 个地市 67 个县（市、区）的 286 个村庄进行乡村旅游发展指导，各个村庄或依托自己的山水环境，或依托农业产业特色，或依托现代创意，因地制宜，形成了自身的特色和发展路径，其中 94 个村庄成功创建省 3A 级景区村庄，安吉余村创建成为国家 4A 级旅游景区。

挑战与问题

浙江省持续推进美丽乡村建设虽然取得了显著成效，也为乡村旅游发展奠定了坚实基础，但与深入实施乡村振兴战略目标相比，仍存在一定差距。一是乡村公共服务薄弱。由于乡村交通道路与停车场、公共厕所、垃圾箱、人居环境以及乡村公共休闲空间的配套建设水平低下，严重影响了乡村整体形象，影响了游客的乡村旅游体验。二是乡村旅游资源没有有效盘活。村民缺乏依靠旅游去辅助农业转型升级、促进农村经济社会协调发展的意识。三是乡村传统文化保护传承不足。散落在乡间的非物质文化遗产缺乏传承、展示与产业化发展的平台。四是乡村空心化问题与老龄化问题没有得到缓解与改善。

措施

为深入实施乡村振兴战略，浙江省推行“万村景区化”创新实践，推动美丽乡村建设成果从“环境美”向“发展美”转型，从美丽景色向美丽经济转变，走出一条以文化和旅游发展激活乡村发展动能、引领乡村振兴的新路。浙江旅游职业学院自2017年5月启动为期五年的“师生助力全省万村景区建设”项目，每年组建师生工作团队，利用课余时间分赴浙江省内各帮扶村庄，开展助力景区村庄创建工作。

1. 实施精准帮扶。“师生助力全省万村景区建设”项目工作启动后，为精准推进帮扶活动，首先确定帮扶村庄及帮扶需求，学校根据专业设置及乡村旅游发展现实需求，将帮扶的内容限定为景区建设对标指导、乡村旅游资源调查与旅游产品策划、乡村旅游商品设计、农家乐菜肴开发、导游词编写、乡村运营管理建议 6 个方面。学校根据各服务团队的专业特长、与所帮扶村庄帮扶需求的匹配度等因素，合理确定各帮扶村庄的服务团队，以优化帮扶效果。

2. 创建科学指导。学校各服务团队严格按照《浙江省 A 级景区村庄服务与管理指南》及评定细则、管理办法指导帮扶村庄创建工作，采用景区开发的方法和成功经验来指导村庄开发建设，在深入调研的情况下制订各帮扶村庄的 A 级景区村庄创建指导方案，明确各帮扶村庄的 A 级景区村庄创建时间表、路线图、责任书，对旅游交通、环境卫生、基础设施与服务、特色活动与项目、综合管理、游客满意程度调查评价等各方面都有明确、详细的指导意见。

3. 培育乡村人才。为助力提升帮扶村庄乡村旅游从业人员的整体素质，助推帮扶村庄乡村旅游人才队伍的建设，学校选派优秀教师分赴各帮扶村庄开展“乡村旅游免费送教下乡”活动，为帮扶村庄负责人、乡村旅游经营者和从业人员免费提供乡村旅游培训。培训内容涉及乡村旅游服务品质提升、乡村旅游经营与管理、A 级景区村庄建设、乡村民宿设计与经营、乡村旅游新媒体技术提升、“百县千碗”工程等多个方面。

成效

1. 推动乡村产业升级，促进创新创业。通过助力景区村庄的建设，在一定程度上推动了乡村的产业升级，促进了乡村地区的创新创业，形成了一批“文旅 + 农业”休闲农场产业、“文旅 + 生态”精品度假产业、“文旅 + 教育”研学基地产业，切实带动了部分乡村村民就地就业，拉长了区域农业产业链，增加了农副产品附加值。如衢州市开化县金星村利用景区村庄建设的契机，发展“文旅 + 农户”民宿客栈产业，现已建有农家乐 6 家、民宿 18 家，年接待游客逾 50 万人次，农民年人均收入超过 3.5 万元；近三年，有超过 2/3 的外出务工青年已经返乡，参与当地民宿、农家乐等小企业的创办或在当地就业。

2. 提升治理管理能力，营造文明乡风。通过景区村庄的创建，提升了景区村庄的乡村治理能力及效果，提高了公共服务设施建设水平，增强了基层党组织号召力，引领出乡村旅游业态与产品，带动了景区村庄乡风文明。如宁波余姚市谢家路村在景区村庄的创建过程中，创新农村基层治理模式，让村级经济不断壮大，不断完善基础设施建设，兴建文化设施丰富村民生活，村民安居乐业、基层和谐稳定，该村也先后获得了“全国文明村”“全国民主法治示范村”等荣誉。

3. 引领乡村文化建设，增强文化自信。通过景区村庄的创建，推动了乡村文化建设，使村民可以享受文化给他们带来的精神洗礼，从而激发他们

的精神力量，让文化自信成为推动乡村发展的动力，带动乡村各项事业的发展。如舟山市普陀区干施岙村通过景区村庄的创建，充分挖掘“五匠”文化、孝文化，利用“五匠”馆和礼孝学堂开发特色旅游产品，并使其成为当地研学教育基地、非遗体验基地、科普教育基地，干施岙村成为当地有名的网红村，成功吸引社会资本参与村庄建设。

经验与启示

1. 因地制宜。遵循乡村自身发展规律，充分体现农村特点，顺应乡村文化肌理，保留乡风、乡味、乡情、乡貌和乡愁，发展有历史记忆、地域特色、品质业态的景区化村庄，防止一窝蜂式的照搬照抄和大拆大建。

2. 生态优先。注重生态环境和人居环境的提升，坚守生态保护的底线，把真山真水真空气、原汁原味原风情作为景区村庄建设最大的优势、最好的品牌，把“绿色惠民、富民强村”的理念贯穿于景区村庄建设的全过程。

3. 创新发展。创新理念，创新思路，创新举措，深化改革，有效突破土地、资金等瓶颈制约和制度障碍，如推行“公司 + 专业合作社 + 农户”等新型发展模式，带动村民增收致富，提高将乡村旅游资源转化为美丽经济的创新能力。

4. 主客共享。满足游客日益增长的需求，推动乡村旅游的供给侧改革，促进乡村旅游提档升级。充分发挥农民主体作用，发挥以旅兴农的作用。

下一步计划

1. 助力景区村庄推动数字赋能。借助数字科技技术，助力景区村庄智慧智能化。以“互联网 + 旅游 + 乡村”为重点，帮扶景区村庄推动与数字科技的融合，推出具有交互性、沉浸式、体验型特点的数字乡村旅游产品。基于“浙里好玩”，帮扶景区村庄构建乡村旅游“一站式、智能化、个性化”智慧服务系统，推出“一键订单”“一码投诉”“10 秒找空房”“20 秒景点入园”“30 秒酒店入住”等便民服务。

2. 助力景区村庄实施“微改造”。结合全省旅游业“微改造、精提升”，在保留村庄原有纹理和浙派风貌的基础上，助力景区村庄实施“微改造、精提升”行动，打造“环境精美、设施精良、体验精致、服务精心、管理精细”的“五精”村庄，按照主客共享原则，构建宜居宜业宜游生态，塑造高品质的乡村休闲生活。

3. 助力景区村庄拓宽“共富路”。围绕浙江省建设共同富裕示范区、社会主义现代化先行省和乡村振兴示范省的目标，助力景区村庄打通“绿水青山就是金山银山”的通道，培养本土专业管理人才，培育专业运营团队，完善设施维护和商户管理，更新产品业态，推出精品线路，打造乡村旅游品牌，实现可持续发展，带动农民增收致富，拓宽以旅兴农实现共同富裕的道路。

4. 助力景区村庄乡村文化振兴。助力景区村庄坚持文旅融合，守护延续好乡村文化等村庄“灵魂”，引导旅游咨询服务点与文化礼堂、乡村书屋等融合发展。助力景区村庄建设文化主题、非遗主题民宿，推出具有鲜明文化特色的乡村文创产品，不断提升乡村内涵，促进乡村文化振兴。

Abstract

Since the Tourism College of Zhejiang launched the "Teacher-Student Efforts for the Construction of Ten Thousand Scenic Villages in Zhejiang Province"project in May 2017, it has been emphasizing people and quality-oriented principle for targeted assistance in poverty alleviation to develop a more comfortable rural tourism experience with better sophisticated public facilities, exquisite ecological environment, meticulous tourist services and more refined operation management. Over the past five years, the college has provided guidance on the development of rural tourism to 286 villages in 67 counties of 11 prefecture-level cities (cities, districts) in Zhejiang Province. As a result, each village has formed its own development path by adapting to local conditions and natural environment, indigenous agricultural industries and modern creativity. Among these villages, 94 have successfully become provincial 3A-level tourist attractions. Yu Village, a village in Anji County in Zhejiang Province, has developed into a national 4A-level tourist attraction.

Challenges and Problems

Despite the remarkable achievements of the Zhejiang Province in the construction of beautiful villages and the solid foundation underlying the development of rural tourism, a gap still exists between its accomplishments and the in-depth implementation of the rural revitalization strategy. Four reasons behind this are listed as follows: **First,** the province is still weak in rural public services. Its undeveloped supporting facilities — rural traffic roads, parking lots, public toilets, dustbins, human settlements and public recreational spaces — have seriously affected the image of the village and the experience of rural tourists. **Second,** rural tourism resources have not been effectively utilized. Villagers lack the awareness of promoting the agricultural transformation, upgrading and coordinating development of rural economy and society through tourism development. **Third,** efforts in protecting, preserving and bequeathing its rural traditional culture are inadequate. The rural intangible cultural heritage lacks a platform for the display and handing down of its culture and industrial development. **Fourth,** the issues on rural hollowing and aging have neither been alleviated nor improved.

Measures

To further implement the rural revitalization strategy, the Zhejiang Province has initiated the innovative construction of the "Ten Thousand Scenic Villages" for the transformation of its "beautiful environment" into a "prosperous development" by shifting the focus from picturesque scenery to economic progress. When the Tourism College of Zhejiang launched the five-year project of "Teacher-Student Efforts for the Construction of Ten Thousand Scenic Villages in Zhejiang Province" in May 2017, it organized a team of teachers and students to conduct an annual development work on the scenic villages in Zhejiang Province in their spare time.

1. Implement targeted assistance. After the initiation of the "Teacher-Student Efforts for Construction of Ten Thousand Scenic Villages in Zhejiang Province" project, it's important to identify first the villages in need of assistance and those that will be getting it to ensure a targeted system. The college provides aid based on their professional benchmarks and the actual needs of rural tourism development. The scope for this is limited to six aspects: benchmarking guidance for scenic spots construction, survey on rural tourism resources and planning of tourism products, design of rural tourism products, cuisine development for agritainment, compiling of tour commentaries, and suggestions on rural operation and management. To improve its chance of success, the college determines the service team for each assisted village based on the matching skills and professional expertise of each service team and the needs of the village.

2. Provide scientific guidance. The service team assists with the scenic village development in strict compliance with the *Service and Management Guide of Zhejiang A-level Scenic Villages,* the evaluation criteria and management rules. Based on its experience, it guides the development and construction through the tried and proven methods of scenic spots development. Also, it formulates guidelines for the development of A-level scenic villages based on in-depth research, and clarifies the timetable, route map and letter of responsibility of the A-level scenic villages. Further more the service team offers clear and detailed guidance on tourism transportation, environmental sanitation, infrastructure and services, special activities and projects, comprehensive management, survey and evaluation on tourist satisfaction.

3. Train rural talents. To help improve the quality of rural tourism workers in assisted villages and train a team of rural tourism talents, the college selects outstanding teachers to carry out the "Free Education on Rural Tourism into Rural Areas" program and provide free rural tourism training for local leaders, rural tourism operators and manpower. The training involves many aspects: improvement of rural tourism service quality, operation and management of rural tourism, construction of A-level scenic villages, design and operation of rural B&Bs, improvement of new media technologies in rural tourism,

and the "One Thousand Dishes of One Hundred Counties" project.

Results

1. Promote the upgrading of rural industries for innovation and business startups. Assistance in the construction of scenic villages has promoted the upgrading of rural industries for innovation and business startups and formed the "cultural tourism + agriculture" leisure farm industry, "cultural tourism + ecology" boutique holiday industry, "cultural tourism + education" research and study base industry. In some rural areas it has facilitated local employment opportunities, extended the regional agricultural industry chain, and further increased the added value of agricultural byproducts. For example, Jinxing Village, Kaihua County, Quzhou City, Zhejiang Province spare no effort in developing the "cultural tourism + peasant households" B&B industry. Now there are six agritainment sites and 18 B&Bs, with the annual reception of more than 500,000 tourists and the per capita income of farmers of over RMB 35,000. For the past three years, more than two-thirds of young migrant workers have returned to their hometowns to operate small businesses such as local B&Bs and agritainment, or to find jobs in local areas.

2. Improve capabilities in governance and management for a civil rural environment. The construction of scenic villages has helped enhance village governance capabilities and has positively affected the locals and their livelihood. It has enhanced the quality of the construction projects of public service facilities, boosting the appeal of grassroots party organizations. It has also successfully guided the rural tourism industry development and products, promoting its culture. For example, during the construction of scenic villages in Xiejialu Village, Yuyao City, Ningbo City, Zhejiang Province, it developed a model of rural grassroots governance, promoted village-level economy, improved infrastructure construction, and built cultural facilities to enrich the life of villagers, ensuring a satisfactory, harmonious and stable grassroots. These villages have also successively won honors such as the "National Civilized Village" and the "National Democracy and Rule of Law Model Village."

3. Guide the construction of rural culture for enhanced cultural self-confidence. The construction of scenic villages has helped advance rural culture, allowing villagers to reap its benefits. It has instilled cultural pride and confidence among them, driving rural development and inspired advocacy for rural causes. The construction of scenic villages for the in-depth utilization the "Five Craftsmen" and filial piety culture, along with the productive use of the "Five Craftsmen" Hall and Rite and Filiality Academy in Ganshi'ao Village, Putuo District, Zhoushan City, Zhejiang Province, has resulted in the development of native tourism products. More importantly, it has become a base for local research and education, intangible heritage experience, science, particularly the well-known local Internet celebrity village. Also, it has enhanced the village's social capital.

Experience and Inspirations

1. Adapt measures to local conditions. Development laws for the countryside development must be followed to reflect the essence of the rural culture, conform to its development path, preserve local customs and maintain the hometown flavor and appearance. Historical scenic villages must be developed while maintaining its regional features and quality businesses. Absolute duplication of other development models, large-scale demolition and construction are forbidden.

2. Ecology as a top priority. We should emphasize the improvement of the ecological environment and human settlements, and strictly adhere to the precepts of ecological protection. Also, the natural environment should be developed. Local, original features must be maintained and promoted for maximum advantage and an appealing brand image must be created. The principle of "green development for people's benefits and well-off villages" throughout the construction of scenic villages must be implemented.

3. Adhere to innovation for development. We should develop new concepts, ideas and measures. Reforms must be thorough to overcome the bottlenecks and institutional land and capital barriers. For example, the practice of new development models such as "companies + professional cooperatives + peasant households" can increase the income of villagers and enhance their innovative talent in transforming rural tourism resources into a prosperous economic development.

4. Co-sharing by hosts and guests. We should meet the increasing demands of tourists, implement the supply-side reform of rural tourism and move forward with its upgrade. With farmers at the center in tourism for agricultural development, all efforts should be made to educate and guide them.

Next Steps

1. Facilitate the digital empowerment of scenic villages. The digital technology is adopted to facilitate the intelligent development of scenic villages. On the premise of "Internet + tourism + countryside" mode, we will assist in the integration with digital technologies. Digital rural tourism products with interactive, immersive and experiential features must likewise be introduced. Based on the "Zhe Li Hao Wan," a public service platform for tourism information of Zhejiang Province, we will help build a "one-stop, intelligent and personalized" service system for rural tourism in scenic villages. Convenience services will be launched as "one click to order," "one

code to complain," "10s for room vacancy," "20s for scenic spot entry" and "30s for hotel check-in."

2. Help implement the "micro-renovation" of scenic villages. Guided by the principles of micro-renovation and refined improvement" principle in Zhejiang's tourism industry, we will assist scenic villages in the implementation of the "micro-renovation and refined improvement" practices based on the preservation of the original Zhejiang-style look of village. We will create a village with "exquisite environment, sophisticated facilities, cozy experience, meticulous service and refined management." In accordance with the principle of co-sharing by hosts and guests and for a quality rural life, we will build an ecological environment appropriate for living, working and traveling.

3. Offer opportunities for the booming development of scenic villages. The goal of Zhejiang Province is to build a common prosperity zone and a pioneering prototype in socialist modernization and rural revitalization. The optimum use of the natural resources in its scenic villages also represents the flourishing development of rural areas. Local professional management talents and operation teams should be nurtured and trained to improve facility maintenance and merchant management. We should update products, launch boutique routes and build rural tourism brands to achieve sustainable development, increase household income of peasants and widen the road of common prosperity through agricultural tourism development.

4. Promote the rural culture revitalization of scenic villages. We will promote the integration of culture and tourism in scenic villages, protect and maintain the essence of rural culture, and guide the integrated development of tourism information service sites, cultural auditoriums and rural bookstores. The intangible heritage-themed B&Bs in scenic villages should also be developed, and rural cultural and creative products with distinctive features should also be launched.

四川阆中市：
凤舞天宫乡村旅游发展模式

Langzhong City, Sichuan Province:
Rural Tourism Development Model of Fengwu Tiangong

摘 要

凤舞天宫旅游度假区通过探索“政府主导、社会主体、国企主力、协会主管、农民主业”的旅游扶贫模式，充分发挥国有企业的社会责任感和带动引领力，采取“三产促一产、一村带多村”的发展运营模式，以逐步丰富阆中旅游休闲度假产品为目标，以特色文化和乡村田园为载体，精心打造了雎鸠婚恋小镇、桥亭康养旅游小镇、五龙村田园生活小镇、天宫风水文化小镇、临江镇村轻奢度假小镇等特色小镇，创建了集生态观光、乡村田园、精品度假、户外运动和文化创意 5 大功能于一体的特色乡村旅游度假区。凤舞天宫旅游度假区着力把乡村打造成环境优美、特色鲜明、吸引力强、生态平衡且持续发展的全国性知名乡村旅游目的地，让贫困户通过入股分红、安排就业、销售农特产品等方式，实现稳定脱贫增收。

挑战与问题

四川阆中市凤舞天宫旅游度假区涉及沿线四个乡镇（街道）9 个村，环线达 40 公里。整个区域贫困人口较多，贫困程度较深，存在交通不畅、环境不美、产业不兴等问题。凤舞天宫旅游度假区在建设中面临着诸多问题：房屋租赁难；征地拆迁难；由于农村房屋分散导致的污水排放系统环境保护压力大、建设难；由于农村道路较窄，货物运输难，等等。

措施

1. 试点先行，示范带动。凤舞天宫旅游度假区采取“先试点、再推开”的模式，即：先在天宫镇五龙村进行试点打造，待形成示范带动效应后，再进行全面推开、全域推动。这样，既缓解了一次性资金投入的压力，又能更好地调动当地群众的参与热情和积极性。

2. 借鉴学习，培养人才。组织学习考察团队到天宫风水文化小镇、临江镇村轻奢度假小镇等地进行学习考察，充分借鉴其他地区成功案例的发展思路、经营理念、发展模式，汲取经验教训，并结合自身实际加以筛选、总结、提升，走出了一条特色发展之路。在此过程中，也培养了一批视野宽、思路多、能力强的人才。

3. 创新合作，共赢多赢。通过与各区域村集体达成战略合作关系，建立“国有企业 + 村集体资产”“国有企业 + 民营企业”合作联营机制，进一步强化各村集体经济的“造血”功能，拓展利益链条。这样既解决了建筑施工土地使用性质的问题，又将公司发展与村民利益进行了捆绑，实现共赢、多赢。

4. 保护环境，绿色优先。凤舞天宫旅游度假区在建设运营过程中始终坚持“绿水青山就是金山银山”的发展理念，最大限度地保留乡村的原始风貌，保护乡村的优美环境。自开展建设以来，共恢复耕地面积 5000 余亩，新建苗圃基地 300 余亩，新建污水处理厂 5 处，做到了保护与开发并重。

5. 完善基础，提升服务。目前，凤舞天宫旅游度假区已修建农耕博物馆 1 处，建有便民活动中心 5 处，文化集散中心 6 处，网红打卡地 12 处，民宿 300 余间，停车位 5000 余个；引进商户 50 家，另有餐饮服务单位 30 家，拥有餐位 500 个，能够满足 800 人同时用餐；新增农家乐 100 余家，新增农业种植面积 20000 余亩，新增业态商户 100 余家。乡村旅游基础设施、商业业态日趋完善。

6. 内练修养，外树形象。凤舞天宫旅游度假区要求工作人员坚持每日晨读《易经》《诗经》《增广贤文》等经典著作，并通过举办“书香万家”“读书班”等活动带动当地居民养成爱阅读的习惯，营造浓厚的学习氛围，不断提高群众的文化知识素养。制定规范的礼仪着装标准，度假区工作人员全部“着古装、行古礼”，树立良好的对外形象。

成效

凤舞天宫旅游度假区年接待游客逾 10 万人次，接待参观考察 500 余批次，年收入达 1000 万元。近三年，凤舞天宫旅游度假区共接待游客 200 万人次，实现旅游综合收入 0.5 亿元，平均年增速达 12%（人数增长比例）、18%（收入增长比例），创造就业岗位 500 余个，带动 30 余户贫困户就业，当地群众年人均收入增加 4000 元。整个区域交通发达、环境优美、产业振兴，乡村面貌焕然一新。凤舞天宫旅游度假区的吸引力和带动力日益凸显，已成为全省接待能力最强、产品体系最丰富、辐射带动群众最多的乡村旅游度假区。2018 年，成功创建为国家 3A 级旅游景区。

经验与启示

1. 健全体制机制，构建标准体系。一是建立引导机制，充分发挥好平台优势，整合智力、资金和技术等资源向乡村倾注。二是建立订单机制，通过公司自营的业态，与农业和农副产业形成订单化机制，建立“销售—采买”一体化平台，进一步提升经营质量。三是建立联营机制，形成“国有企业 + 村集体资产”“国有企业 + 民营企业”合作联营机制，增强村级“造血”功能，延伸村集体经济的利益链条。

2. 优化经营管理，提升发展质量。经营业态方面：大力开拓和打造乡村旅游品牌，打通产品销售渠道，走“农村包围城市”路线，将农村品牌和乡村产品推向庞大的城市经济市场。运营团队方面：优化人员结构，用好用活人才，提高服务质量，全力打造一支专注运营的精英管理团队。宣传营销方面：瞄准目标客户群体，通过制订个性化、定制化宣传营销方案，广泛通过传统媒体、新媒体平台加强宣传营销推广，构建立体宣传营销格局。

下一步计划

凤舞天宫旅游度假区通过建立“三产促一产、一村带多村”的发展运营模式，即以具备优势旅游发展条件的村落发展乡村旅游、以旅游产业促进传统农业和种养殖业的发展，通过一个村发展旅游服务经济、其他多个村落发展旅游供给产业，带动不具备优势资源的村落共同发展，进一步改善提升了乡村基础设施条件，优化美化了乡村自然生态环境，丰富完善了乡村文化旅游产品，辐射带动了当地群众就近就业、稳定增收，走出了一条以乡村旅游带动乡村脱贫致富的新路子，对实施乡村振兴战略、推动农业农村现代化进行了有益探索。下一步，我们将深入挖掘凤舞天宫旅游度假区的优秀经验，不断深化总结，以期整理形成一套完整的规划、设计、建设、运营方案，再适时将我们成熟的建设经验和运营理念带出去，带向全国各地乡村旅游市场，不断推动“凤舞天宫乡村旅游发展模式”在全国各地落地生根、开花结果。

Abstract

By exploring the tourism alleviation model of "government leading, society as the main body, state-owned enterprises as the main force, association in charge, and farmers' main business," Fengwu Tiangong Tourism Resort has given full play to the sense of social responsibility and leading force of the state-owned enterprises, and adopted the development operation model featuring "agriculture, industry, and service industries promoting the development of agriculture, one village leading multiple villages." With the intention of gradually enriching Langzhong tourism leisure products and with distinctive culture and rural scenery as the carrier, the city has orchestrated Jujiu Love and Marriage Town, Qiaoting Eco-Healthcare Tourism Town, Wulong Village Pastoral Life Town, Tiangong Geomancy Cultural Town, Linjiangzhen Village Entry Luxury Resort Town, and other characteristic towns, becoming a special rural tourism resort integrating ecological sightseeing, rural gardens, boutique vacation, outdoor sports, and cultural creativity. The tourism resort has strived to make the village a nationally renowned rural tourism destination with a beautiful environment, distinctive characteristics, strong attractiveness, ecological balance and sustainable development, so that impoverished households can realize stable poverty reduction and income growth through ways such as benefit-sharing compensation, arranged employment, as well as sales of agricultural and sideline products.

Challenges and Problems

Fengwu Tiangong Tourism Resort, Langzhong City, Sichuan Province, involves nine villages in four townships (sub-districts), with a loop of up to 40 kilometers. There are a large number of impoverished people in the region, with deep level of poverty, and local people are plagued by problems such as inconvenient traffic, unsatisfactory environment, and unprosperous industries. In the construction of the tourism resort, it is confronted with numerous problems, such as hardship of house renting, difficulties in land acquisition and demolition, bigger pressure upon environmental protection of the sewage discharging system due to scattered rural houses, and difficulty to transport goods because of narrow rural roads.

Measures

1. Pilot goes first and demonstration sets an example. The tourism resort has adopted the model of "first pilot, and push later," that is, to firstly conduct a pilot project in Wulong Village of Tiangong Town, and the project will be rolled out in the region after the demonstration effect is formed. This resolves the pressure brought by one-off capital investment and better arouses local people's enthusiasm for participation.

2. Learn from examples and foster talents. It has organized a study tour to investigate places such as Tiangong Geomancy Cultural Town and Linjiangzhen Village Entry Luxury Resort Town, learn from development ideas, business philosophy, and development modes of successful cases in other places, and draw lessons.

Based on its own reality, it has embarked on a path of characteristic development through screening, conclusion and improvement. At the same time, it has cultivated a number of talents with broadened vision, active mind and strong capability.

3. Innovative cooperation to gain win-win and multi-win. It has reached a strategic cooperation relationship with village collectives in various regions and established a cooperative joint operation mechanism featuring "state-owned enterprises + village collective assets" and "state-owned enterprises + private enterprises" to further strengthen the self-reliance of each village collective economy and expand the interest chain. This has solved the problem of the nature of land use for construction, and bundled its development with the interests of villages to achieve win-win and multi-win.

4. Protect the environment and give priority to green development. During the construction and operation, the tourism resort has been upholding the development concept of "lucid waters and lush mountains are invaluable assets," preserved rural original style to the greatest extent, and protected rural beautiful environment. Ever since the commencement of the construction, a total of more than 5,000 *mu* of arable land has been restored, over 300 *mu* new nursery bases have been built, and five new sewage treatment plants have been constructed, so that protection and development have been given equal importance.

5. Improve the infrastructure to enhance service level. At present, it has built a farming museum, five convenient activity centers, six cultural distribution centers, 12 internet-famous sites, over 300 B&Bs, and more than 5,000 parking berths. It has introduced 50 commercial tenants and 30 catering service units with 500 dining seats, capable of catering for 800 people at the same time. As over 100 new agritainment, new agricultural planting area of more 20,000 *mu*, and over 100 new business forms of commercial tenants are increased, the rural tourism infrastructure has been improved, with increasingly perfect business forms.

6. Self-cultivation to establish external image. It has required its staff members to insist on morning reading of classic works, such as *I Ching, Book of Songs,* and *Popular Collection of Traditional Chinese Wise Sayings,* and encouraged residents to develop a love of reading through organizing "Books for All," "Reading Class" and other activities, creating a strong atmosphere for learning and improving the cultural knowledge to the public. What is more, it has formulated the standards for etiquette and dress, and its staff members are required to wear ancient clothes to perform ancient rituals, thus establishing a sound external image.

Results

The tourism resort receives more than 100,000 tourists annually, with more than 500 batches of visits and an annual income of RMB 10 million. In the past three years, it has received a total of 2 million tourists, achieving a comprehensive tourism income of RMB 50 million with an average annual growth rate of 12% in tourist arrivals and 18% in annual income, and created more than 500 jobs, boosting more than 30 poor households into employment, increasing the per capita annual income of local people by RMB 4,000. The whole rural area

has shown a new look with developed transportation, charming environment, and prosperous industries. The increasingly obvious attraction and driving force have enabled the tourism resort to become one with the strongest reception capacity, the richest product system, and the largest population affected by its radiation in the province. In 2018, a national 3A-level tourist attraction was successfully created.

Experience and Inspirations

1. Improve the institutional mechanism and build a standard system. First, it sets up a guiding mechanism, gives full play to advantages of the platform, and integrates intellectual, financial and technical resources for rural areas. **Second,** it establishes an order mechanism, forms an order-based mechanism with agricultural and sideline industries through its self-operated business forms, and establishes an integrated platform for sales and purchases to further improve the operational quality. **Third,** it establishes a joint operation mechanism to form a "state-owned enterprises + village collective assets" and "state-owned enterprises + private enterprises" cooperative joint operation mechanism, enhances the village-level "blood-making" function, and expands the interest chain of the village collective economy.

2. Optimize business management and improve development quality. In terms of business forms, it will expand and build rural tourism brands, open up product sales channels, and embark on a line of "encircling the cities from the rural areas" to introduce rural brands and products into the vast urban economic market. In terms of operational team, it will optimize staff structure, make good use of talents, improve service quality and make every effort to build an elite management team centered on operations. In terms of advertising and marketing, it will aim at target customer groups, develop personalized and customized publicity and marketing plans, and extensively strengthen publicity and marketing through traditional media and new media platforms to build a three-dimensional publicity and marketing pattern.

Next Step

First, based upon the development operation model of "agriculture, industry, and service industries promoting the development of agriculture, one village leading multiple villages," the tourism resort has developed rural tourism at villages with superior tourism development conditions, and promoted the development of traditional agriculture and planting and breeding industry with tourism industry. It will develop tourism service economy at a village while developing tourism supply industries at other multiple villages to boost the common development of villages without superior resources. With the aforesaid measures, it can further improve and upgrade rural infrastructure, optimize and beautify rural natural eco-environment, enrich and improve rural cultural tourism products, and drive local people to work in the vicinity, steadily increasing their income. It has embarked on a new road of boosting rural people out of poverty with rural tourism and made beneficial exploration for implementing rural revitalization strategy and boosting modernization of agriculture and rural areas. **Second,** excellent experience and practices of the rural resort will be explored to develop a complete set of planning, design, construction and operation programs by incessant conclusions and arrangements. Furthermore, as appropriate, it is important to bring out our mature construction experience and operational concepts to the various rural tourism markets across the country, and continue to promote "the development model of Fengwu Tiangong Rural Tourism Resort" to take root and bloom around the country.

陕西西安市长安区南堡寨村：
长安唐村项目的探索与实践

Nanbuzhai Village, Chang’an District, Xi’an City, Shaanxi Province:
Exploration and Practice of Chang’an Tang Village Project

摘 要

长安唐村项目通过实施美丽乡村改造、基础设施建设、生态环境修复、农业产业升级、一二三产融合等系统工程，整合区域内以农业旅游、历史文化景观为核心的生态人文旅游资源，针对文旅产业采取保护文物古迹、传统村落、农业遗存、文化遗迹，传承和复兴乡村优秀传统文化等一系列措施，打造集农业旅游、人文旅游、休闲旅游、健康养生、商务会议、乡村休闲等多项功能于一体的全国知名的生态人文旅游名村。

挑战与问题

陕西省西安市长安区南堡寨村始建于清朝嘉庆年间，村内有戏楼、孙氏祠堂、药王庙、七星庙等诸多历史悠久的民居建筑，是具有代表性的典型关中民居。20 世纪 90 年代，由于交通不便，电力和水资源匮乏，村民住在 30 多米高的塬上，而土地大部分在塬下，日常劳作很辛苦，村庄生活环境差。2000 年，为了解决生产生活不便等问题，南堡寨村决定整村搬迁至塬下，原来的老村子房屋老旧，土地闲置，农地荒废，变成了名副其实的“空心村”。一边是历史积淀深厚、文化和旅游价值巨大、可供开发的“空心村”，一边是搬迁至塬下后在基础设施建设、村庄可持续发展等方面亟待破冰的新村落，如何把这一新一旧的村落结合起来，使古老村镇焕发出新的生机、找到新的发展道路，是南堡寨村面临的难题。

措施

2017 年，以南堡寨古村落修复保护为载体的长安唐村项目开始规划建设。长安唐村项目带动南堡寨村乡村以及附近连片区域村镇综合治理与产业发展，正在努力建设成为国家乡村振兴战略实施的先行区与示范区。

1. 改善村庄面貌。一是破解区域内交通不便等诸多问题，实施唐村产业园道路及供水、供气等配套设施建设工程，并持续优化路网结构，建成一批带动产业发展、激活乡村旅游、助力群众脱贫的示范路。二是通过落实农村人居环境整治三年行动计划，实施新建农房管控，开展田园建筑示范，推进宜居宜业美丽乡村建设。为南堡寨村村民打造户前景观，美化户外景观墙、村口老池塘及村民活动场地，美化大田景观，种植当地特色品牌“桂花球”大米，配套观景平台和田内游览步道等。三是在保留原有风貌的基础上，对村落中老旧的土坯房进行现代化改造，修旧如旧，并将闲置的土地流转，将废弃的老旧土坯房屋改造为高档民宿、咖啡馆、茶室等，让旧时老墙庭院、篱笆藤蔓、溪桥流水之景逐步重现。

2. 促进村民参与。一是在由传统农业向规模型农业转型的过程中，主要采取农业公司 + 村集体合作社模式，村集体合作社以“保底 + 分红”的方式对村民土地进行流转合并，增加农民的股权性收益；二是实施订单农业，农业公司利用市场、资金优势扶持“乡村带头人”发展家庭农场或农业专业

合作社，公司对其产品加工销售，实现互惠互利、良性发展；三是组织挖掘乡贤、文化能人、民间艺人，成立相关协会，如乡贤协会、乡村厨师协会、红白理事会等，培训组织村庄文化活动。

3. 挖掘村落文化。一是建立南堡寨村乡愁记忆馆，编写村史《堡寨物华忆长安——南堡寨史话》，对村落规制、人文礼仪、农业生产、农耕信仰等方方面面进行梳理，以期让农耕中国传统村落里的文明乡风得以薪火相传，将南堡寨村打造成乡村历史文化和村落特色的展示基地；二是南堡寨村以村落文化、民俗民风、农耕文化、特色产业等为展示内容，以乡创展厅、乡愁记忆馆、时光记忆馆、柳青陈列馆为文化展示载体，将南堡寨村打造成乡村文化的传承地和乡风文明的弘扬地。

成效

长安唐村经过 4 年的规划建设，带动区域内 3 万多名农村群众实现了从传统农业向乡村文化旅游产业的转变，让古老村庄重新焕发活力。吸纳当地劳动力 30000 人次以上，村民月均增收 2000 元，返乡大学生就业 100 人以上。2021 年第一季度，长安唐村接待游客 15 万人次。2020 年，长安唐村被评为全国乡村旅游重点村，获得陕西省文化产业“十百千”工程重点文化产业园区等多项省市级荣誉。

经验与启示

1. 机制创新。围绕实施乡村振兴促进城乡融

合发展、文旅融合发展，设立省级农村改革试验区。积极建立地方政府、村集体和社会资本“三元共建”的发展模式，三方构建合作平台，共同实施区域建设与产业发展；与村集体合作社建立合资公司进行开发建设，让村集体、村民与社会企业共同受益。创建区街合一、封闭运行、市场运作、三元共建的运作模式，破解体制机制障碍，充分汇集土地、资金、政策等资源，为乡村旅游发展创造空间和机遇。

2. 合作升级。在农业转型升级的过程中，长安唐村一方面采取“农业公司＋村集体合作社”模式，由村集体合作社以“保底＋分红”的方式对村民土地进行流转合并，并组织村民接受相关培训，培训考核合格后安排相关农业生产用工。另一方面实施订单农业，农业公司利用市场、资金优势扶持“乡村带头人”发展家庭农场或农业专业合作社，公司对其产品进行加工销售，从而实现互惠互利、

良性发展。

3. 三产融合。利用社会资源丰富的市场资源优势，构建综合性农业产业发展平台，通过推动农文旅融合发展，坚持以“乡村＋”为主线，推动城乡融合与文旅融合，重点发展现代农业、休闲农业、文化创意、乡村创意、乡村旅游等新型乡村产业，实施两新田园（田园更新、产业更新）建设，构建全链条、全循环乡村产业体系，实现传统乡村产业的全面升级和一二三产融合发展，打造自然山水和历史人文交相辉映的世界级乡村。

下一步计划

长安唐村项目立足于当前发展实际，围绕产业发展定位及目标，进一步推进长安唐村数字化发展，打造以数字技术和互联网为依托的新型文旅产业。接下来，计划在周边的杜曲街道、王莽街道、太乙街道推广“樊川道三区联动”模式，搭建“樊川·唐诗故里”“王莽·稻地水乡”“太乙·长安道”三大产业板块，打造红色研学体验环线和乡村振兴旅游环线，与西安市“三河一山”环线绿道体系有效衔接，带动周边村民共同参与乡村振兴战略发展的进程中，实现区域整体基础设施、特色产业、群众收入、基层治理的大幅度提升，打造乡村振兴战略实施的“西安样板”。

Abstract

By implementing systematic projects such as the rural area transformation, the Chang'an Tang Village project has created a business model that incorporates the traditional culture of the village. This project includes infrastructure and agricultural upgrades, and ecological restoration. At the core of this project is the region's history and culture. This is achieved by taking into consideration the resources in the village. Also, by protecting the cultural relics, traditional villages, and ancient agricultural heritage, the village provides an excellent opportunity for the cultural tourism industry to instruct people about its history. The aim of the project is to build a nationally known village featuring agricultural, humanistic and leisure tourism that can be used for business meetings or relaxation.

Challenges and Problems

Nanbuzhai Village, Chang'an District, Xi'an City, Shaanxi Province, were all built during the reign of the Jiaqing Emperor of the Qing Dynasty. It is home to a great number of typical historical Guanzhong residential houses, theaters, and temples. In the late 1990s, poor transportation infrastructure and lack of basic resources such as water and electricity made the living conditions here terrible. Villagers lived on a 30-meter-high plateau, with most of the farmland under the plateau. This made it hard for the locals to work the land. This unfortunate situation led the Nanbuzahi Village to move the whole town in 2000. During this move, old homes were left behind and the farmland was deserted, turning Nanbuzahi into a "hollow village." The village's long history and fantastic culture would have been ideal for cultural tourism. But infrastructure construction was needed to make it more sustainable. Connecting the two villages to breathe new life into the old village to find a practical and actionable path to development was the problem facing Nanbuzhai.

Measures

In 2017, planning and construction in the Chang'an Tang Village began. The basic purpose was to restore and protect this historic village. Because this project is the driving force for the comprehensive management and industrial development of Nanbuzhai and nearby areas, it was hoped that the project would become a demonstration national rural revitalization strategy.

1. Improving the infrastructure. The top priorities

for the project were to upgrade the infrastructure for water and gas supplies, increase local tourism, and reduce poverty. A three-year action plan for better living conditions was formulated with the focus of building new homes and transforming Nanbuzhai into a more livable and beautiful village. "Guihua ball" is a special local brand of rice that was planted so that tourists can view the plants in their natural habitat. In addition, the old adobe homes in the village were restored and modernized while preserving their original style and appearance. Some of these homes were then converted into high-class B&Bs, Cafés, and tea rooms. The view of fences and vines in the courtyard were recreated so that streams running under the bridges were accessible to all visitors.

2. Promoting villagers' participation. The process of transformation from traditional agriculture to large scale agriculture was adopted to increase farmers' equity. This was accomplished through the model of agriculture companies + villagers coming together to guarantee base pay and dividends for the farmers. Agricultural companies used market opportunities and financial advantages to support "village leaders" in promoting

family farms or agricultural cooperatives. The companies were also responsible for product processing and sales. Also, the villagers, intellectual folks, and other members came together to organize training sessions and village cultural activities with the hope of establishing different associations.

3. Discovering village culture. The first step was turning Nanbuzahi Village into a showcase of rural history and preserving its village culture through the establishment of the Memory Hall of Nanbuzhai and the creation of a history book, which called *A Bountiful Land — The History of Nanbuzhai.* The goal of this project was to pass on the rural culture of traditional villages in China.

Included in this project are rural etiquette, agricultural production and farmers' beliefs. The second step was to upgrade Nanbuzhai so it could serve as a model of village culture and folk customs by displaying different aspects of rural culture in such venues such as the rural creation exhibition hall, the nostalgia hall, the memory hall, and the Liu Qing exhibition hall.

Results

Four years of planning and building allowed the Chang'an Tang village to assist more than 30,000 rural residents in the regions. This was made possible through the transformation from traditional agriculture to rural

cultural tourism. Overall, this project added more than 30,000 job opportunities, increased villagers' monthly income by 2,000 yuan, and attracted more than 100 college graduates to return for employment. In the first quarter of 2021, the village drew 150,000 visitors. It has also won many provincial and municipal honors including the "Ten Hundred Thousand" project award which is a great honor in the cultural industry. In 2020, the village won the award of Key Village of National Rural Tourism.

Experience and Inspirations

1. Mechanism innovation. A provincial-level rural reform pilot zone is important to the revitalization of rural land and the development of cultural tourism. The development mode of "three-tier construction" among local government should be established to create a platform that will jointly implement regional construction and industrial development. Moreover, joint venture companies with village personnel should be established for the benefit of all village enterprises. In addition, for rural tourism to grow, a three-party market agreement free from manipulation should be created to eliminate the institutional barriers.

2. Scaling up cooperation. Agricultural transformation and upgrading has resulted in the Chang'an Tang Village adopting a business model of agricultural companies + village cooperatives. The agreement transfers and merges the villagers' land by giving them guaranteed base pay + dividends, relevant training sessions and agricultural production jobs after they pass an assessment. Implementation of order-oriented agriculture was developed to generate market and financial advantages for the support of village leaders. This process promotes family farms or agricultural cooperatives, making companies responsible for product processing and sales.

3. Integration of primary, secondary and tertiary industries. Rich market resources should be fully utilized, and a comprehensive industry development platform should be created. Through promotion, the integrated development of agriculture, with countryside as the core, the culture-tourism model can be advanced. By focusing on the development of modern and leisure agriculture and creative enterprises, the village and its industries can be confidently elevated. Traditional rural industries can be comprehensively upgraded, and the integration and development of primary, secondary, and tertiary industries can be achieved, resulting in a world-class village featuring natural landscape, history, and culture.

Next Steps

Centered around industrial positioning and development goals, the Chang'an Tang Village project is based on its current developmental needs. It has also promoted the village's digital development, with a digital technology and internet reliant cultural tourism industry.

The next step is to promote the "Fanchuandao Three-District Linkage" model in the surrounding Duqu Street, Wangmang Street, and Taiyi Street, and three more corresponding industries. By creating a studying tour route and a rural revitalization tourism loop that effectively connects the three rivers and one mountain greenway system of Xi'an City, the locals are encouraged to participate in the development of the rural revitalization process. These measures will lead to income increase and a substantial advancement in the overall infrastructure, special industries, and grassroot governance which will hopefully be a model for the implementation of the rural revitalization strategy.

新疆乌鲁木齐市乌鲁木齐县：
以民宿为抓手、以产业融合为路径推进全域旅游

Urumqi County, Urumqi City, Xinjiang Uygur Autonomous Region:
All-for-one Tourism Development with B&Bs as the Means and Industrial Integration as the Path

摘 要

新疆乌鲁木齐市乌鲁木齐县围绕自然生态和特色文化，依托南山得天独厚的自然资源和水西沟特色小镇，以民宿发展为抓手，大力推进"旅游＋文化""旅游＋农业""旅游＋体育""旅游＋康养"等全域旅游，2020年被评为"中国县域旅游综合竞争力百强县""中国乡村旅游发展名县"和"冰雪旅游十强县"，走上了乡村振兴之路。

挑战与问题

乌鲁木齐县总面积 3970 平方公里，耕地 28.7 万亩、草场 450.8 万亩，县域森林覆盖率 19.5%。全县总人口 5.27 万人，其中农业人口 4.36 万人，占 82.7%，以哈萨克族、回族为主体的少数民族人口占总人口的 65.3%。乌鲁木齐县旅游业起步相对较晚，丰富的旅游资源尚未得到充分整合，旅游资源串点成线的融合还需要进一步加强；旅游要素中“购”的元素尤其薄弱，农副土特产品有待进一步完善，旅游纪念品也需要升级塑造品牌，文创产品、特色旅游纪念品的升级打造还有待扶持和研发。

措施

1. 大力改善乡村面貌。在国道、省道、县乡道等公路沿线两侧打造景观大道，推进“路边经济”，鼓励和支持村民开办具有农家特色的民宿和农家乐特色的旅游项目，如田园采摘、花海南山等，按照“乡村面貌景观化、农牧生活旅游化、乡风民俗产品化、农副产品商品化”的要求和“村中有景、前后有院、内外有闲”的标准规范不同主题特色的景观村、休闲居和乐活场。

2. 大力发展民宿。把旅游民宿作为推动脱贫攻坚与乡村振兴有效衔接的重要抓手，以带动农牧民创业增收为目标，发展多种经营模式的旅游民宿，形成布局合理、规模适度、特色鲜明的民宿业发展格局。以民宿、农家乐为基础，以养生、休闲、采摘、田园农耕、山水人家等为主题，现已发展各类特色旅游民宿近 200 家；着力提升旅游民宿品质，对符合评定标准的旅游民宿做好等级评定和复核工作，带动旅游民宿提档升级；推动民生共享发展，通过家庭自助、短期租赁等方式，盘活农

牧民房屋院落，确保农牧民持续增收，使其共享旅游发展成果。

3. 大力推进“旅游+”。推进“旅游+农业”模式，发展休闲观光农业，实施万亩花海及绿化项目、万亩杏花林套种油菜项目，全县各乡镇及公路沿线种植花草近5万亩，逐步引导农业向休闲观光型过渡。推进“旅游+康养”模式、“旅游+体育”模式、“旅游+文化”模式，积极落实水西沟冰雪运动休闲小镇试点工作，打造体育旅游精品线路；按照全域旅游标准，重点在甘沟乡、托里乡发展民俗旅游，打造民俗文化旅游品牌。

成效

乌鲁木齐县通过近两年民宿产业的快速发展，已创造新就业岗位逾800个，吸纳当地就业人数千余人，旅游民宿产业的兴起，让当地农牧民群众得到了实实在在的实惠。据统计，经营民宿和在民宿打工的农牧民群众，人均年增收逾2万元。

实践证明，旅游业的发展，在乡村振兴过程中起着不可替代的作用。继水西沟镇平西梁村被列为“国家乡村旅游重点村”之后，水西沟镇庙尔沟村、板房沟镇八家户村、甘沟乡西白杨沟村也称为“自治区级乡村旅游重点村”，南浦坊民宿、南山雅集民宿被自治区评为精品民宿。乌鲁木齐县先后被评为“2020年度中国县域旅游综合竞争力百强县”“中国乡村旅游发展名县”，并入选“2021年冰雪旅游十强县”。

经验与启示

1. 民宿运营。乌鲁木齐县的旅游民宿运营模式呈多样化发展：一是“农户自主经营”模式，由

农户自己出资对房屋进行装修后打造民宿；二是“农户＋经营业主”模式，农户将自家院子出租给经营业主，由其打造民宿；三是“农户＋公司运营”模式，公司为主体租用多家农户的房屋进行统一装修、管理；四是“农户＋村集体＋公司运营”模式。

2. 民宿打造。以乌鲁木齐县水西沟镇平西梁村为例，该村在整体改造的过程中充分挖掘当地历史、文化资源，突出民族风情以及人文、休闲、养生内涵，还有一系列农事体验项目，有效传承了农耕文化、民俗文化等，使得民宿因为文化而更有温度。这样一来，不仅让人居环境、人文环境、自然环境有机融合，更让美丽乡村有了“美丽经济”。

3. 民宿管理。针对不同区域的具体情况，引导各乡镇、各村结合自身优势，全面发展民宿经济。县民宿管理领导小组联合审批，上门服务，实地指导、审批，对存在问题的经营户下达整改告知单，跟踪服务。民宿开业后，由乡镇人民政府继续做好对已开业民宿的日常服务管理工作，各相关部门根据各自职责做好业务上的服务指导工作。

下一步计划

1. 进一步加强产业融合。推动“旅游＋文化”，打造“昆仑之约”实景演艺；推广民俗文化、民俗产品、民族刺绣、民族餐饮等体验活动；做好非物质文化遗产、文物保护工作，加强非遗传承人队伍建设，支持非物质文化遗产、丝绸之路相关文创产品、匠人工坊等项目进驻景区；推动“旅游＋农业”，鼓励和支持农村集体、农业合作社、农牧民与美食品尝、田园体验、农业科普、果蔬采摘等旅游活动充分结合，以大庙村文旅综合体建设为试点，创新田园综合体建设，促进农村经济发展，抓好休闲农业示范园区的提档升级；发展“旅游＋体育”，充分利用得天独厚的旅游休闲度假资源和冰雪资源，举办冰雪风情节、冬夏季马拉松等体育节庆赛事活动；培育“旅游＋康养”，构建“医、养、休、游”四位一体康养旅游服务生态系统，大力发展旅游休闲、健康养老。

2. 进一步发展全域旅游。紧紧围绕全域旅游，形成旅游民宿与景区、滑雪场、特色美食节、文化街的联动，有效对旅游民宿、景区、花海、村庄、田园综合体、休闲观光园进行串联，形成“景区观光—亲子采摘—品鉴美食—休闲徒步—观看演出—住在民宿”的旅游闭环，在不断满足游客“食、住、行、游、购、娱”等基本旅游需求的基础上，逐步向“商、养、学、闲、情、奇”等要素方向拓展。

Abstract

The Urumqi County, Urumqi City, Xinjiang Uygur Autonomous Region is focused on natural ecology and characteristic culture. It relies on the unique natural resources of Mountain Nan and takes B&Bs as the means of implementing "tourism + culture." It also focuses on "tourism + agriculture," "tourism + sports," and "tourism + health" to promote the all-for-one tourism development. In 2020, it was rated one of the top 100 counties with comprehensive competitiveness in China's county tourism, China's famous rural tourism county and top 10 snow and ice tourism counties, embarking on the road of rural revitalization.

Challenges and Problems

Urumqi County covers a total area of 3,970 square kilometers and has 287,000 *mu* of arable land. In addition, it has 4.508 million *mu* of grassland, and its forest coverage rate is 19.5%, with a total population of 52,700, of which 43,600 agricultural population for 82.7%, of the total. Its ethnic minorities are dominated by Kazak and Hui people, accounting for 65.3% of the total population. The county's tourism industry started late, and its rich tourism resources have not been fully integrated.

The "shopping" element is weak, while agricultural and sideline local products need to be improved. Tourism souvenirs need to be upgraded to create brands, with the characteristic ones needing support and R&D. The quality of its cultural and artistic products also need to be elevated.

Measures

1. Improve the look and appearance of the village. The county has built landscape avenues on both sides of the national highway, provincial highway, county and township roads and other roads. It has also promoted roadside economy by encouraging and supporting villagers to set up country-style B&Bs and agritainment projects. These include crop picking and flower fields on Mountain Nan. In addition, it has a standardized landscape village, leisure residences and entertainment centers as required by "turning rural appearance into landscape, agriculture and animal husbandry life into tourism program, folk custom into products, and agricultural and sideline products into commodities" and the standards of "scenery in village, courtyards at front and back, and leisure inside and outside."

2. Promote the development of B&Bs. The county has applied multiple business models with practical locally-adapted layout in developing its tourism B&B. This was done by recognizing the importance of B&B tourism in promoting the effective connection between poverty alleviation and rural revitalization. The appropriate scale and distinctive characteristics were utilized in motivating farmers and herdsmen to start businesses to increase their income. Based on B&Bs, agritainment and revolving around themes such as health maintenance, leisure, crops picking, pastoral farming and residence in the nature, nearly 200 characteristic tourism B&Bs were developed. It has worked hard to improve the quality of tourist accommodation facilities and made efforts in increasing the quality of B&Bs in the hopes of meeting the needs of the people. Through a shared development, people's livelihood has been improved. Houses and courtyards of farmers and herdsmen have been revitalized through family self-help and short-term leasing programs. The shared fruits of tourism development help ensure the continuous increase of the income of farmers and herdsmen.

3. Advance the "Tourism +" model. With the advancement of the "tourism + agriculture" mechanism, the county has developed leisure agriculture. They have also implemented the project of 10,000 *mu* of flower fields and greening. In addition, the project of 10,000 *mu* of apricot flower forest interplanted with oilseed rape has resulted in nearly 50,000 *mu* of flowers and grass in all towns and villages and along the roads in the county.

This will gradually guide the transition from agriculture to leisure and sightseeing. Moreover, by promoting the

"tourism + healthcare" model, the "tourism + sports" model and the "tourism + culture" model, the county has advanced the pilot work of Shuixigou Ice and Snow Sports Leisure Town to build high-quality sports tourism routes. Also, this has brought to the center the folk tourism in Gangou and Tuoli Townships according to all-for-one tourism standards.

Results

Urumqi County has created more than 800 new posts and absorbed more than 1,000 local employees through the rapid development of the B&B industry in the past two years. The rise of B&Bs has brought tangible benefits to local farmers and herdsmen. According to statistics, the annual per capita income of farmers and herdsmen who operate and work in B&Bs can potentially reach more than RMB 20,000.

Practice has proven that tourism development plays an irreplaceable role in rural revitalization. It is worth noting that after this multi-step revitalization program Pingxiliang Village in Shuixigou Town won the title of "National Key Village of Rural Tourism," Miaoergou Village of Shuixigou Town, Bajiahu Village of Banfanggou Town and Xibaiyanggou Village of Gangou Town won the title of key village of rural tourism at the autonomous region level. And Nanpufang B&Bs and Nanshan Yaji B&Bs were rated boutique B&Bs by the autonomous region. The county was rated one of the "top 100 counties with comprehensive competitiveness of county tourism in China 2020," "famous county for rural tourism development in China" and "top 10 counties of ice and snow tourism in 2021."

Experience and Inspirations

1. B&B operation. Diversified operation models of tourist B&Bs in the county have been developed. **First,** peasant households build B&Bs after home renovations that are funded by the farmers themselves. **Second,** farmers rent their own yards to business owners for the building B&Bs through the "peasant households + business owners" model. **Third,** the company rents homes of multiple farmers for unified decoration and management through the "peasant households + companies" model. **Fourth,** the "peasant households + village collectives + companies" model is also developed.

2. B&Bs construction. By taking the whole-village reconstruction of Pingxiliang Village, Shuixigou Town, Urumqi County as an example, it is evident that it is important to make full use of local historical and cultural characteristics. National customs, humanities, leisure and agricultural experiential projects of the local areas must likewise be emphasized. This is invaluably helpful in

preserving, protecting and promoting the local agricultural and folk culture for the tourists. Its B&Bs reflect the county's warm, welcoming culture. More importantly, this will go a long way toward a seamless, organic integration of human settlements, cultural and natural environment. In the end, the economy will develop into a "flourishing economy" in a thriving village.

3. Management of B&Bs. According to the specific conditions of different regions, villages and towns are guided to develop the B&B economy in combination with their own advantages. The county's B&B Management Leading Group conducts joint examination and approval, provide door-to-door service, on-site guidance and signs off the project. They also issue, as a tracking service, rectification notice to the operators with problems. After opening, the town-level people's government continues to provide daily service and management to the newly-opened B&Bs. All relevant departments also serve and guide the operators according to their respective responsibilities.

Next Steps

1. Strengthen industrial integration. More efforts should be made to promote "tourism + culture" and in organizing live performances of the "Kunlun Mountain appointment." We must also promote folk culture, folk products, ethnic embroidery, ethnic catering and other indigenous experiential activities. In addition, it is important to protect intangible cultural heritage, cultural relics and cultivate successors who will eventually pass on their traditions. By supporting intangible cultural heritage and creative products related to the Silk Road, craftsmen workshops can settle in the scenic spot. It is equally important to promote the "tourism + agriculture" model and to encourage the full integration of rural collectives. The agricultural cooperatives, farmers and herdsmen, and tourism activities will also be integrated into this. By taking the construction of cultural and tourism complex in Damiao Village as a pilot, the pastoral complex construction will be innovated to promote rural economic development and upgrade the leisure agriculture demonstration park. Additionally, the county will continue the development of "tourism + sports" to make full use of its unique tourism attributes. They will also highlight the leisure and vacation resources and hold seasonally-related festivals and activities such as the Ice and Snow Customs Festival and marathon in winter and summer. The "tourism + healthcare" model will also be cultivated and a four-in-one healthcare tourism service ecosystem featuring "medical care, healthcare, rest and tourism" tourism, leisure and healthy elderly care development should be created.

2. Develop all-for-one tourism. The village will focus on all-for-one tourism by linking B&Bs with scenic spots, ski resorts, special food festivals and cultural streets, sea of flowers, villages and pastoral complexes. Leisure and sightseeing parks will also be connected to create a closed loop tourism of sightseeing, parent-child crop picking, food tasting, leisure hiking, performances watching and B&B living. All these can continuously meet tourists' basic needs of "meal and dining, living, transportation, travelling, shopping, and entertainment." All these are expected to gradually expand developments in "business, healthcare, research, leisure, emotion and curiosity."

内蒙古呼伦贝尔市额尔古纳市恩和俄罗斯族民族乡：
文旅融合打造俄罗斯族民俗文化小镇

Enhe Russian Nationality Township, Ergun City, Hulunbuir City, Inner Mongolia Autonomous Region:
Cultural and Tourism Integration Creates a Russian Folk Culture Town

摘 要

恩和俄罗斯族民族乡是全国唯一的俄罗斯族民族乡，近年来，该乡把俄罗斯民俗节日“巴斯克节”“泼水节”打造成为地区旅游品牌，创建“油画小镇”精品旅游文化品牌，不断挖掘民族文化，探索旅游与文化融合的新模式，对俄罗斯族传统节日、饮食、游戏、歌舞等进行开发，形成旅游产品，打造俄罗斯民俗文化小镇，做亮旅游品牌。恩和乡 2013 年被列入“中国传统村落名录”和“中国少数民族特色村寨”；2015 年成为特色景观旅游名镇；2020 年被评为“全国乡村旅游重点村”。恩和已成功探索出一条文旅融合的乡村振兴之路。

挑战与问题

内蒙古额尔古纳市恩和俄罗斯族民族乡共1213户，户籍总人口2790人，俄罗斯族及华俄后裔1276人，约占总人口的46%。行政辖区总面积2068平方公里，隔额尔古纳河为界与俄罗斯相望，边境线长75公里。境内原始林地约120万亩、草原40万亩、耕地20万亩，林草覆盖率80%以上，自然环境优越，全生态、原生态保持完好，野生动植物、矿产资源丰富。

恩和现有旅游资源丰富，包括：民俗馆、列巴房、沿街木刻楞（百年民居）、俄罗斯族民俗体验活动；制彩蛋、套娃、列巴、俄罗斯族歌舞表演、俄罗斯族游戏抢棍、马车游、骑马游等旅游体验项目；自然风光白桦林、哈乌尔河、油菜花田、芍药坡、麦田观光、卧龙山等自然景观；巴斯克节、泼水节、柳条节等节庆活动。俄罗斯族传统节日“巴斯克节”已列入“国家级非物质文化遗产名录”，俄罗斯族传统民间舞蹈已列入“内蒙古自治区非物质文化遗产名录”；俄罗斯族非物质文化传承人现有7人。但另一方面，恩和优质旅游资源尚待开发保护，项目资金少，基础设施薄弱，环境整治、垃圾处理、污水处理、环境美化等问题亟待改善。且该乡冬长夏短，每年旅游旺季仅有3个月，经济发展动力不足，冬季旅游项目有待开发。年轻人外出上学、务工人员较多，村落空心化日趋严重，原始俄罗斯族文化日益流失，缺少系统的载体来保留和弘扬俄罗斯族原始民俗文化。

措施

1. 活动助推旅游发展。一是深挖民俗文化，成功把民俗节日“巴斯克节”“泼水节”打造成地区旅游品牌，每年举办庆祝活动。举办啤酒节暨千人篝火晚会活动，发展恩和夜经济，发展周边游，多元化增加商户收益，促进旅游经济发展。二是自2017年起创建“油画小镇”精品旅游文化品牌，探索旅游与文化融合的新模式。三是加强旅游宣传

推介，积极参加旅游推介会，协助配合多家卫视及主流网络媒体拍摄乡域旅游文化宣传片，通过运营“魅力恩和”公众号，发布恩和动态、自然风景照片和视频，制作俄罗斯族民俗文化、家庭游介绍等专题内容，增加关注量，做亮恩和旅游品牌。

2. 项目促进环境美化。一是传统民俗街基础设施建设项目，完备旅游基础设施、景观雕塑、旅游厕所等，改善了旅游环境，为推动旅游业的发展提供了必要的保障。二是通过落实排水沟盖板及架设路灯项目、道路改造项目、污水处理厂项目、环境美化项目等，不断改善居民生活质量和环境质量，改善地区旅游形象。

3. 制度规范旅游市场。一是开展执法检查工作，保障旅游市场健康有序运行。二是规范经营。合理规范骑马游经营户在固定区域内的经营活动，为经营户免费提供俄式观光马车供其使用。三是管理培训。制定家庭游疫情防控公约及标准，组织旅店业召开电商、服务标准化、法律法规知识等培训会，不断规范旅游市场，保障旅游产业朝着健康有序的方向发展。

成效

恩和乡 2019 年接待游客人数 70 万人次，实现旅游综合收入 2800 万元，家庭游年户均纯收入约 6 万元，带动了农牧民就业，增加了农牧民收入。2020 年，即便受疫情影响，旅游接待人数仍达 36 万人次，实现旅游综合收入 1600 万元。恩和乡最开始仅有 4 户家庭游，如今已发展至 127 户，大力带动了全乡的经济发展，该乡现有五星家庭游 5 家、四星家庭游 1 家、三星家庭游 1 家、红色民宿 2 家，家庭游接待床位数 3800 余张，列巴房 20 余家，投资千万元以上的宾馆有 5 家，旅游纪念品店 20 余家。

经验与启示

1. 加强文旅融合。恩和乡注重游客的俄罗斯族民俗体验感，把民俗节日“巴斯克节”“泼水节”打造成为地区旅游品牌。“油画小镇”精品旅游文化品牌持续发挥作用，恩和乡依托油画小镇，四年内共举办艺术交流、区域合作等活动 10 余次。先后有 130 多名来自全国各大美术院校的教授、各地知名油画家、俄罗斯画家等在恩和采风交流，创作油画 500 余幅。他们通过写生活动深度推广和展示了恩和小镇的艺术魅力，不仅提升了恩和文化品质，还带动了地区经济及旅游产业的发展。

2. 加强旅游推介。恩和积极参加旅游推介会，通过推介平台向各大旅行社整体推介旅游资源；积极配合各卫视以及主流网络媒体采访宣传；建立微信公众平台持续更新动态，发布民俗、人文、景观推荐等内容，进行广泛宣传。

下一步计划

下一步，恩和乡要大力实施“全域旅游”“四季旅游”战略：一是继续打造俄罗斯族民俗文化小镇、“民俗一条街”旅游品牌，对列巴制作、俄罗斯族民间歌舞、俄罗斯族婚礼、俄语课堂、传统游戏、俄式马车游等活动设置固定时间节点，将其作为俄罗斯族民俗体验项目，增加游客的参与度和体验感，进一步弘扬和宣传俄罗斯族民俗文化。二是继续扩大“油画小镇”品牌效应，谋划与文化传媒企业、艺术团队等载体的融合，积极推进“油画小镇”良性有序发展，助推地区产业升级。三是积极争取非物质文化保护展示中心建设项目的落地。四是创新和拓展现有旅游产品，促进文化与旅游融合，扩大旅游推介，推进管理服务标准化，开拓恩和乡文化旅游发展空间，助力乡村振兴。

Abstract

In recent years, as the only Russian nationality township in China, the Enhe Russian Nationality Township in Ergun City, Inner Mongolia Autonomous Region, has developed the Russian folk festivals of "National Basque Festival" and "Water Splashing Festival" as regional tourism brands. The township has also crafted its cultural brand of "oil painting town" boutique tourism. It has made full use of a national culture in creating a new tourism model and cultural integration. Also, it has developed traditional Russian festivals, food, games, singing and dancing, etc. into tourism products, leading to the establishment of a Russian folk culture town with well-known tourism brands. In 2013, the Enhe Township was on the list of "traditional Chinese villages" and "village with Chinese ethnic minority characteristics." It became a famous tourist town with characteristic landscapes in 2015 and was rated a national key village for rural tourism in 2020. It has woven the culture and tourism integration into its journey to rural revitalization.

Challenges and Problems

There are 1,213 households in the township, with a total registered population of 2,790 people, among whom 1,276 people are of the Russian Nationality and Chinese-Russian descendants, accounting for 46% of the total. It covers an area of 2,068 square kilometers and faces Russia across the Ergun River. The border line is 75 kilometers long. There is about 1.2 million *mu* of original woodland, 400,000 *mu* of grassland, 200,000 *mu* of arable land, with a forest and grass coverage rate of more than 80%. Clearly, the township boasts a superior natural environment, well-preserved original ecology and abundant resources of wild animals, plants and mineral products.

There are rich tourism resources in the township, including folklore museums, Russian bread houses, Mukeden along the street (century residences) and Russian folklore experiential activities. The town is also known for the following: color egg-making spots, matryoshka dolls, Russian bread, Russian singing and dancing performances, Russian game of scrambling for sticks, carriage-driving tours, horse-riding tours, and other tourism projects. Its natural landscapes such as the birch forest, Hawu'er River, rape flower field, Chinese herbaceous peony hillside, wheat field sightseeing, and Wolong Mountain are all major tourist attractions. Festivals such as the National Basque Festival and Water Splashing Festival attract many tourists. The National Basque Festival is included on the national intangible cultural heritage list and the Russian traditional folk dances are included in the intangible cultural heritage list of Inner Mongolia Autonomous Region. The Russian intangible cultural heritage has seven successors. Few development and protection of high-quality tourism resources, meager project funds, weak infrastructures and inadequate attention to environmental remediation, garbage treatment, sewage treatment, and environmental beautification are some of the problems restricting its growth. Additionally, the township's long winter and short summer results in a peak tourist season of only three months. There is little momentum for economic development. In view of its limited tourist season, more efforts should be made for the development of winter tourism. Adding to the township's woes are the many young people who go to school or work outside, resulting in the villages increasingly becoming more hollowed. This leads to the incremental loss of primitive Russian folk cultures and a shortage of systematic carriers for their preservation and promotion.

Measures

1. Activities promote tourism development. First, the Russian folk culture has been fully utilized to build the "National Basque Festival" and "Water Splashing Festival" into regional tourism brands that are celebrated every year. Beer festivals and bonfire parties have been also organized to develop the night economy and surrounding tours. This means that overall income is increased for the merchants, boosting the tourism economy. **Second,** the cultural brand of "oil painting town" boutique tourism has been in place since 2017 as a blueprint for a new tourism and cultural integration. **Third,** tourism publicity has been strengthened. The township has participated in tourism promotion conferences and has worked with a number of satellite TVs and mainstream online media to shoot cultural promotional videos for rural tourism. Moreover, it has also produced special content such as Russian folk culture and introduction to family tours by operating the official account of "Meili Enhe." The town has published dynamics, photos and videos of natural scenery in the

township to increase the awareness of its tourism brand.

2. Projects advance environmental beautification. First, the construction of traditional folk streets has enhanced tourism facilities, landscape sculptures, and other projects necessary for tourism. Overall, the tourism environment has been improved which helps guarantee the tourism industrial development. **Second,** projects such as drainage ditch covering, streetlamps, road renovation, sewage treatment plants and environmental beautification have improved the standard of living of the villagers and promoted the image of the township.

3. Systems regulate tourism markets. Law-enforcement have begun inspections of the facilities to ensure a healthy and orderly tourism market. Operations have also been standardized. These include horse-riding tour operations and free Russian-style sightseeing carriages. Management training has also been provided. The township has formulated epidemic prevention and control conventions and standards for family travel. It has also organized the hotel industry to hold training sessions on e-commerce, service standardization and knowledge of laws and regulations to regulate the tourism market. The village thus ensures that the tourism industry develops in a healthy and orderly manner.

Results

The township received 700,000 visitors in 2019 which resulted in a total income of RMB 28 million. The family tour has helped achieve an average household annual net income of about RMB 60,000, which promoted the employment of farmers and herdsmen and increased their income. As it was adversely affected by COVID-19 in 2020, it received only 360,000 tourists, with a comprehensive tourism income of RMB 16 million. The transition from the original four households engaged in the family tour to the current 127 households has greatly driven the township's economic development. There are five 5-star family tour hotels, one four-star family tour hotel, one three-star family tour hotel, two red culture B&Bs, with more than 3,800 beds, more than 20 Russian bread houses, five hotels with an investment of more than RMB 10 million and more than 20 tourist souvenir shops.

Experience and Inspirations

1. Strengthen cultural and tourism integration. The township has developed the "National Basque Festival" and "Water Splashing Festival" into regional tourism brands. This was done to ensure that the tourists are fully aware of the culture of the village they are visiting. To capitalize on its "Oil Painting Town" boutique tourism cultural brand, it held art exchanges and regional cooperation within four years. This has attracted more than 130 professors from national fine art colleges, well-known oil painters and Russian painters to collect materials for art creation and exchange ideas in the township. Overall, the town created more than 500 oil paintings. These sketching activities have promoted the township's local arts, which helps improve its cultural quality while promoting at the same time the development of the regional economy and tourism industry.

2. Increase rural tourism publicity. The township has participated in tourism promotional conferences and popularized tourism resources to major travel agencies through promotional platforms. It has also cooperated with various mainstream online media platforms for interviews and publicity. WeChat has also been used to create a public platform trends of the township, publish details including folk customs, humanities and landscape recommendations for extensive publicity.

Next Steps

Next, the strategy of "all-for-one tourism" and "four-season tourism" will be implemented. **First,** the Russian folk culture town and the "folk street" tourism brand will be further developed and fixed timelines for the Russian folklore experience projects such as Russian bread production, Russian folk songs and dances, Russian weddings, Russian classrooms, traditional games, and Russian carriage-driving tours will be set, to increase tourists' sense of participation and realize the promotion and publicity of the Russian folk culture. **Second,** the township will continue to expand and enhance the "oil painting town" brand and integrate it with cultural media companies. This will hopefully result in regional industrial upgrades. **Third,** more efforts will be made to implement the construction of intangible cultural protection and exhibition centers. **Fourth,** existing tourism products will be innovated and expanded for the integration of culture and tourism to advance tourism promotion and standardization of management services, and broaden cultural tourism development space in the township, hereby driving rural revitalization.

贵州黔南布依族苗族自治州荔波县朝阳镇洪江村：
艺旅融合探索乡村扶贫新路径

Hongjiang Village, Chaoyang Town, Libo County, Qiannan Buyi and Miao Autonomous Prefecture, Guizhou Province:
Integration of Art and Tourism Explores a New Model of Rural Poverty Alleviation

摘 要

贵州荔波县洪江村结合村落资源提炼出了“非遗洪江、艺术洪江、匠人洪江、生态洪江”的发展定位。围绕废旧房、闲置地、贫困户做文章，实现了废旧房变身文创房、闲置地变身生财地、贫困户变身示范户、从“空心村”向网红村的蜕变。洪江村以乡土文化为灵魂，以乡村田园为图景，以生态农业为基础，以艺术扶贫为抓手，以旅游富民为目标，以村民闲置老房和传统村落遗存为媒介，探索出了一条艺术扶贫新路径。

挑战与问题

贵州荔波县洪江村全村共有 9 个自然寨，2014 年洪江村在册精准贫困户 168 户 651 人，贫困发生率 29%，是一个典型的深度贫困村。洪江村基础建设薄弱，村庄环境脏乱、道路狭窄，村里资金短缺，无法改善基础条件。洪江村地貌以山地、高山为主，耕地面积少，全村耕地面积仅有 924 亩，人均耕地面积不足 1 亩，农业机械化产业化难度大，大部分山地荒坡不适宜种植果林经济树种，村民收入来源以务工为主。因大量劳动力外出务工，村内剩下老弱病残留守，缺乏活力和创新，是真正的“空心村”。留守老人大多思想观念老旧，难以接受新思想观念，拒绝学习新思想和新事物。

措施

洪江村围绕荔波县全域旅游发展战略，结合村落资源提炼出了“非遗洪江、艺术洪江、匠人洪江、生态洪江”的发展定位思路。

1.“废旧房”变“文创房”。利用村落闲置、干栏式建筑，结合“民宿”“集体建设用地试点”等政策，邀请美国、西班牙、瑞士和中国各地的艺术家来到洪江，对复建老房进行艺术工作坊兼居室改造，全面激活闲置破败老房。目前，已收储老房屋及宅基地使用权 81 宗，宅基地面积 1.86 万平方米。入驻洪江的艺术家有 88 人，其中以认养 30 年方式入驻的有 11 位，以有偿使用方式入驻的有 77 位。改造修复老房 48 栋，使艺术和乡村在洪江发生了奇妙的“化学反应”。

2.“闲置地”变“生财地”。充分利用黔南州农村集体建设用地使用权制度改革试点村政策，积极探索集体建设用地有偿使用和农村宅基地退出补偿机制，提高土地利用率。目前，村委会已收储废旧房屋和宅基地 103 宗，引进哈尔滨显著医生集团，与洪江村集体经济富洪实业有限公司合作建立洪江康养基地，激活洪江自然资源。

3.“贫困户”变“示范户”。按照“支部 + 公司 + 农户”的产业扶贫推进模式，聚焦贫困户，坚持在推动产业兴旺过程中推进“志智”双扶，把贫困户培育成脱贫示范户。引进企业发展蔬菜、金线莲、大蒜、蚕桑等产业 850 亩，全村 187 户群众在土地流转中受益。组建房修复队 7 支 80 人，其

中贫困户 48 人，每天每人 200 元务工费，月人均收入逾 3000 元。艺术家工作室提供房屋保洁、安保等就业岗位逾 70 个。

4.“空心村”变“网红村”。着力推进文艺扶贫试点建设，主动保护和传承民族文化、乡土文化资源。著名艺术批评家贾方舟、当代艺术家李向明、中央美院艺术家崔国泰等来自国内外的艺术家，齐聚洪江进行艺术创作，村中先后举办“中国—东盟教育交流周之 2020 洪江论坛暨洪江当代艺术邀请展”“写生中国走进洪江”“国际动漫走进洪江艺术展”等大型艺术活动，中央、省及州媒体平台已报道 100 余次，先后吸引美国、法国、德国、瑞典等国内外艺术家到访，实现了生态经济和文化经济的融合发展。

成效

洪江村的探索与坚持，有力推进了农村文旅产业经济的发展。近年来，洪江村年接待游客 7 万人次，旅游年收入 300 万元，旅游带动村民就业 173 人，基本建成 15 个艺术家工作室、46 家民宿客栈，2020 年已实现全村脱贫。艺术家进驻后，与原住民共同生活，逐步加强互动、彼此滋养，重塑传统村落的人文价值观和产业链，让洪江村传统村落遗存的艺术活化起来。随着艺术家的入驻及结合当地土布文化的布艺培训班的开设，洪江的旅游产品由单一的山水风景，转向以多元的文化支撑为主，现今群落式的洪江布依族干栏式建筑风貌，如艺术交流中心、土语南居艺术活动广场、雁西书院文艺交流中心、小梅摄影写生馆、国泰当代美术馆等，已成为洪江的一道风景线。

经验与启示

洪江村的初步成功实践证明：保护乡村农耕文化独特性、保住乡村文化根脉、增强群众文化自信、深化农业农村改革，对振兴乡村至关重要。

1. 独特的文化魅力，是吸引艺术家的核心要

素。洪江村展现出的贵州农耕文明所具有的独特价值，滋养出具有贵州特色的耕读文化和山地文化、乡土文化，其所体现的多样性、包容性、审美性特点，与艺术家希望实现艺术创作的愿望十分契合，使艺术家在心灵和情怀上找到了归属感。

2. 促进乡村振兴要保住乡村文化根脉。洪江村的探索证明：乡村原始风貌和优秀传统文化本身就是一笔财富，蕴藏着发展的优势和资源。这启示我们：一是在村庄规划上，要更加注重保护村庄原有的历史风物遗存，让农村更具人文情怀，为保护、传承、弘扬村庄文化留下足够空间。二是在村庄建设过程中，要坚决杜绝大拆大建，充分挖掘整理好村庄历史文化遗存和非遗技艺，加以合理改造，既保留历史痕迹，又融入现代便利和审美因素，实现活态化传承和发展。

3. 促进乡村振兴要提高农民文化自信。洪江村民通过耳濡目染，通过和艺术家之间的融洽生活，其生活方式和精神面貌也得到了改观。这启示我们：一是要通过深入挖掘整理、展示本村的村落遗存，让村民从文化艺术价值的角度去感知村庄的存在感。二是要发挥好群众主体作用，发动村民参与村庄文化的传承与保护，从参与中获取文化自觉

和文化自信。三是要讲好乡村发展故事，营造浓郁乡愁，让村民看到村庄的发展前景，让更多年轻人愿意留下来建设美丽乡村。

4. 促进乡村振兴，要深化农业农村改革。洪江村抓住有利契机，用改革创新的办法盘活自身资源，取得了初步成果。这启示我们：一是要在盘活利用农民闲置宅基地和闲置农房上下功夫，在保障农民权益的前提下探索宅基地退出和“三权分置”，实现资源再利用，实现效益最大化。二是要在农业产业革命上下功夫，积极探索农业产业结构调整，多样化发展助推农民增收。三是要在农文旅融合发展上下功夫，探索将农事活动体验、农耕文化体验与乡村旅游发展结合起来，带动农村发展。

下一步计划

洪江村将在未来工作的开展中探索三种模式，创建三个示范：一是探索艺术家与扶贫相结合模式，创建艺术扶贫示范；二是探索当代艺术与乡村文化相碰撞模式，创建乡村文化振兴示范；三是探索文化与旅游深度融合的发展模式，创建文旅融合示范。

Abstract

Based on village resources, the brand positioning of "intangible cultural heritage, art, craftsmanship, and ecology" has been determined for the development of Hongjiang Village, Libo County, Guizhou Province. After determining the main tasks, arduous efforts have been made to transform dilapidated houses into cultural and creative houses, idle land into wealth-generating sites, impoverished households into demonstration households, and a "hollow village" into an internet-famous village. With local culture as the soul, rural pastoral landscape as the blueprint, ecological agriculture as the foundation, poverty alleviation through art as the means, enriching people through tourism as the goal, and idle old houses and remains of traditional villages as media, the village has explored a new path for poverty alleviation through art.

Challenges and Problems

There are nine natural villages in the village. In 2014, there were 651 people from 168 archived impoverished households with a poverty incidence of 29%, making it severely impoverished. Due to backward infrastructures, dirty and chaotic environment, narrow roads, and a shortage of funds, the basic conditions in the village could not be improved. Mostly dominated by mountain land and high mountains, with a small arable land area of 924 *mu* and a per capita arable land area of less than one *mu*, the village was not suitable place for an economic fruit forest development. Agricultural mechanization and industrialization were impossible to attain. Many villagers chose to work outside for their livelihood. In no time it turned into a "hollow village" as the elderly, weak, sick and disabled who lacked vigor and energy for innovation were the ones left behind. Most of the elderly were clinging to traditional ideas, refused to learn new things. Typically, they found it difficult to accept new ways of thinking to improve their own lives.

Measures

Centered on the development strategy of all-for-one tourism in Libo County, and on the basis of village resources, the positioning of promoting "intangible cultural heritage, art, craftsmanship, and ecology" has been determined for the development of Hongjiang Village.

1. Transform dilapidated houses into cultural and creative houses. Through the utilization of idle stilt style architecture and based on "B&Bs" and "collective construction land pilots" policies, artists from the United States, Spain, Switzerland and all over the country were introduced to revitalize and renovate the old houses and living rooms into art workshops, and living rooms. Today, 81 old houses and homestead use rights have been purchased and stored which covers an area of 18,600 square meters. A total of 88 artists have settled in the village, 11 of whom have owned their houses for 30 years. Seventy seven of them have paid for the use. Additionally, 48 old houses have been renovated and restored with the amazing results of art and countryside integration in full display.

2. Transform idle land into wealth-generating sites. To improve the land utilization rate, the policies for pilot villages on rural collective construction land use rights system reform in Buyi and Miao Autonomous Prefecture of Qiannan were leveraged. Mechanism for the paid use of collective construction land and compensation on the withdrawal of rural homesteads were also explored. Presently, the village committee has collected and stored 103 dilapidated houses and homesteads to improve the village economy. It has also introduced LXZMG Significantly Medical Group in Harbin City of Heilongjiang Province, and established Hongjiang Healthcare Base in cooperation with Fuhong Industrial Development Co., Ltd. to revitalize the village.

3. Transform impoverished households into demonstration households. In accordance with the poverty alleviation model through industrial development of "Party branches + companies + peasant households," and focused on impoverished households, a change of attitude and educational support were also required to achieve industrial prosperity and transform impoverished households to demonstration households. Enterprises were introduced to develop industries such as vegetables, anoectochilus formosanus, garlic, and sericulture which covered an area of 850 *mu*. One hundred eighty seven (187) village households benefited from the land transfer. Seven house repair teams with 80 people were set up, 48 of whom came from impoverished households. Each could earn RMB 200 per day, with a monthly per capita income of more than RMB 3,000. The artists' studios provided at least 70 jobs in house cleaning and security.

4. Transform a "hollow village" into an internet-famous village. Efforts have been made to promote the construction of pilot projects for poverty alleviation through literature and art to protect and pass on its national culture and local cultural resources. Famous art critic Jia Fangzhou, contemporary creator and artist Li Xiangming, the Central Academy of Fine Arts artist Cui Guotai and other artists at home and abroad gathered in the village for creative endeavors. Large-scale art events were held: the *China-ASEAN Education Cooperation Week — The Hongjiang Forum 2020 & Hongjiang Contemporary Art Invitation Exhibition, Sketching China into Hongjiang* and *International Animation into Hongjiang Art Exhibition.* Publicity coverage from national, provincial and prefecture-level media platforms exceeded 100, enticing domestic and foreign artists from the United States, France, Germany, and Sweden, etc. to visit the village and see for themselves the integrated development of ecological and cultural economy.

Results

The exploration of the village and the perseverance of the local community have promoted the economic development of the rural cultural and tourism industry. In recent years, the village welcomed 70,000 tourists annually, with the annual tourism income of RMB 3 million. A total of 173 villagers have been engaged in tourism, and 15 artists' studios and 46 B&Bs have been built. The village has been lifted out of poverty by 2020. After the settling in the village, the artists live together with the aboriginal people for more interaction and better understanding of each other. This practice has reshaped humanistic values and the traditional village's industrial chain. It has also revitalized the legacy art here. With the arrival of artists and the fabrics training courses established according to the local textile culture, tourism products in the village have been developed as supported

by diverse cultures from the original unitary landscape. Currently, there are community-patterned architectural stilt style of the Buyi Nationality, art exchange centers, Tuyu Nanju Art Activity Plaza, Yanxi Academy Literature and Art Exchange Center, Xiaomei Photography and Sketching Gallery, and Guotai Contemporary Art Museum in the village.

Experience and Inspirations

The village's successful preliminary practice proves that protecting the uniqueness of rural farming culture, preserving the roots of rural culture, enhancing the cultural confidence of people, and deepening the reform of agriculture and rural areas are vital to rural revitalization.

1. Unique cultural charm is the core element of attracting artists. The Guizhou farming civilization displayed in the village boasts a unique value and nourishes both farming, reading, mountainous and local cultures with distinctive Guizhou characteristics. Its diversity, inclusiveness, and aesthetics are in line with the artists' desire for creative expression while giving them a sense of belonging.

2. Preserve the roots of rural culture for rural revitalization. The exploration of the village has proven that the original rural landscape and excellent traditional culture are a fortune, rich in advantages and resources for development. It has enlightened us a lot. **First,** the original historical heritage should be protected in village planning to develop a more humanistic countryside, and further protect, inherit and carry forward the village culture. **Second,** large-scale demolition and construction should be eradicated in village construction to tap historical and cultural relics and intangible cultural heritage for reasonable transformations, which can preserve the historical traces, and also integrate modern convenience and aesthetics, thus achieving the inheritance and development of cultural liveliness.

3. Enhance the farmers' cultural confidence in rural revitalization. Since local villagers and the artists have lived harmoniously with each other, they have influenced the lifestyle and mental attitude of the former. **First,** this living arrangement has resulted in the in-depth exploration, analysis and display of the village's cultural legacy. In the process, the villagers gain a new perspective on value of their culture and artistic traditions.

Second, the role of the masses as the main body should be emphasized to mobilize villagers to preserve, protect and hand down their village culture. Giving them an important role helps them gain cultural awareness and confidence. **Third,** it's important to convey the rural development story, create a nostalgia-evoking environment and help villagers see the full potential of their village. Seeing this, more young people will decide to stay in their hometown and become active role player in its construction and beautification.

4. Expand the rural agricultural reform for revitalization. The village has taken advantage of its opportunities and revitalized its resources through reform and innovation with tentative results. This tells us that **first,** more efforts should be made to revitalize idle homesteads and the farmers' idle houses and explore the withdrawal of homesteads and the system of "separating rural land ownership rights, contract rights, and management rights" on the premise of protecting the farmers' rights and interest for resource reuse and maximum benefits. **Second,** more emphasis should be placed on the agricultural industrial revolution for the structural adjustment of the agricultural industry and diversified resources to increase the farmers' income. **Third,** the integrated development of agriculture, culture and tourism should be highlighted to find new ways to integrate agricultural, farming culture and rural tourism experiences for rural development.

Next Steps

The village will explore three models and develop three demonstrations in future work. **First,** the model of combining artists and poverty alleviation through art will be explored. **Second,** the collision and collusion model of contemporary art and rural culture should be examined for rural cultural revitalization demonstration. Third, a development model integrating culture and tourism should be explored.

四川阿坝藏族羌族自治州九寨沟县：
全域旅游促进乡村脱贫奔小康

Jiuzhaigou County, Aba Xizang's and Qiang Autonomous Prefecture, Sichuan Province:
All-for-one Tourism Drives Rural Poverty Alleviation and Prosperity

摘要

自脱贫攻坚以来，九寨沟县充分依托生态优势和九寨沟国家5A级旅游景区的资源优势，不断创新旅游扶贫新模式，以全域旅游为方向，构建“一主两核三带”新布局，优化旅游产业结构，走出了一条生态旅游发展齐头并进的新路子，实现了从“木头财政”到“旅游财政”、从“资源大县”到“旅游强县”、从“深度贫困”到“小康富裕”的重大转型。自1953年建县以来，全县GDP增长了122倍，财政收入增加了118倍，以旅游业为主导的第三产业对GDP贡献率逾60%，成为全国首批、四川省唯一的“中国旅游强县”。

挑战与问题

九寨沟是中国重要生态屏障和水源涵养地，属于川滇森林及生物多样性保护国家重点生态功能区，是四川省第二大林区，森林覆盖率达 58.65%，森林植被覆盖率 73.78%。然而与此同时，九寨沟县也是四川 88 个贫困县之一，是“三区三州”深度贫困县，是四川省脱贫攻坚“高原藏区”的主战场。九寨沟的旅游业过度依赖于九寨沟风景区，如何打破单一业态、单一景区的模式，如何借助旅游消费转型升级倒逼供给侧结构性改革，让更多困难群众享受到旅游业发展带来的红利，便成为九寨沟县探索的方向。

措施

九寨沟县充分发挥旅游优势，不断创新旅游扶贫机制，以全域旅游为方向，以“一主两核三带”为路径，优化旅游产业结构、促进转型升级，走出了一条“旅游 +”的新路径。

1. 推进景区景点建设。对照省级旅游扶贫示范区创建标准，打造 12 个旅游扶贫重点村，落实停车场、旅游漫道、旅游厕所、观景台、农副产品销售点、游客接待中心旅游基础服务设施的“六小工程”项目建设。目前，九寨沟县已成功创建“四川省旅游扶贫示范区”，成功创建 6 个“四川省旅游扶贫示范村”、107 户“四川省乡村民宿达标示范户”，初步形成“一核多点”彼此带动的全域旅游格局。

2. 推动农旅产业融合。实施“九寨沟 +”品牌培育计划，明确双河镇河坝村和罗依坝村、白河乡太平村、勿角镇苗州村、黑河镇达舍寨村、南坪镇双龙村 5 个农旅融合示范园为九寨沟县现代农业产业融合示范园区。着手打造大录乡油菜大地景观基地和黑河镇七里村甜樱桃采摘园，完善步道、观景台、旅游厕所、标识标牌等旅游配套设施，为第三产业扶贫打下基础。

3. 促进手工旅游发展。充分挖掘县域内特有的饮食文化和手工技艺，探索旅游产品订单式加工模式，引导九寨祥巴、阿布镥孜、奉巫餐饮等公司共同打造一个旅游商品研发基地，发掘旅游食品和旅游手工艺品等特色旅游商品；培育旅游商品企业和品牌，开发“小九九”系列文创产品 180 多种；定向选择 200 余名贫困群众派发旅游商品生产订单，持续带动其增收。

4. 培育发展旅游服务产品。依托九寨沟景区的优势资源，全县共开业藏（农）家乐 39 家。发挥乡村旅游发展优势，成功将罗依乡九寨庄园建设成为“四川省乡村旅游创客基地新业态示范品牌”，目前已接待县内外游客 3600 余人次，实现经济收入 40 余万元。间接带动贫困人口参与就业 900 余人，拓宽了贫困群众增收渠道。

5. 打造旅游精品线路。立足“全域九寨”深度游工程，成功推出环神仙池一日游、秦川文化白马藏族风情一日游 2 条全域九寨休闲度假游线路。以柴门关驿站、罗依产业园区自驾游营地、白河乡太平农庄及县城周边特色农家乐为载体，向游客提供食宿等旅游接待服务，在九环沿线设置以游客体验为主的水果采摘点，带动周边群众发展乡村旅游增收致富，推动九寨环线旅游由景点旅游向串珠式全域旅游、由传统观光游向“旅游 +”综合立体游的转变。

成效

九寨沟县依托全域旅游走上了致富路，2019 年，九寨沟县累计接待游客 185.51 万人次，实现旅游综合收入 17.6 亿元。2020 年，全县通过旅游脱贫人数逾 5500 人，占全县脱贫总人数 5638 人的 97%。目前，九寨沟县已成功引进项目 20 余个、协议投资近 200 亿元；全县共有星级酒店 11 家、非星级酒店 88 家，乡村客栈 700 余家，(藏)农家乐 14 家，演艺场所 10 家，餐饮 2230 家，超市 572 家，带动数万人就业创业。

经验与启示

1. 串珠成线，破解景区高度集中“窘境”。坚持多点布局全面提升，加快构建以九寨风景名胜区为核心、多景区互为支撑、多点多级发展的全域旅游格局：一是推进景点建设。将全县科学划分为全域旅游发展示范带、休闲度假旅游发展带、生态文化旅游培育带，全力打造县域内其他景区景点，促进全域旅游高质量发展。二是提升基础设施水平。全力构建“对外畅达、内部通达”的立体综合旅游交通体系；落实对停车场、旅游厕所、游客接待中心等“六小工程”的建设，塑造美丽乡村新面貌。三是打造精品旅游线路。立足全域九寨深度游工程，精心设计全域旅游专线，实现 A 级景区“串珠成线”，运营好县域旅游线路。

2. 深度融合，多维提升旅游综合“质感”。积极推动农旅、文旅、体旅等产业融合发展：一是实施差异发展。鼓励旅游饭店、地方餐饮品牌、旅行社实施品质化建设，支持旅游市场主体开发丰富多彩的旅游新业态。引导企业打造旅游商品研发基地、旅游创客基地等新业态示范品牌。二是丰富开发模式。深入挖掘民族民俗文化，积极筹办系列节庆活动，推动 6 大类种养基地和 5 个农旅融合示范园建设，精心打造集“农业 + 文化”创意、特色饮食体验和观光旅游为一体的“农业 + 文化”创意基地。三是坚持招大引强。多举措强化全域旅游宣传推介，先后举办了文化旅游联盟品牌战略发布会、文旅发展联盟大会、“文旅品牌之夜”等系列活动，以优质旅游资源吸纳高质企业入驻。

3. 精准衔接，助推贫困群众搭上“便车”。坚持“旅游、扶贫发展”大扶贫模式，多举措促进贫困群众持续增收。一是壮大集体产业。按照“村有支柱产业、户有致富项目、人有一技之长”的要求，以小额贴息贷款、产业发展基金为保障，以九寨沟旅游市场为支撑，积极发展优势中药材和特色种养殖业，120 个村全覆盖建立集体经济，成功创建省级旅游扶贫示范村 6 个，彻底消灭“空壳村”。二是打造村企同盟。通过“百企联百村、百企圆百梦”等活动，动员组织宾馆饭店、藏（农）家乐、演艺市场、旅行社等旅游企业积极参与脱贫攻坚，在就业创业、项目投资、农特产品宣传销售、从业人员技能提升等方面发挥帮扶作用，增强贫困村、贫困户的“造血”功能。

下一步计划

以全域旅游发展为目标，深入推进乡村振兴工作：一是科学制订乡村旅游建设详规，合理布局产业要素，实现乡村产品的全域化。二是打造特色“农旅 + 文旅”新业态，拓宽乡村关联产业融合渠道，不断延伸农业产业园区、农产品基地融合、农产品加工、传统手工业制造，农产品销售平台、乡村文创产品融合等特色业态，带动乡村旅游消费。三是进一步完善乡村交通枢纽网，规划建设产业路、生态路、文明路、致富路。四是加大对乡村旅游从业人员服务技能的培训力度，并建立本地外出人员联络机制，发掘一批“田秀才”“土专家”“乡创客”和能工巧匠，为乡村振兴汇聚人才。

Abstract

Since its fight against poverty was initiated and with full reliance on its ecological advantages and the tourism resources of the 5A-level tourist attraction of Jiuzhai Valley, the Jiuzhaigou County continues to innovate the poverty alleviation through tourism model. Its new paradigm puts Jiuzhai Valley Scenic Area squarely at the core. With all-for-one tourism as the guiding framework, it has put into motion "the Jiuzhai Valley Scenic Area as the mainstay, enhancing the core driving force of Zhangzha Charming Town and Nanping Livable Town, and building All-for-one Tourism Development Demonstration Belt, Leisure Vacation Tourism Development Belt, and Ecological Cultural Tourism Fostering Belt" concept.

They have optimized the tourism industry structure and embarked on a new eco-tourism development parallel to its goal of realizing a major transformation from "timber finance" to "tourism finance," "large resources county" to "strong tourism county" and "extreme poverty" to "well-off and prosperous." Since the county was established in 1953, its GDP has increased 122 times and its financial revenue 118 times. The tourism-dominated tertiary industry has contributed more than 60% to the GDP, leading to the Jiuzhaigou County being recognized as the national first batch and Sichuan Province's sole "China's Strong Tourism County."

Challenges and Problems

Jiuzhaigou is a national major ecological screen and water conservation area that belongs to the national key ecological function zone for forest and biodiversity conservation in Sichuan and Yunnan provinces. It is the second largest forest zone in Sichuan Province, with a forest coverage rate of up to 58.65% and a forest vegetation coverage of 73.78%. As the main battleground in the fight against poverty in the "Plateau Xizang's Area" in Sichuan Province, the county is one of 88 poverty-stricken counties in Sichuan Province. It is also one of the counties with extreme poverty in Xizang's Autonomous Region, the four southern administrative districts of Xinjiang Uygur Autonomous Region, Xizang's areas of Qinghai, Sichuan, Yunnan and Gansu provinces, Linxia Prefecture, Liangshan Prefecture and Nujiang Prefecture. Since its tourism industry is overly dependent on the Valley Scenic Area, the county has been exploring ways to break away from the single business and single scenic area model and pivot to the supply-side structural reform through the transformation and upgrading of tourism

consumption. This economic shift allows villagers who are facing financial difficulty to benefit and share in the dividends from tourism development.

Measures

The county has given full play to its tourism advantages and continued to innovate the mechanism of poverty alleviation through tourism. With the all-for-one tourism as the direction and Jiuzhai Valley Scenic Area as the mainstay, it has optimized its tourism industry structure, facilitated transformation and upgrade and embarked on the path of "Tourism +." This was accomplished by enhancing the core driving force of Zhangzha Charming Town and Nanping Livable Town and building an All-for-one Tourism Development Demonstration Belt, Leisure Vacation Tourism Development Belt and an Ecological Cultural Tourism Fostering Belt.

1. Accelerate the construction of scenic spots. In compliance with the standard requirements for the construction of provincial tourism poverty alleviation demonstration zones, 12 key villages have been built to implement the construction of "Six Small Projects" which include the following: parking lots, tourist roads, tourist toilets, viewing platforms, agricultural and derivative side products points of sale, tourist reception centers and other basic tourism service facilities. The county has successfully established the "Sichuan Province Tourism Poverty Alleviation Demonstration zone," six "Sichuan Province Tourism Poverty Alleviation Demonstration Villages" and 107 "Sichuan Province Rural B&Bs

Standardization Demonstration Households," initially forming an all-for-one tourism pattern driven by "one core and multiple points."

2. Promote the integration of agricultural and tourism industries. The brand development plan of "Jiuzhaigou +" has been implemented and the five agricultural and tourism integrated demonstration parks in Heba Village and Luoyiba Village of Shuanghe Town, Taiping Village of Baihe Township, Miaozhou Village of Wujiao Town, Dashezhai Village of Heihe Town, and Shuanglong Village of Nanping Town have been earmarked as the county's modern agricultural industries integration demonstration zones. Great efforts have been made to construct a ripe produce landscape base in Dalu Township and a sweet cherry picking garden in Qili Village, Heihe Town. All these are designed to pave the way for poverty alleviation through a tertiary industry and to improve tourism at supporting facilities that include trails, viewing platforms, tourism toilets and increase brand awareness through logos and signage.

3. Promote the development of artisanal tourism. Great efforts have been made to optimize the county's unique cooking culture and craftsmanship. Also, work has been done to explore the order-based processing model of tourism products and guide companies such as Jiuzhai Xiangba Culture and Art Co., Ltd., Abu Luzi Xizang's Restaurant, and Fengwu Catering Co., Ltd. to build a tourism product research and development base. Progress has been achieved to develop special products like tourism food and handicrafts and cultivate tourism commodities enterprises and brands that will create more than 180 kinds of cultural and creative products like the "Small Ninety-Nine" series. The county has also guided over 300 impoverished people on distribution orders for tourism commodities production. Implementation of these measures has ensured the continuous growth of income for poor households.

4. Foster and develop tourism service products. With the Jiuzhai Valley Scenic Area and its superior resources as the base, the Jiuzhaigou County has opened a total of 39 Xizang's-styled agritainment industries. Capitalizing on the proven advantages of rural tourism development, it has transformed the Jiuzhai Manor in Luoyi Township into a new business form demonstration brand of rural tourism maker base in Sichuan Province. The township has received over 3,600 visitors from inside and outside of the county, resulting in over RMB 400,000 income for the people. With such measures implemented, it has indirectly driven more than 900 impoverished people to be employed, thus broadening the channels for the poor to grow their income.

5. Develop boutique routes of tourism. Based on the "All-for-one Jiuzhai" in-depth tour project, the county has introduced two routes of all-for-one Jiuzhai leisure and vacation tour such as a one-day tour around the Fairy Pool and one-day tour of Qinchuan Culture Baima Xizang's Customs. With the Chaimenguan courier station, the self-driving camp in the Luoyi Industrial Park, the Taiping farm village in Baihe Township and special agritainment around the county as the carriers, it has provided tourists with food, accommodation and other tourism reception services. Along the ninth ring road from Chengdu to Jiuzhaigou, experiential fruit picking points for tourists have been set up to motivate those living in the surrounding areas to increase their income through rural tourism. With such measures implemented, the transformation of the Jiuzhai Ring Tour from scenic spot to all-for-one tour by stringing various scenic spots together has been realized. Also, it has been successfully converted from a traditional sightseeing tour into a "Tourism +" comprehensive three-dimensional tour.

Results

Based on the all-for-one tourism, the county has embarked on a road to progress. In 2019, it cumulatively received 1.855 million visitors that generated a comprehensive revenue of RMB 1.76 billion. In 2020, more than 5,500 people moved out of poverty through tourism. They account for 97% of 5,638 people lifted out of poverty in the county. Over 20 projects have been introduced, with an agreed investment of nearly RMB 20 billion. Currently, the county boasts 11 starred hotels, 88 non-star hotels, over 700 village inns, 14 Xizang's-styled agritainment enterprises, 10 performing art venues, 2,240

restaurants and 572 supermarkets, resulting in tens of thousands of people being employed or starting their own businesses.

Experience and Inspirations

1. Leverage the high concentration of scenic spots by stringing various scenic spots together. It has upheld the comprehensive improvement of multi-point layout and accelerated the construction of an all-for-one tourism pattern with Jiuzhai Valley Scenic Area as the core. Furthermore, multiple scenic spots that support each other and multi-point and multi-level developments have also begun. **The first step** is to promote the construction of scenic spots. The whole county has been divided into All-for-one Tourism Development Demonstration Belt, Leisure Vacation Tourism Development Belt and Ecological Cultural Tourism Fostering Belt to build other scenic spots and facilitate the high-quality development of all-for-one tourism. **Second,** upgrade the infrastructure level. Great efforts should be made to build a three-dimensional comprehensive transportation system of "externally unblocked, internally accessible" and implement the construction of "Six Small Projects," including parking lots, tourism toilets and visitor reception centers to create an appealing new look for the village. **Third,** build boutique tourism routes. Based on the all-for-one Jiuzhai in-depth tour, an all-for-one tourism special route should be designed to string all A-level tourist attractions together for a smooth and seamless operation of the county tourism route.

2. In-depth integration to enhance the comprehensive "quality" of tourism in all aspects. The integrated development of industries of such industries agricultural, cultural and sports tourism will be proactively promoted. **First,** we will implement differential development. Tourism restaurants, local catering brands and travel agencies should be encouraged to implement quality construction. Tourism market players should be supported to develop diverse new tourism businesses. **Second,** enhance and fine-tune development models. The national folk culture should be explored, festival activities should be organized, the construction of six major planting and breeding bases and five agricultural tourism integration demonstration parks should be boosted. Additionally, an agriculture + cultural creativity base that integrates "agriculture + culture" creativity, special food experiences and sightseeing tourism should be created. **Third,** secure the introduction of big or powerful enterprises. Multiple measures should be taken to expand and elevate the publicity and promotion of all-for-one tourism. Events and activities like the cultural tourism alliance brand strategy conference, the cultural tourism development alliance conference and the cultural tourism brand night should be held, with a view to attracting high-quality enterprises to establish their operations in the county as sign on as partners for quality tourism resources.

3. Precise connection helping poor people catch an "express of getting rich." The "tourism facilitating poverty alleviation development" model should be held high and various measures should be adopted to promote the sustained the income growth of poverty-stricken people. **First,** the collective industry should be strengthened. With the support of the Jiuzhaigou tourism market and through small sums and interest loans from industrial development funds, we will develop superior traditional Chinese herbs, special planting and breeding industries as required by "a pillar industry for each village, a program of getting rich for each household, and a professional skill for each person." Efforts should be made to build the collective economy in all 120 villages under its jurisdiction and create six provincial tourism poverty demonstration villages. The "hollow village" should be eradicated by addressing and finding solutions to the problems facing children, women and the elderly who are left behind in rural villages by rural migrant workers working in cities. **Second,** build village-enterprise alliance. In adherence to the tenets of "enterprises partnered with villages to help the poor realize their dreams," hotels and restaurants, Xizang's-type agritainment enterprises, performing arts venues, travel agencies and other tourism businesses should be organized and coordinated in the fight against poverty. Relevant assistance for employment and entrepreneurship, project investment, publicity and sales of agricultural and

derivative side products and the improvement of skills of the locals must be provided. Impoverished villagers must be motivated and inspired to practice self-reliance to improve their standard of living and move out of poverty.

Next Steps

Rural revitalization will be further facilitated by all-for-one tourism development. **First,** a detailed plan of rural tourism development will be scientifically formulated. Industrial elements will be logically arranged, and rural production should be integrated. **Second,** special "agricultural tourism + cultural tourism" new businesses will be created. The integration channel for rural correlative industries will be broadened. Also, the integration of agricultural industrial parks and agricultural product bases, agricultural product processing and traditional handicraft manufacturing, agricultural product sales platforms and rural cultural creative products, and other special business forms will be extended to drive rural tourism consumption. **Third,** rural transportation hub networks will be further improved and the industrial road, ecological road, civilized road and the road to economic enhancement will be planned and developed. **Fourth,** service skills training for rural tourism practitioners will be intensified. A communication system for local migrant workers will be established. Farming technicians, farming experts, local business operators and skillful craftsmen will be trained and pooled together for rural revitalization.

云南大理白族自治州剑川县沙溪镇：
全域旅游助力乡村振兴

Shaxi Town, Jianchuan County, Dali Bai Autonomous Prefecture, Yunnan Province:
All-for-one Tourism Empowers Rural Revitalization

摘 要

沙溪镇结合沙溪特色小镇创建、沙溪七个传统村落连片示范等项目，着眼于“世界一流、中国唯一”的发展目标，统筹推进大沙溪全域旅游发展战略，助力乡村振兴落地见效。现已初步形成“以寺登为中心、以坝区村落为辐射、以山区村落为补充”的沙溪镇“一镇带七村”全域旅游格局，形成独特魅力、特色鲜明、竞争力强、文化内涵高的精品旅游景区。沙溪镇被评为国家 4A 级旅游景区，先后获评“国家历史文化名镇”“全国最美小镇”。

挑战与问题

云南大理白族自治州沙溪镇是一个以白族为主，汉、彝、傈僳族共居的少数民族聚居镇。下辖14个行政村、49个自然村、76个村民小组。随着古镇旅游环境的提升，古镇保护与发展之间的矛盾逐渐显现，古镇管理的难度加大。另外，古镇旅游产业开发不足，依然以住宿、餐饮为主导，文旅、体验式产业发展缺乏后劲儿，文化内涵优势和民俗体验特点尚未充分发挥其效能。

措施

1. 坚持规划引领。始终坚持规划先行，瞄准"世界一流、中国唯一"的发展目标，以人为核心、以产业为支撑，科学编制特色小镇发展规划。在《沙溪镇总体规划》《沙溪镇区控制性详细规划》《沙溪历史文化名镇保护规划》《沙溪古镇保护管理办法》《沙溪历史文化名镇保护与发展规划》《沙溪传统村落群保护与发展规划》等规划的基础上，编制完成了《沙溪古镇（白族）发展总体规划》和《沙溪古镇（白族）修建性详细规划》。

2. 坚持风貌保护。在保护和保留乡村风貌、乡村文化、历史遗存、田园风光的基础上，突出沙溪特色，坚持修旧如旧，修复了一批白族民居、街道和四方街广场，完成了对古戏台、兴教寺、东寨门、南寨门、老马店等代表性古旧建筑的修复，实施传统村落保护工程，古镇风貌、配套功能、田园风光不断彰显。深化与瑞士相关方面的合作，加强"人文沙溪、生态沙溪、智慧沙溪"建设，使沙溪古镇白族建筑、古镇风貌得到有效保护，同时把古旧建筑修复经验、理念推向世界。

3. 坚持生态优先。牢固树立和践行"绿水青山就是金山银山"的发展理念，合理界定沙溪古镇人口、资源、环境承载力，科学开发旅游文化资源，严格管控各类"红线"，不突破生态红线，不侵占基本农田。强化"一水两污"基础设施建设，建成日处理500立方米的集镇污水处理厂、生活垃圾转运中心，逐步实现污水、生活垃圾100%收集和无害化处理；加强镇区美化绿化，推进绿地面积、水域面积建设；把绿色节能建筑技术积极运用到小镇建设中，建设选材优先选择绿色低碳材料。

4. 坚持企业主体。沙溪古镇采取"1+N"模式推进，确定广东奥园文旅集团有限公司为沙溪古镇特色小镇的投资主体，双方成立平台公司，共同投资经营沙溪古镇。与此同时，大力招引国内知名企业入驻，开启特色小镇社会投资项目建设，一大

批有情怀、有实力的社会企业参与建设，从而使沙溪古镇投资以“1+N”的模式推进，凭借以政府为引导、以企业为主体、市场化运作的方式，累计吸引国内外个体投资者786户，建成客栈258家、饭店118家。

5. 坚持资源整合。探索活化利用“空心村”、众筹参与乡村建设的投融资路径，分别与多家企业合作开展黄花坪“空心村”活化利用试点、田园综合体试点、老粮库改造利用、北龙村庄房开发利用等项目，高效整合各方资源，努力形成推进沙溪古镇建设的强大合力。

成效

自2017年1月1日以来，沙溪镇通过特色小镇的创建，引入15家各类企业入驻，固定宽带家庭普及率、移动宽带用户普及率达95%，生活垃圾收集处理率达95%，生活污水收集率达80%，特色民宿客栈床位数逾1300张，且各项工作逐步由小镇核心区向周边的四联、东南、沙坪、华龙、灯塔、石龙等村辐射。旅游从业人数逾5000人，年接待游客由2016年的13.9万人次增加到2019年的117.793万人次，旅游社会总收入也由2916万元增加到15.33亿元。2020年，实现居民人均可支配收入10686.72元。

经验与启示

1. 在彰显特色上下功夫。突出民族性、唯一性，用好“茶马古道上唯一幸存的古集市”这张“名片”，强化对古民居、古建筑、古院落的活化利用，做好寺登街古戏台铺面活化利用，植入文化

创意产品。挖掘古镇的民族文化内涵，传承好古镇民俗、历史、美食、农耕、歌舞乐等文化，彰显特色小镇“中国风、世界范、沙溪色”，着力打造全国乃至世界上独一无二、不可复制的特色，形成具有影响力的茶马古道文化品牌效应。

2. 在打造产业上下功夫。积极培育产业新业态，加大文化创意设计，优化文化产品结构，丰富旅游小件、伴手礼种类，注重旅游产品本土化，提升特色旅游商品品质。立足于古镇的特色生态、文化资源和古朴宁静的环境氛围，在“静”和“悟”上做文章，打造茶马古道、古镇古村、生态山水、田园风光等“文化名片”，把沙溪古镇打造成生态优美、民风淳朴、文化独特的健康生活目的地。

3. 在追求卓越上下功夫。加快推动古镇保护、建设和管理的制度化、法治化、精细化进程。立足沙溪特色资源和木雕、石刻、布扎等传统手工艺，打造各类文创体验馆，探索建立多元化体验平台，增强游客的参与度和获得感。发扬工匠精神，精雕细琢、精益求精，把特色小镇建设的每个方面都做到极致，着力打造一流的品牌、实施一流的管理、提供一流的体验，全力建设国际化、生态化的低碳休闲特色小镇。

4. 在高效运营上下功夫。按照“政府引导、企业主体、市场运作、互利共赢”的运营管理模式，大胆创新和尝试，打破古镇传统的管理模式，

创建古镇新的管理模式和运营机制，彻底革除政府管理工作中存在的管理人员紧缺、管理经费紧张、管理效率低下等弊端，全面实现特色小镇的高效管理，为游客提供全方位、高质量服务。

下一步计划

1. 深化全域旅游建设。全域旅游作为一种新型旅游发展模式，以全域范围内新的资源观、时空观、产业观为管理创新理念，不仅注重区域内的自然资源开发、保护和利用，还强调其特色人文资源的保护与宣传，从而形成独特的全域旅游模式。沙溪镇持续挖掘当地民俗、节庆、生活劳动行为等各个方面作为全域旅游的重要资源，进一步促进城乡一体化发展，实现区域经济可持续发展。

2. 深化发展智慧旅游建设。切实抓好智慧水务、智慧停车场、智慧旅游厕所等基础设施的建设。通过 VR 技术在古戏台上再现太子会、火把节、本主节等民俗文化和剑川白曲、霸王鞭等非物质文化遗产，让游客切身感受到沙溪文化的魅力。全面完善提升“一部手机游云南”平台功能，实现游客“食、住、行、游、购、娱”的全面智慧化，把沙溪古镇打造成“一部手机游云南”的智慧旅游新标杆，打造成古朴宁静和创新智慧完美结合的茶马古道文化小镇。

Abstract

Projects such as the creation of characteristic towns and the demonstration of seven continuous traditional villages have led Shaxi Town to focus on its goal of becoming "first class in the world and unique in China." It promotes the all-for-one tourism strategy and puts into practice the "one town leading seven villages" concept. Consequently, the town formed "Sideng Street as the center, villages in basin areas as the areas to influence and mountain villages as the supplement." Also, a boutique scenic spot with unique charm, distinctive characteristics, strong competitiveness and profound cultural connotations was also created. As a result, the town has been rated a national 4A-level tourist attraction. It has also been selected a "national famous historical and cultural town" and "the most beautiful town in China."

Challenges and Problems

Shaxi Town in the Dali Bai Autonomous Prefecture, Yunnan Province, is inhabited mainly by the Bai Nationality and co-inhabited by the Han, Yi and Lisu nationalities. It includes 76 villager groups from 49 natural villages in 14 administrative villages. Improvements and the development of the tourism environment of ancient towns inevitably led to a conflict that has increased the difficulty of managing them.

Adding to this disadvantageous position is the fact that the tourism industry is not sufficiently developed as it is still dominated by accommodation and catering rather than authentic culture and experiences. The advantages of cultural connotations and folk experience characteristics are not brought into full play.

Measures

1. Planning first. The town consistently adheres to the principle of "planning first" which is aimed at transforming it into a place which is "first class in the world and unique in China." It also prepares a people-oriented and an industry-supported plan for a characteristic town based on *The Master Plan of Shaxi Town, Detailed Regulatory Plan of Shaxi Town, Protection Plan of Shaxi Famous Historical and Cultural Town, Measures for Protection and Management of Shaxi Ancient Town, Protection and Development Plan of Shaxi Famous Historical and Cultural Town, and Protection and Development Plan of Shaxi Traditional Village*

Groups, Overall Development Plan of Shaxi Ancient Town (Bai Nationality) and *Detailed Construction Plan of Shaxi Ancient Town (Bai Nationality)*.

2. Style and features preservation. The town has highlighted its distinctive characteristics and worked on full recovery as much as possible. It also repaired several Bai folk houses, streets and the square at Sifang Street. This has led to the completion of the ancient stage, Xingjiao Temple, East Village Gate, South Village Gate, old caravansary and other representative ancient buildings and protected traditional villages. This has highlighted the style of the ancient town, supporting functions and rural scenery. It has also strengthened its cooperation with Switzerland in developing a humanistic, ecological and intelligent Shaxi Town, protect the Bai architecture and style of Shaxi ancient town and promote the experience and concept of ancient architectural restoration to the world.

3. Ecological priority. The town has practiced the development concept of "lucid waters and lush mountains are invaluable assets." It has defined its population, resources and environmental carrying capacity and developed tourism and cultural resources. Also, it controlled all kinds of "warning line" and constrained ecological warning line and basic farmland for itself. In addition, it has constructed infrastructure for urban and rural water supply, sewage and garbage treatment, building a sewage treatment plant and domestic waste transfer center with a daily treatment capacity of 500 cubic meters. This gradually helped in attaining the complete collection and harmless treatment of sewage and domestic waste. Also, it has highlighted the beautification and afforestation of the town, expansion of the green area and water area. At the same time, it has applied green and energy-saving building technologies and has given priority to green and low-carbon materials in selecting construction materials.

4. Enterprises as the main body. The town has adopted the "1 + N" model, and determined Guangdong Aoyuan Culture and Tourism Group Co., Ltd. as the main investor for the building of the characteristic town. Both sides have set up a platform company for joint investment and operation. The village has also attracted domestic well-known enterprises to settle in and started social investment projects. A large number of ambitious and powerful social enterprises are involved

in the construction, advancing the investment in the town based on the "1 + N" model. It has also created a market-oriented operation with government as the guide and enterprises as the main body. It has attracted 786 individual investors at home and abroad, with 258 inns and 118 hotels built.

5. Resource integration. It has explored ways to revitalize the "hollowed village" and mobilize villagers to engage in rural construction through crowdfunding. This has also led to the village carrying out projects such as "hollowed village" activation and utilization pilot in Huanghuaping Village. A pastoral complex pilot, transformation and utilization of old grain depots, as well as development and utilization of Beilong Village houses with enterprises help integrate resources for the town's construction.

Results

Since January 1, 2017, 15 enterprises have been introduced and incorporated into the town. The coverage rate of fixed broadband households and mobile broadband users has reached 95% and the domestic garbage collection and treatment rate is at 95%. Also, the domestic sewage collection rate is 80%, and the number of beds in characteristic B&Bs and inns is more than 1,300. This gradually radiates from the core area of the town to the surrounding villages such as Silian, Dongnan, Shaping, Hualong, Dengta and Shilong. Tourism employees also reached more than 5,000 as the annual tourists received from 139,000 in 2016 increased to 1,177,930 in 2019. The total social income of tourism increased from RMB 29.16 million to 1.533 billion. In 2020, the per capita disposable income of residents reached RMB 10,686.72.

Experience and Inspirations

1. Highlight characteristics. It is necessary to highlight the national characteristics and uniqueness of the village. The project should make good use of its calling card as the only surviving ancient market on Ancient Tea Horse Road and revitalize ancient residences. The buildings and courtyards should also be renovated as well as the ancient shop facades and stages along Sideng Street. Certain cultural and creative products should also get a new look while preserving and maintaining their essence. Continuous efforts should be made to utilize the national cultural connotation of the ancient town. Folk customs, history, food, farming, song, dance and music should be handed down and its "Chinese style, international model, and Shaxi charm" should be tastefully showcased. Also, it must strive to create a unique and unrepeatable characteristics across the country, and even the world, to build an influential brand out of the Ancient Tea Horse Road culture.

2. Build industries. The town has cultivated new industrial business models, boosted cultural and creative design and optimized the structure of cultural products. They have also enhanced certain types of small souvenirs, highlighted the localization of tourism products and improved the quality of characteristic tourism commodities. Moreover, based on its native ecology, cultural resources and tranquil environment, the town has explored the "quietness" and "enlightenment" themes. This helps create cultural cards such as Ancient Tea Horse Road, ancient towns and villages, ecological landscape and pastoral scenery. More importantly, this will result in the town's transformation into a healthy lifestyle destination with beautiful ecology, simple folk customs and unique culture.

3. Pursue excellence. The village has accelerated the institutionalization, legalization and refinement of the protection, construction and management of the ancient town. Based on its local resources and traditional handicrafts such as wood carving, stone carving and fabric handicraft, the town has built various cultural and creative experiential pavilions and established diversified experiential platforms. This has enhanced tourists' participation and has instilled in them a sense of accomplishment. Additionally, it has meticulously carried forward the craftsman spirit for the improvement of its characteristic town. It is working hard to achieve first-class brands, management and experience to build an international and ecological low-carbon leisure town.

4. Operate efficiently. It is important to initiate bold innovations and break away from traditional management models for the ancient town. Existing weak points such as personnel shortage, tight budget and low government management efficiency must be eliminated. Doing this can lead to the efficient management of the characteristic town and the creation of comprehensive high-quality

services for tourists.

Next Steps

1. Improve all-for-one tourism. All-for-one tourism model is an innovative management concept that encompasses resources, time, space and industry. It focuses on the development, protection and utilization of natural resources in the region and emphasizes the protection and publicity of its characteristic cultural attributes. Shaxi Town will continue to capitalize on its local folk customs, festivals and lifestyle and labor characteristics as important resources of all-for-one tourism. This will promote the integrated development of urban and rural areas for a sustainable regional economic development.

2. Develop intelligent tourism. Infrastructure such as intelligent water-related enterprises, intelligent parking lots and intelligent tourism toilets should be emphasized. Through VR technology, local folk festivals and intangible cultural heritage are reproduced on ancient stages to allow tourists to appreciate the charm of the Shaxi culture. Also, more efforts will be made to enhance the function of "traveling around Yunnan through one mobile phone" platform for a comprehensive intelligence in tourists' meals + dining, lodging, transportation, travel, shopping, and entertainment. Transforming the town on Ancient Tea Horse Road into a cultural oasis powered by a new intelligent tourism setup and the combination of simple tranquility and innovative advances should be a top priority.

华侨城：
林芝华侨城南山国际汽车营地助力乡村振兴

Overseas Chinese Town Holdings Company:
Nanshan International Motor Camp in Nyingchi Assists Rural Revitalization

摘 要

林芝华侨城南山国际汽车营地是广东省重点异地产业扶贫项目。汽车营地在建设发展的过程中，始终立足于高端精品的市场定位，通过坚持生态保护、强调产品与自然融合、持续进行产品优化改良、积极开展精细化管理和塑造营地品牌形象等举措，形成了特色化经营。目前，华侨城南山国际汽车营地已成为林芝市新的旅游目的地、高端营地产业的先行探索者，其持续打造的品牌文化提升了营地业态的营销方式和影响力，获得了良好的社会效益，差异化战略对营地行业的良性健康发展起到了积极的促进作用。

挑战与问题

产业结构单一、村民增收渠道少，是西藏林芝市贫困的主要原因之一。林芝虽在农畜产业上有所发展，但受制于规模小、缺少龙头企业支撑、市场对接差、抗风险能力差等原因，产业发展困难重重。另外，贫困家庭面临着文化素质低、生产技术缺乏等问题，直接导致家庭贫困。成人教育未受到足够重视，导致贫困人口始终徘徊于贫困线以下。当地群众的成人文化素质和生存技能亟待提高。

措施

1. 精准扶贫，帮扶到户。按照习近平总书记“实事求是、因地制宜、分类指导、精准扶贫”的要求，以低收入群体、有劳动能力、有开发条件的低保户为主要对象，以改善民生、增加贫困人口收入、增强贫困人口自主发展能力为主线，村委会联合当地政府和驻村工作队，选择最需要帮扶的贫困户，结合当地村民的实际经济情况，有针对性地在营地入口的农田上进行青稞种植。双方协商进行收益分成，主要收成归村民个人所有，这就使村民获得了稳定的经济来源。同时，营地还向游客展现了当地工布藏族农耕生态的原始风貌。

2. 科学规划，突出特色。华侨城以企业的大力支持为后盾，将贫困户“靠山吃山、靠水吃水”的传统思想与林芝的资源特色结合起来，为其摆脱贫困创造契机。林芝华侨城通过《汽车主题公园旅游总体规划》，对项目的远期（“一带一路”）、中期（环湖战略）以及近期（空间站战略）进行规划，与周边村庄联动，利用村庄特有的资源，形成旅游环线，配合当地政府发展环多布湖全域旅游，真正做到“靠山吃山、靠水吃水”，带动了当地经济发展，通过产业扶贫实现了可持续发展。林芝华

侨城南山国际汽车营地自试营业以来，通过全新人文旅游目的地的打造，增加了新的人文景点和住宿设施，丰富了当地的旅游资源和接待设施业态，成为林芝旅游形象的标志。它改善了当地旅游环境，带动了周边旅游经济的发展与产业升级，已经成为川藏线上冉冉升起的崭新旅游目的地。

3. 保护生态，因地制宜。华侨城牢固树立和践行“绿水青山就是金山银山”的发展理念，始终强调保护自然环境，秉承低碳绿色、生态环保的原则，坚持走保护和开发并重、生态与经济双赢的发展道路，坚持绿色发展、生态发展、因地制宜、精准发力。林芝由于区位特殊，植被单纯、生态环境脆弱，再加上高原的气候环境特殊，植被一旦破坏将极难恢复。汽车营地在规划设计和建设的过程中，始终秉持着保护环境和生态建设的理念，实施生态型开发，采用因地制宜、依山就势的方式，尽可能保留原有地块上大面积的松树、青冈树及原生态灌木，减少对当地植被的影响；并且结合景观、产品、流线，利用现有的地形和植被设计安装装配式建筑，把对环境的影响降低到最小，使人文设施与自然景观实现完美融合。

成效

林芝华侨城南山国际汽车营地作为扶贫项目之一，本着“取之于民，用之于民”的理念，从藏文化中来，到藏文化中去。作为近年来新兴的旅游业态，其以高体验性和与当地环境的高互动性，实现了汽车露营地产业与自驾游行业以及当地经济社会发展的共荣共生，促使林芝产业生态链不断丰富。

林芝华侨城南山国际汽车营地还通过提高成人文化素质和生存技能，达到扶志扶贫的目的：帮助村民在“家门口”就业，有效解决了 40 户家庭的就业问题；为员工提供系列专业化技能培训，以助其适应营地的工作标准和现代化社会对人才的素质要求。目前，汽车营地项目共有员工 40 位，其中藏族员工 13 位（包含多布村村民 7 位、西藏籍大学生 6 位），其他少数民族（侗、白、彝族）员工 3 位，少数民族员工人数占营地总人数的 40%。这种通过结合当地实际情况和藏区需求开发人力资源的方式，既解决了藏区贫困人口的就业问题，又将扶贫与扶志、扶智结合了起来，为藏区改变贫困现状持续助力。

经验与启示

1. 因地制宜。扶贫工作的开展，首先要因地

制宜，整合资源。一切方案的制订、措施的落实，都要从实际出发，唯有以现有的条件资源为依托，才能确保扶贫工作见成效。

2.“造血”为主。扶贫工作要以“造血”为主、以“输血”为辅，扶贫一定要解决好内因问题，扶志气、扶观念、扶产业、扶技术，才能持续发展，防止脱贫之后又返贫。

下一步计划

为使林芝这片土地更加富饶、人民生活更加富足，华侨城携手深圳市南山区人民政府，积极承担央企的社会责任，投身到精准扶贫的宏伟事业中。汽车营地从立项伊始，便确定了高品质、高规格、优服务的战略目标，融合社会各界力量形成合力，励志打造精品营地。首先，强调产品的人性化和舒适度，对营地现有的常用住宿产品进行优化和提升，包括设计优化、户型改良、增加设备、顶级配置、软装提升、节能环保，等等，使同样的原材料达到最佳效果。其次，强调产品与自然的融合，让人文性的营地设施成为自然和谐的一部分，使游客在藏区相对极端的气候和自然环境下也能实现都市般的舒适休憩，换来片刻的宁静冥想，增加度假营地的人文气息。最后，强调精细化管理和服务创新，让游客能深度体验藏风和当地特色，提升游客满意度。

Abstract

Overseas Chinese Town Holdings Company (OCT Group) — Nanshan International Motor Camp in Nyingchi City is a key poverty alleviation project for non-local industries in Guangdong Province. The auto camp has always had a foothold in the high-end market. It has operated through ecology protection, product and nature integration, product optimization and a management style that has successfully elevated its brand image and reputation. It has become Nyingchi's new tourist attraction and a pioneer in high-end camp industry. It has continuously upgraded its marketing programs and broadened its influence by focusing on its unique selling proposition. It owes its success to this differentiation strategy.

Challenges and Problems

One of the main causes of poverty is the industrial structure and irregular income channels in Nyingchi City, Xizang Autonomous Region. Despite some progress in the agricultural and livestock industry, Nyingchi City faces many difficulties due to its small scale, lack of support from leading enterprises, poor market connection and lack of resources to overcome its disadvantageous position. Impoverished families are not familiar with production technology and adult education has not drawn enough attention.

Measures

1. Targeted poverty alleviation for assistance to households. As General Secretary Xi Jinping emphasized "seeking truth from facts, adjusting measures according to local conditions, classified guidance and targeted poverty alleviation," the local government and village-led task force helped the village committee in identifying poor households that were in most need of assistance. To increase the income of impoverished households, aid was provided to enable them to plant highland barley in the surrounding fields at the camp's entrance. The two sides negotiated an income-sharing agreement that provides the village with a stable source of livelihood. The main harvest is owned by the villagers, while the camp shows tourists the original local Gongbu Xizang's style of farming ecology.

2. Scientific planning to highlight features. With the support of enterprises, the OCT Group has created opportunities with the traditional characteristics of Nyingchi City. Through *Tourism Master Plan for*

Motor Theme Park, the OCT Group of Nyingchi City made a long-term plan (Belt and Road), midterm (lake surrounding strategy) and near term (spaceport) strategy for surrounding villages. Making use of the village's unique resources, it cooperated with the local government in forming a tourism ring route and to develop tourism for the whole area around Duobu Lake. Since its soft opening, the motor camp has new cultural attractions and accommodation facilities that have come to symbolize Nyingchi's emergence as a tourist destination. It has improved the local tourism environment, fueled economic growth and tourism upgrade in surrounding areas. Now it is known as the new tourist destination on the Sichuan-Xizang highway.

3. Protect ecology and adjust measures according to local conditions. The OCT Group applies the concept of "lucid waters and lush mountains are invaluable assets" for environmental protection. It strives to accomplish green goals of low-carbon emission, ecological and environmental protection while balancing it with economic growth for a win-win outcome. Its location, fragile ecology and highland climate make it extremely difficult to restore ruined vegetation. It adapts measures according to local conditions to retain the original plot on a large area of pine trees, oriental white oak and native shrubs to reduce the impact on local vegetation. Combined with the landscape and products, the prefabricated buildings were designed and installed based on the existing topography and vegetation to minimize their environmental impact and to integrate the cultural facilities with the natural landscape.

Results

As one of the anti-poverty projects, Nanshan International Motor Camp in Nyingchi City is committed to the concept of "from the people and for the people, from Xizang's culture and to Xizang's culture." It recognizes common prosperity and symbiosis with self-driving tour to promote local economic and social development through environmental engagement.

The motor camp helps the poor by improving their skills. It offers jobs to local villagers and has solved the

employment problems of 40 families by providing them with professional skill training programs that meet the camp's work standards and modern society's criteria. There are currently 40 employees in the camp, 13 of whom are Xizang's (seven from Duobu Village and six Xizang's college students included) and three of whom are from other ethnic minorities — Dong, Bai and Yi nationalities. Ethnic minority employees account for 40% of the total. Optimizing human resources and tailoring anti-poverty programs according to local needs help lift Xizang people out of their impoverished situation.

Experience and Inspirations

1. Adjust measures according to local conditions. To carry out poverty alleviation work, we must first adjust measures according to local conditions. Integration of resources is always an important element. The formulation of plans and the implementation of all measures should proceed from reality and rely on existing conditions and resources for them to succeed.

2. Self-reliance. The fight against poverty should focus on "blood generating" supplemented by "blood transfusion." The work of poverty alleviation must focus on finding out the internal causes first before addressing industrial support and technological adoption. A sustainable development is achievable, and a relapse into poverty after successfully getting rid of it is also preventable.

Next Steps

To improve Nyingchi City and the lives of its villagers, the OCT Group and the Shenzhen Nanshan District People's government have undertaken the social responsibility of central enterprises, assuming an active role in the grand cause of targeted poverty alleviation.

Since its initiation, the motor camp has set the strategic goals of high quality, high specification and excellent service. It has gathered together all sectors of society to form a collective force to build a topnotch camp. **First,** to achieve the maximum effect using the same raw materials, it stresses the comfort of its products and optimizes the existing common products in the camp industry: design, home improvement, additional equipment, soft decoration, energy conservation and environmental protection. **Second,** it emphasizes product and nature integration. Humanistic camp facilities have become part of nature, offering tourists a comfortable urban-style rest facility in Xizang's' extreme climate and natural environment. **Third,** to improve tourist satisfaction, it emphasizes quality management and service innovation, allowing visitors to experience authentic Xizang's culture and lifestyle.

山东临沂市兰陵县卞庄镇代村：
“农文旅”三位一体构建乡村振兴“共同体”

Dai Village, Bianzhuang Town, Lanling County, Linyi City, Shandong Province:
Trinity of “Agriculture, Culture, and Tourism” Builds a Community for Rural Revitalization

摘 要

山东省临沂市兰陵县代村通过“擘画蓝图，推进项目落地”“农业旅游迭代升级，壮大集体经济”“连片辐射带动，打造夜经济”等方式，“农文旅”一体开发，构建乡村振兴“共同体”。代村在实现自身脱贫致富的基础上，对乡村振兴先行样板进行了有益探索，具有很强的借鉴意义和启示作用。

挑战与问题

山东临沂市兰陵县代村有 1700 多年的历史，现居住人口 1 万多人，村域面积 3.6 平方公里，经营土地 10000 亩。20 世纪 90 年代，代村是出了名的“散、乱、差”村，村集体负债 380 多万元，人地不均、零散经营。代村旅游业起步较晚，统筹规划薄弱，现有资源潜能挖掘不充分，未能有效“串联”，旅游线路较为单一，且服务理念、服务意识、服务质量等供给层面与游客需求间存在一定差距，旅游业发展滞后，农民收入普遍较低。

措施

1. 科学擘画，全力推进建设。2006 年，《山东省苍山现代农业示范园总体规划》编制完成；2012 年，《兰陵国家农业公园旅游总体规划及重点项目控制性详细规划》编制完成。这些都为代村发展指明了方向。

2. 迭代升级，壮大集体经济。代村土地规模化经营，为农业生产的园区化、集约化和现代化奠定了基础。发展农业观光游，打造了农田景观、竹林水岸、荷花湿地等自然风景；利用沂蒙红色旅游资源优势，打造了建党 100 周年展览馆、幸福家园展馆；运用农业新技术，打造农业体验游，建设了农业科技馆、华夏菜园等集景观与技术推广于一体的室内场馆，使得农业科技互动、农事体验、休闲采摘等休闲旅游内容更加丰富。与此同时，代村不断拓宽旅游产业链，开发“代村优品”，逐步实现了农区、园区、公园、景区的升级迭代。

3. 连片带动，打造夜游经济。代村以农业休闲旅游为主体，发展红色旅游、古镇旅游、田园旅游、工业旅游等多元旅游项目，丰富旅游业态。规划“田园新城”，带动周边方圆 20 平方公里的 12 个村加入“乡村振兴”共同体。培育旅游新业态，投资 2 亿元，打造“印象代村”，融入旅游夜经济

元素，将代村打造成集小吃、百货、休闲娱乐等多功能于一体的夜游目的地。

成效

代村依托兰陵国家农业公园，打造了农业旅游、古村旅游、红色旅游等旅游项目，形成“农业 + 文化 + 旅游”一体发展模式，目前累计已帮助200多个村10000多个贫困户脱贫。即便在疫情防控常态化的2020年，代村仍安全接待游客100万人次，全年旅游综合收入7000多万元，门票纯收入2600余万元。代村人在代村党委书记王传喜的带领下，将一个负债近400万元的贫困村，发展为2020年村集体各业总产值36亿元、村集体纯收入1.5亿元、村民年人均纯收入7万元的先进村，实现了“幼有早育、学有优教、劳有多得、病有良医、老有颐养、住有宜居、弱有善扶”的民生目标。通过可持续发展，代村先后荣获“中国最美休闲乡村”“全国十佳休闲农庄”“全国休闲农业与乡村旅游五星级企业”等称号。

经验与启示

“农文旅”一体开发构建乡村振兴“共同体”，是代村在实现自身脱贫致富的基础上，对乡村振兴先行样板进行的有益探索，具有很强的借鉴意义和启示作用。

1. 发挥领头雁效应、全民参与，是全面脱贫、乡村振兴的内生动力。乡村能人在基层社会中扮演

着重要角色，能够聚拢村民形成合力。代村党委书记王传喜团结带领全体村民，以创新农村经济经营管理模式为抓手，探索构建农业与二、三产业融合的现代产业体系，使代村从一个“脏乱穷差”的贫困落后村，发展成为乡村振兴的“排头兵”。

2. 坚持以农促旅、农旅示范，是全面脱贫、乡村振兴的有效路径。代村利用城乡结合部的区位优势，在发展农业的同时，重视旅游业发展。兰陵国家农业公园是全国第一个试点，是现代新型农业旅游区、乡村旅游综合体，集新农村建设、观光农业、农产品消费于一体，有机融合了农耕田区、农村社区、农业园区、农业景区、农业展区。以代村为中心辐射周边区域经济发展，有利于构建全农业产业链条，可以使农民不离土、不离农、不离产、不离乡，村民共同脱贫致富，从而实现农村美、农民富、农业强的愿景。

3. 深化文旅融合、筑基强魂，是全面脱贫、乡村振兴的重要抓手。文化是灵魂，红色历史与现代科技为代村旅游业发展提供了持久生命力与影响力。在革命战争年代，代村曾是沂蒙红色堡垒村。

而今，村中有占地 1600 余平方米的村史馆，将红色文化融入乡村文明，填补了红色旅游的空白。2020 年，代村新建“百年大党　风华正茂”纪念建党 100 周年主题展馆，进一步丰富了红色旅游的内容。一代又一代代村人在长期生产实践中不断发扬中华民族优秀传统文化、传承沂蒙精神，谱写出“爱国爱村、大气谦和、朴实守信、勇于拼搏”的代村篇章。

下一步计划

“农文旅”开发模式，是现代农业发展的必然走向，为乡村发展提供了广阔的发展空间，是推动乡村振兴的有力引擎和新的增长点。进入新阶段，代村将切实巩固脱贫攻坚成果，并将其与乡村振兴有效衔接，全面实现乡村振兴：一是打造一个国家先行样板区。把区域旅游范围扩大到 20 平方公里以外，使旅游项目更加丰富多元、服务乡村振兴作用更加突出、带动作用更加明显。二是建设现代农民共享城。打造城市休闲旅游“后花园”，落地实施覆盖 12 个村庄、1 个国营农场的“田园新城”规划，培育“田园”特色旅游。集中力量打造一座“亦城亦乡亦园，宜居宜业宜游”的农民之城。三是构建全链系统物联网，融入“低碳理念”，推行规模化和集约经营，提高市场开发和运营效率。构建物联网平台终端系统，形成“终端订货—农贸园区—物流配送”链条，创新多元化运营模式，让农民能更多地分享农产品流通带来的利润。

Abstract

The Dai Village in Lanling County, Linyi City, Shandong Province, has undertaken projects based on scientific planning. It has also upgraded agricultural tourism for a robust collective economy and created a night economy through the integrated development of "agriculture, culture, and tourism." Also, it has explored a pioneering information-based model for rural revitalization.

Challenges and Problems

With its more than 1,700 years of history and a population of more than 10,000 people, the village covers an area of 3.6 square kilometers with a usable land of 10,000 *mu*. In the 1990s, it was a "scattered, chaotic and poor" village. A collective debt of more than RMB 3.8 million, uneven distribution ratio between its population and land and haphazard management contributed to its lack of development. Weak overall planning, inadequate utilization of resources, failure to integrate these resources, single tourism route and the gap between service concept, awareness and quality at the supply level and the tourists' demand were among the problems that led to the village's lagging tourism development and low income of its farmers.

Measures

1. Promote construction through scientific planning. In 2006, the village compiled the *Master Plan for Cangshan Modern Agriculture Demonstration Park in Shandong Province* and in 2012 it compiled the *Master Plan for Lanling National Agricultural Park Tourism and Detailed Planning on Key Project Regulation* which clarified the direction for its development.

2. Boost the collective economy through upgrade. The scaled operation of the village's land area has laid a foundation for the zoning, intensification and modernization of agricultural production. To develop agricultural sightseeing tours, it enhanced natural scenery such as farmland landscapes, bamboo forests on the riverbanks and lotus wetlands. It has also developed the Exhibition Hall for the 100th Anniversary of the Founding of the Communist Party of China and the Happy Home Exhibition Hall by capitalizing on the red culture tourism resources of the Yimeng mountainous area. Moreover, it has applied new agricultural technologies to develop experiential tours and established indoor venues by promoting the landscape and technology integration in places such as the Agriculture Science Museum and the Huaxia Vegetable Garden. All these have enriched leisure tourism, including agricultural technology interaction, agricultural experience and leisure picking. The village has expanded its tourism industrial chain and developed "superior products," which has led to the gradual upgrade of farming areas, industrial parks, parks, and scenic spots.

3. Develop a night tour economy through contiguous driving. With agricultural leisure tourism as the main body, the village has developed diversified tourism projects such as red tourism, ancient town tourism, rural tourism, and industrial tourism. It has planned "new pastoral towns" to encourage 12 surrounding villages with 20 square kilometers to join the rural revitalization community. Also, it has fostered new business tourism models with an investment of RMB 200 million to create an "Impression Village" and integrate the elements of a night tourism economy. Through these measures, the village has been transformed into a night tour destination, offering snacks, general merchandise, leisure and entertainment.

Results

With the Lanling National Agricultural Park as the foundation, the village has implemented projects such as agricultural tourism, ancient village tourism, and red tourism. More importantly, it has formed an integrated development model of "agriculture + culture + tourism," helping more than 10,000 impoverished households in over 200 villages move out of poverty. Despite the regular epidemic prevention and control in 2020, the village still managed to welcome 1 million tourists, generating a comprehensive tourism income of more than RMB 70 million and a net income from ticket sales exceeding RMB 26 million. Under the able leadership of Wang Chuanxi, the poverty-stricken Dai Village that was saddled with a debt of nearly RMB 4 million was developed and became a progressive place. In 2020, it had a total output value of RMB 3.6 billion from all industries in the village collective, a net income of RMB 150 million from the village collective and a per capita net income of RMB 70,000. It has improved people's livelihood through "early childbearing, quality education for study, more pay for work, qualified doctors for the sick, care for the elderly, livable residences and assistance for the weak." Its sustainable development has earned the village awards such as the "Most Beautiful Leisure Village in China," "National Top Ten Leisure Farms," and "National Leisure Agriculture and Rural Tourism Five-star Enterprise."

Experience and Inspirations

The village has promoted the integrated development of "agriculture, culture, and tourism" to build a rural revitalization community guided by a pioneering model based on an enlightened leadership.

1. Leading role players and mass participation are the driving force for poverty alleviation and rural revitalization. Capable people are the grassroots of poverty alleviation and rural revitalization. They play an important role in forging a strong collective force of villagers. Wang Chuanxi, Secretary of the Party committee of Dai Village, led all villagers in exploring the construction of a modern industrial integration system that melds together agriculture, secondary and tertiary industries. Through an innovative rural economic operation and management model, the village has transformed into a rural revitalization "vanguard" from a "dirty, chaotic, poor, and backward" village.

2. Perseverance in promoting tourism through agriculture and developing an agricultural tourism model is an effective way for poverty alleviation and rural revitalization. By utilizing the location of the urban-rural fringe area, the village has emphasized tourism development while developing agriculture. The Lanling National Agricultural Park is the first pilot in China. It is a new, modern agricultural tourism area and a rural tourism complex which combines new rural construction, agricultural sightseeing and product consumption. The Park organically integrates farming areas, rural communities, agricultural parks, scenic spots and exhibition areas. With it at the center, Dai Village has radiated economic development to the surrounding areas and built an entire agricultural industrial chain to ensure the continuous engagement of farmers in their hometown's agricultural industries. Through this mechanism, the villagers can move out of poverty and fulfill its potential of becoming a beautiful village with high-income farmers and a flourishing agriculture.

3. Strengthening cultural tourism integration is an important means for poverty alleviation and rural revitalization. While culture is the soul, red history, modern science and technology are the lifeblood that provide lasting vitality and influence for the village's tourism development. During the Revolutionary War, the village was a red fortress with the Yimeng mountainous area as its protective wall. The Village History Museum covers an area of more than 1,600 square meters; it's a showcase of the integration of red tourism and rural culture. In 2020, a new exhibition hall with the "Centenary Party in its Prime" as the theme was built to commemorate the 100th Anniversary of the Founding of the Communist Party of China. Through long-term production and practice, generations of villagers have carried forward the excellent traditional Chinese culture, nurtured the Yimeng spirit, and cultivated the "country-loving, village-loving, generous, modest, honest, trustworthy, and courageous" spirit.

Next Steps

The "agriculture, culture, and tourism" integrated development model represents a modern trend that

provides a sizable space for rural development. It is a powerful, new engine that drives rural revitalization. After entering a new phase, the village will consolidate the results of poverty alleviation and rural revitalization. **First,** a national pilot model area will be created. The area of regional tourism will be expanded to more than 20 square kilometers for the enrichment and diversification of tourism projects. **Second,** a modern shared city for farmers will be built. The village will develop a "back garden" to support urban leisure tourism, implement the "new pastoral towns" plan for 12 villages and one state-owned farm. Also, it will develop characteristic "pastoral" tourism, focusing its efforts on building a town of peasants. Such will be characterized by the concept of "integration of a town, a township, and a garden, and suitability for living, working and traveling." **Third,** a full-chain system based on the Internet of Things will be developed. The "low-carbon concept" should be incorporated for a scaled and intensive operation to improve the efficiency of market development and operation. Additionally, a terminal system anchored on the Internet of Things platform will be established to form a chain of "terminal ordering-agricultural trade parks-logistics distribution." This will also be utilized for the development of new diversified operation models that will help farmers earn more profits from the circulation of agricultural products.

宁夏贺兰山东麓葡萄产业园区管理委员会：

葡萄酒文旅融合模式

Administrative Committee of the Grape Industrial Park in the Eastern Foot of Helan Mountain, Ningxia Hui Autonomous Region:

"Integration of Wine and Cultural Tourism" Model

摘 要

宁夏葡萄产业的综合发展，在带动产区村民脱贫致富、农业增效、企业获利等方面发挥了巨大的作用，它将宁夏本土文化、葡萄酒文化、“绿进沙退”治沙文化等与旅游产业发展相结合，是一产、二产、三产有机结合的特色产业。宁夏贺兰山东麓葡萄产业园区管理委员会为葡萄酒产业提供创新内生动力，走出了独特的葡萄酒文旅融合创新开发助力乡村振兴之路，不仅有效突破了发展瓶颈，还形成了一系列引领产业发展的“三产”融合创新模式。

挑战与问题

宁夏贺兰山东麓产区在酿酒葡萄种植方面有着得天独厚的自然地理环境。作为受欧盟保护的中国首批地理标志，宁夏贺兰山东麓葡萄酒已经被《世界葡萄酒地图》和《全球葡萄酒旅游最佳应用》两本国际刊物收录。自 2014 年宁夏贺兰山东麓葡萄产业园区管委会成立至今，产区已有建成投产的酒庄 101 家，酿酒葡萄种植面积 49.2 万亩，年生产优质葡萄酒 1.3 亿瓶。在国际、国内广泛关注贺兰山东麓产区的情况下，如何高效发挥葡萄产业一、二、三产业高度融合的特质，做好葡萄种植、酿造生产和文旅体验融合发展，满足市场多元需求，实现产业高效可持续发展，就成了管委会面临的主要挑战。

措施

1. 聚集葡萄酒产业发展人才。葡萄酒三产融合创新发展，需要从业人员既具有一定的葡萄种植和葡萄酒酿造储存专业知识，又能对当前文旅市场热门趋势拥有敏锐的嗅觉，更需要有接轨国际著名产区发展模式的国际化视野，所以它对人才的整合与创新能力要求非常高。管委会广泛吸引来自浙江大学、复旦大学、南开大学、中山大学、美国普渡大学等国内外近 30 名专家，共同为宁夏葡萄产业综合开发提供智力支持。

2. 建立葡萄酒产业发展智库。创新宁夏本地与东部沿海城市的联动机制，探索建设葡萄酒指数研究院，研究发布产业指数、消费指数、品牌指数和葡萄酒文旅指数等指数体系；制定葡萄酒旅游服务标准，开发葡萄酒文化创意产品；开展葡萄酒产业链延伸的模式和策略研究、葡萄酒旅游融合创新的机制和模式研究、葡萄酒旅游市场研究、葡萄酒旅游融合创新的产品和服务设计、葡萄酒康养目的地研究等，全面推动和促进宁夏贺兰山东麓葡萄酒产业向文旅融合的方向高质量创新发展，提升葡萄酒产业竞争力。

3. 建立葡萄酒产业发展联盟。贺兰山东麓葡萄酒虽然在全球主要消费国有相当大的知名度，但主流产品价格偏高，在银川、中卫等宁夏本地市场和国内其他地区的消费量不大，且酒庄及周边文化旅游设施和服务配套相对滞后，现有葡萄酒相关的文化旅游体验活动以采摘、品酒和酒窖参观游览为

主。在文旅市场消费以休闲度假和亲子体验等为主的情况下，管委会积极联系沙坡头、黄河宿集、镇北堡影视城等主要旅游和度假景区，以及张裕摩塞尔、源石、西鸽等主要旅游酒庄，加强合作，丰富和提升葡萄酒旅游产业体验型产品与服务的内容与质量。

成效

产区葡萄产业综合开发的观光旅游模式、亲子休闲模式、节事驱动模式、经销商接待体验模式等逐渐成为全国范本，张裕摩塞尔十五世酒庄、志辉源石酒庄、巴格斯酒庄、贺东庄园、米擒酒庄、玉泉国际酒庄、森淼酒庄 7 家酒庄被评为 A 级景区，且已在农村环境治理、农民就业增收、农业增产提效等方面发挥了显著的作用。葡萄产业综合开发提供就业岗位已超过 12 万个。

在管委会的长期努力下，联合产区酒庄创新推出一系列推广行动，如在本地产区举办国际葡萄酒旅游博览会，在外部客源市场举办葡萄酒品鉴体验推广会，在互联网渠道设立葡萄酒虚拟体验展厅，最大限度确保产区信息的立体化展示。2019 年新冠肺炎疫情暴发前以及 2021 年疫情得到有效控制后，贺兰山东麓产区酒庄接待游客数量，始终是自治区休闲旅游接待量的重要组成部分，志辉源石酒庄、张裕摩塞尔十五世酒庄等，游客年接待量增长率始终保持在 20% 左右。

经验与启示

1. 确定发展思路。宁夏将发展葡萄产业作为脱贫的根本之策，依托葡萄产业这一“紫色名片”发展特色优势产业，因地制宜，把发展葡萄酒产业同加强黄河滩区治理、加强生态恢复结合起来，提高技术水平，增加文化内涵，加强宣传推介，打造知名品牌，不断增加附加值、提高综合效益。用葡萄酒文旅高质量发展模式，为乡村脱贫和振兴提供引领示范。

2. 明确发展模式。宁夏产区依托中国（宁夏）贺兰山东麓国际葡萄酒博览会永久会址、红酒一条街、闽宁扶贫（葡萄酒）产业园、中国酒业协会葡萄酒培训中心、贺兰红酒庄、贺兰山东麓葡萄酒教育学院等，探索建设葡萄酒工业旅游基地、文商旅综合体、研学基地、酒庄民宿、酒庄设计酒店等文旅新业态，将闽宁镇打造成贺兰山东麓葡萄酒全产业链聚集展示中心，使其成为集历史观光、文化体验、文创产品展示、研学教育、品酒活动等于一体的产区文化地标。

下一步计划

2021 年，国务院批准《宁夏国家葡萄及葡萄酒产业开放发展综合试验区建设总体方案》，该试验区是国务院批准设立的我国西部第一个国家级农业类开放试验区。目标到 2025 年，贺兰山东麓酿酒葡萄基地总规模达到 100 万亩，年产葡萄酒 3 亿瓶以上，实现综合产值 1000 亿元。为确保实现发展目标，管委会将在自治区党委和政府的领导下，进一步发挥产区资源、政策优势，加强与东部沿海地区高校和市场的联动，推动“葡萄酒 + 文旅”产业融合发展，整合贺兰山东麓的史前文化、农耕文化、西夏文化、黄河文化和移民文化，做强做透“葡萄酒 + 文旅”产业链，形成具有中国特色的葡萄产业综合开发示范样本。

Abstract

The grape industry in Ningxia Hui Autonomous Region has achieved comprehensive development and played a prominent role in lifting villagers in the wine region out of poverty. It has improved agricultural efficiency and increased profit from enterprises. The industry integrates Ningxia's local culture, wine culture, and sand containment through "afforestation for desertification control." Rural tourism development has organically created a new enterprise which is a combination of the primary, secondary and tertiary industries. The Administrative Committee of the Grape Industrial Park in the Eastern Foot of Helan Mountain, Ningxia Hui Autonomous Region, has provided the endogenous push for innovation in the wine industry. It blazed a unique path to rural revitalization through the integration of wine and cultural tourism. This breaks through the bottleneck on development and creates the innovative three industries' integration to spearhead development.

Challenges and Problems

Ningxia Wine Region at Helan Mountains' Eastern Foot boasts a unique natural and geographical environment for wine production and grape planting. At Ningxia Wine Helan Mountains' Eastern Foot, the first batch of geographical indications in China protected by the European Union have been included in two international publications. Since the establishment of the administrative committee in 2014, 101 wineries have been built and put into production in the region, with a grape planting area of 492,000 *mu*, and an annual production of 130 million bottles of quality wine. The attention the village has received has led to more challenges for it. The Ningxia Region at Helan Mountains' Eastern Foot faces administrative committees that seek to utilize the highly integrated characteristics of the primary, secondary, and tertiary industries of the grapes. In addition, the committee is focused on developing the planting of grapes, brewing effective developments for a sustainable industrial development.

Measures

1. Assemble talents for wine industry development. The development of this industry requires that the village employees possess certain expertise in grape planting, winemaking, and storage. Also, it requires people who are skilled in current cultural tourism and international trends. Thus, employment requirements are demanding. The administrative committee has widely attracted nearly 30 experts from home and abroad, including Zhejiang University, Fudan University, Nankai University, Sun Yat-sen University, and Purdue University in the US, to jointly provide intellectual support for the comprehensive development of the wine industry in Ningxia Hui Autonomous Region.

2. Establish a think tank for wine industry development. The administrative committee has developed a new linkage mechanism between Ningxia and other cities. The goal of this project is to establish a wine index research institute that would study index systems, consumption index, and brand index. The committee has also formulated wine tourism services and has developed wine cultural and creative products. In addition, it has conducted research into the model and strategy of wine industry chain, extension and the mechanism, of wine tourism integration and innovation. The goal of this is to promote the high-quality innovative development of Ningxia wine industry at Helan Mountains' eastern foot into the cultural tourism integration and enhance the competitiveness of the wine industry.

3. Form alliances for wine industry development. The Ningxia Wine at Helan Mountains' Eastern Foot is well known in major consumer countries worldwide. However, the prices of mainstream products are relatively high in the local Ningxia markets such as Yinchuan City and Zhongwei City. The cultural tourism and supporting service facilities of wineries are not as advanced as they should be. However, the industry of wine tasting, grape picking and winery visits are considered major rural tourism experiences. The administrative committee has contacted major tourist consumption markets such as Shapotou, Huanghe Suji, and the China Western Film Studios, as well as major tourist wineries such as Chateau Changyu Moser XV, Yuanshi Vineyard and Xige Estate for better cooperation and to enhance the experience-oriented products and services of the wine tourism industry.

Results

The models, developed based on the wine industry in Ningxia Wine Region at Helan Mountains' Eastern Foot, have become national models for sightseeing, parent-child leisure, and festival driven events. Chateau Changyu Moser XV, Yuanshi Vineyard, Chateau Bacchus, Chateau Hedong, Chateau Miqin, Chateau Yuquan, and Chateau Senmiao, have been rated A-level tourist attractions. These seven tourists' wineries played a prominent role in rural environmental governance, farmers' employment, income increase, agricultural production and efficiency growth. The comprehensive development of the grape industry has provided more than 120,000 job opportunities.

The administrative committee has joined hands with wineries in the local region with long term efforts in

mind. In addition, they have held wine expos and tasting experiences. The committee has established relations with external customer markets and set up virtual experience halls to ensure the three-dimensional display of informing the public about the project. Before COVID-19, the tourists reception by the wineries in Ningxia Wine Region at Helan Mountains' Eastern Foot has always constituted an important part of leisure tourism reception of the autonomous region. And the growth rate of the annual reception of the wineries such as Yuanshi Vineyard and Chateau Changyu Moser XV is maintained at about 20%.

Experience and Inspirations

1. Determine development ideas. The high quality development model of wine cultural tourism is adopted to guide rural poverty alleviation resources. This is done through the development of the grape industry and the reliance on the "purple brand." This brand is characteristic and advantageous to industrial development and Ningxia has locally-adapted measures based on the native environment. They have also combined the development of the wine industry with the management of the Yellow River beach area and ecological restoration. This is expected to lead to improved technology, enhanced cultural connotation, and increase in publicity. The model of high quality development of wine and cultural tourism is adopted to guide rural poverty alleviation and revitalization.

2. Clarify development models. The Ningxia wine region has explored new cultural and tourism business modes such as the wine industry tourism bases, culture, business and tourism complexes, research bases, winery B&Bs, and winery design hotels. This was done in reliance to the Ningxia (China) International Wine Expo at Helan Mountains' Eastern Foot, a red wine street, Minning Poverty Alleviation (Wine) Industrial Park, Wine Training Center of China Alcoholic Drinks Association,

and Chateau Helanhong. The goal is to build a mining town that will serve as an assembly exhibition center for the entire wine industry chain at Helan Mountains' Eastern Foot. This spot will also be the wine region's cultural landmark that integrate historical sightseeing, cultural experiences and wine tasting.

Next Steps

In 2021, the State Council approved the General Plan for *the Construction of Ningxia National Open Development Comprehensive Pilot Zone for Grape and Wine Industry*. This was the first national level agricultural open pilot zone in Western China that was approved by the State Council. By 2025, the total scale of wine brewing at the base of the Helan Mountains' Eastern Foot is expected to reach about 1 million *mu* generating more than 300 million bottles of wine with a value of RMB 100 billion. The administrative committee will work to achieve this goal by giving full play to the resources in the wine region and policy advantages and strengthened interactions with colleges and universities. It will also promote the integrated development of "wine+cultural tourism" industry. In addition, it will focus on the prehistoric culture, farming culture, and immigration of Western Xia culture at the Yellow River.

重庆酉阳土家族苗族自治县车田乡：

规划发动　示范带动　文化驱动　融合联动　改革推动

Chetian Township, Youyang Tujia and Miao Autonomous County, Chongqing Municipality:

Planning Pioneering, Demonstration Leading, Culture Driving, Integration and Interaction, Reform Propelling

摘要

2017 年，车田乡被确定为重庆市深度贫困乡镇，重庆市文化旅游委扶贫集团入驻车田乡，着力实施规划发动、示范带动、文化驱动、融合联动和改革推动五大扶贫系统工程，全力助推脱贫攻坚，布局衔接乡村振兴。车田乡依托资源禀赋优势，坚持政府引导、市场主导、群众主体，因地制宜、因势利导，科学编制规划，完善配套设施，深入挖掘土苗文化，大力发展乡村旅游，坚持“一乡一业”“一村一品”的发展思路，构建起村村有特色产业、户户有增收项目、人人有致富门路的产业格局。

挑战与问题

重庆市酉阳县车田乡距离酉阳县城75公里，辖区面积72平方公里，下辖4个行政村22个村民小组，总人口8414人，土家族、苗族居多，占总人口的95%以上。辖区森林覆盖率高，生态环境好，冬暖夏凉，气候宜人，土苗文化底蕴浓厚，历史文化底蕴深厚。车田乡虽有得天独厚的优势，但群众等靠要思想依然严重，主动性不强；注重眼前利益得失，缺乏长远发展思维，眼界不广；旅游业态单一，旅游产品开发不足、体量小。

措施

1. 规划发动，为脱贫攻坚谋划。市县乡共同制订了车田乡《脱贫攻坚三年发展规划》《旅游度假区规划》和《集镇风貌改造规划》，聚焦解决“两不愁三保障”突出问题，着眼产业发展和乡村振兴，围绕“游客为什么来？”“怎样来？”“来干什么？”等系列问题，为脱贫攻坚装上“加速器”，使发展步入快车道。

2. 示范带动，为集体经济造血。车田乡在4个村开展示范带动运营，建成“村级旅游示范点”，作为村集体资产，辅以土苗民居旧危房保护改造和人居环境打造，完善提升示范运营的软硬件水平，建立起管用一体化机制。示范旅游村带动全乡“桃源人家”民宿发展233家、“森林人家”20家，其中贫困户70多户，带动村民就业、产业发展和农产品销售。

3. 文化驱动，为旅游产业夯基。车田乡通过“保护一座天龙山”“挖掘一个lia娲洞”“呈现一座土司城”“建设一个文化中心”“建立一个苗绣非遗扶贫工坊”“原创一首《lia娲她是谁》歌曲”等文化驱动工程，挖掘整理车田乡的历史文化资源，为旅游发展提供文化支撑、讲述历史故事、涵养互动场所，使车田的旅游立得住、走得远。

4. 融合联动，为产业发展赋能。市、县、乡、村四级联动，农、文、旅融合联动，各部门单位合力联动，着眼“一村一品、一组一特”，着力形成生态康养、田园综合、农林观光、农耕体验的特色化、差异化发展格局，使车田乡望得见山、看得到水、留得住乡愁。

5. 改革推动，为“三农”改革加速。在文旅融合中“政府搭台、市场运作、群众参与”，引入国有和民营主体，以“市场主体+专业合作社+

农户”的方式，探索“三变”改革和“租金 + 薪金 + 股金”的“三金”模式，加强集体经济与农户、贫困户的利益联结，力求形成可持续发展的体制机制，增强发展的内生动力。

成效

通过以旅游为抓手，车田乡推动脱贫攻坚取得全面胜利：3 个行政村顺利摘帽，脱贫 624 户 2797 人，年人均纯收入从 2014 年的 6005 元增长到 2020 年的 11000 元；建成“桃源人家”民宿 233 家、森林人家 20 家，年均接待游客 70000 余人次，户均增收 10000 余元；被重庆市评为“乡村旅游示范乡镇”。

经验与启示

1. 构建工作合力。脱贫攻坚是一项系统工程，要统揽整合各方力量，构建起“专业扶贫、行业扶贫、社会扶贫”互为补充的大扶贫格局；既要发挥帮扶作用，又要充分调动贫困群众自身的积极性，坚持同心协力，形成合力。

2. 挖掘全乡资源。车田乡围绕乡村旅游和特色产业发展，精准施策，对症下药，统筹指导全乡的产业扶贫，积极转变发展观念，拓展创新思路，

充分挖掘全乡资源禀赋特色。采取政府引导、国企引领、市场带动、群众主体的办法，规模化、产业化发展油茶等绿色有机特色农业；依托优良的自然生态、优美的田园风光、凉爽的气候条件，大力发展乡村旅游，打造农旅融合示范园，不断提升贫困地区发展的内生动力。

3. 强化资金保障。三年来，市县各级各部门全力倾斜支持，共投入 6 亿多元用于脱贫攻坚基础设施、乡村旅游、产业发展、公共服务等多个方面的建设，构建起“新增脱贫攻坚资金优先满足、新增脱贫攻坚项目优先布局、新增脱贫攻坚举措优先集中”的政策保障体系。

下一步计划

一是加强市场机制培育和改革创新。要想确保产业发展早见规模、早出成效，龙头引领是关键。坚持国有企业示范引领、各类市场主体广泛参与，深化农村“三变改革”，全面流转荒地，建设果园、茶园、花园，落实政策支撑、财政撬动，发挥市场主体、市场资金在产业发展中的关键作用，持续推动旅游经济发展壮大。二是推动特色产业可持续发展。坚持因地制宜、因势利导，全域规划布局特色产业。充分发挥生态和旅游资源禀赋优势，科学确立以油茶、茶叶和乡村旅游为主攻方向，以中药材、叶用枸杞、经果林等小品种产业为有效补充，长短结合、全域发展、整体推进的产业发展思路。

Abstract

When the Chetian Township in Chongqing Municipality was categorized as severely impoverished in 2017, the Poverty Alleviation Group of Chongqing Culture and Tourism Development Commission began to settle there. They were tasked to implement the poverty alleviation projects on five aspects of "planning pioneering, demonstration leading, culture driving, integration and interaction, and reform propelling," for poverty alleviation and rural revitalization. Endowed with abundant resources, the Chetian Township has formulated scientific plans, improved supporting facilities, adapted measures according to local condition and explored the Tujia and Miao cultures for the prosperous development of rural tourism by adhering to the principles of government guidance and market leadership. The township upholds the "one industry for one township" and "one product for one village" concepts. It has developed an industrial pattern featuring "distinctive industries for each village, income-increasing projects for each household, and prosperity-achieving ways for each villager."

Challenges and Problems

The Chetian Township is 75 kilometers away from Youyang County, with an area of 72 square kilometers. It includes four administrative villages and 22 groups of villagers with a total population of 8,414—of which the Tujia and Miao minorities account for more than 95% of the total. With extensive forest coverage and beautiful ecological environment, it enjoys fair weather conditions, warm in winter and cool in summer. It boasts profound historical and cultural assets, owing to the rich cultural backgrounds of the Tujias and Miaos. Despite its unique advantage, the masses still rely on national aid and fiscal appropriation or poverty alleviation funds. Lacking the necessary skills for advancement and local gainful activities, they focus on immediate, short-term benefits.

Measures

1. Poverty alleviation planning. The township, county and city, have jointly formulated *Three-Year Development Plan for Poverty Alleviation, Planning on Tourism Resorts* and *Renovation Plan on Town Look and Style* for the Chetian Township. It is focused on ensuring that rural poor people will not have to worry about food and clothing, access to compulsory education, basic medical services and safe housing with the goal of

industrial development and rural revitalization. Answers to such fundamental questions as "why do tourists come," "how do they come" and "what do they come here for" are important for the planning and implementation of poverty-alleviation measures.

2. Demonstration-led collective economy transformation. Four villages in Chetian Township have tried the demonstration-led operation, building it into the "village-level tourism demonstration site" as their collective asset. They work hard to protect and transform old dilapidated houses of the Tujia and Miao villagers and build human settlements. This has resulted in the improvement of the software and hardware of demonstration operations, and the establishment of a management-use integration mechanism. The demonstration tourism village has promoted the development of 233 "Taoyuan Renjia" B&Bs and 20 "Senlin Renjia" B&Bs in the township, including more than 70 impoverished households, facilitating the employment of villagers, industrial development and sales of agricultural products.

3. A culture-driven foundation for the tourism industry. The Chetian Township has fully utilized its historical and cultural resources by implementing culture-driven projects such as the protection of Tianlong Mountain, Liawa Cave excavation, Tusi Town presentation, building of a cultural center, establishment of a poverty alleviation workshop for intangible cultual heritage such as Miao embroidery and the *Who Is Liawa* composition. The cultural support, historical stories and interactive sites for tourism development assure a lasting development for the Chetian Township.

4. Integration and interaction to empower industrial development. The interaction among the village, township, county and city; the integration of agriculture,

culture and tourism; and the joint efforts of various departments and units, have resulted in a localized and differentiated development template featuring ecological health, rural complex, agriculture and forestry tourism and farming experience. The focus on "one product for one village, one specialty for one team," is designed to ensure the Chetian Township retains its original natural environment.

5. Accelerating the reform of "agriculture, rural areas and farmers." To comply with the principle of "government bridging, market operation, and mass participation" in the culture-tourism integration, state-owned and private entities are brought together to explore the "three changes" reform (turning resources into assets, villagers into shareholders, and capital into equity) and the "three funds" model (rent + salary + equity capital) through "market entities + professional cooperatives + peasant households." The interaction among various agencies and local villages enhances endogenous sphere of influence and puts in place a sustainable development system for the benefit of farmers and poverty-stricken households.

Results

Tourism development has facilitated the all-round success of the Chetian Township in the battle against poverty. A total of 2,797 people from 624 households in three administrative villages have been lifted out of poverty. The per capita net income has increased from RMB 6,005 in 2014 to RMB 11,000 in 2020. Two hundred thirty three (233) "Taoyuan Renjia" B&Bs and 20 "Senlin Renjia" B&Bs have been established, with an average annual reception of more than 70,000 people. The average income increase of households is over RMB 10,000 and the township has been rated a rural tourism demonstration township in Chongqing Municipality.

Experience and Inspirations

1. Make joint efforts in work. Since poverty alleviation is a systematic project, it's necessary to integrate all forces to build a poverty alleviation pattern in which poverty alleviation through expertise, poverty alleviation through industrial development and poverty alleviation through social assistance are supplemented with each other. In addition, it's necessary to play the role of assistance and fully mobilize the enthusiasm of impoverished people, thus making joint efforts for poverty alleviation.

2. Full utilization of the township's resources. With the development of rural tourism and characteristic industries as its anchor, the Chetian Township has implemented spot-on policies for specific issues. Through collaborative and coordinated activities, it has implemented poverty-alleviating measures, changed development concepts, expanded innovative ideas and explored the characteristics of resources. Additionally, the township has adopted the "government guidance, state-owned enterprises leading, market driving, and the main body of the masses" framework to develop green and organic local agriculture through large

scale industrialization. It is working hard to develop rural tourism and create demonstration parks with the integration of agriculture and tourism based on its sound ecological environment, idyllic scenery and cool climate.

3. Provide strong funding support. Over the past three years, the municipal and county departments at all levels have given their full support and have invested more than RMB 600 million in infrastructure construction for poverty alleviation, rural tourism, industrial development and public services. They have established a policy support system prioritizing the allocation of new funds, arrangements for new projects and new measures focused on poverty alleviation.

Next Steps

First, strengthen the development of market mechanisms, reform and innovation. It is crucial to adhere to the guidelines of flagship-led enterprises to ensure the scale of industrial development and early attainment of results. We will persist in the demonstration and leadership of state-owned enterprises and extensive participation of various market entities. To promote tourism economy and industrial development, we will strengthen the "three changes" reform in rural areas, transfer wasteland in an all-round manner, build orchards, tea gardens and gardens, provide policy support and financial support. **Second,** boost the sustainable development of characteristic industries. We will adapt measures to local conditions for more benefits, focus on the layout of characteristic industries across the township. We will also optimize ecological and tourism resources, give full play to an industrial development system characterized by a combination of advantages and disadvantages, all-for-one development and overall promotion with the camellia oleifera, tea leaf and rural tourism as the main focus, and traditional Chinese medicinal materials, leaf-used wolfberry fruit, economic fruit forest and other small industries as effective supplements.

湖北荆州市松滋市卸甲坪土家族乡：
文旅融合、农旅融合、康旅融合、电旅融合

Xiejiaping Tujia Township, Songzi City, Jingzhou City, Hubei Province:
Integration of Culture and Tourism, Agriculture and Tourism, Healthcare and Tourism, and E-Commerce and Tourism

摘 要

湖北省荆州市松滋市卸甲坪土家族乡以创建“国家全域旅游示范区”为契机，以脱贫攻坚特色旅游发展三年规划为蓝本，大力发展文旅融合、农旅融合、康旅融合、电旅融合，紧密结合脱贫攻坚，深入推进“旅游+”产业融合发展，旅游扶贫效果明显。2019 年，卸甲坪成功创建了国家 3A 级旅游景区，年接待游客量突破 36 万人次，旅游总收入突破 8000 万元。目前，卸甲坪正努力争创国家 4A 级旅游景区。卸甲坪减贫成效突出，整体经济水平大幅提升，已蜕变为湖北省旅游名镇。

挑战与问题

湖北省荆州市卸甲坪土家族乡地处武陵山脉东麓，最高海拔 815 米，素有“荆州屋脊”之称。全乡面积 110.3 平方公里，其中耕地面积 1.7 万亩、山林面积 11.2 万亩，下辖 8 个行政村和 1 个社区，总人口 1.47 万人，其中土家族占 63%。卸甲坪是湖北省 12 个散居少数民族乡镇之一，也是一个偏远山区乡、深度贫困乡。卸甲坪有着得天独厚的青山绿水美景、独具特色的民族民俗文化、引人入胜

的农副旅游产品，这些都是卸甲坪旅游发展中的特色亮点。然而，如何夯实产业基础、丰富经济模式、兼顾生态保护，成了卸甲坪旅游带动脱贫的新挑战；交通和旅游基础设施不完善、旅游开发不够深入、旅游专业人才匮乏，仍是制约卸甲坪旅游发展的主要问题。

措施

1. 推进“文旅融合”，风俗变风景。美丽的风景因文化而有灵魂。在文旅部门的指导下，卸甲坪乡挖掘土家族风土人情，植入文化基因，凸显人文之美。挖掘“土因子”：以“山歌大王”宁远俊和“荣誉乡民”邓和平为代表的文化工作者挖掘和收集散落民间的土家族民俗文化资源，先后出版《深溪土司研究》《松滋土家歌谣故事集成》《松滋土家族史考》和《荆南土家族研究》等系列丛书十余套，成为传承土家族文化的“活化石”。传唱“土调子”：文化进课堂，组织“卸甲坪山歌”培训班和年轻干部夜学班，常态化开展土家歌舞与土家语教学；文化进校园，摆手舞、竹竿舞、打莲湘等民族舞蹈丰富校园大课间，押加、蹴球等民族体育项

目走进训练基地；文化进乡村，新建土家民俗文化博物馆，策划庆卸公路“十里文化长廊”，土家族文化逐渐绽放生机。唱响“土牌子”：自 2016 年起，连续四届民俗文化节均上榜“荆楚乡村旅游名线”，曲尺河村和覃睦庄社区更是在 2019 年跻身“中国少数民族特色村寨”。

2. 推进“农旅融合”，山货变俏货。着力发展生态种养等特色农业，产业发展活力迸发，乡村“旅游后备厢”不断升级：一是培育新业态。依托“基地 + 农户”，支持培育晶地农业、村晖农业等 28 家新型市场经营主体，开发了葛根、蜂蜜、香菇、坛酱等 10 余种特色农产品。二是擦亮新品牌。2019 年，“卸甲坪葛根”成功申报国家农产品地理标志。2020 年起，卸甲坪每年规划 200 万元产业基金，全力扶持壮大“葛根 + 山羊”循环产业，打造荆州“葛根之乡”。市委、市政府出台了《卸甲坪葛根产业发展三年行动方案（2021—2023）》，大力支持葛根产业的发展。三是拓宽新渠道。依托“旅游后备厢工程”，借着消费扶贫、农村电商的东风，土家蜂蜜、传统酱菜、葛根制品等“土疙瘩”成了俏销货，走出深山，走向全国。

3. 推进“康旅融合”，资源变财源。卸甲坪天然温泉资源得天独厚，依托曲尺河温泉度假邨，打造集温泉养生、康养度假、田园休闲为一体的乡村旅游典范：一是“借鸡下蛋”大开发。引进宜昌民生集团建设了曲尺河温泉度假邨，带动本乡就业 200 多人，“好山好水真温泉”的名号叫响大荆州、火爆湘鄂边，年接待游客 20 多万人次。二是立足康养再定位。卸甲坪温泉富含硫化物、钙、镁等多种有益于人体健康的微量元素，卸甲坪土家族乡锁

定康养胜地的远景目标，丰富游客新体验，提升旅游附加值。三是打造温泉第一乡。定位湘、鄂两省第一温泉康养小镇，融合中医疗养、运动健身、土家美食等元素，做实“温泉 + 酒店 + 养生 + 运动 + 美食”等融合大文章。

4. 推进“电旅融合”，滞销变畅销。2018 年，卸甲坪土家族乡成立了松滋首家农村电子商务运营中心，线上销售葛根制品、传统酱菜、熏制腊肉、土鸡、山羊、蜂蜜等 27 种农特产品，自营业以来，已销售产品近 3 万件，实现销售额 300 多万元。随着旅游热度上升，各地游客纷至沓来，传统酱菜、葛根制品、熏制腊肉、土鸡、土豆等以前的“土疙瘩”成了网红抢手货，生态种养的禽、畜、葛、蔬等农副产品走出深山，走进城市，走上了餐桌。

成效

2020 年，卸甲坪全乡旅游就业人数突破 1000 人，年游客接待量突破 36 万人次，旅游总收入突破 8000 万元，创历史新高。设立 400 万元产业扶贫基金，支持龙头企业、专业合作社与贫困户建立稳定联结机制，引导贫困户参与种养。截至目前，全乡共培育农民专合组织、农家乐、客栈和传统食品店 60 余家，建成 2000 亩葛根基地、1000 亩花卉苗木基地、500 亩高山蔬菜基地、300 亩生态大米基地、100 亩岩泉水产养殖基地、20 万筒香菇基地、10 万斤土家坛酱基地。产业扶贫已覆盖全乡 80% 以上的贫困户，户均增收 2500 元以上。全乡 5 个省级贫困村全部出列，889 户 2689 人建档立卡贫困人口全部脱贫。

经验与启示

1. “旅游 + 民俗”，突出民族特色。深入挖掘卸甲坪境内自然山水、天然温泉、民俗文化、红色教育等文旅资源，打造以土家民俗文化为本底、以“赏土家风情，泡天然温泉”为主题的乡村旅游点，走出了一条“旅游 +”的乡村旅游发展新路子。

2. “旅游 + 产业”，构建产业链条。随着卸甲坪旅游的蓬勃发展，文旅融合，农旅融合，康旅融合，电旅融合，各种业态形式百花齐放，完善并拓展了卸甲坪全域旅游的发展。

下一步计划

1. 积极破解交通瓶颈。加快推进沲水至卸甲坪旅游公路的建设；打通卸甲坪至江南高速王家畈出口的连接线、杨树坪至宜张高速连接线，让卸甲坪融入宜昌 1 小时经济圈，成为宜昌、张家界旅游的驿站和节点，成为荆州旅游的西部桥头堡。

2. 持续推进景点开发。拓宽融资渠道，引进实力强、有旅游开发经验的大公司进行战略合作，有序推进曲尺河康养小镇、黄林桥生态小镇、江西观避暑、曲尺峡游玩、天生桥观景等景点的开发。

3. 大力培育特色产业。支持乡内小型农家乐、民宿产业发展，提升旅游服务能力；培育卸甲坪葛根、源溪洞生态虾蟹、村晖生态粮油等特色农业产业品牌，逐步将农产品变成旅游产品。充分发挥旅游的综合效益，进一步巩固脱贫成效，助推乡村振兴。

Abstract

Xiejiaping Tujia Township, Songzi City, Jingzhou City, Hubei Province has the opportunity to create a "national all-for-one tourism demonstration zone" which is based on the three-year plan for poverty alleviation and special tourism development. It has advanced the integration of tourism for agriculture, healthcare and e-commerce. Due to the tight integration of its poverty alleviation goal with the in-depth promotion of integrated development of the "Tourism +" industry, remarkable achievements have been made. In 2019, the township created a national 3A-level tourist attraction, with an annual tourist reception exceeding 360,000 and a total tourism revenue exceeding RMB 80 million. Currently, it's striving to become a national 4A-level tourist attraction. Owing to its outstanding performance in poverty reduction and improved overall economic level, Xiejiaping has become a well-known tourist township in Hubei Province.

Challenges and Problems

Located in the eastern foot of Wuling Mountain, with its highest elevation at 815 meters, the township is known as the "Roof of Jingzhou." It covers an area of 110.3 square kilometers, including 17,000 *mu* of arable land and 112,000 *mu* of mountain forests. It includes eight administrative villages and one community with a population of 14,700, 63% of whom are Tujia minority group which accounts for 63% of the total. As one of the 12 scattered ethnic minority townships in the province, Xiejiaping is a severely impoverished remote mountainous township. Despite its tourism advantages such as unique natural sceneries, distinctive ethnic folk cultures, and fascinating agricultural and sideline tourism products, the township faces the challenge of how to achieve consolidated industrial foundations. It's also confronted with the problem of an economic model in need of enrichment and an inadequate ecological protection for poverty alleviation through tourism. Undeveloped transportation and tourism infrastructures, insufficient tourism development and lack of tourism professionals have limited its growth.

Measures

1. Promote the "integration of culture and tourism" to change customs into landscapes. Picturesque scenery will be vested with abundant cultural connotation and support. With the guidance of cultural and tourism departments, the township has made full use of the customs of the Tujia Nationality, blending the best of its native elements to showcase its unique essence and beauty. It has explored the Tujia culture. For example, cultural workers represented by the "Folk Song King" Ning Yuanjun and "Honorary Villager" Deng Heping tapped and collected Tujia folk cultural resources scattered among the people and successively published more than ten series of books such as *Research on Chieftain's Culture of Shenxi Town, Tujia Ballad Story Collection, Historical Study on the Tujia Nationality of Songzi City,* and *Research on the Tujia Nationality of Jingnan (also* *named Nanping Kingdom, one of the Ten States* (902-979) that controlled southern China during the first half of the ninth century, the so-called Five Dynasties period). These books were developed into "living fossils" for the preservation and promotion the Tujia culture. Moreover, the Tujia culture has been integrated into courses for "Xiejiaping Folk Songs" which consist of classes for young cadres to train them to belt out Tujia songs and perform traditional dance Tujia language is spoken regularly to promote cultural development in the campus. Ethnic dance like hand-waving dance, bamboo pole dance, and Lianxiang beating dance (traditional folk dance with a bamboo pole to pray for peaceful villagers and prosperous country) have enlivened the school's breaktime activities. Ethnic sports projects such as Yajia, a tug-of-war to pull the rope by leg, waist, shoulder and neck and Cuqiu, a traditional ball kicking sports, have been brought into the training base. They have also driven cultural immersion into rural areas to build a new Tujia folk culture museum and plan the "Ten-li Cultural Corridor" of Qingxie Highway (Qinghesi-Xiejiaping Highway of Songzi City, Jingzhou City) to reinvigorate the Tujia culture. It has also promoted local brands. Consequently, four consecutive folk culture festivals have been on the list of Hubei Famous Rural Tourism Routes since 2016. And Quchihe Village and Qinmuzhuang Community were among the ethnic minority villages with Chinese characteristics in 2019.

2. Promote the "integration of agriculture and tourism" to make local products popular. With its characteristic agriculture such as ecological planting and breeding at the core, the industry has developed a method to provide for the continuous support for tourism development. New business formats have been created in response to the "bases + peasant households" model. The township has cultivated 28 new types of market entities such as Jingdi Agriculture and Cunhui Agriculture. It has developed more than 10 special agricultural products, including pueraria lobata, honey, shiitake mushrooms, and altars of sauce. New brands have also been promoted. It successfully applied for the National Geographical Indication Agricultural Products for the brand of "Xiejiaping Pueraria Lobata" in 2019. It has been allocating since 2020 an industrial fund of RMB

2 million annually for the development of the recycling industry of "Pueraria lobata + goat." This led to the creation of a "township of Pueraria lobata" in Jingzhou City. The municipal party committee and government have issued a three-year action plan for the industrial development of Pueraria lobata from 2021 — 2023 to provide their support. What's more, new channels have been broadened. In the context of poverty alleviation through consumption and rural e-commerce development and with the unceasing tourism development support, the Tujia Nationality's local products are sold throughout the country. They include honey, traditional pickles and Pueraria lobata products.

3. Promote the "integration of healthcare and tourism" to transform resources into wealth. The township has utilized Quchihe Hot Spring Resort to create a rural tourism model that integrates hot springs for health, vacation and pastoral leisure. The unique advantages have been leveraged for large-scale development and it has introduced the Yichang Minsheng Group to build the Quchihe Hot Spring Resort, generating more than 200 jobs in the township. The slogan of "lucid waters, lush mountains, and authentic hot springs" resound throughout Hubei and Hunan provinces. This resulted in an annual tourist reception of more than 200,000. More healthcare-focused goals have also been set. As the Xiejiaping hot springs are endowed with abundant health-beneficial microelements such as sulfides, calcium and magnesium, the township is determined to build a healthcare resort for the enrichment of tourists' new experience and boost the added value of tourism. It has worked hard to transform into the No. 1 Hot Spring Township. Branded as the first hot spring healthcare town in Hunan and Hubei provinces, the Tujia Township has deftly combined elements such as traditional Chinese medical care, sports and fitness, and Tujia delicacies, embodying an integrated blueprint of hot springs, hotels, healthcare, sports and delicacies.

4. Promote the "integration of e-commerce and tourism" to turn slow sellers into best sellers. In 2018, the township established the first rural e-commerce operation center in Songzi City. This station sells 27 kinds of special agricultural products such as Pueraria lobata products, traditional pickles, smoked bacon, native chicken, goat and honey. Nearly 30,000 products have been sold since its operation, registering a revenue of more than RMB 3 million. With the increase in tourism publicity, it has attracted a large number of tourists from all over the world. This means local products such as traditional pickles, Pueraria lobata products, smoked bacon, native chicken, and potatoes have become internet-famous best sellers. Agricultural and other corollary products, including ecologically developed poultry, livestock, Pueraria lobata, and vegetables have made their ways from the mountains, into the city and onto the table.

Results

In 2020, the township reached a new tourism high with more than 1,000 people employed tourism, an annual tourist reception exceeding 360,000 and a total tourism revenue of over RMB 80 million. A poverty alleviation fund through industrial development of RMB 4 million has been set up to support a stable correlation mechanism among leading enterprises, professional cooperatives and impoverished households. They help guide these

households to engage in planting and breeding. To date, it has cultivated more than 60 farmers' professional cooperatives, agritainment, inns, and traditional food stores. They have built a Pueraria lobata base of 2,000 *mu*, created a flower and seedling base of 1,000 *mu*, a mountain vegetable base of 500 *mu* and an ecological rice base of 300 *mu*. They have also created a rock spring aquaculture base of 100 *mu*, a shiitake mushroom base of 200,000 tubes, and a Tujia sauce base of 100,000 *jin*. As a result, more than 80% of poverty-stricken households have been covered by the poverty alleviation project through industrial development, with the average household income increase of more than RMB 2,500. Five provincial-level poverty-stricken villages in the township have eliminated poverty and 2,689 people of 889 archived impoverished households have also been lifted out of poverty.

Experience and Inspirations

1. "Tourism + Folk Customs" to highlight national characteristics. The township has explored cultural tourism resources such as ecological landscape, natural hot springs, folk culture, and red cultural education to create a rural tourist spot based on Tujia folk culture and themed with "appreciating traditional Tujia customs and enjoying natural hot springs." It has become a trailblazer of a rural tourism development path with the "Tourism +" model.

2. "Tourism + Industries" to build industrial chains. With the robust tourism development, various business models such as cultural and tourism integration, agriculture and tourism integration, healthcare and tourism integration and e-commerce and tourism integration have emerged and flourished, expanding the all-for-one tourism development in the township.

Next Steps

1. Break the traffic bottlenecks. The township will speed up the construction of the tourist road from Weishui

River to Xiejiaping and open up the connection from Xiejiaping to the Wangjiafan Exit of Jiangnan Expressway (a part of Yueyang-Yichang Expressway, located in the South of the Yangtze River of Jingzhou City) and the connection from Yangshuping to Yizhang Expressway (Yichang-Zhangjiajie Expressway), so that Xiejiaping can be integrated into the one-hour economic circle in Yichang City and become a tourism station and node of Yichang City and Zhangjiajie City, serving as a western gateway for tourism of Jingzhou City.

2. Develop scenic spots. It will broaden financing channels, introduce large companies with considerable cash and clout and abundant experience in tourism development for strategic cooperation. It will steadily promote the development of scenic spots such as Quchihe Healthcare Town, Huanglinqiao Ecological Town, Jiangxiguan Summer Resort, Quchixia Recreation, and Tianshengqiao Viewing.

3. Nurture characteristic industries. Continuous support will be provided to develop small-scale agritainment and B&Bs industries in the township for robust tourism capabilities and services. It will cultivate special agricultural industry brands such as Xiejiaping Pueraria Lobata, Yuanxidong Ecological Shrimp and Crab, and Cunhui Ecological Grain and Oil. They will attempt to turn agricultural products into tourism products. Most importantly, it will give full play to the comprehensive performance of tourism for consolidated poverty alleviation results and rural revitalization.

广西南宁市马山县古零镇乔老村小都百屯：
“共商、共建、共管、共享”的乡村旅游模式

Xiaodubai Village, Qiaolao Village, Guling Town, Mashan County, Nanning City, Guangxi Zhuang Autonomous Region:
Rural Tourism Model of “Consultation, Co-Construction, Co-Governance, and Sharing”

摘 要

广西省南宁市马山县古零镇乔老村小都百屯以打造“水车之乡”为特色，坚持“社区即景区、乡村即旅游”的发展理念进行示范村建设，着力把小都百综合示范村建设成为环弄拉生态旅游区满足“食、住、行、游、购、娱”需求的一站式时尚生活、休闲农业旅游基地。小都百屯群众通过“共商、共建、共管、共享”的“休闲农业 + 乡村旅游 + 扶贫”模式，成立小都百旅游服务公司，家家受益，人人共享，带动社会资本投入近 5000 万元发展种养产业、果蔬特色优势产业、生态观光产业、民宿农家乐、农特产品销售等旅游扶贫开发产业。全屯农户通过直接参与、间接带动、股权带动等模式参与发展乡村旅游产业，2017 年，小都百屯实现整屯脱贫摘帽，成为集度假、美食、观光休闲旅游于一体的新型农村。

挑战与问题

广西南宁马山县古零镇乔老村小都百屯地处马山县环弄拉生态旅游核心区，为古零镇乔老村 19 个自然屯之一，属典型的喀斯特山区。2013 年以前，全屯种地靠天、条件恶劣，群众主要通过外出务工和种植玉米、蔬菜等旱地作物维持生活。全屯有 72 户共 290 多人，民族以壮族和瑶族为主，耕地总面积 561 亩，贫困发生率达 31%。2013 年人均收入仅为 3200 元，被列为“马山县扶贫开发整村推进村”。

措施

1. 统筹规划打造特色村庄。2013 年，小都百屯被确定为南宁市综合示范村建设项目。小都百屯利用固有的山水打造天然生态人文景观，在规划布局上强调场地的低开发、高档次建设；结合富有地方民族特色的、简洁大方的建设风格，对全屯 86 栋房屋进行外立面改造，建筑采用“灰白”主色调，设计水波窗花，融入水车元素图案，建设白墙灰瓦的壮乡特色民居；对全屯房屋进行庭院改造、绿化美化彩化工作，打造农家院落特色。同时，在示范村建设进程中突出挖掘、保护和传承发展小都百物质、非物质文化遗产，并在人文景观和自然景观等方面体现独具魅力的民族特色文化。示范村内划分有观光农业园、风情百家园、水车园、百花园、百乐园、百香园 6 个文化园区，建设小都百记忆展示馆，挖掘保护传承水车园历史文化，打造有利于旅游业发展的壮、瑶民族特色文化。

2. 完善设施建设生态新村。2014 年，马山县积极整合各部门资金，编制完成《小都百创五星级乡村旅游区发展规划》；完善小都百基础设施，建设完成游客服务中心、生态停车场、旅游厕所；实施排水工程、道路工程、电气工程、园林景观改造工程、公共设施建设工程、环卫工程、人畜分离安置工程等，改造小都百乡村环境；改造农家乐，提高农家乐的档次和水平；稳步推进乔老半岛村集体经济项目、星级汽车营地及青少年户外活动基地建设等。建成后的小都百综合示范村基础设施完善，面貌焕然一新。

3. 农旅融合打造乡村旅游新模式。小都百重视生态农业与旅游产业融合发展，坚持“共商、共建、共管、共享”理念，实施旅游扶贫战略：一

是“共商”开展土地确权工作，完善了农村土地承包经营权制度，依法保障农民土地承包权益，采取“基地 + 专业合作社（公司）+ 农户”的经营模式，打造果蔬药材生态农业基地等；广西乔老爷农业开发有限责任公司进驻乔老村小都百屯，将全屯土地进行流转，建立现代农业示范基地，建立果蔬有机种植大棚 130 个，发展休闲农业。二是“共建”发展乡村旅游，拉长乡村旅游产业链条。依托青山绿水，紧扣生态与旅游发展的融入点，2014 年引进马山中凯乡村旅游发展有限公司，采取“公司 + 农户”的模式，由屯里出土地、公司出资金，共同建设农家旅馆，发展休闲旅游业。三是“共管”乡村旅游，探索小都百资产收益模式。2015 年成立小都百旅游服务公司，设立董事会，确定“土地租金、劳力薪金、信贷 + 人力入股”的经营模式和“统一经营、统一管理、统一收益、统一分配”的管理模式。四是“共享”小都百资产收益，实现全屯脱贫致富。当地群众通过土地租金、劳力薪金、人力等资本入股，当地银行向贫困户发放扶贫贴息贷款，帮其入股共享收益。

成效

2013 年以来，小都百屯以打造“水车之乡”为特色，本着“社区即景区、乡村即旅游”的发展理念进行示范村建设，着力把小都百综合示范村建设成为环弄拉生态旅游区满足“食、住、行、游、购、娱”需求的一站式时尚生活、休闲农业旅游基地。示范村于 2014 年年底建成并投入使用，带动社会资本投入近 5000 万元发展种养产业、果蔬特色优势产业、生态观光产业、民宿农家乐、农特产品销售等旅游扶贫开发产业，全屯农户通过直接参与、间接带动、股权带动等模式参与发展乡村旅游产业，带动旅游从业人数 60 多人，近三年年接待游客 70 多万人次，实现年旅游收入约 4000 万元，人均收入大幅增加。2017 年，小都百屯实现

整屯脱贫摘帽，并成为集度假、美食、观光休闲旅游于一体的新型农村，全屯农民年人均纯收入由 2013 的 3200 元，增加到 2020 年的 13000 元。小都百成为国家 3A 级旅游景区和“中国最美休闲乡村”。

经验与启示

1. 抓住机遇，部门合力开发。2017 年中央一号文件指出：鼓励农村集体通过与社会资本联办乡村旅游企业、创办乡村旅游合作社等方式发展乡村旅游；国家旅游局等部门也陆续发布了一系列乡村旅游扶贫政策。当地党委政府充分把握政策机遇，积极整合各级、各部门资源优势，指导小都百不断探索创新旅游脱贫致富新模式、新路子，延长旅游产业链，为贫困户创造更多收益方式，真正做到乡村旅游与消除贫困同时进行、同步发展。

2. 突出特色，提升旅游扶贫内涵。在打造乡村旅游项目时，必须注重挖掘一村一品一韵，依托自身生态环境、民俗文化、资源优势，突出特色，提升内涵，避免低端化、单一化、同质化和生搬硬套。应从自身实际情况出发，注重特色旅游产品的创新和提升，赋予其丰富的文化内涵，明确旅游扶贫发展定位，从而达到“以特取胜”的效果，力争成为特色鲜明、别具一格的乡村旅游品牌标杆，使乡村旅游扶贫实现可持续发展。

3. 村民自治，达成发展乡村旅游共识。村规民约制度的建立与规范，是乡村实行自治的重要手段，是村民开展群众活动应遵循的规章。小都百屯通过建立村级协商自治机制，指导村民制定村规民约制度，引导群众积极参与示范村建设，化解矛盾纠纷，同时积极探索示范村建设的后续管理工作，研究出台了旅游开发、公共卫生保洁、公物管理、电费收取、表彰奖励、激励等一系列制度措施，从而达到规范旅游市场秩序的目的。这样一来，既促进了和谐文明乡村的建成，又能提升乡村旅游地的品质与口碑，为示范村可持续发展奠定了基础。

下一步计划

马山县将继续坚定不移地走农旅融合的旅游扶贫道路，依托秀丽的山水优势和丰富的人文资源，强化旅游基础建设，继续谋好思路、盘活资源，升级打造旅游品牌，增强旅游内生动力，大力发展特色优势旅游产业，做大做强特色旅游品牌，为巩固脱贫成果、助力乡村振兴持续贡献旅游力量。

Abstract

A demonstration village with "a township of waterwheels" as its distinctive characteristic and "turning communities into scenic spots, and villages into tourism destinations" as its guiding development philosophy is being planned in Xiaodubai Village, Qiaolao Village, Guling Town, Mashan County, Nanning City, Guangxi Zhuang Autonomous Region. This will be a one-stop life and agricultural tourism center for "eating, lodging, transportation, travel, entertainment, and shopping" in Nongla Ring Eco-Tourism Tourist Area. Local villagers have established the Xiaodubai Tourism Service Company through the "leisure agriculture + rural tourism + poverty alleviation" model and on the philosophy of "Consultation, Co-Construction, Co-Governance, and Sharing" for benefit sharing. To date, it has attracted RMB 50 million social capital for the development of poverty alleviation industries through tourism. It includes industries in planting and breeding, local fruit and vegetable cultivation, ecological tourism, B&Bs, agritainment and agricultural local product sales. They're intended to ensure the engagement and direct participation of peasant households in indirectly-driven and equity-led rural tourism development. By adhering to this concept, the village was lifted out of poverty in 2017 and has been transformed into a countryside tourism destination that integrates leisure vacation, delicacy and sightseeing.

Challenges and Problems

Located at the center of Nongla Ring Eco-Tourism Tourist Area, the village is one of 19 natural villages in Qiaolao. Its area is characterized by a karst mountain. Prior to 2013, the planting conditions were backward as the harvest yield relied heavily on local climate. At the time, villagers made their living by working outside and planting upland crops such as corn and vegetables. The village has more than 290 people in 72 households, dominated mainly by the Zhuang and Yao nationalities. It has a total arable land area of 561 *mu* and a 31% poverty incidence. In 2013, the per capita income was RMB 3,200, clearly indicating its impoverished condition and its urgent need for advancement and poverty alleviation measures.

Measures

1. Overall planning to build characteristic villages. The village was identified as a comprehensive demonstration village construction project in Nanning City in 2013. Natural ecological and cultural landscapes were developed based on its intrinsic mountains and waters. Low-impact development and high-end construction of sites were emphasized in planning and layout. The façade of 86 village houses in the village was renovated with local ethnic characteristics and construction styles. Gray and white colors were used in water wave window grilles designs that integrated waterwheel patterns. White walls and gray tiles of the Zhuang Nationality were used in residential buildings. All courtyards were renovated, and more efforts were made for the

greening and beautification of characteristic farmyards. At the same time, the exploitation, protection, heritage, tangible and intangible cultural legacy were highlighted in the construction of the demonstration village. The landscape reflected the village's charming ethnic culture.

To establish the Xiaodubai Memory Exhibition Hall, protect and promote the Waterwheel Park's cultural heritage and the culture of the Zhuang and Yao nationalities, the demonstration village is divided into six cultural parks: Sightseeing Agriculture Park, Fengqing Baijia Park, Waterwheel Park, Baihua Park, Baile Park, and Baixiang Park.

2. Improvement of facilities to build ecological new villages. In 2014, Mashan County integrated the funds of various departments to complete the *Development Plan on Building Xiaodubai into a Five-star Rural Tourist Area.* It improved village infrastructure and constructed the tourist service center, ecological parking lot and toilets for tourists. To improve the village's environment, it implemented engineering systems for water supply and drainage, road construction, electric, landscape renovation, public facility construction. environmental sanitation, resettlement, human and livestock separation, etc. These have all led to an increase in the grade and level of agritainment in the village and promoted the construction of its collective economy in Qiaolao Peninsula, star-level car camps and outdoor youth activity centers in an orderly manner. As a result, the Xiaodubai comprehensive demonstration village has been equipped with infrastructure that has given it a completely new look.

3. Integration of agriculture and tourism to create a new model of rural tourism. With emphasis on the integrated development of ecological agriculture and tourism industry and with "Consultation, Co-Construction, Co-Governance, and Sharing" as its guiding policy, the village has implemented a poverty alleviation strategy through tourism. **First,** to improve rural contracted management rights of land system and protect farmers' land contracted rights in accordance with the law, land rights confirmation was carried out through consultation. A business model of "bases + professional cooperatives (companies) + peasant households" was adopted to build ecological agricultural bases integrating fruits, vegetables and medicinal materials and bamboo rat breeding professional cooperatives. The Guangxi Qiaolaoye Agricultural Development Co., Ltd. was introduced, and the village land was transferred to establish modern agricultural demonstration centers and 130 organic fruit and vegetable greenhouses for the development of leisure agriculture. **Second,** rural tourism was developed through a joint construction to extend the rural tourism industrial chain. Based on the lucid waters and lush mountains concept, and the integration of ecological and tourism development, the Mashan Zhongkai Rural Tourism Development Co., Ltd. was introduced in 2014. To develop the leisure tourism industry, the "companies + peasant households" model was adopted. Villagers provided the land and companies provided funds for the joint building of rural hotels. **Third,** rural tourism was developed through a co-governance to explore the assets income model of the village. The Xiaodubai Tourism Service Company was established in 2015 and a board of directors was formed to assess the business model of "land rents, labor salaries, credit + human resources' equity participation" and the management model of "unified operation, unified management, unified profit, and unified distribution." **Fourth,** the income assets of the village is distributed through sharing to help all villagers shake off poverty and improve their lives. Local people pooled their capital from land rents, salaries &

wages and human resources as shares. Local banks issued subsidized loans to impoverished households so they can participate in equity building and profit sharing.

Results

With "a township of waterwheels" as its characteristics and "turning communities into scenic spots, and villages into tourism destinations" as the guiding philosophy, the demonstration village was completed in 2013 and has been put into use at the end of 2014. It has generated RMB 50 million social capital derived from industries in planting and breeding, fruit and vegetable cultivation, ecological tourism, B&Bs, agritainment and agricultural local product sales. More than 60 people have been engaged in the tourism industry. Over the past three years, the village has received more than 700,000 tourists, achieving an annual tourism income of about RMB 40 million and a substantial increase in per capita income. In 2017, the village was lifted out of poverty. It has been transformed into a countryside tourist destination that integrates vacation, delicacy, sightseeing in its development. The per capita net income of farmers increased from RMB 3,200 in 2013 to RMB 13,000 in 2020. More importantly, it has become a national 3A-level tourist attraction and has been rated as the most beautiful leisure village in China.

Experience and Inspirations

1. Seize opportunities for a concerted development. In the No. 1 Central Document issued in 2017, rural collectives were encouraged to develop rural tourism social capital cooperation, establish rural tourism enterprises and create rural tourism cooperatives. The China National Tourism Administration (CNTA) and other departments successively issued poverty alleviation policies through rural tourism. The party committee and government subsequently seized the opportunity to integrate the advantageous resources of all departments at all levels, guide the village to explore new tourism models and new ways to alleviate poverty and extend the tourism industrial chain. This has led to the creation of more income streams for impoverished households and the simultaneous advancement of rural tourism development and poverty elimination.

2. Highlight local characteristics for quality poverty alleviation through tourism. Every special product in every village should be explored for rural tourism initiatives. The local characteristics of the product should be emphasized and reliance on ecological environment, folk culture, and resource advantages should be similarly stressed instead of low-end, simplified, homogeneous and mechanical development. Innovating and improving the village's characteristic tourism products is necessary for the enrichment of its cultural essence to strengthen poverty alleviation through tourism, create a benchmark for the local brand and achieve sustainable tourism practices.

3. Village self-governance for consensuses on rural tourism development. The establishment and standardization of village rules and regulations are necessary for the implementation of self-governance. Villagers must follow them in carrying out activities. Through village-level consultation, autonomy mechanism and guidance from villagers, the framework for rules and regulations must be established. The village has guided the masses in their participation in the construction of the demonstration village. Also, it has helped in conflict disputes and resolutions, monitored the management of demonstration village construction and issued institutional measures in tourism development, public health and cleaning, public property management, electricity fee collection, commendations, rewards and incentives. All these measures promote the creation of gracious, harmonious villages, boost the quality and reputation of rural tourism destinations and provide a solid foundation for a sustainable development.

Next Steps

By adhering to the proven poverty alleviation measures and relying on its picturesque natural scenery and rich cultural resources, Mashan County will continue to strengthen tourism infrastructure, explore effective ways to revitalize its resources and upgrade its tourism brands. It will enhance the endogenous power of tourism for a vigorous rural revitalization.

福建龙岩市上杭县古田红色旅游区：
红色旅游高质量可持续发展

Gutian Red Tourist Area, Shanghang County, Longyan City, Fujian Province:
High-Quality Sustainable Development of Red Tourism

摘 要

福建省龙岩市古田旅游区积极探索红色旅游发展路径，推动旅游区高质量发展，不断完善和丰富红色旅游产品体系、管理服务体系、基础设施体系、公共服务体系，进一步调动广大群众参与红色旅游的积极性，不断增加其满意度，将古田特色的红色文化资源优势有效转化为发展优势，增强红色旅游对当地经济社会发展的辐射带动作用。

挑战与问题

福建省龙岩市古田红色旅游区是著名的古田会议召开所在地。虽然古田红色旅游越来越火爆，但红色旅游开发的深度远远不够，大部分游客到古田仅是直奔古田会议会址一游。古田旅游需发挥红色文化旅游的优势，以古田国家5A级旅游景区综合提升、红色文化教育培训等项目为支撑，将古田打造成中国最著名的红色文化研学旅游目的地、教育培训基地和国际红色文化旅游交流中心；同时推进红色文化产业和绿色生态产业协同发展，带动文旅康养产业跨越式发展。

措施

1. 强化古田旅游品牌打造。一是优化游览环境。实施了景区（点）提升改造、古田会议旧址群修葺、景区交通改造提升、景区夜景提升等工程项目，持续建设旅游要素，完善景区服务功能，景区面貌焕然一新。二是探索建设古田梅花山文旅康养试验区。为推进红古田、绿步云深度融合，打造“红绿”交相辉映、城乡融合、农文旅融合发展的现代化文旅康养小城市，2019年11月起创新体制机制，用公司化运作打造古田梅花山，将其打造成为“新时代老区苏区振兴发展样板”，进一步提升古田影响力。2020年，梅花山文旅康养试验区多个项目正式落地。三是构建古田红色旅游和环梅花山生态旅游经济圈。在古田镇原有的基础上优化

城市布局，并在古田镇筹划新集镇中心、学校和医院，按县级城市标准打造古田小城市。目前古田已初步明确三大片区，即古田镇、梅花山区和小池片区，全面发展红色旅游、森林康养、地质旅游、研学培训、温泉养生和度假居养。

2. 强化古田培训品牌打造。一是着力打造专兼职多元体系的师资队伍，树立社会“大师资”观念，构建“三位一体”师资格局，借助古田基地合作院校的优质师资力量、教学资源和先进的教学管理经验，实现师资共享。二是加强现场教学点建设，按照“六个有”标准，“成熟一处，实施一处”，提升全市100个现场教学点功能水平，打造现场教学基地集群，并充分挖掘各教学点的听点、看点、悟点、卖点，串点成线，策划不同专题、不同板块的精品培训线路。三是加大对外交流力度，目前，中央国家机关工委、财政部、公安部、国家公务员局、国防大学等156家部门单位在古田设立了教育培训基地或教学点。四是加快培训基地建设，提升培训承载力，积极推进古田干部学院二期、古田干部学院步云分院、古田红色宾馆、福建农商行古田党校四个培训基地的建设。五是拓宽培训市场，积极在厦门、广州、深圳、上海等地开设运营中心，2019年承接培训班5196期，学员约24.13万人次，与2018年同期相比增加了21.6%。

3. 强化古田研学品牌打造。依托古田国家5A级旅游景区及周边红色、绿色、客家、畲族等文化资源，充分发挥全国爱国主义教育基地、全国中小学生研学实践教育基地、港澳青少年游学基地的品

牌优势，着力打造面向全国青少年的综合实践基地，加快推进全国中小学研学营地的建设。目前，已初步形成了以古田为点向外辐射的研学实践教育网络，规划设计了小学、初中阶段的研学实践教育线路，高中阶段研学线路正在考察中。截至 2019 年年底，累计为龙岩市境内中小学校提供了 40 期、近 3800 人次的免费公益研学活动。古田红色培训现已实现对全国 31 个省、市、自治区的全覆盖，中央各部委、央企、民企、高等院校等 160 多家单位在古田设立了教育基地或教学点，前来培训的人数每年逾 20 万人次。截至 2019 年年底，古田共接待研学实践教育培训班 280 余批次，学生约 8.5 万人次。

成效

红色旅游的发展，迅速带动了古田当地餐饮、住宿、服务等相关行业的发展，吸引了一大批有实力的企业入驻，其中“四上”企业 16 家，包括有文化休闲旅游、研学旅游、党性教育培训、养生休闲、购物、商务会展、餐饮、节庆 8 种服务业态，提高了当地群众的生活水平，造福当地百姓。如今的千米古田街和万米古田路，有三星级以上标准酒店 3 家，中档舒适型宾馆快捷酒店 13 家，特色红军客栈、农家乐民宿 33 家，总床位约 2000 张；各类餐饮店 100 余家，可同时容纳 12000 人就餐。沿路沿街 100 多家商铺琳琅满目，立面统一改造为青砖灰瓦，道路统一铺设为沥青路面，招牌统一制作为新式材料，路灯统一设计为火炬…… 一派欣欣向荣的景象。作为“最美乡村”的五龙村，借助毗邻古田会议会址的优势，结合红色旅游，发展生态和乡村旅游，形势喜人，民宿、农家乐和红军客栈人来人往、热闹非凡。据不完全统计，古田红色旅游实现直接就业 1000 余人，间接就业 5000 人；景区群众收入有五成源于旅游。通过发展红色旅游，古田当地形成了一系列旅游产业链，周边村民的收入翻了好几番，村里建起了图书室、篮球场、公园，丰富和方便了村民生活，全村栽种了油菜花、荷花等，四季风景如画，人民生活幸福安康。

经验与启示

1. 活动创新。开展“走出去、请进来、送上门、勤服务、善创新”等多种多样的教育活动，每年举办 10 次以上的临时展览，组织宣传小分队巡回宣讲，并派出专业人员开设讲座近 500 场次。举办奥运火炬传递仪式、激情广场大家唱、全国青少年青春歌会、全国红色旅游经典巡礼、2021 年上杭“红古田”半程马拉松等诸多活动；开展“古田会议万里行”，在新疆昌吉、呼图壁，江苏茅山新四军纪念馆举办“古田会议——党和军队建设史上的里程碑”展览；在福建省海峡民间艺术馆举办“古田会议 90 周年红色文化展”；在澳门举办“客家精神文化展”。

2. 内容创新。古田（吴地）红军小镇通过开展“十个一”活动——“当一回红军战士，缅怀革命先烈”“听一个红军故事，追忆峥嵘岁月”“学一篇主席诗词，陶冶革命情操”“唱一首红色歌谣，激发爱国情怀”“行一段红军路，重温革命历史”“煮一顿红军饭，体验艰苦岁月”“打一场模拟战，接受战争洗礼”“开一次运动会，激发人体潜能”“写一篇红色征文，传承红色基因”“领一枚荣誉勋章，争做时代新人”——让中小学生在重温革命历史、体验艰苦岁月的过程中追忆峥嵘岁月，激发爱国情怀，争做时代新人。影视作品《红色摇篮》《古田会议》《古田 1929》《寻访铸魂之路——走进古田》《长征路，新故事——古田专题》《古田军号》等，从平凡的视角去挖掘革命故事、老区故事的爱国主义闪光点，从而实现爱国主义教育和“好口碑”的双丰收。

3. 形式创新。不断创新古田油菜花节活动内容，耗时一个多月开展汉服周、小红军研学周、非

遗文化周、红色快闪周、文创集市周等活动，充分挖掘出红色、绿色、古典、民俗、文创等文化内涵。2019 年国庆期间，景区通过升国旗、观看国庆盛典、唱支红歌给祖国、瞻仰一次古田会议旧址群、听一回革命历史故事、“我和国旗同框”、红色主题蜡像馆探索、为毛主席献枝花、“我在圣地古田，为祖国祝福”万人签名等活动掀起爱国热潮，受到广大游客的欢迎。2021 年，景区喜迎建党 100 周年油菜花季系列活动的红歌快闪周，同时倾力打造古田油菜花欢乐谷，古田梅花山千亩油菜花海以盛情之姿，献礼中国共产党百年华诞，为古田增添了一抹专属的春季亮色，展现出“圣地党旗红，十里菜花香”的乡村振兴诗画胜景。

下一步计划

继续把古田会议这一“金字招牌”用足、用活，充分发挥红色资源与绿色资源优势，推进红色文化产业和绿色生态产业协同发展，实现“红绿”交相辉映，带动文旅康养产业跨越式发展。通过提升红色旅游景区质量，持续促进周边交通设施提升、生活环境改善，带动景区周边乡村居民，在餐饮业、住宿业、娱乐业、交通业、商业、景区运营参与等方面实现创业富民和就业富民。采取切实可行的措施促进红色旅游与乡村旅游融合发展，实现旅游反哺农业，使农户成为旅游商户、农产品变成旅游商品，实现乡村振兴。

Abstract

Through the active exploration of the quality development path of red tourism, the Gutian Tourist Area of Longyan City has enriched the red tourism products, management services, infrastructure and public services systems. It has enhanced the enthusiasm and satisfaction of the masses to engage in red tourism and transformed the advantages of red cultural resources with Gutian characteristics into developmental advantages for the enhancement of the radiating and leading role played by red tourism on the local economy.

Challenges and Problems

The Gutian Red Tourist Area is the site of the famous Gutian Conference. Despite the popularity of Gutian red tourism, there is still a long way for its development as most tourists just go to Gutian Town for a conference. Supported by projects such as the comprehensive upgrade of the 5A-level tourist attraction and red culture education and training, Gutian's advantages in red cultural tourism should be leveraged to develop it into China's most famous research red culture destination, education and training base and international red culture tourism exchange center. At the same time, the coordinated development of the red cultural and the green ecological industries should be promoted to drive the forward leap of the culture, tourism, and healthcare industries.

Measures

1. Strengthen Gutian's tourism brand building. First, optimize the tour environment. Projects in scenic spots such as the upgrade of scenic areas (spots), renovation of the former site of Gutian Conference, traffic improvement and the night view beautification have been implemented. Also, continuous tourism construction and perfection of service functions have brought a new look to the scenic area. **Second,** explore the construction of Gutian Meihua Mountain Culture, Tourism and Healthcare Experimental Zone. To promote the in-depth integration of Red Gutian (red tourism development of Gutian Town) and Green Buyun (green ecological development of Buyun Township) and create a modern city with culture, tourism, and healthcare industries featuring "red and green" interplay, urban-rural integration, and integrated development of agriculture, culture and tourism, the system and mechanism have been innovated since November 2019 to build the Gutian

Meihua Mountain through corporate operations, develop it into a "model for the revitalization and development of old revolutionary base areas and Soviet areas in the new era," and further enhance the influence of Gutian Town. In 2020, a number of projects in the experimental zone were officially launched. **Third,** develop Gutian's red tourism and eco-tourism economic circle around the Meihua Mountain. The urban layout has been optimized based on the original. It aimed to build new town centers, schools and hospitals in Gutian Town. Small cities of Gutian Town have been developed according to county-level city standards. At present, three areas have been preliminarily identified—Gutian Town, Meihua Mountain Area and Xiaochi Town Area—for the comprehensive development of red tourism, forest recuperation, geological tourism, research and training, hot springs and leisure vacation.

2. Strengthen the Gutian brand building training. First, more efforts have been made to build a diversified system with full-time and part-time teachers, establish the concept of "professional teacher resources" and build a "three-in-one" pattern of teacher qualifications, realize teacher resources sharing by virtue of excellent teachers, quality teaching resources and advanced teaching management experience of colleges and universities in cooperation with Gutian base. **Second,** construction of on-site teaching sites has been strengthened. According to the "six aspects" standards (there is a home field for learning and observation, a place for report interpretation, basic equipment, full-time and part-time commentators, text and video documents, as well as rules and regulations), one site integrating the standards on the six aspects above can be implemented and functions of the 100 on-site teaching sites in the city have been improved, so as to create a cluster of on-site teaching bases, and fully tap their comprehensive potentials, and then plan boutique training routes with different topics and sectors. **Third,** intensify foreign exchanges. Currently, 156 departments and units including the State Organs Work Committee of the CPC, the Ministry of Finance, the Ministry of Public Security, the National Civil Service Administration, and the National Defence University PLA China have set up education and training bases or teaching sites in Gutian Town. **Fourth,** it's important to accelerate the construction of training bases, enhance training capacity, and promote the construction of the four training bases, namely Gutian Cadre College Phase II, Gutian Cadre College Buyun Branch, Gutian Red Hotel, and Fujian Rural Commercial Bank Gutian Party School. **Fifth,** the training market has been expanded to launch operation centers in Xiamen, Guangzhou, Shenzhen, Shanghai and other places. In 2019, 5,196 training courses were undertaken with about 241,300 trainees, a year-on-year increase of 21.6%.

3. Strengthen Gutian's research brand building. In reliance on the cultural resources such as red tourism,

green development, Hakka culture, and the She Nationality customs of the 5A-level tourist attraction and surrounding areas, the brand advantages of the national patriotism education base, the national primary and secondary school student research and practice education base, and the Hong Kong and Macao youth study tour base have been leveraged to build a nationwide comprehensive practice base for youth, thereby accelerating the construction of national primary and secondary school research camps. A research and practice education network radiating outwards with Gutian Town as the core has been formed. Research and practice education routes for primary and secondary schools have been designed, and the research routes for high schools are being examined. As of the end of 2019, a total of 40 free public research activities for nearly 3,800 people had been provided to primary and secondary school students in Longyan City. Also, 31 autonomous regions, cities, and provinces across the country had been covered with training on Gutian red culture. More than 160 units including central ministries and commissions, central enterprises, private enterprises, and institutions of higher learning had set up education bases or teaching sites in Gutian Town, training over 200,000 people every year. Furthermore, more than 280 batches of training courses on research and practice education had been delivered in the town by the end of 2019, offering training to approximately 85,000 students.

Results

The red tourism development has promoted local catering, accommodation, services and other related industries and attracted a large number of powerful companies, including 16 which were above the designated size (namely industrial enterprises above designated size, construction enterprises with qualifications, enterprises above designated size of wholesale, retail sale, catering trades and hotels, service enterprises above designated size), covering the services in eight different kind of businesses: cultural and leisure tourism, research tourism, and Party education training, health preservation, shopping, commercial conventions and exhibitions, catering, and festivals, benefiting the local people and improving their living standards. Nowadays, there are three standard hotels above three-star level on the one-thousand-meter Gutian Street and ten-thousand-meter Gutian Road, 13 middle-grade comfortable budget hotels, 33 characteristic Red Army inns and agritainment B&Bs, with a total of about 2,000 beds. Also, there are over 100 eateries which can accommodate 12,000 people for dining at the same time. A wide variety of products are exhibited in more than 100 shops along the road and on the streets, with uniformed blue bricks and gray tiles in the facade, uniformed asphalt pavement on the roads, uniformed new materials for shop signs, and uniformed torch shape for

street lights, all of which convey prosperity. Adjacent to the former site of the Gutian Conference and relative to the red tourism development, the Wulong Village, the most beautiful village, has developed ecological and rural tourism, achieving satisfactory results and receiving a flood of tourists in B&Bs, agritainment, and Red Army inns. According to an incomplete statistics, the Gutian red tourism has directly helped in the employment of more than 1,000 people and indirectly employed 5,000 people. 50% of the income of people on the scenic spot is derived from tourism. Through the development of red tourism, the tourism industry chains have been formed in the town, redoubling the income of surrounding villagers. Moreover, libraries, basketball courts, and parks have been built in the village to enrich the lives of villagers. Also, rape flowers and lotus have been planted presenting to portray a picturesque all-season scenery and a happy and healthy life.

Experience and Inspirations

1. Innovate activities. Various educational activities such as "go global, call in, deliver door to door, diligent services, frequent innovation" have been carried out. Also, more than ten temporary exhibitions are held every year, so publicity teams are organized to give publicity on the exhibitions and professionals are dispatched to deliver nearly 500 lectures. It's necessary to hold such activities as the Olympic Torch Relay Ceremony, Passionate Singing on Squares, National Youth Songs, National Red Tourism Classic Tour, and "Red Gutian" Half Marathon in Shanghang County 2021; carry out the activity of "Ten-Thousand-Li Spread of Gutian Conference Spirit" and hold the exhibition Gutian Conference — A Milestone in the History of Party and Army Building in Changji Hui Autonomous Prefecture and Hutubi County of Xinjiang Uygur Autonomous Region, and Maoshan Mountain New Fourth Army Memorial Hall; hold the Red Culture Exhibition of the 90th Anniversary of Gutian Conference at Fujian Strait Folk Art Museum; and hold the Hakka Spiritual Culture Exhibition in Macao.

2. Innovate content. Through the implementation of the following ten activities in the Red Army town of Gutian (Wudi Community), that is, to be a Red Army soldier in memory of revolutionary martyrs; listen to a story of the Red Army in remembrance of extraordinary times; read a poem by Chairman Mao to nurture revolutionary sentiments; sing one red ballad to inspire patriotism; take a walk along the Red Army road to experience the revolutionary history; cook a meal of the Red Army to experience the hardships; stage a simulated battle to receive baptism of the war; hold a sports meeting to stimulate potentials of the human body; write an article related to the Red Army to pass on the red genes; earn a medal of honor as a pioneer of the time. Primary and elementary school students can experience the revolutionary history and recollect the extraordinary hardships of those years to inspire their patriotism in the new era. Film and television shows such as *Red Cradle, Gutian Conference, Gutian 1929, Explore Roads to Soul Building — into Gutian, Long March Road, New Stories — Gutian Special,* and *The Bugle from Gutian* have explored the highlights of patriotism in revolutionary stories and stories of old areas from an ordinary perspective, hereby acquiring both patriotism education and "good reputation."

3. Innovate forms. To fully explore red, green, classical, folk custom, and creative cultural themed programs, continuous efforts should be made to innovate the content of Gutian Rape Flower Festival, carry out more than one-month activities such as Han Chinese

Clothing Week, Little Red Army Research Week, Intangible Cultural Heritage Week, Red Song Flash Week, and Cultural and Creative Market Week. At the National Day in 2019, such activities as raising the national flag, watching the National Day celebration, singing a red song to our motherland, visiting the Gutian Conference former site, listening to revolutionary history stories, "National Flag and I," exploring the red-theme wax museum, offering flowers to Chairman Mao, and "I am in Gutian, a holy land, praying blessing for the motherland" signature activities were conducted in the scenic spot, all of which have been hugely popular among a majority of tourists and spurred a surge in patriotism. In 2021, the Red Song Flash Week to celebrate the "100th anniversary of the founding of the People's Republic of China" rape flower blossom season activities were held in the scenic area, and more efforts were made to develop Gutian Rape Flower Happy Valley. The rape blossoms throughout the Meihua Mountain in Gutian cordially paid tribute to the centennial birthday of the CPC, adding a touch of exclusive spring color to Gutian Town and presenting a rural revitalization featuring "red Party flag flying on the holy land permeated with profound rape flower fragrance."

Next Steps

To ensure continuous efforts will be made for the full utilization of the golden brand of the Gutian Conference, advantages of both red and green resources should be given full play and the promotion of the coordinated development of the red cultural industry and green ecological industry. This will ensure the "red and green" interplay and the forward leap development of culture, tourism, and healthcare industries. The quality of red tourist attractions will be further boosted to improve surrounding transportation facilities and living environment, drive rural residents around the scenic area to engage in entrepreneurship and employment in catering, accommodation, entertainment, transportation, commerce, and scenic area operations. Last but not least, practical measures will be adopted to promote the integrated development of red and rural tourism, so it can play an agricultural back-feeding role of turning farmers into tourist merchants and agricultural products into tourist commodities for the realization of its rural revitalization goal.

安徽六安市金寨县花石乡大湾村：
茶旅融合探索乡村扶贫新模式

Dawan Village, Huashi Township, Jinzhai County, Lu'an City, Anhui Province:
Integration of Tea and Tourism for a New Model of Rural Poverty Alleviation

摘要

安徽省六安市金寨县大湾村位于国家级自然保护区马鬃岭脚下，是金寨县 71 个重点贫困村之一。2016 年以来，大湾村的干部群众积极用好扶贫政策，依靠发展“山上种茶、家中迎客”特色产业，探索出一条具有大别山革命老区特色的旅游脱贫致富之路。通过积极开发民宿旅游、十里漂流等旅游项目，2020 年，大湾景区获批国家 3A 级旅游景区，过境游客达 35.8 万人次，真正让大湾村群众吃上了“旅游饭”。

挑战与问题

安徽省六安市金寨县大湾村位于国家级自然保护区马鬃岭脚下，总面积25.6平方公里，辖37个居民组、1032户3778人。2014年，建档立卡贫困户242户707人，贫困发生率29.12%。作为平均海拔800米以上的典型高寒山区村，大湾村基本兼具了深度贫困地区的所有致贫因素，全村没有一条像样的道路，群众消息闭塞，靠山吃山，以砍柴卖树维持生计。环境的恶劣、思想的保守、条件的落后，导致该村发展举步维艰，贫困发生率居高不下，2014年被列为全县重点贫困村。

措施

1.“自力更生”打造样板。2017年，村里成立旅游开发公司，将集体产权房屋改造成民宿，聘请本村村民作为“管家”负责日常运营，不但使村集体年均增收10万元，也为发动群众发展民宿做了示范。“细雨农家”“新云小院”“情宿大湾”，这些都是大湾群众自行开办的民宿，且各有特色。民宿店主通过线上线下相结合的模式，带动贫困户销售茶叶、黑毛猪肉、土鸡蛋等农副产品，实现了销售新突破。

2.“腾笼换鸟”转型升级。大湾村利用帽顶山、百丈岩、十二檀、三官庙等独特的自然景观和六安六区十四乡苏维埃政府旧址、安徽省工委旧址（汪家祠堂）等一批红色旅游资源，依托天马自然保护区秀美景观，融入茶文化元素，打造“基地+休闲”型景点，推进茶产业与乡村旅游、文化、康养等产业深度融合。依托大湾十里漂流，发展富有乡村特色的民宿和养生养老基地，打造乡村旅游精品线路，丰富乡村旅游业态和产品，带动全村观光休闲、旅游、文化、康养收入实现了新的突破。

3.“引凤筑巢”扩大规模。大湾村积极打造

3A 级旅游景区，加快文化旅游与扶贫工作的结合，为乡村旅游发展营造良好环境。引进企业开发“大湾民宿”，实现村集体年收入 7 万多元；引进鸿源集团投资建设 26 栋精品民宿，提升了大湾旅游的游客接待能力；引进社会资本投资开发大湾十里漂流，丰富旅游业态，辐射带动沿线餐饮住宿等服务业发展；引进市级龙头企业安徽蝠牌生态茶业股份有限公司，采取“龙头企业 + 农户”的产业发展模式，改造茶园变游园、生产中心变茶文化体验中心，茶旅融合，实现茶农增收，带动茶农茶厂就业。

4.“百花齐放”各显神通。随着乡村旅游业的逐渐兴起和金寨县旅游的大力对外推介，城里人到乡下休闲度假渐成时尚。在政府的支持下，部分农户开发出了以农家乐为主的乡村休闲旅游产品，目前已发展农家乐 32 家，乡村旅游已呈稳步发展趋势，带动 60 户贫困户实现增收。

成效

1. 基础设施不断完善。2014 年以来，大湾村对未通水泥路的居民组实行道路硬化全覆盖，对之前路面较窄的道路实施“扩面延伸”，修建 5 座桥，铺设完成全长 47 公里的水泥路；通过实施集中供水和高位引水工程，解决了全村饮水问题；积极实施供电线路改造，确保组组通生活用电；新建游客服务中心 1 处、旅游厕所 4 座、生态停车场 6000 平方米、旅游步道 3.5 公里；积极完善大湾 4 个安置点配套工程，结合乡村振兴，彻底解决居住环境的“脏、乱、差”现象，确保其安全、卫生，为广大游客提供干净、舒适的旅游服务。

2. 生态底色不断增亮。大湾村实施美丽乡村建设，开展三清四拆，拆除危旧房屋 95 户 260 间，对桥边街道实施沿街立面改造；开展“三线三边”整治，实施农村垃圾污水厕所整治“三大革命”，改厕 525 户；对文体广场供电、电信、移动、联通等杆线进行全面整改；新建天然林 1000 亩，植树造林 500 亩，并安排生态护林员进行管护；积极引导群众整理院落，使得村落面貌焕然一新。

3. 产业基础不断夯实。大湾村立足花石乡茶产业基础，对村内 1000 亩老茶园进行改造提升，新种植茶园 1000 亩，全村优质茶园扩大到 5000 亩。2018 年，茶叶已达到“一村一品”标准。2020 年茶季，仅大湾茶厂收购六安瓜片鲜叶就有 11 万余斤，实现茶农增收 400 余万元，带动 46 名茶农在茶厂就业，户均年增收 7000 余元。

4. 旅游吸引力不断增强。大湾村修缮红色遗址，开发旅游景区和项目，提供近 100 个就业岗位，村内群众优先就业，就业群众月均增收 2400 元；大湾村以自然资源入股分得门票收入的 40%

作为集体经济收入。2020 年，漂流项目仅试营业一个月，就吸引了近 6 万游客前来体验。

经验与启示

1. 必须通过生态优先实现绿色发展。大湾村拥有得天独厚的自然景观和文化资源，须坚定不移地走生态优先、绿色发展之路，以“景村共建”的模式整村推进乡村旅游开发建设，坚持“原生态”规划建设，着力打造与村民共生共融的开放式景区。在开发过程中，始终围绕“保护、完善、提高”思路，保存景区植被、道路、房屋等原始风貌，为景区和乡村“一体化”发展打下了基础。将小茶叶发展为大茶业，将小茶园发展为游乐园，树立“产业优、百姓富、生态美”的乡村旅游扶贫新形象。

2. 必须通过融合发展带动产业兴旺。充分挖掘贫困村的旅游资源构建产业链条，突出扶贫村旅游特色主题，推进乡村旅游与农业、工业、文化产业、体育产业、养老产业、交通产业、城镇建设等联动，带动蔬菜、畜禽等地方农产品的销售，促进农业种植业结构调整；带动农副产品、土特产品和旅游纪念品等旅游商品的加工销售，促进农村加工业的发展；带动交通运输、商贸物流、观光旅游、休闲度假、房地产等产业的发展，实现一、二、三产业互融互动。总之，要使乡村旅游产业成为拉动贫困村区域经济的“助推器”和“新引擎”，为当地农民创造更多就业机会。

下一步计划

下一步，大湾村将进一步发展乡村旅游产业，牢固树立“绿水青山就是金山银山”的理念，坚持企业主体、市场运作，尊重旅游企业的市场主体地位，更好地发挥政府引导、扶持作用，提升村民自身发展动力，把旅游发展作为乡村振兴的重要举措。通过天堂寨景区与马鬃岭景区辐射带动，以自然风光、红色文物游览为吸引点，以千亩茶园农事体验、农耕民俗文化体验为基础，以民宿体验、自驾旅游、研学旅游为主线，围绕着旅游元素形成丰富的乡村旅游产品体系，进一步使乡村旅游与乡村振兴深度融合，打造特色乡村旅游品牌，把大湾村打造成特色化、品牌化、品质化的乡村旅游样板村。

Abstract

Dawan Village in Anhui Province is one of 71 poverty-stricken villages in the county. It is located at the foot of the Mazongling Nature Reserve, Jinzhai County in Anhui Province. Since 2016, villagers have been actively developing tourism projects that will hopefully reduce poverty throughout the region, including the Ta-pieh Mountains' old revolutionary base. This Dawan scenic area was approved as a national 3A-level tourist attraction in 2020, and received 358,000 transit tourists. Clearly, the villagers can make a living through tourism development.

Challenges and Problems

The Dawan Village includes 3,778 people from 1,032 households. It is located at the foot of the Mazongling Nature Reserve and covers 25.6 kilometers. In 2014, 707 people from 242 households lived in poverty, which is roughly 29.12% of its population. Because the village is high in the mountain, with 800 meters altitude in average, it is impossible for the villagers to live a normal life. With no decent road, the village is blocked off from world news and events. Most of the villagers make ends meet by cutting down firewood which they sell for their income. The poor environment, conservative concepts, and backward conditions have caused development difficulties and led to poverty being a continuing issue.

Measures

1. Developing "self-reliance" for a new model. In 2017, a tourism company was developed to help lead the villagers out of poverty. This was done by training the villagers in how to maintain a B&B, how to become a housekeeper, and how to deal with daily matters of running a tourist attraction. This has resulted in an increase of RMB 100,000 for the local villagers and has set an example how a village can mobilize their members to develop B&Bs. So far, the villagers have operated many B&Bs such as the Xiyu Farmhouse, Xinyun Courtyard, and Qingsu Dawan. Each B&B has their own culture and is unique in their own way. More importantly, this has worked to drive poverty-stricken villagers to make more money and create unique products such as tea, pork, native eggs, thereby making sales breakthrough.

2. "Vacating the cage to change the birds" for transformation and upgrading. By taking advantage of the village's unique natural resources such as the Maoding Mountain and Baizhang Rock, it is able to integrate elements of tea culture and develop "the leisure + base" scenic spots. Other parts of the village that will be repurposed include Shi'ertan Ancient Village, Sanguan Temple, and red tourism resources in shisi Village, Liu Areas in Lu'an City. By centering the resources on industries such as rural tourism, culture and rehabilitation the tea industry of the village is heavily promoted. Another important part of the village is to focus on its natural resources. This involves rural tourism development and the creation of unique boutiques and the dissemination of its culture beyond its boundaries.

3. "Attracting the phoenix to build nests" for scale expansion. The village has actively built a 3A-level tourist attraction and accelerated the integration of cultural tourism and poverty alleviation. This works to create a sound environment for rural tourism development. Enterprises were also introduced to develop the Dawan B&Bs. These two projects work to create a collective income of more than RMB 70,000. The Hongyuan Group was introduced to build 26 boutique B&B clusters that will enhance the tourism capacity in the area. Another part of the village is earmarked for the creation of social capital. Private capitals were also introduced to invest in rafting areas in Dawan. This will entail investing and creating industries such as catering and accommodation along the route. In addition, the city-level leading enterprise Anhui Fupai Ecological Tea Co., Ltd. is introduced to transform tea gardens through industrial development model of "leading enterprises + peasant households." This will hopefully work to integrate tea and tourism which will lead to increasing the tea farmers' income by helping them find jobs at tea factories.

4. "All flowers bloom together" for common development. Rural tourism is a trend that many people are beginning to appreciate and enjoy. This is due to the recent rise in publicity of Jinzhai County. Many urban residents have made their ways to this part of the country with the goal of taking a relaxing vacation. In addition, the government is working to create a support system for this type of tourism. They have worked with farmers to

develop rural leisure and tourism related products related to agritainment. Currently 32 sites for agritainment have been developed. Rural tourism has also steadily developed during this time, resulting in the increase of income for 60 poverty-stricken households.

Results

1. The infrastructure is improved. Over the past 7 years, the village has implemented many projects that seek to build up the infrastructure of the village. For example, a new project was recently undertaken to reinforce the roads that were previously inaccessible to those who live near narrow roads. This resulted in five roads and 47 kilometers of new cement roads being built, which created pavement of new accessible roads. Another project was focused on building a centralized water supply and high-level water diversion which have helped solve the villages' drinking water problem. Yet another was focused on upgrading the existing power supply of the village. This helps the villagers get more access to electricity and also ensures that the tourists will have electricity. Another tourist center was also built along with infrastructure upgrades to existing buildings. In all, 6,000 square meters of ecological parking lot and 3.5 kilometers of side walk are newly built. More importantly, upgrades to the current living conditions of the villagers have also been developed. Most villagers no longer live in dirty, chaotic, and poor living conditions. The aim of rural revitalization, however, is to ensure the safety and hygiene for the villagers and the tourists.

2. The ecology is developed. The village has undergone cleanups and demolitions of 260 houses of 95 households. Streets have been renovated and villages are under construction with the goal of creating a better ecological habitat. The renovation on Three Lines, Three Arounds (environmental governance along the railway line, highway line and river line, as well as around the city, inter province and scenic areas) has also been constructed. In addition, the Three Revolutions of rural garbage, sewage, and toilet systems have been implemented and 525 toilets were built. Power supply, China Telecom, and China Mobile and other rod lines in the cultural and sports square have been comprehensively rectified. 1,000 *mu* of natural forests are newly built and 500 *mu* of land has also been utilized for management and protection. The tourists are guided to clear their courtyard which will present a completely new village look.

3. The industrial foundation is consolidated. The foundation of the tea industry in Huashi Township has transformed and upgraded old tea gardens. This resulted in new gardens that are over 1,000 *mu* and therefore created over 5,000 *mu* of tea gardens for the village. This is successful because the village tea was known as the "one product for one village" standard in 2018. More importantly, vendors love the products that come from the village. In 2020, the Dawan Tea Factory purchased more than 110,000 *jin* of fresh Lu'an Guapian leaves. In turn, this has helped the villagers increase their income by more than RMB 7,000.

4. The tourism attractiveness is enhanced. The village has taken steps to increase the income for the local villagers. One important aspect of the tourism business is to prioritize local villagers when looking for

new employees. This has provided nearly 100 jobs and has increased their income by RMB 2,400. Also, 40% of income from ticket sales through equity participation based on natural resources is taken as a collective economy income. In 2020, the one-month trial operation of rafting attracted nearly 60,000 tourists.

Experience and Inspirations

1. Ecology and green development are the pillars of this project. Because the village is full of scenic areas, the village must prioritize its natural landscape. As well, the cultural resources of the area provide a great escape for those who are willing to take in the views. One important part of the village is also the local villagers. It would be great if the local villagers were able to interact with the tourists and offer them a true experience. Developments are currently underway that seek to improve existing infrastructure including vegetation, roads, and homes. The protection, improvement, and upgrade of the village is important to its development as this will be beneficial to the local villagers as well as the tourists. In addition to buildings, there have been efforts to build up existing tea farms into a big industry which will hopefully serve for poverty alleviation and new recreational parks.

2. Another important part of the industry is integrated development. This is important because we must fully utilize the tourism resources of poverty-stricken villages for industrial chains. The highlight of the industry would be to promote the linkage of rural tourism with agriculture, industry, and culture. In addition, the vegetation, livestock, and homes in the village will be among the featured highlights. It is important to drive sales of local items that are unique to this village. By driving the development in transportation, commerce, and sightseeing, the natural integration of the village will hopefully be on full display. Overall, the rural tourism industry should become a booster and new engine to stimulate the regional economy of impoverished villages.

Next Steps

With the natural beauty of its lucid waters and lush mountains, the Dawan Village will further develop rural tourism in conjunction with the support and guidance of the government. This will hopefully enhance its development and lead to rural revitalization. Driven by the Tiantangzhai Scenic Area and Mazongling Scenic Area, attracted by natural sceneries and red cultural relics, based on tea planting experience and farming culture experience, guided by the main line of B&B experience, self-driving tours and research tours, and revolving around the tourism elements for a rich rural tourism product system, rural tourism will be further integrated with rural revitalization to develop a characteristic rural tourism brand, hereby building the village into a model of rural tourism with characteristics, branding and quality.

北京门头沟区清水镇梁家庄村：
“门头沟小院”文旅赋能绿色发展模式

Liangjiazhuang Village, Qingshui Town, Mentougou District, Beijing Municipality:
“Mentougou Courtyard” Cultural Tourism Empowers a Green Development Model

摘 要

北京市门头沟区梁家庄村坚定践行“两山”理论，坚定走好绿色转型发展之路，将精品民宿作为推动乡村振兴的突破口，持续推进“门头沟小院”绿色发展，通过“门头沟小院”文旅产业赋能帮扶脱低，全面实现了门头沟区梁家庄村整村脱低摘帽的攻坚目标，打造出首都生态涵养区生态富民、绿色发展的新模式，成为引领门头沟区域旅游发展的精品民宿新样板。

挑战与问题

北京门头沟区梁家庄村土地 387 亩，全部是退耕还林地，种植杏树。2016 年，梁家庄村认定低收入农户 94 户 165 人，被列为市级低收入村。村庄虽然位于龙门涧风景区南部，但属于深山区，交通不便，旅游基础设施薄弱，“食、住、行、游、购、娱”旅游六要素缺乏，文旅体验项目少，旅游可持续发展动力不足，壮大村集体经济面临巨大挑战。

措施

1. 提升人居环境。梁家庄村 2019 年累计清理木柴、乱堆乱放杂物 80 余吨，栽种花草 1300 余棵，完成街坊路石板铺装及观景台亮化工程，探索形成垃圾分类“定人定时、上门收集”模式，固定 2 名垃圾分类指导员，实现“垃圾不落地”。联系帮扶企业投资 160 万元，新建 394 平方米服务中心，广泛为村民开展插花、茶艺、编织、面点等志愿服务培训。村庄人居环境不断提升，2020 年 9 月被评为“2020 年中国美丽休闲乡村”。

2. 导入“门头沟小院”。梁家庄村抓牢精品高端民宿这个突破口，采用“村集体 + 公司”的模式，与帮扶单位合资成立高端民宿开发运营公司——北京梁家庄创艺乡居文化有限公司，发展“门头沟小院”精品民宿产品。合资公司中，村集体占股 51%。2019 年，帮扶单位投入 1600 万元改造完成 17 套闲置房屋。截至目前，累计 19 套房屋已投入运营。

3. 打造“高端精品蔬菜种植基地”。2018 年，梁家庄村在北京市农林科学院的大力支持下，利用新开发的 90 亩土地，投入 334 万元低收入帮扶资金实施芦笋种植项目，采取村企合作模式打造高端精品蔬菜种植基地。一方面，由农林科学院专家及专业种植公司对土壤检测、项目设计、种植管理、后期采收等各个环节进行全过程跟踪指导，着力解决人才技术问题。另一方面，为保证芦笋后期取得

稳定持续收入，村集体与京研益农公司签订了收购协议，采取保底价和市场价两种收购方式，有效避免了因市场价格波动带来的损失，确保了村集体与农户的收益。在招标项目施工过程中，梁家庄村及周边村民有 60 余人参与了基地建设，带动 28 户低收入农户就业增收。

成效

1. 经济效益。2018 年，梁家庄“门头沟小院”项目实现村民增收 35 万元，解决 55 户脱困、97 人脱低。2019 年，民宿综合收入 150 多万元，实现农户年租金收入 14.3 万元，解决 82 户脱困、137 人脱低，提前半年完成了全年全村脱低攻坚目标。2020 年，克服疫情严重影响，通过建立市场化的运营机制，带动村民就业 40 余人，发放工资 16 余万元。

2. 社会效益。三年来，梁家庄村按照美丽乡村规划，新增加了道路、河桥、观景台等景点，帮扶公司积极协助实施了梁家庄村委会花坛摆放、墙壁挂花、主路街景绿化、村内 81 盏红灯笼亮化、24 幅墙壁画等工程，提升和美化了梁家庄村的产业运营环境，村容村貌得到极大改善。2020 年梁家庄村获评“2020 年中国美丽休闲乡村”。

经验与启示

1. 盘活存量是乡村振兴的潜在动力。梁家庄村虽然地处大山、交通不便，但在村庄发展上，村党支部发挥主观能动性，将闲置农房、村集体土地等存量资源充分盘活，借助帮扶单位力量，把民宿产业和精品农产品产业做出了特色、做出了名气。

2. 绿色发展是乡村振兴的必由之路。“绿水青山就是金山银山”，发展必须处理好人与自然的关系，促进人与自然的和谐共生。梁家庄村始终坚定不移地走生态优先、绿色发展道路，因地制宜探索发展精品民宿和特色农业，使良好生态成为乡村振兴发展的重要支撑、重要保障。

下一步计划

下一步，梁家庁村将继续落实践行“两山”理论，充分发挥国有企业资源、技术、资金、团队优势和区域自然生态环境优势，聚力打造“门头沟小院 +”田园综合体模式，丰富区域旅游产品和旅游吸引力，为村经济体持续造血赋能，形成保障农民长期增收的有效形式，将梁家庄村打造成具有示范意义的特色村、富裕村、文明村，为建设新时代美丽乡村做出更大贡献，让梁家庄人过上幸福安康的新生活。

Abstract

The village has a firm practice that is focused on green transformation and development. This is done by using the Two Mountain Theory and by expanding the boutique B&Bs. In addition, the breakthrough for rural revitalization in Liangjiazhuang Village, Mentougou District, Beijing Municipality is aimed at poverty alleviation through the Mentougou Courtyard cultural tourism. This new development model features more green and ecological enrichment in the capital's ecological conservation area.

Challenges and Problems

The village covers an area of 387 *mu*, it is focused on rebuilding farmland for the planting of apricot trees. In 2016, the village was designated low income with 165 people of 94 households falling into the below poverty area. Despite the beautiful and scenic views, the village is not sustainable for rural tourism. The village has poor infrastructure, poor transportation, and limited entertainment options resulting in the immense number of challenges for a strong village collective economy development.

Measures

1. Improve human settlements. Since 2019, the village has cleaned up more than 80 tons of firewood and heaped sundries. Villagers have also planted 1,300 flowers and plants which serve to brighten the appeal of the village. It has moved garbage collection model with two people leading it. There is a fixed "personnel and fixed time for door-to-door collection" to ensure that the village streets remain clean and free of garbage. The village has also invested RMB 1.6 million into building up services for the villagers, built a new service center of 394 square meters, and provided villagers with volunteer services, tea art, and pastry cooking training. As a result of these improvements, the village was rated as China's Beautiful Leisure Village in September 2020.

2. Introduce the "Mentougou Courtyard." To build upon the existing boutique B&Bs, village leaders have joined hands for an enterprise with Beijing Liangjiazhuang Chuangyi Rural Culture Co., Ltd. This firm is a high end boutique B&B development and operation company which focuses on creating luxurious B&Bs. The village collective holds 51% of shares in the joint venture company. In 2019, the enterprise helped by investing RMB 16 million which went towards the renovation of 17 idle homes. To date, 19 homes have been put into operation.

3. Develop a "high-end quality vegetable planting base." By partnering with the Beijing Academy of Agriculture and Forestry Sciences, the village has developed about 90 *mu* of land, most of which have been invested into the low-income assistance fund. The village and the academy focused on making asparagus and hoped to build high-quality vegetables. The experts helped the villagers by guiding them through the process of planting — beginning with soil testing, project management, and harvesting. Village leaders have also formed a separate agreement with Jingyan Yinong (Begin) Seed Sci-Tech Co., Ltd. and has adopted acquisition methods of guaranteed low price and market price. This can help its farmers avoid losses and ensure a stable income from its vegetable harvest. During the bidding process, more than 60 people from the village and the surrounding areas came together to help build a new base. This project was beneficial to the low-income villagers as they were able to get income from this project.

Results

1. Economic performance. In 2018, the "Mentougou Courtyard" project in the village registered an income increase of RMB 350,000 for villagers, lifting 97 people out of poverty and helping 55 households increase their income. In 2019, the comprehensive income in B&B operation reached more than RMB 1.5 million and the annual rental income of peasant households was RMB 143,000, helping 137 rise out of poverty. In addition, 82 households also saw a year-on-year increase in income. Thus, its goal of increasing the income of the low earners was achieved. However, in 2020, the COVID-19 epidemic has hurt the industry very badly. In response, a new mechanism that focused on assisting villagers find jobs was created.

2. Social benefits. Over the past three years, the village has added roads, river bridges, and viewing platforms in accordance with the beautiful village construction planning. The companies offered active assistance in projects such as the Liangjiazhuang Village committee parterre putting, flower hanging on the wall,

streetscape greening of main roads, and 81 red lanterns lighting and 24 wall paintings, thereby improving the industrial operation environment of the village and its look. Last year it won the "Most Beautiful Leisure Village in 2020" trophy.

Experience and Inspirations

1. Tapping existing resources is a potential driving force for rural revitalization. The village is inconvenient for transportation because it is in a mountainous region. This has led to the initiative that seeks to tap into the potential of the village by using existing resources such as idle farmhouses and village collective land for development.

2. Green development is inevitable for rural revitalization. The relationship between nature and man must be cultivated at every opportunity. The village has lucid waters and lush mountains which are invaluable assets to the collective and must therefore be properly addressed. It has been taking steps to ensure it developing the area's unique culture. Also, it has followed the path of ecological priority and green development and developed boutique B&Bs and characteristic agriculture according to local conditions to support and ensure rural revitalization.

Next Steps

The next step is to use the enterprise relationships that have been made and take advantage of the natural resources of the village. Further more, the Two Mountain Theory will be used to build a pastoral complex model of Mentougou Courtyard. Using this model will result in regional tourism products and tourism attractiveness that will empower the village economy and create an effective production system for the village. Village farmers will also benefit from this program as they will earn more income and contribute to the development of their locality.

广东茂名市高州市根子镇元坝村：
丰富完善荔枝特色产业链，助推乡村振兴

Yuanba Village, Genzi Town, Gaozhou City, Maoming City, Guangdong Province:
Perfected and Characteristic Industrial Chains of Litchis Drive Rural Revitalization

摘 要

广东省茂名市根子镇元坝村盘活农村土地资源，发展优势特色产业，完善产业链，促进产业融合发展，大力发展旅游业，以乡村旅游助推乡村振兴。元坝村的特色产业为荔枝，凭借荔枝走出了“一果兴、百业旺”的富民兴村之路。产业规模化、组织化、品牌化，通过“龙头企业＋农民合作社＋专业户＋农民”模式，在完善荔枝标准化种植、加工、仓储、物流、电商、科研的基础上，发展养蜂、文化旅游、观光采摘、民宿、康养、餐饮等新业态。打造根子河碧道、红荔胜境、水墨桥头、初心广场等众多网红打卡景点，使元坝村成为八方宾客品游千年荔乡文化的旅游目的地。

挑战与问题

广东省茂名市根子镇元坝村地处粤西山区，下辖 12 个自然村，有 519 户 2522 人，地处大唐荔乡核心区——世界上最大的连片荔枝林中心地带。该村始建于东晋年间，是岭南道教先驱、东晋名医潘茂名行医制药之地，有木偶戏、山歌、粉皮、豆饼角等诸多非物质文化遗产留存至今。元坝村虽然有着丰富的自然和文化资源，但存在很多问题：一是基础设施落后，村里的道路窄，行车、会车不便，荔枝成熟的时候，自驾来采摘的游客多，因缺少停车场，导致车辆乱停乱放，交通阻塞；二是产业结构单一，村里的支柱产业是荔枝，荔枝上市时间是 5—7 月，除了荔枝村里没有其他产业，而且荔枝主要是鲜果销售，销售产品单一；三是群众发展意识不强，不了解乡村发展政策，思想守旧，对农村的发展缺乏前瞻性。

措施

1. 发挥党员作用。为更好地推进乡村振兴工作，元坝村对全村 74 名党员进行精准管理，坚持“因地制宜、按需设岗、人岗相适”原则，按照每位党员的年龄、特长以及履职能力等设定了组织员、宣传员、助理员、调解员、联系员、清洁员 6 种岗位，带动群众积极投入乡村旅游业和其他产业的发展。例如村组织员培训村民学会电商销售，创新开展“荔枝 + 订制”扶贫带货活动，吸引消费者现场订制村中贫困户的荔枝树，实现荔枝预售。

2. **打造荔枝品牌。**元坝村被列为广东省特色农产品优势区，其生产的白糖罂荔枝、储良龙眼、桂圆肉均为国家地理保护标志产品；全村有 3 种产品为全国名特优新农产品；村内注册商标 8 个，分别为“蒸姑娘”“树鲜森”“好利皇家”“果滋佳”“绿滋佳”“绿礼坊”“绿美农”“绿滋山庄”；打造了“根子贡荔”“根子有荔”“蒸姑娘”等根子元坝特色品牌；设计有冷链包装箱 7 款。实现了整村产业“统一技术、统一加工、统一品牌、统一宣传”四个统一。

3. **提升荔枝产业。**元坝村大力培育发展农业龙头企业和农民专业合作社，发挥联农带农作用，推动荔枝生产、销售、品牌打造提档升级。深入推进“三变”改革，通过“龙头企业 + 农民合作社 + 专业户 + 农民”模式，大力发展荔枝标准化种植、深加工、仓储、物流、电商等环节。目前，元坝村已发展成为国家级电子商务进农村综合示范县示范村建设点，80% 的荔枝鲜果通过电商进行外销，剩余的 20% 鲜果供应省内高端市场。荔枝干、龙眼干、桂圆肉等干果加工设备 150 多套，每天鲜果加工能力达 200 吨；荔枝深加工产品有荔枝酒、荔枝汁、荔枝发酵型饮料、荔枝酥等。

4. **整治乡村环境。**元坝村通过召开村民代表会议、村级“大喇叭”宣讲、入户动员等方式，因地制宜首创了“小三园”模式，即：发动村民利用清拆后的空地种植时令蔬菜、栽花种草或种植小果树，打造小花园、小菜园、小果园。目前该村已建

成错落有致的“小三园”265 个。农村无害化卫生户厕改造普及率达 100%，建设标准化公厕 3 座；自然村配备保洁员和建立生活垃圾收运处理体系覆盖率达 100%。扩改公路 6 公里，新建双车道水泥路 3.5 公里，新建停车场 8 个。

成效

元坝村以 6 公里的荔乡景观大道和 4 公里的根子河碧道为主轴，将整村打造成为极具岭南乡村风貌的甜美荔乡，拥有根子河碧道、红荔胜境、水墨桥头、初心广场等诸多特色景点，凭借独有的自然和文化景观吸引国内外游客前来参观。2020 年，该村接待游客超 100 万人次，荔枝季逢周末，每天接待游客超 3 万人次；各类产业总产值约 3.8 亿元，农民年人均纯收入 5.8 万元。元坝村已获得国家森林乡村、首批广东省美丽乡村精品线路、茂名市乡村振兴“精彩 100 里”的精华所在地、广东省十大美丽乡村等荣誉，已成为茂名市乡村振兴的“样板村”。

经验与启示

1. 大力发展特色产业。元坝村形成以荔枝产业为龙头、带动三产融合发展的产业发展模式。荔枝产业实现了规模化、组织化，产业链完整、产业配套完善，吸引大学生、外出务工人员返乡创业，

荔枝产业实现可持续发展。

2. 全面规划村庄建设。元坝村及早规划、统一设计，三年前就已经部署开展了农房管控、风貌提升工作。尊重群众意愿，发挥群众主体作用，引导村民积极参与精品民宿、特色土作坊建设。元坝村结合“三清三拆三整治”工作，因地制宜首创了“小三园”模式。实现让山水、田园、村落、产业和谐共生、相得益彰。

下一步计划

元坝村继续加强对产业链的延伸，发挥利用好元坝村的自然和文化特色资源，探索特色旅游业态，整理和发掘当地丰厚的历史文化、荔枝文化、红色文化和民俗风情，以“古色、红色、绿色”为主题，整合水利河道治理、农村乡村振兴、交通乡村道路建设等各方资金，一盘棋推进，将元坝村建设成为“产业兴旺、生态宜居、乡风文明、治理有效、生活富裕”的美丽乡村。

Abstract

Yuanba Village, Genzi Town, Maoming City, Guangdong Province has revitalized industrial chains with the goal of promoting rural revitalization for rural tourism. Litchi is a characteristic product of the village, and it has enriched the quality of many people's lives. By following the principles of "industrial socialization, systematization, and branding," through the "leading enterprises + farmers' cooperatives + professional households + farmer" the village has been able to develop news businesses. These businesses include warehouse logistics, e-commerce, and scientific research. The goal of these projects is to create better ways to promote bookkeeping, cultural tourism, and sightseeing. The village also contains many popular tourist destinations such as Genzi River Green Road, Red Litchi Wonderland, Ink Bridgehead, and Chuxin Square. Because of this, the village has been able to draw thousands of tourists.

Challenges and Problems

Yuanba Village is located at the center of the Datang Lixiang (litchi growing region in the Tang Dynasty) and has one of the largest areas of litchi forest in the world. The village population consists of mountain people from 12 natural villages, 2,522 people and 519 households. It is famous because Pan Maoming practiced medicine in this village during the Eastern Jin Dynasty. Many intangible cultural heritage such as puppet shows, folk songs and bean starch sheets have all been developed in this area. While the village is culturally rich, it is facing several challenges. One of these is poor roads and lack of parking spaces. One adverse effect this has on the village is that people tend to park on the side of the road, causing traffic delays and congestion. Another issue is that the village relies upon one product for their industry: litchi. The litchi is sold in markets from May to July which makes other months difficult for the villagers. The final issue that the villagers must deal with is that they are not skilled in rural development as they lack the necessary skills to turn the industry into a profitable business enterprise.

Measures

1. Play the role of Party members. The goal of the village is to train the villagers on how to properly run the industry. This was done by "adjusting measures according to local conditions, setting up posts according to needs, and matching people to posts." In addition, the village has elected decision-making seventy-four party members, six organizers and staffs. In addition, assistants, mediators, liaisons and cleaners have all been formed to encourage the people to promote the rural tourism industry better. The villagers are trained in e-commerce which will hopefully help alleviate the poverty throughout the village.

2. Develop litchi brands. The village is listed as an advantageous area with characteristic agricultural products in Guangdong Province, with the Baitangying litchi, Chuliang longan, and dried longan pulp as the

geographic national products. Three agricultural products in the village are classified as nationally famous, special and new. There are eight registered trademarks, namely Zheng Gu Niang, Shu Xian Sen, Hao Li Huang Jia, Guo Zi Jia, Lv Zi Jia, Lv Li Fang, Lv Mei Nong and Lv Zi Shan Zhuang. In addition, the village has also created characteristic brands of Yuanba Village, Genzi Town, such as "Genzi Gongli," "Genzi Youli" and "Zheng Gu Niang." It has designed seven types of cold chain packaging boxes for unified technologies, processing, brands and publicity for the industry of the village.

3. Improve the litchi industry. The villagers have focused on compensating the farmers that develop leading agricultural enterprises as they have guaranteed to give full pay to the farmers. This is good for the village because by developing new ways to grow litchi, the village will get more income. The standardization of litchi planting has been improved through three in-depth reforms of "leading enterprises + farmers' cooperatives + professional households + farmers." The village is also successful in the e-commerce sector as 80% of litchi sales have come from online sales while the other 20% is from high-end markets. There are more than 150 sets of equipment for dried fruit processing such as dried litchi, dried longan and dried longan pulp, with a daily processing capacity of 200 tons of fresh fruits. Deep-processed litchi products include litchi wine, litchi juice, litchi fermented beverages and litchi cakes.

4. Renovate the rural environment. A new model has been implemented, which seeks to provide the villagers with more representation and mobilization. They are mobilized to use the cleared land to plant seasonal vegetables, flowers, and grass. Sometimes they are asked to grow small fruit trees that will supply the food for small villages. The village has also moved beyond planting as they have renovated three household toilets. In addition, they have created cleaners, waste collection and transportation. It has also expanded 6 kilometers of roads, built 3.5 kilometers of two-lane roads and built eight new parking lots.

Results

The village has developed into a beautiful, productive place with litchi farms driving its growth. Since it is made up of 6 kilometers of litchi township avenue and 4 kilometers of Genzi River Green Road as the main axis, it has attracted many domestic tourists. In 2020, the village welcomed more than 1 million visitors. During the peak litchi season, the village was averaging 30,000 tourists per day which had a positive effect on the financials of the village as they gained about RMB 380 million. Because of this, the farmers income also increased to RMB 58,000. It was awarded national honors such as the first batch of

beautiful village boutique routes in Guangdong Province, essence of "wonderful 100 *li*" of the rural revitalization project in Maoming City and top ten beautiful villages in Guangdong Province. It has also become a model village for rural revitalization in the city.

Experience and Inspirations

1. Develop characteristic industries. The village has developed a multi-step approach that focuses on primary, secondary, and tertiary industries that play a leading role in the litchi industry. This systematic approach facilitates the industrial chain necessary for the litchi business to become profitable. College students and migrant workers have been attracted to live and work in the village, helping in its sustainable development.

2. Scheme village construction. By applying the principles of unified designs, the village has started to renovate old rural homes. Local villagers had expressed their wish to keep their buildings look the same. With this in mind, homes are designed to ensure to have a uniformly modern look. In combination with the work of "cleansing and elimination, demolition and removal, environmental renovation and improving," the village has created the "small three gardens" model according to local conditions, achieving the harmonious coexistence and mutual development of landscape, rural cultures, villages and industries.

Next Steps

Yuanba Village will continue to explore characteristic tourism businesses and explore its rich historic local culture, litchi culture, red culture and folk customs by extending its industry and taking advantage of its native resources. Several construction projects are underway that will help modernize the village. Some of these villages include rural revitalization, rural road constitution and water conservation efforts. The goal is to make the village beautiful as a whole, while retaining aspects that have made it great: livable ecology, civilized style and effective governance.

浙江丽水市景宁畲族自治县大均乡：
文旅融合绽放“五朵畲花”

Dajun Township, Jingning She Autonomous County, Lishui City, Zhejiang Province:
Integration of Culture and Tourism for Development of Five Villages with the She Nationality Characteristics

摘 要

浙江省景宁畲族自治县大均乡始终坚定“绿水青山就是金山银山”的发展理念，优化空间布局和环境协调融合，着力构建全域旅游发展新格局，逐步形成三杆大均、水韵泉坑、田园伏叶、畲寨李宝、古驿新庄“五朵畲花”齐绽放的局面，有效促进了民族区域社会经济又好又快发展，让乡村旅游成为乡村振兴新引擎，为旅游助力乡村振兴提供了生动的畲乡样本。

挑战与问题

浙江省景宁畲族自治县大均乡面积 86 平方公里，森林覆盖率 89%，下辖 5 个行政村 60 个自然村，户籍人口 4479 人，全乡畲族人口占总人口的 35.4%。大均乡民族风情浓郁，自然景观秀丽，历史文化悠久，但是由于地处浙西南山区，交通等基础设施滞后，旅游资源开发程度较低，年轻劳动力大量外出务工，一些农户人走屋空，甚至一度出现“空心村”现象。如何壮大农村产业基础、吸引年轻群体回流、激活乡村振兴，就成为大均乡发展所面临的难题。

措施

1. 传承古风古韵。大均乡 5 个行政村中，现有省级历史文化古村落重点村 1 个、一般村 2 个。为加强对自然景观和文物古迹的保护，大均乡坚持修旧如旧，投资 1900 余万元开展历史文化古村落建设，目前已完成大均、伏叶、李宝 3 个村的保护和提升工程。充分利用古村、古宅、古道、古树等资源打造有品质的景观，如将大均村村口有着 1100 余年历史的古樟打造成“迎客唐樟”景观；充分开发利用大均古街，将其打造成为“中国畲乡之窗”景区的核心景点，让古风古韵成为大均乡的金字招牌。

2. 坚持村景融合。依托各村资源优势，按照“一村一品”进行村庄规划，还原农村“看得见山，望得见水，记得住乡愁”的本色，成功打造三杆大均、水韵泉坑、田园伏叶、畲寨李宝、古驿新庄“五朵畲花”齐绽放的局面。目前，全乡 5 个行政村中，已建成大均村、李宝村、伏叶村三个 3A 级景区村。

3. 联动串联景点。大均乡距县城 13 公里，为进一步完善交通圈，开通专班公交，每日在县城和大均乡之间往返 28 趟，以满足游客和当地居民的出行需要。此外，还有畲乡绿道从县城延伸至大均泉坑村，有效串联起了景宁县城、凤凰古镇、畲乡之窗景区等区块，形成美丽小环线，游客可利用公共自行车、观光游览车等绿色交通工具沿绿道骑行游玩。畲乡绿道不仅提升了大均的知名度和美誉度，也串联起了沿线大量的优质民宿，有效带动民宿经济的发展，成为助推村民致富和乡村振兴的“致富绿道”。

4. 引导民宿迭代升级。大均乡创新民宿发展模式，全面提升民宿产业的核心竞争力，打造大均

乡“品质旅游，民宿担当”这一金名片，走出了一条从无到有、从弱到强、从俗到精的嬗变之路。伏叶村民宿农家乐产业完成了从“食在农家的 1.0 版本”到“兼具旅游六要素的 2.0 版本”，再到“有文化有内涵的 3.0 版本”的三次升级，形成了高、中、低农家乐民宿发展层次，可同时满足不同消费层次、不同文化背景游客的需求。

5. 开发畲族特色业态。以国家级非物质文化遗产项目畲族婚嫁体验为核心，定期举办农民畲歌赛、梅山西瓜节、伏叶民族乡村百花大会、畲族渡亲节、洗井泼水节、彩虹跑、花园跑、中国畲乡国际铁人三项赛等畲族传统民俗活动；为游客增设民族书屋、畲画馆、畲药馆、畲族服饰体验馆、畲绣馆、畲茗工坊等文化场馆和工艺品游购馆。

6. 发展特色水域经济。立足优越水环境，积极打造浮伞漂流、天然沙滩烧烤、游泳池、露营目的地等休闲游基地，推出泼水节、冬泳联赛等品牌亲水活动，深度开发水上瑜伽康养、桨划游船体验等项目。以涉水救援业务培训为载体，成功吸引 IRIA 国际搜救教练联盟急流救生训练基地、省消防应急救援基地落户大均，成为全国四个水域救援培训基地之一。

成效

1. 民生保障、百姓安居。大均乡强力推进危旧房改造工作，共拆改十余栋危房；完成畲乡之窗 4A 级景区提升工作；5 个行政村均全面完成饮用水达标提标建设工程，实现村村饮用水安全；大力推进垃圾分类，推进垃圾分类试点乡镇建设，新建四分类垃圾收集房 8 个、户内外二分桶 2498 套，建立垃圾兑换回收便民服务站 1 个；全面完成厕所革命，完成全乡 15 个公厕修缮；配齐各类设施 168 个，粉刷墙面 500 多平方米。大均乡实现了乡村的美丽蜕变，人居环境不断改善，群众和游客的幸福感倍增，满意度不断提升。

2. 集体增收，百姓致富。大均乡 2020 年 5 个行政村全年实现村集体经济总收入 182.33 万元，较 2014 年增长 169%。农村人均可支配收入

25377 元，较 2014 年增长 132%。2020 年全乡接待游客 148.12 万人次，实现营业收入 2379.74 万元，其中农家乐民宿营业收入 1650 万元。

3. 文旅支撑，产业兴旺。大均乡现已形成以文旅产业为支柱，以水域救援产业、精品研学产业为补充的生态产业集群。全乡共有民宿 33 家，农家乐 58 家，餐位数 3000 余个，床位数 557 张，其中金宿 2 家、银宿 2 家。水域救援产业规模不断扩大，2018 年至今，水域救援培训基地已完成各类培训 120 余班次，培训学员 3500 余人，创收培训费用 2100 余万元。

大均乡产业振兴和畲乡之窗效应已经初步显现，先后入选“省级旅游风情小镇”“浙江省 AAAA 级景区镇”等。

经验与启示

1. 深挖文化底蕴。大均乡畲族文化底蕴深厚，文化传统悠远，人文优势鲜明，是畲族文化的重要聚集地。如李宝村以“魅力畲寨”的理念指导规划，紧抓“风情畲寨”的定位，助推洞宫畲王寨项目开工建设，带动村庄整体发展。

2. 改善人居环境。依托“小城镇综合整治”“六边三化三美”“厕所革命”“美丽乡村建设”等重点工作，开展环境整治，进一步改善景区周边乡村的基础设施、公共服务和人居环境，夯实乡村旅游发展基础。开展美丽庭院、花样农家评比等活动，最大限度地调动村民的积极性，激发村民的“爱美之心”。深入开展“五水共治”，清理河道逾 15 公里，清理出垃圾逾 45 吨，治理黑臭河 1 条、小微水体 5 条。通过 4A 级景区乡镇建设，让大均的广大群众和外地游客共享发展成果，主客之间真正实现了“美人之美、美美与共”。

3. 融合数字技术。作为全市首个开通 5G 网络的乡镇，大均创新推出智慧旅游导览系统，在为游客提供智能化自助服务的同时，也为农家乐民宿提供了宣传推广的平台。如：伏叶村根据“田园”定位，发展数字农业休闲体验园，打造鱼菜共生现代化农业实践体验、数字共享菜园；泉坑村引入采用以色列 MABR 技术进行污水处理的系统，不仅可在旅游旺季满足全村污水处理的需求，还将污水处理点打造成乡村景观，供村民和游客休憩游览，此乃全市首例。诸多相关举措全面提升了旅游服务品质，实现“数字 + 旅游”，使数字赋能乡村振兴。

下一步计划

旅游助力乡村振兴之路，任重而道远。在新时代的新起点上，大均乡将继续集水域救援、山林经济和文旅融合的产业发展于“一体”，以“5G 通信 + 智慧生态治理平台”和“两山金融服务 + 乡村生态信用评定体系”为技术与金融的“两翼”，推动“两山”理论在大均乡域的创新实践，加速融合发展，拓宽致富之路，进一步彰显民族文化特色，全力打造乡村振兴畲乡新样板。

Abstract

In adherence to the concept of "lucid waters and lush mountains are invaluable assets," the Dajun Township, Jingning She Autonomous County, Lishui City, Zhejiang Province has optimized the layout and coordinated integration of its environment. It hopes to build a new all-for-one tourism template by gradually advancing the common development of the five villages with the cultural and traditional elements of the She ethnic group. Emphasis on education, business and punting in Dajun Village, charming Quankeng Village, idyllic Fuye Village, the She minority village — Libao Village, and the ancient courier station — Xinzhuang Village are among those covered in a comprehensive plan which has advanced the sound and rapid social and economic development of ethnic regions. It has effectively developed rural tourism into an efficient engine for rural revitalization and facilitated rural revitalization through the development of the elements of the culture, tradition, heritage and history of the She minority group.

Challenges and Problems

With an area of 86 square kilometers and a forest coverage rate of 89%, Dajun Township includes 60 natural villages with five administrative villages. With a registered population of 4,479 people, 35.5% of which consists of the She ethnic minority. Despite rich native customs, picturesque natural landscapes and long history and culture in the township, it has limited infrastructure, including transportation and tourism resources due to its mountainous location in the southwest Zhejiang Province. A large number of young laborers have opted to work outside. Some peasant households left their hometowns and a number of "hollow villages" have appeared. Strengthening the rural industrial base has been a problem in the township, along with attracting the young to return to their hometowns so they can become proud participants in the development and vitalization of the rural lifestyle.

Measures

1. Ancient styles and charm. Among the five administrative villages in the township, one is a provincial-level historical and cultural ancient village and two are general villages. To enhance the protection of natural landscapes, cultural relics and historical sites, the township has invested more than RMB 19 million in the construction of historical and cultural ancient villages and restored them to their original form. Dajun Village,

Fuye Village and Libao Village have been successfully protected and upgraded. Resources like ancient villages, ancient residences, ancient roads, and ancient trees have been fully utilized to create quality landscapes. For example, the 1,100-year-old ancient camphor tree at the entrance of Dajun Township has been developed into a guest-greeting venue. What's more, the ancient streets of Dajun Township have been thoroughly explored as a core scenic spot of the "Window of the She Township in China," making antique styles and charm into the township's "golden brand."

2. Emphasize the village-scenery integration. In reliance upon the advantages in resources of each village, in accordance with concept of "one product for one village" in village planning, and to restore rural nature as a "wonderland bearing lucid waters, lush mountains and nostalgia," remarkable achievements have been achieved in the five villages with the She Nationality characteristics that emphasizes education, business and punting in Dajun Village, charming Quankeng Village, idyllic Fuye Village, the She minority village — Libao Village, and the ancient courier station — Xinzhuang Village. Currently, among the five administrative villages in the township, three are 3A-level scenic villages — Dajun, Libao and Fuye.

3. Improve the connectivity of scenic spots. As Dajun Township is 13 kilometers away from the county, 28 shuttle buses from the county to the township are opened daily for residents and travelers alike. In addition, the She Township greenways extend from the county to Quankeng Village of Dajun Township, and connect such blocks as Jingning County, Phoenix Town, and the scenic spot of the "Window of the She Township." This forms a beautiful loop line, allowing tourists to ride along the greenways through green transport such as public bicycles and sightseeing buses. The greenways have boosted the popularity and reputation of the township and increased the interconnectivity of quality B&Bs along the route. This has substantially improved the economic development of the B&Bs and created a "rich greenway" for rural revitalization and the prosperity of the villagers.

4. Guide the iterative upgrading of B&Bs. Through the innovative development of B&Bs and enhancement of the industry's core competitiveness, the township has created its golden brand of "Quality Tourism, B&Bs Responsibility" which has evolved from scratch, from weakness to might and from basic to refined. The agritainment industry of Fuye Village has been upgraded from its basic version 1.0 in food supply to version 2.0 which integrates the six elements of tourism. From there, it has been elevated to version 3 which signifies a wealth of cultural products and offers. The gradual elevation of scale has stratified B&Bs at high, middle and low levels, allowing it to the varying demands of tourists at different consumption levels and with different cultural backgrounds.

5. Develop the She Nationality native businesses. Anchored on the She Nationality wedding experience and the national intangible cultural heritage and traditional customs such as singing contests of farmers, Watermelon Festival of Meishan Village, Hundred Flowers Conference of Fuye Village, Bride Escorting Festival of the She Nationality, Well-Washing and Water-Sprinkling Festival, Color Run, Garden Run, and the International Triathlon

Race of Chinese She Township are regularly staged. Moreover, cultural venues and craft shopping halls, ethnic bookstores, She Nationality galleries, She Nationality medicine halls, She Nationality costume experience halls, She Nationality embroidery halls, and She Nationality tea workshops are also set up for tourists.

6. Develop the local water economy. Leisure activities such as rafting, natural beach barbecues, swimming pools and camps are created based on the superior water environment. Similarly, it can be optimized to launch the Water-Sprinkling Festival, Winter Swimming League and other branded activities and projects such as water yoga rehabilitation and boat paddling. The IRIA rapids life-saving training base and the provincial fire emergency rescue base are also successfully launched in the township with water rescue training as a carrier, making the township one of the four such training bases in China.

Results

1. Improve people's livelihood for peaceful life. The township has demolished and renovated more than ten dilapidated houses through vigorous renovation; upgraded the 4A-level tourist attractions of the "Window of the She Township"; five administrative villages have been covered by up-to-standard safe drinking water; promoted the construction of pilot towns for garbage sorting, resulting in the building of eight four-class garbage sorting rooms and 2,498 two-class bins indoors and outdoors. A garbage exchange and recycling service station has been established; 15 public toilets in the township have been renovated for a complete overhaul; 168 facilities of various types have been equipped, and more than 500 square meters of walls have been painted. Significant improvements have been achieved in the township, resulting in a desirable living environment that boost the satisfaction and well-being of locals and tourists alike.

2. Increase the collective income to enrich people. In 2020, the five administrative villages of the township registered a total income from their collective economy of RMB 1.8233 million, an increase of 169% over 2014. The per capita disposable income in rural areas was RMB 25,377, an increase of 132% over 2014. The township received 1,481,200 tourists and registered an operating income of RMB 23,797,400 in 2020, RMB 16.5 million of which came from the operating income of agritainment and B&Bs.

3. Support cultural tourism for a flourishing industry. The township has now formed an ecological industry cluster with cultural tourism as the pillar and water rescue and quality research and education industries as the supplement. In the township there are 33 B&Bs and 58 sites for agritainment, with more than 3,000 seats for meals and 557 beds, including two gold-ranked B&Bs (high-end standard) and two silver-ranked B&Bs (ordinary standard). The scale of the water rescue industry continues to expand. Since 2018, more than 120 training courses have been completed in the training base. More than 3,500 people have completed their training, at a total cost of more than RMB 21 million.

The industrial revitalization and the success of the window of the She Township has generated accolades and awards. It has been successively honored with such titles as a provincial-level town with tourism styles and a 4A-level scenic town in Zhejiang Province.

Experience and Inspirations

1. Maximize the cultural theme & messaging. The township is an important showcase for the She culture and traditions. The Libao Village, for example, guided the planning on the concept of a "charming She minority village," and highlighted the positioning of a "fascinating village," to facilitate the construction of the Donggong Shewangzhai project (located at Libao Village) and the overall development of villages.

2. Improve human settlements. Relying on the key tasks outlined in the "Comprehensive Renovation of Small Towns," "Six Sides, Three Improvements, Three Beauties (to achieve the goal of beautiful cities, villages, and houses at the roadside, railway side, waterside, mountain side, city side, and countryside through cleaning, greenery, and embellishment)," "Toilet Revolution," and "Beautiful Village Construction," environmental enhancements have been implemented for the improvement of rural infrastructures, public services and human settlements in the surrounding scenic spots of the villages and the consolidation of the developmental foundation of rural tourism. Activities such as the appraisal of beautiful courtyards and diverse rural residences are also conducted to spark the enthusiasm of villagers and stimulate their passion for beauty. The work on "Five Water Governance (involving sewage treatment, flood control, drainage, water supply, water conservation)" is implemented. As a result, more than 15,000 meters of riverways and more than 45 tons of garbage have been cleared and one fouling river and five small and micro waters have also been controlled. The construction of 4A-level scenic towns has helped the masses of Dajun Township and tourists are benefiting from the development. They have become active partners and participants in "appreciating the culture of others for the prosperity of human civilization" between hosts and guests.

3. Integrate digital technologies. As the first township with 5G coverage in the city, the Dajun Township has launched a smart tour guide system to offer tourists intelligent self-service and also provide a publicity platform for the agritainment and B&Bs. For example, the Fuye Village has developed experiential digital agricultural leisure parks based on its positioning as an "idyllic development." It has provided a modernized agricultural experience in aquaponics, and also created digitally shared vegetable gardens. The Quankeng Village has introduced the city's first sewage treatment system using the Israeli MABR technology. This can adequately meet the demands for sewage treatment during the tourist season. It has built sewage treatment plants in rural landscapes for the use of villagers, visitors and tourists. This has improved the service quality of tourism and achieved the goal of "digital + tourism" and rural revitalization through digital empowerment.

Next Steps

There is still a long way to go for rural revitalization through tourism development. At the threshold of the new era, in adherence to the integration of the industrial development of waters rescue, forest economy and culture-tourism integration with "5G communications + smart ecological governance platform" and "two mountains financial services + rural ecological credit rating system" as the "two wings" of technology and finance, the township will promote the innovative practice of the "Two Mountains Theory," accelerate integrated development, pave the road to prosperity, demonstrate the native ethnic culture and strive to create a new model for the rural revitalization of the She Township.

山西晋中市平遥县段村镇横坡村：
横坡生态园打造古村旅游“横坡梦”

Hengpo Village, Duancun Town, Pingyao County, Jinzhong City, Shanxi Province:
Hengpo Ecological Park Realizes the “Hengpo Dream” of Ancient Village Tourism

摘要

横坡村以集体合作社为基础，与县龙头企业煤化集团合作开发包括采摘体验区、生态景观区、军事拓展体验区、国学文化体验区、水上项目体验区、窑洞文化体验区、民俗风情体验区、农耕文化体验区、生态养殖区和食品加工区 10 个功能区在内的农旅融合产业集聚区，把曾经“迟暮”的古村打造成远近闻名的休闲度假村，走出一条以乡村旅游为龙头、村企共建、三产融合发展的乡村振兴之路。

挑战与问题

横坡村距世界文化遗产平遥古城 15 公里，共有土地面积 3448 亩，其中耕地面积 2200 亩，人口 826 人。横坡村自然生态良好，文化底蕴深厚，黄土高原丘陵山区特色土窑洞、砖窑洞、四合院、古街、古巷、古庙宇等古建古迹保存完好，2016 年被评为“中国传统村落”。但横坡村基础设施薄弱，农户分散的生产经营模式导致土地产出效益低下，是典型的贫困村。

措施

1. 编制实施乡村发展规划。横坡村先后编制实施《横坡村学华西十五年规划》《新农村建设规划（2009—2020）》《横坡村美丽乡村建设规划（2017—2030）》，提升基础设施，改善人居环境。《段村镇全域旅游横坡古村度假区规划》搭起以横坡村为中心、辐射带动周边 2 个乡镇 14 个村发展的古村旅游度假区框架，结合土地利用、产业发展、居民点布局、生态保护和历史文化传承等因素，科学布局乡村生产、生活、生态空间，保护传统村落和乡村风貌，将乡村符号与大众旅游消费需求充分融合起来，因地制宜打造乡村旅游业态。

2. 优化旅游发展环境。一是重构当地生态环境。横坡生态庄园面积 1.2 万余亩：实施农林种植 4700 余亩，其中经济林 3000 余亩、生态林 1700 余亩；荒山造林 7000 余亩。二是完善基础设施和公共服务。庄园 18.5 公里主干街道安装了太阳能路灯，建起了污水处理厂、垃圾填埋点。配套建设游客接待中心、标准旅游厕所、特产超市和停车场，重点景点开通免费 WiFi。修建功能齐全的村民文化教育培训中心、老年人日间照料中心和卫生室。

3. 聚焦增收创新模式。一是创办峰威集体经济合作社，推行土地资金入股生产互助股份合作。合作社产生的收益，60% 对农户分红，40% 用于集体经济积累。二是以“名村 + 名企”模式与县龙头企业平遥煤化集团合作开发生态庄园项目，企业以资金入股，村集体和村民以林地、窑洞入股，集体流转土地以物作价获得动态收益，村民的工资、林地、窑洞分红由合作社发放。

4. 促进产业多元融合发展。横坡生态园是一个农旅融合的产业集聚区，其中包括温家岭林果采摘体验区、苗岭黄土风情生态景观区、军事拓展体验区、道庄庙传统国学文化体验区、鹤里河水上项目体验区、古村窑洞文化体验区、新村民俗风情体验区、现代农业农耕文化体验区、生态养殖区和食品加工区等 10 个功能区，形成了一条集田园观光、农耕采摘、亲子研学、住宿餐饮、特产采购于一体的，农、林、牧、副、工、贸多元循环可持续的产业链，激活自我造血功能。

5. 打造古村文旅品牌。横坡村建设农耕文化博物馆、窑洞文化博物馆、道庄庙儒道佛文化体验区，举办乡村文化节，保护传承农村文化，振兴乡村风气。横坡村借力“平遥中国年”“平遥国际摄影大展”等金字招牌，举办横坡古村春节赏灯会，承办国际摄影大展采风活动，开通微信、抖音等自媒体账号，促进乡村旅游消费，打响“横坡古村”文化旅游品牌。

成效

横坡村通过生态庄园项目，发展乡村旅游，完成“荒山就地变园区，农业就地变工业，农民就地变工人”的华丽蜕变，实现了“土地增效，农民增收，多元发展”的转型跨越，村民过上了打工领工资、土地领租金、股金领分红、过节领福利的美好生活。2016 年至今，横坡村累计接待游客 180 余万人次，旅游综合收入 3600 余万元，村民年人均收入 17000 元，村集体资产逾 980 万元。全村有 1/3 的家庭其家庭资产已达到 100 万元，87% 的家庭在城镇拥有住宅，93% 的家庭拥有一辆小轿车。

经验与启示

1. 农民主体为本。以合作社为纽带，以特色产业为抓手，将乡村旅游产业发展的投资主体、经

营主体和受益主体联结为一体，实现小农户和现代农业发展的有机衔接，保障村集体和全体村民更好地分享旅游发展红利。峰威合作社被国家农业农村部评为“国家级示范合作社”。

2. 村企联建为要。采用“龙头企业 + 集体 + 村民”的合作模式，盘活土地资源，获得政策资金支持，实施连片开发、规模经营，加快三产融合和城乡融合。横坡生态庄园项目流转土地 1.2 万亩，每年可带动周边 14 个行政村土地增收 1200 余万元，直接受益农户达 4000 户。项目投资额达 1.9 亿元，其中享受国家支持资金 4000 余万元。横坡生态庄园项目被列入“全国光彩事业重点项目”。

下一步计划

横坡村提出打造国际乡村旅游度假区的“横坡梦”，启动编制“十四五”发展规划，按照“产业兴旺、生态宜居、乡风文明、治理有效、生活富裕”的总要求，以创建国家 4A 级景区为牵引，升级文化品质，开发“仙坡”品牌特色乡村旅游产品，重点打造美丽乡村文化节和“平遥中国年我在横坡过大年”节庆活动，推进智慧景区建设，提升旅游体验，打响横坡古村文化旅游品牌。进一步完善产业布局和功能分区，丰富乡村经济业态，加快本地能人培育，拓展农民增收空间，培育乡村发展新动能。完善合作社章程制度与村规民约，推动合作化庄园经济与乡村治理协同发展，争当全国乡村振兴的排头兵。

Abstract

The Hengpo Village in Pingyao County, Shanxi Province has joined hands with Shanxi Pingyao Coal Chemical Group Co., Ltd., the county's leading enterprise, to develop 10 agricultural and tourism integration industrial clusters. This involves experiential areas for fruit picking or harvesting, ecological landscape, team spirit buildup, traditional Chinese culture, water project, cave dwelling and folk customs. The cultural farming, ecological breeding and food processing areas have helped develop the backward ancient village into a popular leisure resort — blazing a rural revitalization trail through the prioritization of rural tourism, village-enterprise co-construction and integrated development of the primary, secondary and tertiary industries.

Challenges and Problems

The village is 15 kilometers away from the Pingyao Ancient City, a UNESCO World Heritage Site. It covers a total land area of 3,448 *mu*, including 2,200 *mu* of arable land and a population of 826 people. Endowed with sound ecology and centuries-old culture, it has well-preserved ancient buildings and historic sites on the hilly and mountainous areas of the Loess Plateau. Earthen cave dwellings, brick cave dwellings, courtyard houses, ancient streets, ancient alleys, and ancient temples are some of the village's distinctive characteristics. In 2016, it was rated a "Traditional Chinese Village." The primitive infrastructure of the village and the haphazard production and operational modes of its peasant households have resulted in its low output efficiency, reducing it to a poverty-stricken area.

Measures

1. Prepare and implement plans for rural development. The village has successively compiled and implemented the *Hengpo Village Fifteen-Year Plan in Learning from Huaxi Village, New Rural Construction Plan (2009 — 2020),* and *Beautiful Village Construction Plan in Hengpo Village (2017 — 2030)* to improve infrastructure and human settlements. It has also prepared *Planning on Hengpo Ancient Village Resort of Duancun Town All-for-one Tourism* to set up a framework of ancient village tourism resorts centered on Hengpo Village. This development is expected to expand to 14 villages in the surrounding two towns, protect traditional

villages and their rural features by considering factors such as land use, industrial development, residence layout, ecological protection and historical and cultural inheritance. A scientific layout of rural production spaces, life and ecology are similarly factored to achieve the full integration of rural symbols and tourists' consumption needs and to develop a rural tourism mechanism based on local conditions.

2. Optimize the environment for tourism development. First, the local ecological environment has been reconstructed. The Hengpo Ecological Manor covers an area of more than 12,000 *mu*, of which more than 4,700 *mu* allocated for agricultural and forest planting (including more than 3,000 *mu* of economic forests and more than 1,700 *mu* of ecological forests) and more than 7,000 *mu* apportioned for barren hill afforestation. **Second,** infrastructure and public services have been improved. Specifically, solar streetlights have been installed along the main street of 18.5 kilometers in the manor. Sewage treatment plants and landfill sites have also been established. The supporting facilities of tourist reception centers, standard tourist toilets, specialty supermarkets and parking lots have been equipped and free WiFi in key scenic spots are provided. Moreover, full-featured cultural education and training centers for villagers, day care centers for the elderly and clinics have been built.

3. Innovative models to increase income. First, the Fengwei Collective Economic Cooperative has been created to establish a joint stock partnership through land pooling, capital as shares and mutual production assistance. For cooperative-generated income, 60%

of it is distributed to farmers as dividends and 40% used for collective economic accumulation. **Second,** the ecological manor project has been developed in cooperation with the county's leading enterprise Shanxi Pingyao Coal Chemical Group Co., Ltd. through the "famous villages + famous enterprises" model. The company made a capital investment while the village collective and villagers pooled forest land and cave dwellings as shares. The collective's transferred land was taken as goods to generate a dynamic income stream. Wages and dividends of the villagers from forest land and cave-dwelling pool were distributed by the cooperative.

4. Promote the diversified and integrated development of industries. The Hengpo Ecological Park is an industrial cluster area integrating agriculture and tourism, including 10 functional and experiential areas: Wenjialing Fruit Picking, Miaoling Loess-style Ecological Landscape, Team Spirit Buildup, Daozhuang Temple Traditional Chinese Culture, Heli River Water Project, Ancient Village Cave Dwelling Culture, New Village Folk Customs, Modern Agricultural Farming Culture, Ecological Breeding Area and Food Processing. Altogether they have led to an industrial development chain which integrates rural sightseeing, farming and fruit picking, parent-child research, accommodation and catering and specialty procurement. The circular sustainable development of agriculture, forestry, animal husbandry, sideline production, industry and trade contributed to the overall improvement in the village. They have also instilled in the villagers the virtues of self-reliance and hard work.

5. Build cultural tourism brands of ancient villages. Hengpo Village has built the farming culture museum, cave dwelling culture museum and the Daozhuang Temple — Confucianism Taoist and Buddhist cultural experiential areas. It has organized rural cultural festivals to protect, preserve and pass on its rural culture and revitalize the rural lifestyle. Leveraging the golden brands of the "Pingyao Chinese Year" and "Pingyao International Photography Exhibition," the village holds the Spring Festival lantern appreciation events in Hengpo Ancient Village. It has hosted the International Photography Exhibition and opened its own social media accounts such as WeChat and Tik Tok to promote the rural tourism consumption and the cultural tourism brand of "Hengpo Ancient Village."

Results

Through the ecological manor project and the development of rural tourism, the village has turned barren hills into parks, agriculture into industries and farmers into workers. It has also achieved its goal of "land efficiency improvement, farmers' income growth and diversified development." As a result, villagers have elevated their standard of living by earning wages through jobs, obtaining rents from land, receiving dividends from stocks and reaping the cultural benefits from festivals. Since 2016, the village has received more than 1.8 million tourists, with a comprehensive tourism revenue of more

than RMB 36 million, an annual per capita income of RMB 17,000 and collective assets of more than RMB 9.8 million. One-third of the village households have assets of RMB 1 million, 87% of which own houses in cities and towns, 93% of them own a car.

Experience and Inspirations

1. Farmers are the core of rural development. With cooperatives as the link and characteristic industries as the means, the village has integrated investment, business and beneficiary entities for rural tourism industry development. It fortified the organic link between small peasant households and modern agricultural development to ensure that the village collective and all the villagers can share the dividends of tourism development. Notably, its collaborative partner, the Fengwei Collective Economic Cooperative, is rated a "National Demonstration Cooperative" by the Ministry of Agriculture and Rural Affairs of the People's Republic of China.

2. Village-enterprise co-construction is vital. Based on the cooperation model of "leading enterprises + collectives + villagers," the village has revitalized land resources, obtained policy support for funding and conducted continuous development and large-scale operations to fast-track the integration of the three industries and urban and rural areas. The transferred land of 12,000 *mu* in the Hengpo Ecological Manor Project increases the income of 14 surrounding administrative villages by more than RMB 12 million each year, directly benefiting 4,000 peasant households. Total investment for the project is RMB 190 million, of which more than RMB 40 million is subsidized by the government which has listed it as a "National Key Project of Glorious Causes."

Next Steps

With the "Hengpo Dream" of developing an international rural tourism resort proposed, the village is scheduled to compile the development plan for the "14th Five-Year Plan." In accordance with the general requirements for "prosperous industry, livable ecology, civilized rural customs, effective governance, and affluent life" and guided by the creation of a national 4A-level tourist attraction, the village will upgrade the quality of its cultural offers. It will also develop the characteristic rural tourism products of the "Xianpo" brand which will be focused on the creation of beautiful rural cultural festivals and the "Pingyao Chinese Year" festivities. Also, it will promote the construction of smart scenic spots, boost tourism experience to promote the cultural tourism brand of Hengpo Ancient Village. As well, it will improve its industrial layout and functional zoning, enrich the business systems of rural economy, accelerate the training of capable locals, expand the channels to increase the income of farmers and foster new drivers for rural development. It will also enhance the cooperative's charter system and village regulations and rules. More importantly, it will proactively promote the coordinated development of cooperative manor economy and rural governance and endeavor to be a vanguard of rural revitalization in the country.

天津蓟州区穿芳峪镇小穿芳峪村：
“小穿乡野公园”发展模式

Xiaochuanfangyu Village, Chuanfangyu Town, Jizhou District, Tianjin Municipality:
“Xiaochuan Countryside Park” Development Model

摘 要

天津市蓟州区穿芳峪镇小穿芳峪村通过打造全景式乡野公园，整体推进民俗民宿、现代园林、乡村景区和节庆活动四个旅游板块融合，采用集体管理、抱团发展的运营模式，抓住机遇，将乡村旅游产业链向纵深延伸，发展文化产业和特色农业，将“小穿乡野公园”打造成有市场价值、相互关联、布局合理的复合型产业体系。

挑战与问题

天津市蓟州区穿芳峪镇小穿芳峪村是典型的半山区，地形地貌条件较好，风景秀丽，全村共有农户 82 户 274 人。小穿芳峪村地处山区，山多地少，农业生产率低下，且产业单一，缺乏特色产业。村庄基础设施差，环保意识弱，经济落后，是有名的穷村。

措施

1. 制订发展规划。为确保历史文化与现代文明实现良性对接，小穿芳峪村制订了“一园、二景、四板块”的文化强村规划，即：打造全景式乡野公园，建设卧牛山和望牛岭两个风景区，整体推进民俗民宿、现代园林、乡村景区和节庆活动四个旅游板块的融合。

2. 确定发展模式。为提升产业竞争力，小穿芳峪村确立了“集体＋公司＋农户”的发展模式，成立了股份有限公司。一是将村民的土地流转到村集体，二是盘活村民宅基地，村民用农地和宅基地入股，村集体统一规划，公司统一经营，实现了由小农经济向规模化发展的转化，壮大了集体经济实力。

3. 发展特色民宿。在占地 600 亩的乡野公园内建设了 11 个房车基地及 4 栋邵窝（陕北窑洞）、1 个云杉餐厅，打造了集餐饮、住宿、会议、婚庆等服务于一体的乡村文旅全产业链。全村还建成精品徽派四合院（民宿）17 个（包院），目前还有 7 座精品民宿正在建设中，村内发展风格统一的民宿，分散经营，统一监管。

4. 建设特色农业。将土地规模化经营作为改革突破口，将全村土地全部流转到村集体，成立种植专业合作社，统一栽植高收益的白蜡等优质苗木，发展景观植物培育、生态农产品种植。这样一来，不仅让特色农业具备了观赏和体验功能，还借助于现代物流手段发展出定制化的配送服务，既增加了旅游活动的维度，又为传统农业拓宽了市场。

5. 举办节庆活动。利用冬季的特殊天气条件，依托小穿乡野公园的场地优势和综合服务能力，秉承绿色健康发展理念，以特色乡土文化为核心，开展冰雪旅游活动。具体包括五个部分：一是冰雪景观展示；二是魔幻灯光夜景；三是冰上游乐活动；四是特色食宿与休闲娱乐；五是特色乡村文化展示与体验。通过这些活动，突破冬季乡村旅游活动单调匮乏的瓶颈，为游客带来冬季冰雪活动的快乐体验，为本地乡民带来有品位的年节文化活动，扩大优秀地域文化的社会认知，增加小穿乡野公园的活动内容与范围，提高“小穿旅游”的品牌影响力，增加小穿乡野公园及区域内民宿业的冬季经营收入，实现乡村旅游的全时、全景式发展。

成效

小穿芳峪村的年人均收入，从 2012 年的

8400 元增加到 2020 年的 4.01 万元；村集体收入，也从 2012 年的 0 元增加到 2020 年的 100 万元。该村先后被评为“全国休闲农业与乡村旅游示范点”“全国美丽宜居乡村”“国家 3A 级旅游景区”“中国美丽休闲乡村”“天津市美丽宜居乡村”和“全国乡村治理示范村”。

经验与启示

1. 统一思想，明确发展方向。小穿芳峪村党支部带领村民走出家门，先后到北京、陕西、保定、成都等地的中高端特色民宿参观考察，开阔眼界、统一思想，将乡村旅游作为该村长远发展的支柱型产业，大力发展中高端旅游民宿。

2. 推进改革，增强发展活力。2015 年，小穿芳峪村抓住土地制度改革试点的契机，村内村外统筹考虑、统一规划，实现了村庄规划、土地利用规划、产业规划、基础设施规划“四规合一”，为小穿芳峪村的发展注入了生机和活力。通过建设村民住宅楼，使现有村台全部变成乡村旅游产业用地，全村实现居住产业分离，壮大了集体经济。

3. 拓宽渠道，增加收入来源。小穿芳峪村的发展，为村民带来了多渠道的收入来源：一是老百姓的土地保值增值款；二是合作社入股分红的收入；三是宅基地流转后的租金收入；四是宅基地抵押贷款入股股份公司的红利收入；五是在公司和合作社的打工收入。

下一步计划

借力乡村振兴战略，助推产业发展：一是加大基础设施建设。完成 88 户、1.2 万平方米的农民住宅小区建设。二是打造田园综合体。整合区域资源，提升“小穿乡野公园”景区功能，建设污水处理、雨水收集系统，启动夏季漂流、冬季雪乡增收项目。三是挖掘文化资源价值。规范“唐槐”旅游景点；寻源“邵窝”文化、明清“隐逸”文化，恢复“龙泉园”“响泉园”“问源草堂”等穿芳园林。

Abstract

Through the creation of a panoramic countryside park to advance the integration of the four tourism sectors of folk customs and B&Bs, modern landscape, rural scenic spots and festivals, and the adoption of collective management for common development, the Xiaochuanfangyu Village, Chuanfangyu Town, Jizhou District, Tianjin Municipality, has seized the opportunity to extend its rural tourism industry chain for the development of cultural industries and agriculture to build the "Xiaochuan Countryside Park" into an interconnected composite industrial system with market value.

Challenges and Problems

Located in a typical semi-mountainous area with sound topographical landform and picturesque scenery, the Xiaochuanfangyu Village encompasses 274 people in 82 peasant households. Due to its mountainous terrain and limited arable land, the village lags behind in agricultural productivity. With poor infrastructure, weak awareness of environmental protection and a disadvantaged economy, the village is known for being impoverished.

Measures

1. Formulate a development plan. In order to ensure a healthy connection between traditional customs and modern civilization, the village has formulated the "one park, two scenery, and four sectors" plan to develop a powerful cultural village. Through a panoramic countryside park and the development of the two scenic areas of Woniu Mountain and Wangniu Ridge, it aims to promote the integration of the four tourism sectors of folk customs and B&Bs, modern landscape, Shaowo (cave dwelling of northern Shaanxi) and historical culture.

2. Determine a development model. The village has determined the development model of "collectives + companies + peasant households" and established joint stock limited companies to enhance its industrial competitiveness. **First,** transfer villagers' land to village collectives. **Second,** revitalize villagers' homesteads. Leasing or shareholding can be adopted in the operation, and villagers can invest in shares through their agricultural land and homesteads for a unified planning of village collectives and unified operation of companies. Transformation of the small-scale peasant economy into large-scale development can be achieved and the collective economy can be strengthened.

3. Develop culturally authentic B&Bs. Eleven RV

bases, four cave dwellings and a Yunshan Restaurant have been built in the countryside park with an area of 600 *mu*, creating an industrial chain of rural cultural tourism services such as catering, accommodation, conferences and wedding. In addition, 17 boutique Hui-style quadrangle courtyards (B&Bs) have been built in the village, and seven boutique B&Bs are under construction. The village aims to develop B&Bs with unified style, decentralized management and unified monitoring.

4. Develop native agriculture. Parcels of land are transferred to village collectives to establish professional planting cooperatives as a reform breakthrough. Quality nursery stocks such as high-yield ash trees are uniformly planted to cultivate landscape plants and ecological agricultural products. The planting can enjoy the functions of viewing and experience, and also facilitate to develop customized distribution services by virtue of modern logistics. This increases the variety of tourism activities and expands the market for traditional agriculture.

5. Stage traditional festivals. Based on the special weather in winter, advantageous sites and comprehensive service capabilities of Xiaochuan Countryside Park, ice-snow tourism activities are according to the concept of green and healthy development with the authentic local culture as the core. Activities are categorized into five parts: ice and snow landscape program, astro-tourism (stargazing, night sky viewing), special accommodation, leisure entertainment and experiential rural culture activities and exhibits. These activities promote an all-season program, especially during winter when tourism activities are sparse. Also, this promotes traditional Chinese New Year festivities and other local festivals. They are vehicles of expanding the knowledge, understanding and appreciation of regional culture, further increasing the depth and breadth of exciting activities at the Xiaochuan Countryside Park. More importantly, they elevate the Xiaochuan Tourism brand image and improve the operating income of the park in winter and the B&B industry in the region.

Results

The per capita income of the village has increased from RMB 8,400 in 2012 to RMB 40,100 in 2020, and the village collective income has also increased from RMB 0 in 2012 to RMB 1 million in 2020. The village has been

successively rated as a national demonstration site of leisure agriculture and rural tourism, a national beautiful and livable village, a national 3A-level tourist attraction, a beautiful leisure village in China, a beautiful and livable village in Tianjin, and a national demonstration village of rural governance.

Experience and Inspirations

1. Unanimous agreement for clarity in development direction. Tourism has been regarded as a pillar industry after the visit of the Party branch of the village and the local villagers to high-end B&Bs in Beijing Municipality, Baoding City, Shaanxi Province, Chengdu City, etc. They recognize the importance of the tourism industry for the village's long-term development and for the medium and high-end B&Bs.

2. Promote reforms to enhance development vitality. In 2015, the village took the opportunity to reform the land system with coordinated and unified planning for land use, industries, infrastructure planning, infusing vitality into its development. Construction of residential buildings for villagers has helped transform all the existing village sites into a piece of land for rural tourism. The separation of residence and industry resulted in a stronger collective economy.

3. Expand income streams to increase purchasing power. The development of the village has broadened the sources of income for its residents. The main five channels of income streams are funds from land value preservation and appreciation, income from cooperatives' share dividends, rentals from the transfer of homesteads, dividends from joint-stock company shares through mortgage on homesteads, and income from working in companies and cooperatives.

Next Steps

The strategy of rural revitalization is leveraged to boost industrial development. **First,** increase the construction of infrastructure and complete the construction of residential communities with an area of 12,000 square meters for 88 households. **Second,** build a rural complex. Integrate regional resources to enhance the function of the "Xiaochuan Countryside Park" as a scenic spot, establish sewage treatment and rainwater collection systems and launch the income-boosting programs of rafting in summer and snow village tourism in winter. **Third,** maximize the utilization of cultural resources. Develop and standardize the "Tanghuai" tourist attraction (a miracle in which an ancient locust tree, originated in the Tang Dynasty). Discover the source of "Cave Dwelling" (Shaowo in Chinese) culture, "Seclusion" (Yinyi in Chinese) culture of the Ming and Qing dynasties, and restore gardens such as "Longquan Garden," "Xiangquan Garden," and "Wenyuan Cottage."

湖南张家界市武陵源区：
“世界自然遗产旅游 +” 的脱贫之路

Wulingyuan District, Zhangjiajie City, Hunan Province:
Road to Poverty Alleviation through “World Natural Heritage Tourism +” Model

摘 要

脱贫攻坚以来，湖南省张家界市武陵源区围绕“把景区旅游效益辐射到乡村中去”“把农民带进旅游产业链上来”“把游客带到农户家中去”“把农民带到旅游致富路上来”四大路径，探索出以“四带动、四转变”为特征的旅游扶贫模式：实施核心景区带动，促进农业向旅游业转变；实施乡村民宿带动，促进农村向乡村旅游目的地转变；实施旅游企业带动，促进农民向旅游从业者转变；实施旅游产品带动，促进农产品向旅游商品转变。武陵源区演绎了经济社会质、量齐升的蜕变，实现了从“养在深闺”到享誉世界、从偏僻山区到宜居宜游、从“靠山吃山”到生态优先的转变，将旅游产业发展与精准扶贫有机结合，为贫困群众打开了致富之门。

挑战与问题

武陵源区位于湖南省西北部武陵山脉中的张家界市境内，1988 年 5 月经国务院批准设立为县级行政区，总面积 397.58 平方公里，其中核心景区 217.2 平方公里。建区初期，由于自然、历史、文化等各种因素，全区 5 万多人口大多在温饱线上挣扎，年人均收入不足 200 元，脱贫攻坚的任务艰巨而繁重。1992 年，联合国教科文组织将武陵源作为中国首个“世界自然遗产”列入《世界遗产名录》。武陵源区以此为契机，开始大力发展旅游业，走上了乡村振兴之路。

措施

1. 绘就产业发展新蓝图。武陵源区通过做优做强乡村旅游、农业、文创三大带贫产业，绘就“旅游＋扶贫”产业发展蓝图，出台了《武陵源区乡村旅游发展实施指导意见》《武陵源区产业精准扶贫规划》等一系列政策文件，投入财政产业扶持资金逾 1.5 亿元，调动特色民宿、农家乐、农业龙头企业、农民专业合作社、文创企业等带贫主体的积极性，撬动社会投资逾 30 亿元，通过打造武陵源峰林峡谷特色民宿体验区和实施“一县一特”“一乡一业”“一村一品”“一户一产”等带贫项目，培育带贫主体强劲的造血功能，确保贫困人口真正脱贫。

2. 发展乡村旅游。充分利用秀丽的山水风景和浓厚的民俗文化，大力发展乡村旅游，让农民变成旅游从业者，实现农民区内“内循环”，抓住乡村旅游“点、线、面”布局，通过推出乡村旅游精品线路和特色民宿，为当地农民提供“家门口就业”的机会，确保了旅游产业发展红利有效释放、真金白银尽快“落袋”。目前，“张家界市—中湖—天子山”和“张家界市—协合—索溪峪—张家界村”两条精品线路上有特色民宿、农家客栈、农家乐 700 多家，带动 8000 多位农民从事乡村旅游服务业，每年带动农民增收逾 2000 万元。

3. 发展农业产业。将创新产业扶贫模式融入“创建湖南省农村一二三产业融合发展示范县”之中，建成鱼泉贡米、天子山剁辣椒、湘阿妹菜葛、武陵源头茶叶 4 个省市级产业园，培育发展省级农业龙头企业 1 家、市级农业龙头企业 11 家、农民专业合作社 76 家。龙头企业产业链融合、农业功能融合、农业渗透融合走上良性轨道，带动建档立卡贫困户大力发展优质水稻、精品果蔬、绿色茶叶、特色养殖等扶贫农业产业，近年来脱贫户享受“区、乡、村”三级产业累计分红资金逾 1000 万元。如菜葛产业，近年来武陵源区整合扶贫资金 2000 万元支持菜葛种植、产品提质和品牌创建发展，全区葛根种植面积 4000 亩，直接受益农民 5000 多人，每年带动脱贫户 2300 人，年人均增收逾 1000 元。

4. 发展文创产业。走“文旅融合发展，产业带动扶贫”的特色路子。投入扶贫资金 491 万元引进乖幺妹土家织锦产业，其产品涵盖艺术品收藏、居家装饰、服装、服饰和实用类产品 600 多种，申请专利 122 件，公司累计培训土家织锦技

师1200多人次，现有产业工人180多名，是目前武陵山片区最大的土家织锦研发中心和生产基地，带动索溪峪街道1463名脱贫人口致富。投入扶贫资金410万元引进扶持熊风雕塑产业做大做强，流转土地86.5亩，在索溪峪街道双文村打造大湘西第一个兼具人文历史价值、民俗风情的雕塑公园，使其成为大湘西最专业的写生、创作、实习、培训、接待基地，解决了4个村31户脱贫户的务工就业问题。

5. 健全发展机制。武陵源区建立健全“全域旅游+扶贫”“四跟四走”产业扶贫带动机制，“劳动务工型、土地流转型、订单收购型、入股分红型、种养托管型、合作帮扶型”等产业帮扶模式得到广泛运用，产业扶贫变输血为造血，贫困户和村集体长期获得产业发展红利。据统计，2020年武陵源区农村居民年人均可支配收入达15621元，同比人均增收逾1200元。各村级组织在农民自愿的基础上，采取反租倒包、租赁承包、土地入股等多种形式流转土地，发展特色民宿、旅游店铺、特色产业，增加村级集体经营性收入；并依托项目优、发展快、前景好的产业主体，以土地使用权等资源形式参股，增加村集体股份合作收入。协合村、李家岗村、土地峪村等5个村与张家界湘阿妹食品有限公司签订菜葛土地流转协议，公司统一经营管理，每年村产业分红资金3万元；双文、双星、田富、金杜4个村资金入股熊风雕塑产业园，每年村集体分红32万元。

成效

2016年，武陵源区率先在湖南省整区脱贫，2017年、2018年、2019年连续三年持续巩固，

武陵源区旅游扶贫之路越走越宽广。据统计，全区农村居民年人均可支配收入由2015年的10000元，增加到2020年的15621元，全区人民最大限度地享受到了旅游发展的红利。武陵源区充分利用世界自然遗产资源大力发展旅游产业，将产业扶贫与精品景区、特色城镇、美丽乡村“三位一体”的全域旅游进行高质量融合，成为“国家首批全域旅游示范区”，每年带动农民增收逾4亿元，其中5119名脱贫人口增收总额逾4000万元。

经验与启示

1. 注重农民技能提升。武陵源区编印《武陵源区产业扶贫技能培训资料汇编》《武陵源区产业发展实用技术手册》，采取技术单位、龙头企业、合作社相结合的方式，对全区扶贫产业进行“点对点”“一对一”的巡回培训。2016年以来，累计组织各类产业技能培训班200多期，培训农民2万余人次，其中贫困户8000多人次。

2. 注重乡村品牌培育。天子山剁辣椒、湘阿妹菜葛、禾田居茄子、天门红茶、天子绿茶等16个产品获得绿色食品认证；系列扶贫产品获得专利13件；湘阿妹菜葛获评“国家葛根种植标准化示范区”；“天子名翠”和“鱼泉贡米”获评湖南省著名商标；金毛猴红茶获评米兰世博会金奖；“两品一标”认证和基地创建占比耕地面积比例，均位居全省前茅。

3. 注重农业产品营销。积极参加农博会、展览会、年货节、扶贫日活动等，以多种形式促进线下产品营销，并通过众创空间、供销云商、农村淘宝等电商企业和智慧武陵源、微信、抖音、京东等电商平台促进线上销售。各经营主体紧跟科技新前沿，瞄准消费新趋势，将“互联网+”“生态+”等现代新理念引入生产经营活动中，创新生产方式、经营方式和资源利用方式，将“旅游+产业”的边界扩展到更广的范围，实现生产、生活、生态共赢。

下一步计划

脱贫攻坚取得全面胜利、实现全面小康后，武陵源区在新的历史起点上提出了“把武陵源美丽乡村打造成武陵山片区乡村振兴的样板”目标，大力实施乡村产业提质、乡村建设升级、人居环境整治提升、公共服务保障行动、乡风文明培育行动、乡村治理示范6大行动26项工程100项重点任务。力争到2025年，实现农业总产值达10亿元，乡村旅游接待430万人次、综合收入66亿元，农村居民年人均可支配收入逾25000元的新目标。

Abstract

Wulingyuan District, Zhangjiajie City, Hunan Province has explored a poverty-alleviation model through tourism based on four major paths: promoting the tourism benefits of scenic spots to rural areas; driving farmers to engage in the tourism industry chain; attracting tourists to farmers' homes; helping farmers become prosperous through tourism.

It has also become a core scenic spot in the agriculture-to-tourism transformation. It has also served as a model for rural B&Bs in driving the transformation of rural areas into tourist destinations. Furthermore, it has become a model for tourism enterprises in the transformation of farmers into tourism practitioners. Finally, the village also serves as a model in the transformation of agricultural products into tourist commodities. The district has changed significantly as its economy, quality and way of life have undergone an unprecedented change from little-known to world-renowned. The village used to be a remote mountainous area, but it has transformed into an ideal living and travel destination. It has also switched from relying on local resources utilization to focusing on ecological priority. As a result, it has realized the organic integration of tourism industry development and targeted poverty reduction, offering poverty-stricken people the opportunity for a more prosperous life.

Challenges and Problems

Located in Zhangjiajie City in Wuling Mountain of northwestern Hunan Province, Wulingyuan District was established by the approval of the State Council in May 1988 with a total area of 397.58 square kilometers. It includes core scenic spots of 217.2 square kilometers. In the early days of the district's establishment, a majority of the population of more than 50,000 were impoverished. People were struggling for food and clothing and lived off an annual average income of less than RMB 200. The task of poverty alleviation was arduous and onerous. In 1992, Wulingyuan was inscribed by UNESCO as China's first "World Natural Heritage Site." Capitalizing on this prestigious badge of honor and recognition, the district began to develop its tourism industry and took on the mission of rural revitalization.

Measures

1. Deploy industrial development. The district has drawn up a blueprint for the development of "tourism + poverty alleviation." This will be done by strengthening the three poverty-reduction industries of rural tourism, agriculture and cultural and creative industries. It has created policy documents, such as *Guiding Opinions on the Implementation of Rural Tourism Development in Wulingyuan District* and *Targeted Poverty Alleviation Plan through Industrial Development in Wulingyuan District*. In addition, it has invested heavily with the financial support funds of more than RMB 150 million to stimulate the building of characteristic B&Bs, agritainment, leading agricultural enterprises, farmers' professional cooperatives, cultural and creative enterprises and other poverty-reduction entities. By leveraging the social investment of up to RMB 3 billion and through the creation of the Wulingyuan Fenglin, it has cultivated poverty-reduction entities with strong function in upgrading. This is to ensure that the impoverished people are lifted out of poverty.

2. Develop rural tourism. The district has made full use of its stunning landscape and rich folk culture to develop rural tourism. This also entails turning farmers into tourism practitioners and realizing the "inner recycle" in rural areas. To accomplish this, it launched boutique routes and incorporated rural tourism into the layout, scaling it up from micro to macro. The village characteristic B&Bs provide local farmers with job opportunities and ensure that they can obtain dividends from industrial development and increase their income. At present, there are over 700 characteristic B&Bs, farm inns, and agritainment along the two boutique routes of "Zhangjiajie City – Zhonghu Township – Tianzi Mountain" and "Zhangjiajie City – Xiehe Township – Suoxi Valley – Zhangjiajie Village." This helps over 8,000 farmers engage in rural tourism services and increases their annual income to more than RMB 20 million.

3. Develop agricultural industries. It has incorporated

the poverty alleviation model through innovative industries. This was done through the initiative of "creating demonstration counties with integrated development of rural primary, secondary and tertiary industries in Hunan Province." Four provincial and municipal industrial parks on Yuquan Gongmi, Tianzishan Chopped Pepper, Xiang A Mei Caige (a new type of vegetable, cultivated from pachyrhizua angulatus), and Wuling Yuantou Tea were built. In addition, a leading agricultural enterprise at the provincial level, 11 leading agricultural enterprises at the municipal level, and 76 farmers' professional cooperatives were also developed. The integration of

leading enterprises' industrial chains with agricultural functions and agricultural penetration was a guaranteed path to follow. The archived impoverished households were motivated to develop quality rice, boutique fruits and vegetables, green tea, special breeding and other poverty-alleviation agricultural industries. In recent years, households that were lifted out of poverty have enjoyed a cumulative dividend of more than RMB 10 million in the three-tier industry in the "village, township, and district." For example, in recent years, the district has integrated the poverty-alleviation funds of RMB 20 million to support Caige planting, product quality improvement, brand creation and development. The planting area of Pueraria lobata in the region is 4000 *mu*, benefiting more than 5,000 farmers and lifting 2,300 people out of poverty every year, with the annual per capita income increase of more than RMB 1,000.

4. Develop cultural and creative industries. The village has followed the path of "integrated development of cultural and tourism, and industry-driven poverty alleviation." It invested the poverty-alleviation funds of RMB 4.91 million to introduce the Guaiyaomei Tujia brocade industry. These products cover more than 600 kinds of art collection, home decoration, clothing, costume and practical products. The company has also applied for 122 patents and trained more than 1,200 Tujia brocade technicians. With more than 180 industrial workers, it's currently the largest Tujia brocade R&D center and production base in Wuling Mountain area as it helps 1,463 people in Suoxiyu Sub-district rise out of poverty and make some money. It invested the poverty-alleviation funds of RMB 4.1 million to introduce and support the vigorous development of Xiongfeng sculpture industry, with the transferred land area of 86.5 *mu*. The first sculpture park featuring cultural history and folk customs has been built in Shuangwen Village, Suoxiyu Sub-district, which is the most professional sculpture park in western Hunan Province. A base for sketching, creation, internship, training and reception has also been constructed.

5. Improve the development mechanism. The district has established and improved the "all-for-one tourism + poverty alleviation." In addition, the "Four Follows (Funds follow the poor, the poor follow the capable people, the capable people follow the industrial projects, and the industrial projects follow the market)" poverty alleviation mechanism driven by industrial development has also been implemented. The industrial assistance models characterized by "labor work, land transfer, order purchase, dividend sharing, planting and breeding trust, and cooperative assistance" have been widely applied. The poverty alleviation through industrial development has transformed the model from

continuous supply to self-upgrading. This means that the impoverished households and village collective can obtain long-term dividends from industrial development. Statistically, the per capita disposable income of rural residents in the district reached RMB 15,621 in 2020, a year-on-year increase of more than RMB 1,200. Based on farmers' voluntary efforts, village-level organizations have adopted various forms of land transfer, such as subcontracting, lease contracting and pooling of land as shares to develop characteristic B&Bs, tourist shops and other local industries that would increase the operating income of the village collective. The village has relied on industry entities with excellent projects, rapid development and bright prospects. Because of this, it has participated in shares in the form of resources such as land use rights to increase joint stock income of the village collective. Five villages, including Xiehe Village, Lijiagang Village, and Tudiyu Village have signed the Caige land transfer agreement with Zhangjiajie Xiang A Mei Food Co., Ltd. The company has conducted a unified operation and management over village industries with an annual dividend from industries of RMB 30,000. The four villages of Shuangwen, Shuangxing, Tianfu and Jindu have invested in Xiongfeng Sculpture Industrial Park, generating an annual dividend for the village collective of RMB 320,000.

Results

In 2016, the district took the lead in reducing the poverty levels in Hunan Province. It continued to consolidate its poverty alleviation achievements for three consecutive years from 2017 to 2019. According to statistics, the per capita disposable income of rural residents in the district increased from RMB 10,000 in 2015 to 15,621 in 2020. This means that local people enjoyed the maximum benefits of tourism development. The district has made full use of world natural heritage resources to develop the tourism industry based on the high-quality integration of poverty alleviation through industrial development and the all-for-one tourism featuring boutique scenic spots, characteristic towns, and beautiful villages. It has become the first batch of national all-for-one tourism demonstration zones, which increased local farmers' income by more than RMB 400 million each year. Overall, 5,119 people were lifted out of poverty and the village income increased by more than RMB 40 million.

Experience and Inspirations

1. Improve farmers' skills. The district compiled and printed *Skills Training Materials Collection on Poverty Alleviation through Industrial Development in Wulingyuan District* and *Practical Technical Manual on Industrial Development in Wulingyuan District.* It has adopted a combination of technical units, leading enterprises and cooperatives to provide "one-to-one" itinerant training on poverty-alleviation industries in the region. Since 2016, it has organized more than 200 training courses on various industrial skills, offering training to more than 20,000 farmers, including more than 8,000 impoverished households.

2. Develop rural brands. A total of 16 products, including Tianzishan Chopped Chili, Xiang A Mei Caige, Hetianju Eggplant, Tianmen Black Tea, Tianzi Green Tea, were granted Green Food Certification. Thirteen patents were granted to a series of poverty-alleviation products. Xiang A Mei Caige was awarded "National Caige Planting Standardization Demonstration Zone," "Tian Zi Ming Cui" and "Yu Quan Gong Mi" were awarded the famous trademarks of Hunan Province, and Golden Monkey Black Tea was awarded the Gold Medal of Expo Milano 2015. The certifications of green food, organic agricultural products, and geographic agro-product indications, as well as their base establishment were ranked first in terms of the proportion of arable area in the province.

3. Promote agricultural products. In addition to participating in the "Agricultural Expo," exhibitions, New Year's Shopping Festivals, and Poverty Alleviation Day, the village leaders have promoted online sales through Markerspace. They also used supply and sales cloud business, rural Taobao and other e-commerce companies such as Wulingyuan, WeChat, Tik Tok, and JD.com to grow their business. All business entities have kept up with new frontiers in science and technology by staying on top of new consumption trends. They have introduced modern concepts of "internet +" and "ecology +" into production and business activities, and innovated production methods, operational and resource utilization. The extension of the boundary of "tourism + industry" into a wider range has achieved a win-win situation in production, life and ecology.

Next Steps

Once poverty alleviation is achieved and the local villagers attain a prosperous standard of living, the district will aim at "making the beautiful village into a model for rural revitalization in the Wuling Mountain area" a new historical starting point. They will implement 26 new projects and 100 key tasks. These will take place in the six key activities: the improvement of rural industrial quality, the upgrading of rural construction, the improvement of human settlements, the support for public services and the cultivation of rural traditions and customs. By 2025, it hopes to achieve a total agricultural output value of RMB 1 billion, with a rural tourist reception of 4.3 million people, a comprehensive income of RMB 6.6 billion, and a per capita disposable income for rural residents of more than RMB 25,000.

贵州黔南布依族苗族自治州龙里县龙山镇龙山社区：

丰富旅游业态，打造文旅品牌

Longshan Community, Longshan Town, Longli County, Qiannan Buyi and Miao Autonomous Prefecture, Guizhou Province:

Enrich Tourism Industry & Build Cultural Tourism Brands

摘 要

贵州省龙里县龙山镇龙山社区依托区位优势，有效盘活自然和人文旅游资源，完善基础设施建设，引进龙头企业，丰富旅游业态，带动全社区 61 户 194 人脱贫致富。通过乡村旅游助力，使得龙山社区成为“生态美、产业兴、百姓富”的美丽乡村。

挑战与问题

龙山镇龙山社区位于龙里县西南部，距龙里县城 2.5 公里，西距省会贵阳 21 公里，行政区划面积 13 平方公里，耕地面积 1313 亩，全村有农户 667 户 2404 人，其中苗族、布依族等少数民族人口占总人口的 40% 左右。龙山社区交通便捷，自然资源丰富，地处龙架山腹地，山清水秀、风光宜人；少数民族的节日、服饰、习俗等文化事项传承和保护得较为完好，如布依山歌、花灯戏、苗族斗鸡舞、苗族挑花刺绣等。但龙山社区当地群众都以传统的种植业为生，能有效利用自然和人文景观的旅游项目尚开发不足。

措施

1. 完善基础设施，提升公共服务。社区政府 2016 年启动乡村田园式旅游景区建设，不断对旅游基础设施、交通等加大投入，包括河道治理、村庄、城市主干道建设，以及大型停车场、古建景观楼阁、观光旅游等项目建设。目前龙山社区经过改造，有民宿客栈 14 家、农家乐 58 家、在建五星级酒店 2 家；已建成旅游观光步道、骑行步道；有游客服务中心 1 个、停车场 4 个、车位 600 个、旅游公厕 8 座，有城市公交直达；邮电通信、环保等设施也已实现全覆盖。

2. 引进龙头企业，打造文旅品牌。龙山社区依托良好的区位优势，通过政府引导及基础设施建设，撬动企业进驻：引进贵州森鸿置业发展有限公司投资建设龙门镇武侠文化小镇，引进贵州龙里赶乡场置业有限公司投资建设莲花赶乡村项目，引进贵州云龙旅游集团投资建设龙里水乡旅游生态城。龙里水乡旅游生态城自 2020 年 9 月开业以来，引进大型文旅品牌《龙乡水里 · 贵秀》，引爆龙里旅游，带动周边农家乐、民宿快速发展。同时社区建成莲花湿地公园、"云从飞瀑" 网红打卡地、美丽乡村厉家庄、省级甲级乡村旅游村寨坝上村等。

3. 丰富旅游业态，助力脱贫攻坚。龙山社区

依托便捷的交通区位优势和周边丰富的文化旅游资源，围绕“食、住、行、游、购、娱”，重点打造集休闲度假、娱乐观光、民俗体验、文化传承、宜居宜游宜业等于一体的乡村旅游示范点。龙山社区依托丰富的传统文化，于每年的“三月三”“四月八”“六月六”、端午、重阳等当地少数民族比较重视的节日及节日期间举办歌会、舞蹈表演、徒步登山等活动，开展民俗展演，弘扬和传承传统文化；村民自办农家乐、民宿；随着龙门镇武侠文化小镇、“云从飞瀑”、莲花湿地公园、龙里油画大草原、龙里水乡飞跃丛林等一批特色旅游重点项目陆续落地及建设，社区旅游业态不断丰富，已经成为全省旅游的重要承载地。

成效

通过活动聚人气、引人流，近年来，龙山社区累计接待游客 400 余万人次，旅游综合收入 3000 余万元，村民年人均收入逾 19000 元，带动全社区 61 户 194 人脱贫致富。通过乡村旅游助力，使得龙山社区成为“生态美、产业兴、百姓富”的美丽乡村。

经验与启示

1. 在发展规划上，应做好前期的调研工作，聘请专业的设计公司进行规划设计，避免造成因规划不合理而返工的现象。

2. 在品牌营销上，应更加注重培育景区产品的品牌吸引力，加大宣传的力度。

3. 在管理服务上，应更加注重以人为本的服务理念，提高服务水平，让游客有宾至如归的感觉。

4. 在人才配置上，应加大专业管理运营人才的引进力度，景区的开发建设只是前期工作，后续的宣传运营都需要用专业人才来进行经营管理。

下一步计划

一是对景区上游河道进行整治，优化旅游环境，从而吸引更多的游客前来游玩。二是在周边有条件的村寨投资建设乡村旅游项目，扶持农家乐，开发体验式的旅游项目，丰富旅游元素，吸引游客，增加收入，助力乡村振兴。三是加大招商引资力度，争取为旅游业的发展提供一个良好的经济环境，也为乡村振兴工作奠定经济基础。

Abstract

With its advantageous location, the Longshan Community, Longshan Town, Longli County, Guizhou Province has given full play to its natural and cultural tourism resources, helping lift 194 people in 61 households in the community out of poverty through the upgrading of infrastructure, introduction of leading enterprises and multidimensional tourism development. An effective rural tourism program has turned it into a progressive village with "healthy ecology, prosperous industry, and well-off people."

Challenges and Problems

Located in the southwest of Longli County, Longshan Community, Longshan Town is 2.5 kilometers from Longli County, and 21 kilometers from Guiyang, the provincial capital on its west. With an administrative division area of 13 square kilometers and an arable area of 1,313 *mu*, the village has 2,404 people in 667 households, including ethnic minorities such as the Miao nationality and the Bouyei nationality which account for about 40% of the total. The community is located in the hinterland of Longjiashan, boasting convenient transportation, rich natural resources and picturesque scenery. The cultural heritage preservation and protection are manifested in festivals, costumes and customs of ethnic minorities are well maintained and remarkably intact. Examples of this include the Bouyei folk song, Huadeng Opera, cockfight dance, cross-stitch and embroidery handicraft of the Miao. However, local people in Longshan Community still rely on traditional planting for their livelihoods. Development of natural and cultural tourism projects here still have a long way to go.

Measures

1. Improve the infrastructure and public services. In 2016, the community government started the construction of rural scenic spots, and increased its investment in tourism infrastructure and transportation such as river regulation, village renovation, urban arterial road construction, large parking lots, ancient architectures and pavilions, and sightseeing tour projects. After the village renovation, there are currently 14 B&Bs, 58 agritainment sites, two five-star hotels under construction, tourist and cycling trails, one tourist service center, four parking lots, 600 parking spaces, and eight public toilets. More importantly, the community is accessible to city buses, and covered by post and telecommunications

services, environmental protection facilities, etc.

2. Introduce leading enterprises to build cultural tourism brands. With its advantageous location, Longshan Community has earned government guidance and support and investment for infrastructure construction. For example, Guizhou Senhong Real Estate Development Co., Ltd. is introduced for the construction investment of Wuxia Culture Town of Longmen Town; Guizhou Longli Ganxiangchang Real Estate Co., Ltd. for the Lianhua Ganxiangcun Project; while Guizhou Yunglong Tourism Group is introduced for the construction investment of the eco-village of Long Li Watery Town. Since its opening in September 2020, the Long Li Watery Town has introduced a large cultural tourism brand "Longxiang Shuili – Gui Show," which showcases Longli tourism and drives the rapid development of surrounding agritainment and B&Bs. At the same time, the Lotus Wetland Park, the internet-famous scenic spot of "Clouds Traversing the Roaring Waterfall," the beautiful villages of Lijiazhuang and Zhaibashang, a provincial A-level rural tourist village has been also built in the community.

3. Enrich the tourism industry for poverty alleviation. Anchored on convenient transportation and abundant cultural tourism resources in surrounding areas, the Longshan Community strives to create a rural tourism demonstration site which integrates leisure and vacation, entertainment and sightseeing, folk custom experience, cultural heritage, living, traveling and working based on people's needs for dining, accommodations, transportation, traveling, shopping and entertainment. The community's traditional culture is maintained through singing parties, dance performances and hiking during the lunar months of March 3, April 8, June 6, Dragon Boat Festival, Double Ninth Festival and other such festivals celebrated by ethnic minorities. Folk performances promote and preserve traditional culture. Villagers run their own agritainment projects and B&Bs. With the launch and construction of special tourism key projects such as the Wuxia Culture Town of Longmen Town,

"Clouds Traversing the Roaring Waterfall," Lotus Wetland Park, Longli Oil Painting Prairie and Jungle Flight of Long Li Watery Town, the tourism industry is enriched and revitalized, developing the Longshan Community into an important tourism hub in Guizhou Province.

Results

Various activities are conducted to attract more people. The Longshan Community has received more than 4 million tourists in recent years, registering a comprehensive tourism income of more than RMB 30 million, with the annual per capita income of villagers amounting to more than RMB 19. This has helped 194 people in 61 households eliminate poverty. Owing to rural tourism, the community has turned into a productive village with a "healthy ecology, prosperous industry and well-off people."

Experience and Inspirations

1. In the planning development, a preliminary research is essential and hiring a professional design company is equally necessary to avoid a rework due to poor planning.

2. In terms of brand marketing, the brand appeal of products in scenic spots should be developed and broadened to generate publicity.

3. In regard to services, a people-oriented service concept should be strengthened and the quality and service level must be improved to allow tourists to feel comfortable and welcome.

4. In the aspect of talent allocation, more management and operations professionals should be recruited. The development and construction of scenic spots is only the beginning. Professional talents are required for subsequent management, operation and publicity.

Next Steps

First, to attract more tourists, the upper reaches of the scenic spot must be rectified to optimize the environment.

Second, invest in the construction of rural tourism projects in surrounding villages with favorable conditions, provide support for agritainment, develop experience-based tourism projects, and enrich tourism elements to enhance people's income and promote rural revitalization.

Third, attract more investment to provide a conducive environment for tourism development and create a solid economic foundation for rural revitalization.

山东济宁市泗水县龙湾湖乡村振兴示范区：

新型合伙人机制激活乡村文旅新业态

Longwan Lake Demonstration Zone for Rural Revitalization, Sishui County, Jining City, Shandong Province:

the New Partnership Mechanism Activates the New Type of Business in Rural Cultural Tourism

摘 要

山东省济宁市泗水县龙湾湖乡村振兴示范区通过创新“乡村合伙人”机制，打造创客村落、文创小街、儒学讲堂、初心学院等文旅新业态，推动乡村振兴融合发展，形成了绿水青山生态资源与文旅新业态相呼应、生态文明与文化艺术相连接的典型发展模式，走出了一条文旅产业与乡村振兴融合发展的特色道路。

挑战与问题

山东省济宁市泗水县龙湾湖乡村振兴示范区规划面积 7.9 万亩，辖南仲都村、东仲都村、夹山头村等 18 村，现有 3576 户 12255 人。示范区内林木覆盖率达 54.7%，龙湾湖水面 7500 亩，山清水秀、生态较好。但长期以来，生态资源利用不足，村民参与乡村新业态开发的积极性不高，缺少将绿水青山转化为绿色发展的思路和办法。

措施

1. 打造“文创小街”。由村集体牵头，盘活农村闲散宅基地，以租赁形式对房屋进行统一改造，引入等闲谷艺术粮仓等文旅项目，打造具有创客集聚功能的“文创小街”。引入“花筑”等品牌民宿，借助外来优质资源丰富乡村旅游业态。利用当地文化匠人和设计师资源，开展柳编、工艺品制作等培训活动，带动当地农户加盟运营。

2. 创建文创院落。持续开展乡村人居艺术环境提升行动，通过创建文创院落集群，打造新型乡村空间，将乡村生态与创意艺术有机融合，大大提升了乡村气质形象。培育研学旅行产品业态，改造原有民居，建设创客研学基地，打造了龙湾书房、鲁班记忆木工坊、陶艺工坊等创客空间，实现创意活动与艺术村居的深度融合。

3. 创新“乡村合伙人”机制。建构了“基础合伙人—成长合伙人—核心合伙人”晋升机制，进而形成“合伙人招合伙人，合伙人招项目，项目招合伙人，项目衍生项目”的人才与产业联动机制，全面激活乡村人才集聚体制，吸引外部合伙人 33 人，落地业态 40 余个，为当地筹集各类资金 2.5 亿元，带动直接就业 300 余人。

4. 推行“儒学讲堂 + 初心学院”模式。积极推进乡村文化振兴，示范区建设乡村儒学讲堂，开展以孝文化学习为特色的儒学讲解活动，并形成常态化机制；建设了集课堂教学、实践教学、案例教

学于一体的泗水县初心学院，打造符合山区特色的教学课程体系，助力乡村文化振兴。

成效

1. 集体经济显著增收。示范区已落地等闲谷艺术粮仓、龙湾湖艺术小镇等文旅项目 9 个，入驻汇源矿泉水等涉农加工企业 6 家。区内龙湾湖文化旅游特色小镇 2020 年累计接待游客逾 50 万人次，生态采摘等旅游活动农业产值超过 600 万元，产业融合发展格局逐步形成。

2. 民生状态明显改善。受益于旅游业的带动，区内南仲都村在 2017 年实现全面脱贫；2020 年，该村已建立旅游采摘大棚 74 个，产值 645 万元，村民每人每年可旅游分红 1500 元，该村被评为“国家级旅游扶贫试点村”。

3. 环境保护成效显著。通过文旅项目配套，示范区内新增污水处理站 2 处，新修樱花大道、环湖路等生态旅游道路 16.6 公里，实施全面亮化工程，村庄生态保护能力和人居环境都得到极大提升。

龙湾湖乡村振兴示范区获批“中国乡村旅游创客示范基地”“全国乡村旅游重点村”，入选“山东省美丽村居建设省级试点”“山东省政府乡村振兴联系点”等，逐步形成独具特色乡村文旅新业态发展的集聚区和示范区。

经验与启示

1.“乡村合伙人”机制激活市场化运营模式。探索创新“乡村合伙人”机制，利用技术入股、创意合作、直接注资、协助招商、扩充平台等多种形式，激活乡村人才集聚模式，吸引艺术家、行业带

头人、非遗传承人等合伙人 30 余人，产业融资逾 2 亿元，以人才振兴推动乡村产业市场化运营。

2. 文化艺术与生态文明有机融合。示范区充分依托原真村落与生态资源，将现代创意艺术、自然生态、村居环境有机融合起来，以文旅新业态推动乡村三产绿色发展，打造“三生三美”的和谐乡村。

3. 文化振兴与产业振兴有机融合。示范区创意落地项目在传承质朴民风的同时，挖掘和谐、共生、孝道、大美等儒家文化，通过精品民宿、创意农业打造具有齐鲁风韵的现代精品乡村，实现文化振兴与产业振兴的有效融合。

4. 文旅发展与民生诉求有机融合。乡村振兴的落脚点是改善民生，区内文旅产业平台在选择合伙人、引进项目、平台发展等多个环节上都引入了“反哺”乡村的元素：通过创造就业、常态化技能培训等活动，提升村民新业态从业能力；通过举办乡村艺术节、成立乡村合唱团等形式，丰富了乡村文化活动；通过开办研学辅导班、文化辅导课，改善村里儿童的受教育环境，在发展文旅产业过程中解决民生诉求。

下一步计划

1. 持续探索乡村合伙人新场景、新机制。加强与高校、研究机构的合作，总结乡村合伙人机制与现代企业经理人制度间的共性与差异，探索通过产品标准化、服务标准化、管理标准化等措施弥补短板，深入研究乡村合伙人机制的适用场景、创新路径、复制条件，提高成功率。

2. 持续扩大优势项目覆盖范围。扩大区内艺术粮仓、乡村文创街区等优势项目的覆盖范围，发挥片区生态环境、人文禀赋等资源优势，形成文旅产业发展合力。力争在三年内实现：落地产业项目 60 个以上，扶持、培训各类创新创业合伙人 300 人以上，带动就业 4000 人以上。

3. 持续推广乡村文旅新业态发展模式。总结文旅新业态在乡村场景中的发展模式，梳理创意文化商业流程与推广潜力，归纳乡村振兴模式化输出的理论体系，逐步开展文旅新业态模式的复制与商业输出，打造乡村振兴集聚区、示范带，形成集群效应。

Abstract

Longwan Lake Demonstration Zone for Rural Revitalization, Sishui County, and Jining City. Shandong Province has formed a typical development mode in which ecological resources are utilized to develop tourism and rural revitalization. The "rural partnership" entails building new types of businesses such as Maker Village, Cultural and Creative Street, Confucianism Lecture and the Original Aspiration Academy, and has pushed for the development of rural revitalization. These developments create a cultural tourism and ecological civilization that links culture, art, and rural revitalization.

Challenges and Problems

The planned area for Longwan Lake Demonstration Zone is 79 thousand *mu* with 18 villages under its jurisdiction. The total population of the 18 villages is 12,255 people from 3,576 households. The forest coverage rate in the demonstration zone reaches 54.7% as the water covers 7,500 *mu*. It is beautiful as it is surrounded by mountains, its clear waters, and a good ecology. However, some of these ecological resources have not been fully utilized for some time as the villagers here are not too enthusiastic about participating in the development of new forms of business in their community. Further more, they lack the ideas and methods to transform ecological resources such as lucid waters and lush mountains into green development.

Measures

1. Building cultural and creative streets. The demonstration zone will take the lead in redeveloping the use of homesteads and implement the transformation on these buildings by turning them into rental units. Cultural tourism projects such as Leisure Valley Art Granary are introduced to build Cultural and Creative Streets that can gather Makers. Homestay hotels, such as the Floral Hotel, are also introduced to enhance the commercial activities of rural tourism through high-quality external resources. The internal resources of local craftsmen and designers are used to carry out training in crafts and wickerwork manufacturing. This results in local peasant households working together to operate local businesses together.

2. Building cultural and creative clusters. The demonstration zone will work to improve the artistic environment of rural habitats by creating new rural spaces

for Creative and Cultural Clusters. This project will organically integrate the rural ecology with creative arts and hopefully enhance the image of the rural areas. The village has created a study tour product system. This will transform the original folk houses and repurpose them as the base for creative artists and establish creative spaces for Longwan Study, Luban's Memory Wood Workshop and Pottery Workshop, all of which are integrated in artistic village dwellings.

3. Innovating the "rural partnership" mechanism. The promotion mechanism of "basic partner — growing partner — core partner" has been formulated. This partnership has created a linkage mechanism between industry and talents in which "partners recruit other partners, partners attract projects, projects attract new partners, and projects can multiply." This partnership has fully gathered rural talents, attracted 33 external partners, landed more than 40 business models, raised 250 million yuan from various funds for the local area, and driven the direct employment for more than 300 people.

4. Implementing the model of "Confucianism Lecture + Original Aspiration Academy." To actively promote the revitalization of rural culture, the demonstration zone has constructed a rural Confucianism Lecture Hall with the goal of conducting lectures on Confucianism's the filial piety values and mores. The demonstration zone has also constructed the Original Aspiration Academy in Sishui Country, which integrates classroom teaching, practical teaching and case teaching. This process creates a teaching curriculum system in line with the characteristics of mountainous areas.

Results

1. The collective economy has significantly increased its income. The demonstration zone has landed 9 cultural tourism projects. These include Leisure Valley, Art Granary, and Longwan Lake Art Town. In addition, 6 agricultural related processing enterprises have also been settled in the area. Longwan Lake Cultural Tourism Town in the demonstration zone drew a total of more than 500,000 tourists in 2020. Ecological fruit picking and other tourism activities have produced an agricultural revenue of more than RMB 6 million. The developmental pattern of industrial integration is gradually formed.

2. People's livelihood has improved significantly. As a result of the tourism industry, South Zhongdu Village

in the demonstration zone achieved comprehensive poverty eradication in 2017. By 2020, 74 fruit-picking sheds for tourists have been established, generating RMB 6.45 million each year. The South Zhongdu Village was accordingly named the National-level Tourism Poverty Alleviation Plot Village.

3. Effective environmental protection is achieved. The living environment of villagers has been greatly improved through facilities that were created through cultural tourism projects. Two sewage treatment facilities have been added in the demonstration zone and 16.6 kilometers of ecological tourism avenues have also been built. These avenues — the Cherry Blossom Avenue and Ring Lake Road — included comprehensive lighting projects.

Longwan Lake Demonstration Zone for Rural Revitalization has been approved as a demonstration base for Chinese Rural tourism Creators. These creators are a National-level Key Village of Rural Tourism, a provincial-level pilot area of Beautiful Village Construction of Shandong Province, a contact point for rural revitalization of Shandong Provincial Government and others. It has gradually formed a gathering area of demonstration zone for the development of unique villages in rural cultural tourism.

Experience and Inspirations

1. Activating the market-oriented operation mode with the "rural partnership" mechanism. The demonstration zone has explored innovative "rural partnerships" and activated the gathering of rural talents. This has been done through technical shareholding, creative cooperation, direct capital injection, and assistance in investment. More than 30 partners have joined in the endeavor and more than RMB 200 million has been invested as industrial financing to promote the market-oriented operation in rural industries for talent revitalization.

2. Organic integration of ecological civilization with culture and art. The demonstration zone relies on the original villages for their ecological resources and the organic integration of the village's modern creative arts, natural ecology and the environment. It also promotes the green development of three rural industries, with the new cultural tourism mode and creates a harmonious village

of "prosperous production, good ecology, and beautiful life."

3. Organic integration of cultural and industrial revitalization. The culture of the village is fully and effectively integrated into the demonstration zone. Village people are simple and honest folks so this creative project dives into the Confucian values of harmony, symbiosis, filial piety, and greater beauty. As a result, the village hotels and creative agriculture become more modern with the charm of the Qilu area.

4. Organic integration of developing cultural tourism and improving people's livelihood. Rural revitalization is based on the improvement of people's livelihood. The platform of cultural tourism in the demonstration zone has introduced the back feeding of the rural areas in many ways. For example, by selecting the villagers as participants in the new business model, the development zone is able to create employment and help with the development of new skills for the villagers. Traditional rural cultural activities are enriched by holding rural art festivals and forming rural choirs. Children in the village are educated by running classes that focus on the culture of the village. The demand for a better quality of life is addressed in the process of developing cultural tourism.

Next Steps

1. The continuous efforts to explore new scenarios and mechanisms for rural partners. The demonstration zone will seek to strengthen its agreement

with universities and research institutions. They will summarize the commonalities and differences between the rural partnership mechanism and the manger system that is present in modern enterprises. In addition, they will explore measures that make up for shortcomings through product standardization, service standardization, and dive into the applicable scenarios. This exploration project will ultimately serve to seek out new innovative paths, replicate the conditions of rural partnerships, and improve the success rate of such efforts.

2. Continuous efforts to expand the coverage of advantageous projects. The demonstration zone will expand the coverage of advantageous projects such as art granaries, cultural and creative clusters, and give full play to the ecological environment. It will also utilize humanistic endowments and other resources which will help form a synergistic cultural tourism development. The zone will attempt to reach more than 60 industrial projects within three years. During this time, they will seek to support and train over 300 partners of innovation and entrepreneurship and create 4,000 jobs.

3. Continuous efforts to promote the new type of business in rural cultural tourism. The demonstration zone will summarize the development models of the new business in rural cultural tourism. They will also work to sort out the business process including the potential for promotion and the success rate of the replication and output of new cultural tourism modes. In the end, the demonstration zone seeks to form a cluster effect from the summarization of this new business model.

江西宜春市靖安县中源乡：
践行“两山”理论，打造山乡康养度假小镇

Zhongyuan Township, Jing’an County, Yichun City, Jiangxi Province:
Two Mountains Theory for an Eco-healthcare Tourist Town

摘 要

江西省宜春市靖安县中源乡积极践行“绿水青山就是金山银山”的发展理念，全力创建山地乡村休闲旅游度假区，打破旅游的季节性壁垒，实现老百姓收入翻番，让“两山”理论的转化成效越发凸显出来。近两年，中源乡投入 2 亿元打造包含有 600 多家民宿的山乡康养度假小镇，推动全乡实现脱贫率 100%，贫困人口年人均收入达 14006 元，同比增长 21.67%，走出了一条生态富民的乡村振兴发展新路。中源乡先后荣获首批“江西省 AAAA 级乡村旅游点”“江西省第二批特色小镇”“2019 年度江西避暑旅游目的地”等生态旅游“名片”，中央电视台多次走进中源乡拍摄专题片，将该乡誉为“快乐候鸟村”。

挑战与问题

江西省宜春市靖安县中源乡面积 159 平方公里，四周高山矗立，海拔千米以上的山峰有 19 座，中间平坦开阔，下辖 11 个行政村、145 个村民小组，常住人口 11458 人。近年来，中源乡民宿产业发展蓬勃，接待游客人数逐年递增，但在发展过程中，仍存在整体旅游产业业态不够丰富、民宿品位与档次整体较为低端、旅游接待标准不高、群体消费能力较低、配套娱乐设施不多、特色旅游商品较少等问题。淡、旺季游客人流量反差巨大，旅游季节性较强，当地百姓的旅游收入极不稳定。

措施

1. 聚焦规划引领，助推乡村旅游有序发展。以中源特色小镇建设为抓手，依托中源乡产业发展规划、文化旅游项目策划、中源避暑小镇专项规划等，按照“因地制宜、合理布局、突出特色”的原则，充分考虑生态环境的承载能力和区域旅游总体发展等因素，使中源民宿旅游发展与各项规划相协调，逐步完善旅游配套设施，极力促成高山滑雪等龙头项目落地实施，积极探索高端民宿集群化发展模式，大力招引星级酒店入驻运营，全面提升旅游接待能力，努力实现全龄化、全时性、全区域旅游发展目标。

2. 做好多元文章，打造乡村旅游特色品牌。基于现有的资源禀赋，按照“一村一品”发展思路，形成“吃在古竹山下、住在三坪合港、行在港口向务、游在龙坵洞下、购在邱家船湾、娱在垴上”的旅游发展格局，补齐“山上民宿化、山下空心化”民宿产业的发展短板。同时，深入挖掘具有中源本地特色的地域文化、群众文化、传统文化、客家文化等，培育开发形式多样的文娱活动，让中源旅游朝着农耕体验、文体娱乐、旅游观光、休闲度假、健康养老等多种功能拓展，满足游客的多元化需求。

3. 规范经营管理，促进乡村旅游提档升级。切实加强对乡村旅游从业者的培训，提高旅游服务水平和管理规范，促使民宿行业规范有序、安全卫生、诚信经营，打造乡村民宿的“中源样板”。持续开展好“星级民宿”“民宿示范点”评比活动，促使民宿产业不断提档升级，形成“你追我赶”的良好竞争氛围。同时，加大政策扶持，在项目建设、产业发展等方面提供资金保障、技术指导，逐步完善健全乡村旅游产业发展组织体系，及时协调解决发展中存在的问题和困难，通过以点带面、示范引领，整体推进中源乡村旅游高质量发展。

成效

1. 特色小镇建设助力基础设施“好”起来。靖安县中源避暑小镇总投资约 16 亿元，目前已完成投资约 3 亿元。先后完成了 2.3 公里三坪陈家湾至龙头坳农村公路、污水管网及配套处理设施、垃圾压缩站、河堤示范段、四园一礼堂改造提升、智慧旅游公厕、游客集散中心、智慧旅游服务平台等项目建设，小镇基础设施日臻完善，旅游接待水平和承载能力均得到显著提高，受到了当地群众和外来游客的一致称赞。

2. 升级民宿产业助推农村经济“强”起来。中源乡立足生态优势，乘着避暑小镇建设东风，先后打造了九岭山房、三闲居、等闲居、云上九岭等一批高端民宿接待点，引进了牛岗岭、神仙庵等一批高端民宿集群康养项目，推进了悦榕府、怡福居等一批旅游康养项目。目前，全乡登记在册的民宿接待点有 620 余家，接待床铺 2.1 万余张，高峰时段日接待游客 3 万余人次，全年接待游客 120 万

人次，旅游综合收入达 1.3 亿元，全乡年人均收入超 2 万元。

3. 发展乡村旅游带动贫困群众“富”起来。中源乡借力民宿产业的蓬勃发展，全力促进乡村旅游产业升级，找准乡村旅游与脱贫攻坚的结合点，支持和引导贫困户以多种方式参与到乡村旅游开发、建设、经营中，让“旅游红利”真正落到贫困户头上，形成了贫困群众持续、稳定、较快增收和村级集体经济快速发展的良好局面。目前，中源乡旅游从业人员有 2000 余人，旅游带动 345 户 861 人建档立卡贫困人口脱贫。

经验与启示

1. 规范民宿管理发展，助推旅游健康有序发展。为促进乡村旅游民宿产业持续健康发展，中源乡先后出台了《中源乡农家乐休闲旅游实施意见》《中源乡农家乐实施细则》《旅游卫生和食品安全管理办法》《农家乐管理办法》等规章制度，成立了中源乡农宿文化乡村旅游协会，通过“支部 + 协会 + 农户”的方式，把分散的农家乐经营户组织起来，实行统一价格、统一挂牌、统一制度的“三统一”制度，每年定期开展培训班提升从业人员专业技能水平，逐步形成了中源乡农家乐产业自我管理、自我约束、自我发展的新格局。依托特色小镇建设，对原有游客集散中心进行了改造提升，新建了智慧旅游指挥平台、智慧旅游指挥中心、小镇可

视化管控平台及“中源避暑小镇”旅游公共服务平台等多个功能区，实现了基于交通、环保、综治、文旅运营等各行业、各领域的智慧化创新，进一步创新了智慧旅游管理模式。

2. 强化政策资金扶持，拓宽贫困群众长效增收渠道。中源乡紧紧抓住乡村旅游发展机遇，大力扶持贫困村和贫困户开办农家乐、建客栈民宿，乡村旅游已成为贫困群众实现脱贫致富的重要渠道。为激发贫困群众内生动力，中源乡通过组织培训、考察学习等多种方式，提升贫困户脱贫致富的劳动技能，提高贫困群众创业就业“造血”能力。全乡从事农家乐经营的 24 户贫困户，户均增收 2 万余元。

下一步计划

紧盯大南昌都市圈客群，拓展长江中游城市群市场，发挥中源气候优势，挖掘农耕文化和客家文化，导入“年轻化”“亲子游”业态，推进农业、养生、旅游、文化、信息化等产业避暑度假深度融合，大力发展儿童体验、运动营地、文化体验、养老社区等项目，推进中源牛岗岭、枕云谷等精品民宿集群建设，逐步引领普通民宿升级。开发中源九岭高山滑雪和邱家温泉等项目，丰富中源旅游四季体验项目，将中源小镇建设成一个全季节、全龄化的康养小镇，实现从“老年人的朋友圈”到“一家人的欢乐圈”的转变。

Abstract

Following the "lucid waters and lush mountains are invaluable assets" framework, the Zhongyuan Township in Jing'an County, Yichun City, Jiangxi Province endeavors to create mountainous rural leisure tourism resorts. Along with this, it strives to remove the seasonal barriers of tourism and double the income of the locals to achieve the effective transformation of the "Two Mountains Theory." In the past two years, it has invested RMB 200 million to build the township into a mountainous rural eco-healthcare resort with more than 600 B&Bs. As a result, its poverty alleviation rate has reached 100%, while the per capita income of the poor has increased to RMB 14,006 — a year-on-year increase of 21.67%. Evidently, it's on its way to an enriching ecology-centered rural revitalization development path. The township has been successively awarded prestigious eco-tourism honors such as the first batch of "AAAA-Level Tourist Attractions in Jiangxi Province," the second batch of "Featured Towns in Jiangxi Province" and "Jiangxi Summer Resort Tourism Destination in 2019." The China Central Television (CCTV) has frequently filmed feature programs in the township that has become known as a "Happy Migratory Bird Village."

Challenges and Problems

With an area of 159 square kilometers, the township is a flat and open land surrounded by high mountains, 19 peaks of which are more than 1,000 meters above sea level. It has 11 administrative villages under its jurisdiction, with 11,458 permanent residents in 145 villager groups. The local B&B industry has thrived in recent years, with the number of tourists increasing year after year. However, during its development phase some problems occurred. Business models lacking in innovation, substandard B&Bs and tourist reception, weak tourists' consumption capacity, insufficient supporting recreational facilities and scarce special tourism products were among them. The sharp contrasting tourist flow between the low and peak season indicated the immense effects of the seasons on tourism and the unstable derivative income of the locals.

Measures

1. Promote the orderly development of rural tourism with astute planning. As outlined in its strategic plan of building a specialty town involving cultural tourism projects and special planning for the Zhongyuan Summer Resort Town, the township has considered its eco-environmental load capacity and the overall regional tourism development. All these were factored in the B&B tourism development and other relevant plans according to the principles of "adapting to local conditions, rational distribution and highlighting features." It has also improved supporting tourism facilities for leading project such as alpine skiing. Also, it explored the development model of high-end B&B clusters to introduce starred hotels for operation. The measure is expected to improve the multi-faceted tourism reception capacity and achieve an all-age, all-time and all-region tourism development goal.

2. Build a rural tourism specialty brand through multiple approaches. With its abundant resources, the township has adopted a tourism development framework of "eating at Guzhu and Shanxia villages, residing at Sanping and Hegang villages, transportation at Gangkou and Xiangwu villages, traveling at Longqiu and Dongxia villages, shopping at Qiujia and Chuanwan villages, and entertainment at Naoshang Village" as outlined in the "one brand for one village" concept. It has also used the same concept as characterized by "B&B clusters on the mountains, hollow villages down the mountains" to remedy the shortcomings of the B&B industrial buildup. Also, it has explored regional culture, mass culture, traditional culture and the Hakkas culture with local characteristics and created a wide variety of recreational activities. More importantly, it pivoted Zhongyuan tourism towards a multi-functional farming experience, recreational and sports activities, tour and sightseeing, leisure and vacation, and health care for the elderly to meet the demand of travelers.

3. Standardize operation and management for an upgraded rural tourism. In creating a distinctive "Zhongyuan Model" for rural B&Bs, efforts have been made to level up the training of rural tourism practitioners, improve tourism service and management standard, promote the B&B industry operation safely and smoothly. Appraisal activities such as "Starred B&Bs" and "B&B Demonstration Sites" have been conducted to promote the continuous upgrading of the B&B industry and create a competitively healthy atmosphere of "racing each other." Policy support has also been strengthened, fund guarantee and technical guidance in project construction and industrial development have been provided. The organizational system of the rural tourism industry has been improved for the immediate coordination and resolution of issues and difficulties that may arise. All these are geared toward the high-quality Zhongyuan rural tourism progress through a demonstration guidance.

Results

1. Characteristic town construction upgrades infrastructures. The total investment of Zhongyuan Summer Resort Town is about RMB 1.6 billion, with about RMB 300 million of investment already completed. A series of construction projects such as the 2.3-kilometer rural road from Chenjiawan of Sanping Village to Longtou'ao, sewage pipe network and its supporting processing facilities, waste compacting stations, riverbank demonstration sections, the renovation of four parks and one auditorium, smart tourism public toilets, tourist distribution centers and smart tourism service platforms have been successively accomplished. The town's improved infrastructure, enhanced tourism reception and load capacity have won the unanimous approbation from locals and visitors alike.

2. Upgraded B&B industry drives the rural economy. Based on its ecological advantages and the opportunity of developing the Summer Resort Town, the township has successively built a number of high-end B&B receptions such as Jiulingshanfang, Sanxianju, Dengxianju, and Yunshangjiuling. It has also introduced several high-end B&B eco-healthcare cluster projects including Niugangling and Shenxian'an. Additionally, it launched a group of eco-healthcare tourism projects such as those in Yuerongfu and Yifuju. Currently, there are more than 620 registered B&B receptions in the township, with more than 21,000 beds receiving more than 30,000 tourists per day during peak hours. In a year, 1.2 million tourists are received, with the tourism comprehensive income amounting to RMB 130 million and the per capita income of the township exceeding RMB 20,000.

3. Rural tourism development enriches impoverished people. To allow poor households a share in the cash windfall of tourism dividends and attain a stable and sustained income growth and drive the accelerated development of the collective economy of the village, the township is adopting the combination of rural tourism and poverty alleviation. This strategy is also adopted to support and educate the villagers on the various ways they can be involved during the development, construction and operation of rural tourism. As a result, more than 2,000 people have been employed in the township's tourism, helping lift 861 impoverished people in 345 households out of poverty.

Experience and Inspirations

1. Standardize the management and development of B&Bs for a healthy and orderly tourism development. To facilitate the sustained and healthy development

of rural tourism B&B industry, the township has successively promulgated *Suggestions on Zhongyuan Township Agritainment and Leisure Tourism, Enforcement Regulations on Zhongyuan Township Agritainment, Measures for the Administration of Travel Health and Food Safety, Measures for the Administration of Agritainment and other rules and regulations*. It has organized the Association of Zhongyuan Town B&B Cultural Rural Tourism and coordinated agritainment operators in various places to implement the unified prices, unified listing and unified system through "Party branches + associations + peasant households." It has regularly carried out annual training courses to improve the professional skills of practitioners for a new self-management, self-discipline, and self-development for agritainment operational structure. With the construction of a specialty town as its foundation, it has renovated and upgraded its original tourist distribution centers, newly built functional areas — including smart tourism command platforms, smart tourism command centers, visualization management and control platforms and the Zhongyuan Summer Resort Town tourism public service platforms. Consequently, it has achieved smart innovation in all sectors and industries based on transportation, environmental protection, comprehensive governance and cultural tourism operations. Also, it has further innovated the smart tourism management model.

2. Strengthen financial support for broad long-term income growth channels. The township has utilized every possible channel to support poverty-stricken villages and impoverished households. Capitalizing on rural tourism development opportunities to move locals out of poverty and improve their standard of living, it has motivated them to operate agritainment industries, build inns and B&Bs. To this end, it has organized training courses, study seminars and other methods to enhance their labor skills and provide them with the opportunity to shift the source of their livelihood to gainful employment in tourism industries and business startups. Currently, there are 24 poor households engaged in agritainment that are earning an average income increase of more than RMB 20,000 per household.

Next Steps

The township will expand the city cluster market along the middle reaches of the Yangtze River with the Nanchang metropolitan area client base at the center. It will maximize its climatic advantages and explore its indigenous farming culture along with the Hakka culture. It will also introduce "rejuvenation" and "family tourism" and accelerate the thorough integration of agriculture, health, tourism, culture, information technology and other industries. Great efforts will also be made to develop programs such as wholesome children's activities, sports camps, cultural experiences and elderly care communities to facilitate the construction of boutique B&B clusters such as Niugangling and Zhenyungu. Such projects are expected to pave the way for the upgrading of ordinary B&Bs. Moreover, it will develop Jiulingshan alpine skiing, Qiujia hot springs, expand the township's four-season tourism and other experiential programs. All these are expected to transform Zhongyuang into an all-season eco-healthcare town for all ages and from "an exclusive destination for the elderly" to "an inclusive wonderland for a family."

吉林延边朝鲜族自治州敦化市雁鸣湖镇小山村：
“党支部 + 公司 + 合作社 + 农户”的组合模式

Xiaoshan Village, Yanminghu Town, Dunhua City, Yanbian Korean Autonomous Prefecture, Jilin Province:
A Combination Model of “Party branch + companies + cooperatives + peasant households”

摘 要

吉林省敦化市雁鸣湖镇小山村以党支部为引领，通过成立合作社，以村民入股的形式发展乡村旅游产业，走“党支部 + 公司 + 合作社 + 农户”的模式，合理利用资源，统筹谋划，通过开办农家乐、乡村民宿、现代农业、特色文创产品等方式，带动村民共同致富。

挑战与问题

吉林省延边朝鲜族自治州敦化市雁鸣湖镇小山村距离敦化市区 70 公里，距雁鸣湖镇区 18 公里，小山村辖区面积 21.4 平方公里，下辖三个自然组，全村 321 户 1064 口人。全村耕地 16.44 平方公里，水域面积 3.5 平方公里，林地面积 1.38 平方公里。村内的雁鸣湖水质清澈，湖泊面积近 3 平方公里，盛产淡水鱼，同时也是黑鹳、东方白鹳、丹顶鹤、中华秋沙鸭等水禽的重要生态廊道和栖息地。小山村直通 201 国道、鹤大高速，交通便利。小山村虽然自然资源丰富，但开发和利用率不高，在本地区是有名的“脏乱差”村，产业融合不足，带动效益不足，村民收入仍然以种植、养殖、农产品加工为主。

措施

1. 改善基础设施。自新农村建设实施以来，小山村对基础设施、公共设施、人居环境设施进行了升级改造，路面硬化率、安全饮水率、亮化率、有线电视网络覆盖率、室内卫生厕所普及率等均达到 100%，提高了村民幸福生活指数，缩小了城乡生活质量。

2. 搞活发展机制。小山村因地制宜，逐步形成了本村独有的“党支部 + 公司 + 合作社 + 农户”经营模式，实现了一、二、三产业融合发展的新业态，形成“农民变股民，村民变职工，离土不离乡，家家有产业，人人有活干”的良好局面。

3. 盘活旅游资源。小山村由党支部引领，以合作社为主体，实行村民入股机制，充分利用好村庄山、水、林、田、湖、草等丰富的自然资源，凭借天然的生态景观、优异的地理位置，打造现代农业观光采摘园和集水上娱乐、水上游船、湿地观光、民宿住宿、农家美食于一体的综合性场所，增加游客驻足时间。

4. 挖掘乡村文化。小山村充分挖掘本村的“雁鸣湖文化”“知青文化”“红色文化”等，致力于打造“村史博物馆”“知青大院”等文化景观，让小山村“看得见青山、望得见绿水、记得住乡愁”，做到讲好山村故事、带动村民致富。

成效

小山村路面硬化率、安全饮水率、亮化率、有线电视网络覆盖率、室内卫生厕所普及率等均达到100%，提高了村民幸福生活指数，缩小了城乡生活质量差距。小山村每年接待游客近15万人次，为当地提供就业岗位100个。2016年人均收入16000元，2020年人均收入达22000元，年人均收入五年内增加了37.5%，全村建档立卡贫困户12户18人均已实现脱贫。2020年，村集体收入123.4万元，比2019年增加了10%。小山村先后获得“全国生态文化村”“全国乡村振兴示范村”“全国文明村”“全国乡村旅游重点村”“全国乡村自治示范村”等荣誉称号。

经验与启示

1. 基础设施是前提。通过近年来的新农村建设，努力完善了公共设施、基础设施、人居环境设施等，不断提高村民幸福生活指数，极大地缩小了城乡居民生活水平差距。

2. 人才是关键。任何事业的发展都是以人为本，乡村振兴的前提必须是人才振兴。要多方面争取人才、培养人才，把当地有文化、懂经营的党员和群众吸纳为合作社重要成员，合理利用资源，统筹谋划，促进各项事业发展。

3. 产业融合是宗旨。要实现农村一、二、三产业融合发展，把农产品的生产加工与销售渠道融合起来，通过开办农家乐、乡村民宿、现代农业、特色文创产品等方式，突破发展新道路，带动村民共同致富。

下一步计划

下一步，小山村将继续推动农旅文一体化和一、二、三产业融合发展，打造新时代农村小康示范点。一是建设环湖路。为打造休闲旅游乡村、夯实健全旅游基础设施，争取项目资金修建长达6公里的环雁鸣湖观光路。二是建设湿地观光木栈道。因小山村地处雁鸣湖国家级保护湿地腹地，自然景观优美，为有效开发、合理利用自然资源，打造生态休闲观光景区，将在湿地上建设长达5公里的湿地观光木栈道，让游客返璞归真，亲近大自然放松心情。三是建设高光效体验大棚。因小山村地处中国北方，而冬季是乡村旅游短板期，为延长产业链、实现反季旅游，筹备建设占地2000平方米的高光效大棚，内部设置民宿、餐厅、假山、假水、植被等，打造一处实现反季旅游的综合性场所。

Abstract

The Party branch has guided Xiaoshan Village, Yanminghu Town, Dunhua City, Yanbian Korean Autonomous Prefecture, Jilin Province to develop rural tourism in the form of equity participation with the villagers. The establishment of cooperatives such as the "Party branch + companies + cooperative + peasant households" has achieved a logical utilization of resources and helped coordinate the planning of the local village. In addition, the operation of agritainment, rural B&B's, modern agriculture, cultural and creative products have all been developed and implemented. These all come together to facilitate the realization of villagers' well-off life.

Challenges and Problems

Xiaoshan Village covers an area of 21.4 square kilometers and includes three natural groups with 1,064 people from 321 households. Xiaoshan Village is 70 kilometers away from Dunhua City and 18 kilometers away from Yanminghu Town. The village has 16.44 square kilometers of arable land, 3.5 square kilometers of water area, and 1.38 square kilometers of forest land. The Yanming Lake in the village is rich in freshwater and covers an area of nearly 3 square kilometers of limpid water. This body of water is an important ecological habitat for waterfowls like black stork, oriental white stork, red-crowned crane, and Chinese merganser. The village has convenient transportation as it is directly accessible to National Highway 201 and Hegang–Dalian Expressway. Despite the abundant natural resources and transportation, the village has low development and utilization rates. Many people refer to the village as "dirty, chaotic, and backwards." The village has also poor levels of industrial integration, few driving benefits and villagers who still rely on agriculture for their income.

Measures

1. Improve infrastructure and public services. The village has seen significant increases in public facilities due to the upgrade of the existing countryside buildings. For example, safe drinking water is provided to all, cable TV is now available, along with indoor toilets that are also available to all. All these upgrades work to improve the villagers' overall life and helps to narrows the gap between those in urban and rural areas.

2. Invigorate development mechanism. The village has gradually formed its unique model of "Party branch +

companies + cooperative + peasant households" according to local conditions. It has realized a new business opportunity from the integration of the development of primary, secondary and tertiary industries. The result is a balanced model in which the "farmers become shareholders, villagers become employees, and they don't have to leave their hometown as there is an industry for development in each household."

3. Revitalize tourism resources. The Party branch and the cooperatives of the main body created a mechanism of equity participation that aims to see tourists spending time on their tour. The Party Branch and the cooperatives have created a sightseeing, garden picking in modern agriculture and a comprehensive site integrating water games, cruises, wetland sightseeing, B&B accommodation and rural delicacies through the utilization of the natural geography.

4. Explore rural culture. By exploring the Yanming Lake Culture, Educated Youth Culture, and Red Culture, the village is expected to transform into a wonderland of lucid waters, lush mountains and nostalgia. Buildings such as the Village History Museum and Educated Youth Courtyard will help tell stories about the mountain village and help the villagers become prosperous.

Results

Roads across the village have been resurfaced, safe drinking water is now available to all, and indoor toilets are now open. With this upgrade, the villagers can enjoy a better life. Also, this helps to narrow the gap in the quality of life between urban and rural areas. 150,000 tourists visit the village each year and provides 100 jobs for the local people. The per capita income increased from RMB 16,000 in 2016 to RMB 22,000 in 2020, a 37.5% increase within five years. A total of 18 people from 12 impoverished households in the village have been lifted out of poverty. The village's collective income was RMB

1.234 million, an increase of over 10% compared to 2019. More admirably, it has been awarded such honors as the "National Ecological Culture Village," "National Rural Revitalization Demonstration Village," "National Civilized Village," "National Rural Tourism Key Village" and "National Rural Autonomy Demonstration Village."

Experience and Inspirations

1. Infrastructure serves as a prerequisite. Recent construction of new countryside facilities has improved the lives of the villagers. Overall, the goal is to shrink the gap in the quality of life between rural and urban areas.

2. Talent function as a key. Utilizing the talents of the villagers is important as all undertakings for development should be people-oriented. It is necessary to seek and train talents in various skills. Local Party members should develop various undertakings, become proficient in business operation, and maximize the utilization of resources.

3. Industrial integration as the means and end to accomplish its goal. Integrating the development of the primary, secondary, and tertiary industries in rural areas is vital to the work being done. Also, integrating the production and processing of agricultural products is important for sales channels. The operation of agritainment, rural B&B's, modern agriculture, as well as characteristic cultural and creative products should be developed as new ways for the villagers to enjoy a prosperous life are explored.

Next Steps

The village should continue to advance the integration of agriculture, tourism, and culture. The integration of the primary, secondary, and tertiary industries will create a framework for a demonstration village in the new era. In 2021, **the first step** is to build a 6-kilometer ring road around the Yanming Lake for sightseeing. Funding has to be obtained for the building of a leisure tourism village and to improve tourism infrastructure. **Second,** a wooden plank road for wetland sightseeing should be built. This wooden road will be located in the hinterland of the wetland of Yanming Lake national-level nature reserve, an area with picturesque natural landscape, sightseeing, and relaxation. **Third,** a greenhouse to promote photosynthetic efficiency should be created. Since the village is located in the north of China, few people enjoy rural travel in winter. B&Bs, restaurants, rockeries, artificial water, and vegetation should be built on 2,000 square meters of land. This serves to extend the industrial chain and develop a comprehensive venue for out-of-season tourism.

广西百色市德保县城关镇那温村：
农旅融合助推乡村脱贫

Nawen Village, Chengguan Town, Debao County, Baise City, Guangxi Zhuang Autonomous Region:
Integration of Agriculture and Tourism Facilitates Rural Poverty Alleviation

摘 要

那温村依靠得天独厚的自然优势和山水风光，挖掘“稻—花—蜜”生态资源，积极发展乡村生态旅游；同时打造桑蚕、养蜂、旅游、百香果、有机水稻“五大产业”，实现农业产业和旅游产业融合发展，将脱贫攻坚与美丽乡村建设同步推进。该村采用政府引导、企业经营、农民入股的形式，激发农民动力，走出了一条“旅游 + 扶贫”的致富新路，不仅摘掉了贫困村的“帽子”，还成为德保县文化旅游产业的样板。

挑战与问题

广西百色市德保县那温村辖 7 个自然屯，11 个村民小组，317 户 1180 人。经 2015 年精准识别，那温村共有建档立卡贫困户 72 户 246 人，贫困发生率为 8.53%，年人均收入不足 8000 元。村民长期以种植水稻为生，由于人均耕地少、致富渠道单一，年轻劳动力流失严重，留守的多为老人和儿童，乡村振兴建设和产业发展十分困难，被列为“十三五”整村推进贫困村，也是广西壮族自治区乡村旅游扶贫重点村。

措施

1. 成立旅游专业合作社。2016 年 4 月，那温村组织 98 户农户成立了那温旅游专业合作社，以“政府引导、群众主体，合作社经营、农民入股”的模式，带领村民以土地、劳务等要素流转入股参与花海种植和利润分红，吸纳贫困户参与那温旅游资源开发，带领贫困户通过发展赏花旅游增收脱贫。旅游合作社结合“绿水”“青山”生态优势，充分挖掘“稻—花—蜜”生态资源，春夏之际，种植不同品种的水稻绘制图案，打造稻田艺术；冬季则利用冬闲田种植花卉，打造造型多样的田园花海，增加蜜源。组织群众开展山歌对唱、手工舂糍粑、徒手抓河鸭等民俗活动，实现了常年旅游亮点不断的效果，吸引了众多区内外游客前来观光旅游。

2. 成立农业专业合作社。在旅游专业合作社引领带动下，那温村群众积极开发旅游周边产品，先后成立了那温黄美玲种养专业合作社、那温村清水源生态农民专业合作社，建设了那温村百香果种植基地，打造出桑蚕、养蜂、旅游、百香果、有机水稻“五大产业”，形成了“一村五基地”的产业兴旺局面，不断拓宽村民收入渠道。各个合作社通过吸纳贫困群众到基地务工和收购农产品等途径，

覆盖全村 58 户贫困户，实现了让群众在“家门口”就业的目标。

3. 推动旅游产业升级。那温村先后整合中央预算内资金以及扶贫、住建、农业、水利、交通、文旅、旅游专业合作社等各方面资金，通过开展房屋立面风貌改造、景观打造、河堤美化等工作，逐步完善旅游基础设施。开发特色民宿和农家乐、种植观赏花卉等项目，建设推动那温旅游产业发展升级。同时挖掘山歌对唱等传统民俗文化活动，大力发展水果、蜂蜜等农业产业，形成“民俗 + 旅游”“农业 + 旅游”的产业融合模式。开发那温人家生态旅游景区，使旅游品位得以全面提质优化，旅游知名度、影响力和美誉度全面提升，将旅游业打造成为那温村的主导产业。

成效

2016 年以来，那温村通过发展乡村旅游，村容村貌、环境卫生、居住环境等均得到极大改善，年人均收入增加到 17000 多元；2016—2020 年，那温人家乡村旅游区共接待游客 10 万多人次，旅游综合收入 200 多万元。2018 年，那温村各项脱贫指标高标准完成，实现了整村高质量脱贫。2019 年，那温村获评“广西十大最美乡村”和“中国少数民族特色村寨”；2020 年，那温人家乡村旅游区获评“广西四星级乡村旅游区”。

经验与启示

那温村村民不等不靠，发挥自身强烈的发展动力及能人、带头人作用，投入到乡村旅游和相关产业发展工作中，齐心协力探索符合自身条件的产业发展之路和增收致富之路。那温村依托资源禀赋，整合运用各级政府资金形成合力，将那温村乡村建设与乡村旅游同步推进，脱贫攻坚与乡村振兴同步开展，实现了生态文明建设、脱贫攻坚、乡村振兴协同推进，使其形成可复制、可参考、可推广的高质量脱贫示范村。

下一步计划

下一步，那温村将结合乡村振兴建设，继续深入推进乡村旅游产业，并带动其他产业发展。一是围绕“食、住、行、游、购、娱”旅游要素，健全景区功能，挖掘乡土文化资源，进一步完善乡村度假旅游的配套设施，扩大接待能力，提高服务水平。发展休闲垂钓、民族风情、农家食宿体验、漂流等特色旅游项目，着力打造德保旅游新亮点，努力实现“村美人富”新目标。二是精心策划特色旅游产品，在“农、土、俗”上细挖掘，在“新、奇、特”上下功夫，做实“购”字文章，开发具有本村特色的农副产品，进一步提高农副产品的附加值，促进农业增效、农民增收，增加旅游社会经济效益。三是将传统农业、现代农业、生态农业推进到旅游观光农业的新高度，全力提升农村旅游的档次和实力。

Abstract

By relying upon its natural resources, the Nawen Village has created new avenues for poverty alleviation. Rural eco-tourism development has been done through the maximum utilization of rice, flowers, honey, and five other industries that include silkworm, beekeeping, tourism, passion fruit, and organic rice. Agriculture and the tourism industry are simultaneously making great strides in the elimination of poverty from the village. The village is also a model for cultural tourism as it has set a new standard for poverty alleviation as well as cultural tourism.

Challenges and Problems

The Nawen Village has a population of 1,180 people and consists of seven natural villages. A 2015 study determined that 246 people were living in poverty and the annual income was less than RMB 8,000. Considerably less arable land compared to other villages, severe loss of young labor and a greater number of elderly population than young are some of the reasons for the village's relative poverty. Although the village has not yet experienced an economic boom, it is undergoing a Five-Year Plan that seeks to alleviate poverty through rural tourism in the Guangxi Zhuang Autonomous Region.

Measures

1. Establish a Tourism professional cooperative. In April 2016, 98 farmers from the village took the initiative and began to make changes to the way things were done. Some of the changes they made led to the establishment of the Nawen Tourism Professional Cooperative which was focused on empowering the villagers to engage in flower planting and profit sharing. As a result of this, more households have been able to participate in the rural tourism industry which helps to alleviate poverty. In addition, the tourism professional cooperative has fully tapped the ecological resources of rice, flowers, and honey on the basis of ecological advantages of lucid waters and lush mountains. Specifically, different varieties of rice are planted in Spring and Summer to form patterns for the display of paddy art. Flowers are planted in idle fields in winter to develop a sea of vibrant colors in different shapes to attract more bees and increase honey production. Culture and folk customs are a big part of village life, with the elderly engaging in activities that are reminiscent of their indigenous traditions.

2. Establish an agricultural professional cooperative. With the guidance of the tourism professional cooperative,

the villagers have developed tourism related products. In addition, they have also developed Huangmeiling Planting and Breeding Professional Cooperative, Qingshuiyuan Ecological Professional Cooperative. Also, they have found new ways to exploit their natural agricultural resources. Overall, 58 impoverished households have all taken up work in the base and have been earning an income.

3. Promote the tourism industry upgrade. Investors have been generous with their donations and have allowed the village to upgrade the existing infrastructure. This includes, to name a few, an upgrade of housing, water conservation reliance, and transportation. Most importantly, these funds were used to improve the cultural tourism infrastructure through the renovations of homes, creation of new amenities and new entertainment options. On the other hand, the village is also using their culture to attract tourists. These include the signing of traditional songs, agricultural development and engagement in folk activities.

Results

The impact of rural tourism has greatly affected the region. The appearance is much better than before, the living environment has changed for the better, and the annual per capita income has increased to more than RMB 17,000. From 2016 to 2020, the Nawen Family Rural Tourist Area has seen more than 100,000 tourists which has generated an income of more than RMB 2 million. In 2018, the village was lifted out of poverty with high quality standards now being the norm. In 2019, it was awarded the "Top Ten Most Beautify Villages in Guangxi" and "A Village with Chinese Ethnic Minority

Characteristics" and in 2020 the Nawen Family Rural Tourists Area was awarded the four star rural tourist area in Guangxi.

Experience and Inspirations

The villagers have showed intense interest in making their own village better without relying upon government assistance. In addition, they are becoming leaders and are devoted to the rural tourism industry. Funds have been made for the villagers to use for rural construction and infrastructure upgrades without losing sight of its poverty alleviation goal.

Next Steps

Next steps for the Nawen Village include the amplification of the role of its rural tourism industry in driving the development of other industries based on established rural revitalization and construction framework. **First,** efforts will be made, which will perfect the elements of transportation, travel, shopping, and entertainment. More efforts will be made to improve functions of scenic spots, tap local cultural resources, and improve supporting facilities for rural tourism. Projects such as fishing, ethnic customs and rural accommodations will be developed. The Debao County tourism will be showcased for its beauty and the prosperity of its people. **Second,** characteristic tourism products will be meticulously planned with emphasis on "new, rare, and special" characteristics centered on "rural, native, and folk" natures for sales generation. Agricultural and sideline products with village characteristics will be developed to further increase their added value, boost agricultural efficiency and increase the income of farmers. **Third,** traditional, modern agriculture, and ecological agriculture will be upgraded to a new level of tourism agriculture, which will in turn promote the level and strength of rural tourism.

河北张家口市张北县小二台镇德胜村：德胜模式实现从脱贫到振兴的跨越

Desheng Village, Xiaoertai Town, Zhangbei County, Zhangjiakou City, Hebei Province: Desheng Model Drives the Leap from Poverty Alleviation to Revitalization

摘要

河北省张北县德胜村构建了以乡村旅游为主线的融合性产业，开发农业的多功能性，形成农业观光采摘园、平安福农业科技园、光伏经济示范园、民宿餐饮一体化体验园、绿色乡居建筑博览园等村旅游设施。通过企业主导，带动农民，村企共创，延长产业链，提升价值链，用资本整合资源，以市场引领发展，使产业要素深度融合，构建起参与性的增收保障体系，形成了可持续发展的机制。德胜村为可持续发展提供持久动力，农民生活质量不断提升，其获得感、幸福感、安全感不断增强，凭借脱贫攻坚与乡村振兴的有效衔接，全村实现了从脱贫到小康的历史性跨越。

挑战与问题

河北张北县德胜村属于典型的农耕村，下辖 6 个自然村，总面积 20205 亩，其中耕地 5085 亩，全村 549 户 1176 人，其中建档立卡贫困户 145 户 290 人，贫困发生率 1.5%，是张北县典型的贫困村。该村长期处于自然发展状态，建设无规划，农民无产业，产品无品牌，致富无门路，发展无人才，集体无经济。农民收入长期在低位徘徊，人居环境条件较差，村庄破败，道路泥泞，空心化严重。多数农民外出打工谋生，留守人员多为老弱病残，缺少可持续发展的产业、机制和动力，发展缺活力，脱贫少支撑，振兴没路径。

措施

1. 坚持规划先行。将建设乡村旅游与精准扶贫相结合，以打造张北全域旅游的“体验窗口名片”为愿景目标，构建“一环串联、两轴引领、五区联动”的规划格局。设置德胜乡社文化服务区、星光迷境有机康养区、林田艺园景观体验区、润马公社生活体验区、润马牧场互动旅游区五大功能分区。打造三大特色游憩线路和四大客群旅游路线，构建慢行游憩道路闭环。德胜文化广场、德胜印象展馆、德胜农业示范园及“德胜源”餐厅等基础建设项目均已完成，德胜乡村旅游体系初步形成。

2. 坚持产业带动。按照“培育主体，开发主业，形成主导”的思路，进行整体规划；产业增强引领性，实现增值增收；发展落脚持续性，提供长久动力。发展现代生态农业示范园区，开发农业的多种功能，使产业链由单纯的农田种植的生产端向综合产业的体验端转变，效益由产品销售的经济效益向经济、社会、生态、资源效益的全面性转变，产业定位由过去的一产向一、二、三产融合发展的高端化转变，对农民形成综合带动。马铃薯产业增加经营性收入，光伏产业增加流转性收入，民宿产业增加财产性收入，企业就业增加劳务性收入。目前德胜以旅游为核心的综合产业已覆盖全体村民，为村民提供各类就业岗位 300 多个，已有 30 多位农村青年成为企业员工。

3. 坚持品牌先导。民宿品牌：已建成民宿 180 套，形成兼具多种风格的京西北民宿群，即“德胜宿集”。文化品牌：已组建村民文艺队 2 支，设计了公司 logo，实施了《德胜尊老助学办法》，制定了《德胜村民守则》，李勇艺术小院、李易峰音乐工作室落成。策划了《德胜村—揽胜楼联合运营方案》，筹建德胜艺术社。农业品牌：成立德胜平安福生态农业科技发展有限公司，并在中医农业、生态农业微生物种养殖方面取得成效。德胜马铃薯在第十九届中国绿色食品博览会上获得金奖，德胜村获评全国“一村一品示范村”、全国“绿色无公害示范基地”。德胜平安福生态农业科技发展有限公司获评“河北省科技型中小企业”“张家口市市级农业科技园区”。

4. 坚持平台集聚。河北农业大学乡村振兴研究院落地德胜。国家住建部、中国八大院校、中国建材协会等联合打造“绿色乡居建筑博览园”。成立“中国德胜绿色乡居发展联盟”，举办绿色乡居文旅大会。引进教育部农校通，并规划建设德胜食品安全小镇。引进“游帮学”团队，规划建设德胜青少年研学基地等。

5. 坚持人才引进。在德胜村成立了“乡村振兴研究院”，实施文化品牌人才建设。邀请北京崇贤馆世纪文化传媒有限公司董事长、北京崇贤馆创始人李克及张德欣、左宁等知名人士出任德胜实业集团智库专家顾问委员会成员。德胜已成为各类人才创新创业的热土，高端人才的不断加入，为乡村振兴注入了蓬勃活力。

6. 坚持模式引领。“企业带动，农民参与；平台合作，品牌助力；文化引领，同创共享”的模式，使企业回归农村、资本回归农业、农民回归家乡，共创美好生活，建设幸福德胜。通过土地流转、民宿出租和实施田园综合体建设，使资源变资产、资金变股金、农民变股东，农民成为真正意义上的资产权益人，成为德胜模式的践行者和受益者。

成效

德胜村构建了以乡村旅游为主线的融合性产业，开发农业的多功能性，建成农业观光采摘园、平安福农业科技园、光伏经济示范园、民宿餐饮一体化体验园、绿色乡居建筑博览园等村旅游设施。2019 年接待游客 6000 余人次，2020 年接待游客 5 万多人次。通过资源聚集、要素融合、合作发展，生态资源和农业多元化功能得到开发利用，为可持续发展提供了持久动力。农民生活质量不断提升，2020 年，农民年人均收入达到 16400 元，比 2017 年增加了 90.7%；集体经济收入逾 150 万元。脱贫攻坚与乡村振兴的有效衔接，使德胜村实现了从脱贫到小康的历史性跨越。

经验与启示

1. 脱贫攻坚必须形成推动发展的新动能。德胜村受自然及人文条件的限制，不可能有足够的内生动力。德胜集团入驻，首要是促进产业发展，不仅带来投资，更带来市场化的理念方法和运行机制，用企业化的方式管理农业，用现代化的理念引导农民，用工程化的思路实施项目，用科学化的方法参与管理。如此一来，既能提升效率又可对接市场，既能增加收入又可规避风险，找到了城乡融合发展实现乡村振兴的路径。

2. 脱贫攻坚必须有价值理念和情怀。德胜集团以“企业带领农民共同致富，建设幸福美丽德胜新村”为价值理念，第一取向不是开发赢利，而是担当责任。目前，该企业已投入1.3亿元，全部用于德胜村的公共基础设施和产业先期培育，虽然眼下自身收入不多，但却为当地建起了以乡村旅游为核心的新型业态，为农民持续就业增收打下了基础，也为企业未来发展铺平了道路，真正实现了深度融合、合作共赢、同创共享，甘当一支永不撤离的帮扶“工作队”。

3. 脱贫攻坚必须有可复制的模式。德胜模式的核心在于带动与共享。“带动”是将利益留给农民，按照市场的方式引领产业，参与治理，规避风险，保障增收；“共享”是将长远利益与农民共享，在于未来产业和服务收益，在于今后市场和预期，在于模式的有效复制。只有不断地复制并在新的实践中提升完善模式，才会有新的机遇和市场，才能获得品牌信誉，才能持续获得收益。

4. 扶贫攻坚的落脚点必须在于带动农民。只有激发农民积极参与、自我“造血”、持续增收、生活幸福，才能真正体现企业的价值所在，这也符合党的政策和农民的意愿，且更符合发展的价值理念和长远利益。没有农民的主体参与，农村就不可能得到深耕与发展，更不具备生命活力。目前，德胜村以乡村旅游为主线的各产业链条上的就业岗位和产业终端的收入主体，都是德胜村及其周边的村民。

下一步计划

“十四五”期间，德胜村继续按照企业带动、农民主体、市场运作、科技支撑、村企协同的原则，实现“六个新”的发展目标：构建生态种植养殖、农产品加工供应链、民宿康养旅游、绿色装配式建筑和文化产业的“4+1”产业新格局；搭建企业创业、员工创新、农民致富、集聚要素、合作共享的新平台；培育具有市场传播力、诚信守德、绿色生态、健康安全的德胜系列新品牌；提升可复制推广的“企业+农村、平台+品牌、同创+共享”的德胜发展新模式水平；建设乡村振兴研学、农民科技培训、产业发展实践、先进文化传播的多业态教育新基地；打造要素整合、村企共建、创业就业、创新发展的参与性保障新体系。

Abstract

Desheng Village, Zhangbei County, Hebei Province, has built an integrated industry with rural tourism as the focal point. They have developed a multi-functional agricultural system and has built tourism facilities around this such as agricultural sightseeing picking parks, Ping'anfu agricultural science and technology parks.

They have also built B&Bs, catering integration experience parks and green rural residential architecture expo parks. Leadership enterprises have driven farmers to co-create the village based on mutual efforts for extended industrial chains, enhanced value chains, integrated resources through capital, and market-leading development. This helps with achieving in-depth integration of industrial elements, building a participatory income increase guarantee system, and developing a sustainable development mechanism. The Desheng Model has provided a lasting impetus for the sustainable development of the village and has improved the living quality of farmers. It has also enhanced their sense of accomplishment, happiness, and safety. They have also effectively linked poverty alleviation and rural revitalization which has led to an impoverished standard of living to a more prosperous one.

Challenges and Problems

Desheng Village is a typical farming village with six natural villages under its governance. It has a total area of 20,205 *mu*, 5,085 *mu* of which is arable land. There are 1,176 people of 549 households in the village, 290 people and 145 archived impoverished households of which have a poverty incidence of 1.5%. This statistics make it a typical poverty-stricken village in Zhangbei County. For a long time, the village has had no natural development. Nor is there any construction plan. There were no plans for industry for farmers, brand for products, or ways to improve their lives. It also lacks talent for development, economy for collectives, or a way to reduce a dilapidated and hollow village. Most farmers go out to work for a living and leave the elderly, weak, sick, and disabled behind. As a result, there is a lack of industries, mechanisms and motivations for sustainable development, growth vitality, poverty alleviation support and no revitalization path.

Measures

1. Planning-pioneering. The construction of rural tourism has been combined with targeted poverty alleviation to create an "experience window card" of the all-for-one tourism in Zhangbei County. They have also built a planning pattern of "one loop in series, two axes leading, and five areas connected." In other words, five functional areas have been set up. They are: Desheng Community Cultural Service Area, Xingguang Mijing Organic Healthcare Area, Lintian Yiyuan Landscape Experience Area, Runma Commune Life Experience Area, and Runma Ranch Interactive Tourist Area. Also, three characteristic recreational routes have been built so that tourist groups can enjoy recreation. The infrastructure

projects such as Desheng Cultural Plaza, Desheng Impression Exhibition Hall, Desheng Agricultural Demonstration Park and "Deshengyuan" Restaurant have all been completed and the Desheng rural tourism system has been initially developed.

2. Industry-driven. The plan has been carried out in accordance with the idea of "fostering the main body, developing the main business and forming the leadership." In addition, the role of industries in leading has been enhanced for both value and income increase. The sustainable developmental goal has been promoted to provide long-term momentums. The village has developed modern eco-agricultural demonstration parks and explored multiple functions of agriculture to realize the transformation of the industrial chain from the production of single farmland planting to the comprehensive industries. This is an all-round transformation of benefits from the economic benefits of product sales to the economic, social, ecological, and resource benefits. The high-end transformation of the industrial positioning from the primary industry to the integrated development of the primary, secondary and tertiary industries motivates the farmers to advance village development. The village has also developed the potato industry for more operating income, the photovoltaic industry for more circulating income and the B&B industry for more property income. Also, it has promoted corporate employment for more labor income. Presently, the comprehensive industries with tourism as its core cover all villagers, which generate more than 300 job opportunities and help more than 30 rural youth find jobs at enterprises.

3. Brand-leading. The village has built 180 sets of B&Bs and developed a group of B&Bs with multiple styles of Northwest Beijing called the "Desheng B&B Clusters." The village has formed two art teams of villagers for their cultural heritage. They designed company logos and implemented *Methods to Respect the Elderly and Assist Students in Education in Desheng*

Village. They formulated *Desheng Villagers' Code* and completed Li Yong Art Academy and Li Yifeng Music Studio. Also, the *Joint Operation Plan between Desheng Village and Lansheng Building* has been organized to prepare for the establishment of Desheng Art Club. The agricultural brand is Desheng Ping'anfu Ecological Agriculture and Technology Development Co., Ltd. and it has been established. They made remarkable achievements in microbial breeding of traditional Chinese medicine agriculture and ecological agriculture. Desheng Potato has won the gold medal at the 19th China Green Food Expo which make the village a national "One Product for One Village Demonstration Village" and a national "Green Pollution-Free Demonstration Base." Desheng Ping'anfu Agriculture Company was approved as "Hebei Province Science and Technology Based Small and Medium-sized Enterprise" and "Zhangjiakou Municipal Agricultural Science and Technology Park."

4. Platform-Integrating. The Rural Revitalization Research Institute of Hebei Agricultural University has landed in Desheng County. Many platforms, including the Ministry of Housing and Urban-Rural Development, Eight Universities in China, have jointly created the "Green Rural Residence Architecture Expo Park." The "China Desheng Green Rural Residence Development Alliance" was established to hold the Green Rural Residence Cultural Tourism Conference. Also, the "Nong Xiao Tong" of the Ministry of Education has been introduced for the planning and construction of Desheng Food Safety Town and the "You Bang Xue" (means that tourism drives study) team has been also introduced for the planning and construction of Desheng Youth Research Study Base.

5. Talent-introducing. The Rural Revitalization Research Institute has been established in the village to implement the recruitment and cultivation of talents for cultural brands. Li Ke, Chairman of Beijing Chongxiangguan Century Culture Media Co., Ltd. and founder of Beijing Chongxiangguan, Zhang Dexin, Zuo Ning and other celebrities have been introduced as members of the Think Tank Expert Advisory Committee of Desheng Industrial Group. As a result, the village has attracted all kinds of talents for innovation, entrepreneurship, resulting in an energized and revitalized rural revitalization program.

6. Model-guiding. Through the model of "enterprise driving, farmers' participation, platform cooperation,

brand assistance, cultural guidance, co-creation and sharing," and enterprises that develop well in rural areas, the farmers have a higher standard living. The land transfer, B&B leasing, and rural pastoral complex construction have transformed resources into assets. They have also converted capital into equity and turned farmers into shareholders. This means that farmers have become real asset owners and also practitioners and beneficiaries of the Desheng Model.

Results

The village has built an integrated industry with rural tourism as the main driver. It has also developed multi-function agricultural products and has built tourism facilities such as an agricultural sightseeing park. The Ping'anfu agricultural science and technology parks, photovoltaic economic demonstration parks, B&B and catering integration experience parks and green rural residence architecture expo parks have all been constructed. The village welcome more than 6,000 tourists in 2019, and more than 50,000 tourists in 2020. Through resource aggregation, element integration and cooperative development the village is on a path of sustainability. Other ecological resources and agricultural diversified functions have been developed and utilized, thus providing a lasting impetus for sustainable development. More importantly, the quality of life of farmers has been improved. In 2020, the per capita income of farmers reached RMB 16,400, an increase of 90.7% over 2017. The collective economic income reached more than RMB 1.5 million. The complementary linkage between poverty alleviation and rural revitalization has achieved a historic leap from poverty alleviation to a higher standard of living.

Experience and Inspirations

1. New driving force for poverty alleviation. Natural and cultural limitations restrict the endogenous potential of the village. The introduction of Desheng Group can promote industrial development, attract investments and create viable marketing structures. They can also lead to operating mechanisms that include modern agricultural management systems guided by advanced scientific concepts and engineering ideas to improve market efficiency. This will increase income and limit risk exposure. The integrated development of urban and rural areas is another rural revitalization model.

2. Values and feelings for poverty alleviation. The Desheng Group has prioritized responsibility instead of profit. It has done so by applying the concept that "enterprises should lead farmers to become prosperous and build a happy and beautiful new Desheng Village." The enterprise has invested RMB 130 million in public infrastructure and industrial pre-cultivation. Despite its current low profits, it has built a new business model with rural tourism as the core for local areas. It has laid a foundation for continuous employment and income increase for farmers. Also, it has paved the way for the future development of the enterprise. The enterprise is voluntary to provide continuous support for village development to achieve in-depth integration, win-win cooperation, co-creation and sharing.

3. Replicable models for poverty alleviation. The core of the Desheng Model places the role of driving and sharing at the center. "Driving" means that benefits belong to farmers and that market-based management ensures the involvement of farmers in governance. This is expected to limit risk exposure and achieve income growth. "Sharing" signifies that long-term benefits are shared with farmers, in whom lies the future of the industry. Constant iteration also spur improvements and replicability.

4. Driving farmers as a poverty alleviation goal. The motivation, active participation and farmers' self-improvement reflect the value of enterprises, which are in line with the Party's policy and farmers' wishes and long-term interests of development. In-depth exploration and agricultural development cannot be achieved without the participation of farmers. Today local villagers and those from surrounding villages are the primary source of employment at industrial chains for rural revitalization.

Next Steps

During the "14th Five-Year Plan" period, the Desheng Village will work to achieve new developments based on the following: (1) Application of the principles of enterprise driving, with farmers as the main body; market operation, technological support and village-enterprise collaboration, that is, building a new "4 + 1" industrial pattern of ecological planting and breeding, agricultural product processing supply chain, B&B healthcare tourism, green prefabricated construction and cultural industry. (2) Developing a new platform for business entrepreneurship, employee innovation, farmers' enrichment, element aggregation, cooperation and sharing. (3) Fostering Desheng's new brands infused with cultural integrity, green ecology, health and safety. (4) Enhancing a replicable and promotable new Desheng development model of "enterprise + countryside, platform + brand, co-creation + sharing." (5) Establishing new education bases for multi-format businesses for research study on rural revitalization, technology training for farmers and industrial development practice. (6) Dissemination of advanced culture, creating a new guaranteed participatory system characterized by element integration, village-enterprise co-creation, entrepreneurship and employment and innovative development.

辽宁阜新市细河区四合镇黄家沟村：
自然资源与工业遗产的融合模式

Huangjiagou Village, Sihe Town, Xihe District, Fuxin City, Liaoning Province:
Integration Mode of Natural Resources and Industrial Heritage

摘 要

辽宁省阜新市细河区四合镇黄家沟村利用自然资源优势大力发展乡村旅游，黄家沟旅游度假区将松涛湖自然资源与独特的工业遗产资源相结合，使第一产业、第二产业、第三产业相融合，推出“春赏花、夏戏水、秋采摘、冬滑雪”的四季旅游产品，以完善的服务设施和卓越的服务理念，打造出集休闲、观光、度假、游乐于一体的东北地区最大的乡村旅游胜地。通过大力发展旅游业，黄家沟村现已发展成为国家 4A 级旅游景区、国家乡村旅游重点村、辽宁省“图强致富文明带”示范村，成了名副其实的阜新“第一村”。

挑战与问题

辽宁省阜新市细河区四合镇黄家沟村位于阜新市区西北部，距市中心 6.5 公里，占地面积 5.79 平方公里，土地面积 8000 余亩，耕地 4046 亩，属半丘陵地区，下辖四个村民小组，农户 420 户，总人口 1762 人。黄家沟村旅游资源丰富，村内具有得天独厚的自然山水景观资源，区域内有一山、两河、九湖、千亩松林等丰富的自然资源。黄家沟村区位交通条件优越，村内有长深、阜锦等高速公路过境，村口即是阜新北站高速口。2001 年起，黄家沟村开始利用自然资源优势大力发展乡村旅游，但由于缺乏统一规划，建设布局不合理，功能分区不明显，用地与道路间关系凌乱，土地浪费、用地不合理等现象严重；村内道路不成体系，村内道路边沟系统不畅；缺少娱乐健身场地与设施，公用工程设施和环卫设施不健全，村民存在随意丢弃垃圾的现象，影响村子形象和生态环境。

措施

1. 提升村庄环境品质。黄家沟村在维护生态安全的基础上，规划了一系列滨水公园、景观绿带、休闲广场，将山水格局融入整体区域环境，营造绿色、生态、宜居、休闲的乡村环境。村内四季花香，绿树成荫，水乐园、滑雪场、生态农场、五彩花田等成为人们茶余饭后散步休憩之地，黄家沟村被建设成了一个绿色、自然、宜居的新乡村，广大农民深切感受到了生活环境的改善，幸福指数骤然提升。

2. 保障基础设施和公共服务设施。黄家沟村从本区域功能定位出发，合理配置，从不同层面配

置完善的公共服务设施；严格控制市政基础设施用地的位置和规模，保证基础设施规划方案的落实，确保市政基础设施能够满足未来发展的需求，为区域的持续发展提供有力支撑。黄家沟旅游度假区通过完善基础设施，畅通了道路，并在全村各区域安装路灯，实现全面亮化，全面改善了农村人居环境和居民生活质量。

3. 强化社区概念。规划除了对城市级别的公共服务设施进行布局外，还强化了社区和组团的概念，将整个规划区划分为若干规模适中的居住片区和居住组团，在其中配置社区级的生活服务配套设施，包括配套教育、商业服务、体育健身、医疗卫生、文化福利等，以方便居民日常生活。

4. 合理布局村庄公共空间。充足而富有特色的村庄公共空间是提升居民生活品质的关键。规划对区域的公共空间进行了全面设计：一方面构建公园、广场、绿化廊道等公共开放空间体系，打造充满活力的居民活动空间；另一方面，通过确立指标和行政手段干预保证公共空间的实施，从用地性质、功能组成和空间形态等诸多方面规划和引导城市公共空间的建设。

5. 做好旅游景区开发和保护。依靠黄家沟村丰富的自然资源和钢铁铸造企业独特的工业遗产优势，辽宁太克集团—东广产业有限公司与黄家沟村共同创建了黄家沟旅游度假区。度假区坚持贯彻“开发和保护相结合”的原则，大力倡导绿色开发、绿色项目、绿色经营、绿色消费，尽可能地维护和营造良好的自然生态环境和社会人文环境，实现了景区经济、社会、生态环境效应的良性循环。

成效

黄家沟旅游度假区充分发挥旅游业的综合带动作用，特别是与太平沟村两村融合，带动了周边贫困村的经济增长，在建设宜居乡村、农民增收、拉动就业、推动地区经济发展等方面取得了实实在在的成效。黄家沟旅游度假区 2019 年接待游客 50 万人次，实现旅游收入 8500 万元，利润 1050 万元，税金 320 万元。度假区景区安置员工 1000 余人，其中 80% 是本村适龄安置人员。2010 年，黄家沟村年人均收入 11000 元，黄家沟旅游度假区的员工月平均工资 2500 元；2020 年，年人均收入已达到 25900 元，黄家沟村已经从原来的贫困村变为比较富裕的村子。该度假区已经成为带动农民致富、改善生态环境、促进产业转型、拉动地方经济发展的生力军。

经验与启示

1. 产业融合。黄家沟村放弃了落后的农业生产模式，形成土地规模化、集约化生产。控制工业企业发展规模，取缔环境污染严重的工业用地，对其进行生态升级，使其成为黄家沟的特色景点。将生态底蕴和优势进行合理配置，将初具规模的乡村旅游经济延伸到农副产品加工、影视文化带动等，彰显其个性和特色。

2. 公司运营。公司运营模式能起到用好外力、激发内力，用好能人、带动闲人，形成干事创业合力的作用。黄家沟村采用公司运营的模式，激活乡村资产价值，激发村民发展热情，用市场配置资源的方式大力发展乡村旅游。

下一步计划

一是培养人才，把想干事、能干事的人培养成专业人才，更新其发展理念，促使其更好地发挥示范带头作用。二是发挥乡村旅游在乡村振兴中起到的关键作用，通过乡村旅游引领相关产业健康发展，使村民走上脱贫致富的新路子。三是持续抓好地域民俗文化传承。黄家沟旅游度假区还拥有独特的人文环境，区内每一幢建筑、每一座桥梁、每一条路都以石头为主，同时点缀有木艺造型。悠远的人类文化和淳朴的乡村民风，诠释了辽西这座美丽的“石头小镇”——黄家沟村。四是加强乡村治理，培育文明村风。从改善人居环境、提高幸福指数入手，探索建立村规民约、文明超市、文明户奖励等制度，加强村风治理，激发群众内生动力。五是打通旅游产品销售流通环节，在消费对接、商贸物流、组织引领及生产加工上力争有所创新。

Abstract

Huangjiagou Village in Sihe Town, Xihe District, Fuxin City, Liaoning Province, is developing rural tourism around its natural resources. The Huangjiagou Resort Area combines the natural resources of Songtao Lake and its unique industrial heritage. It integrates the primary, secondary and tertiary industries for a year-round tourism product of "appreciating flowers in spring, playing with water in summer, harvesting in autumn and skiing in winter." The largest rural resort in Northeast China that integrates leisure, sightseeing, vacation, and recreation was built with excellent service facilities and concept. Through vigorous efforts, Huangjiagou has developed into a national 4A-level tourist attraction, a national rural tourism key village and a demonstration village that is "striving to become rich and ethical" in Liaoning Province. It has worthily earned its reputation as the "No.1 Village" in Fuxin City.

Challenges and Problems

The village is located in the northwest of Fuxin City, 6.5 kilometers away from downtown. It covers an area of 5.79 square kilometers, with a semi-hilly land area of more than 8,000 *mu* and an arable land of 4,046 *mu*. It has jurisdiction over four villager groups with 1,762 people in 420 households. Also, it boasts rich tourism resources, a unique hill landscape, two rivers, nine lakes, thousands of *mu* of pine forests, etc. The village has a developed transportation system with the Changchun — Shenzhen and Fuxin–Jinzhou expressway. Moreover, it is conveniently located as the exit to Fuxinbei Railways is just at its entrance. Since 2001, it has begun to make great use of its natural resources to develop rural tourism. However, haphazard planning, ill-conceived construction layout, indistinct functional divisions, irregular utilization of land and roads, land waste, land usage and other serious problems have stymied its progress. Roads within the village are fragmentated and its roadside ditch network is uneven. Its sparse recreational areas and fitness centers, substandard sanitation facilities and other sanitary issues have affected its image and ecological environment.

Measures

1. Improve quality of village environment. The village plans a series of waterfront parks, green belts and leisure squares to integrate into the overall regional environment for a livable green rural environment. Its shades of lush green trees complement the year-round fragrance its lovely native flora exudes. Waterfront parks, ski resorts, ecological farms, vibrant flower fields — all offer a warm welcome for those seeking rest and relaxation. It has been built into a livable green, new village. More significantly, majority of farmers have felt the dramatic improvement of their standard of living and happiness index.

2. Ensure infrastructure and public services. The village allocates public service facilities at different levels based on regional functional positioning. It strictly controls the location and scale of the plot for municipal infrastructure and ensures their proper implementation for future development and for a sustainable regional development. The Huangjiagou Tourist Resort has enhanced the rural living environment and the quality of life of the locals through improved infrastructure and roads. It has also installed streetlights to illumine the village and increase its curb appeal.

3. Strengthen the community concept. In addition to the strategic layout of public service facilities at the municipal level, the village also strengthens the concept of community and group. The whole planning area is divided into several residential areas and groups. Life service supporting facilities at the community level are configured, including education, business services, sports and fitness, medical and healthcare and cultural welfare to provide order and structure to the daily lives of residents.

4. Reasonably arrange the public space. Adequate distinctive public spaces are the key to improving the quality of life of village residents. All-encompassing regional public spaces such as parks, squares and green corridors are established to provide them with dynamic activity areas where they can spend wholesome time with their family and friends. This also implements the precept of public space through indicator establishment and administrative means, and the plans and guidelines for the construction of urban public spaces with the nature of land usage, functional composition and spatial form as the framework.

5. Focus on development and protection of scenic spots. With the village's rich natural resources and its industrial heritage left by iron and steel casting enterprises as the cornerstone, the Liaoning Taike Group — Dongguang Industry Co., Ltd. and the village jointly established the Huangjiagou Resort Area. It adheres to the principle of combining development and protection, advocates green development, green projects, green management and green consumption. Also, it maintains and creates a sound natural, social and cultural environment and fulfills the effects of the scenic spot's virtuous cycle.

Results

The Huangjiagou Resort Area has achieved tangible results in constructing livable villages, increasing farmers' income, stimulating employment and promoting regional economic growth by giving maximum play to the driving role of tourism. Specifically, it cooperated with Taipinggou Village and spurred the growth of surrounding poverty-stricken villages. In 2019, the resort area received 500,000 tourists, achieving RMB 85 million of tourism

income, RMB 10.5 million of profit and RMB 3.2 million in tax revenues. It has provided employment for 1,000 local farmers, 80% of whom are age-appropriate villagers who need government-arranged job placement.

In 2010, the annual per capita income of the village reached RMB 11,000 and the average monthly salary of the resort staff was RMB 2,500. In 2020, the annual per capita income of the village reached RMB 25,900. Evidently, it has been lifted out of poverty and has become relatively prosperous. The resort area has turned into an economic engine that provides villagers with an additional income stream. It represents a sustainable opportunity for them to improve their standard of living. Enhancement of the ecological environment, industrial transformation and the stimulation of the local economy are some of the palpable results the resort has had on the village and its residents.

Experience and Inspirations

1. Industrial integration. The village abandoned the backward agricultural production mode and explored large-scale and intensive production. It controls the scale of industrial enterprises, bans high-polluting

industries and has implemented ecological upgrades to build a characteristic scenic spot. It rationally allocates ecological heritage and comparative advantages, extends the emerging rural tourism economy to the processing of agricultural and side products, film and television to showcase its distinctive characteristics.

2. Company operations. A company's operation mode can capitalize on external forces, stimulate internal forces and organize a skilled talent pool for entrepreneurship. The village adopts the mode of company operation to activate the value of rural assets, stimulate villagers' enthusiasm. Also, it develops rural tourism through a strategically measured allocation of market resources.

Next Steps

First, cultivate talents. We should recruit and train those who are capable and interested in pursuing a professional career. The development concept of leading by example should be demonstrated. **Second,** give maximum play to the role of rural tourism in rural revitalization. We can lead the healthy development of relevant industries through rural tourism and lead villagers to embark on a new path to poverty alleviation and prosperity. **Third,** pay constant attention to regional folk culture, its qualities and time-honored legacy. The Huangjiagou Resort Area boasts a unique cultural environment. A great number of buildings, bridges or road guides in the area are made of stone and decorated with wood. Its unique rural folk customs and architecture can transform it into a beautiful "stone town" in western Liaoning Province. **Fourth,** strengthen rural governance and establish an ethical village. With an eye to the improvement of the living environment and the happiness index of village residents, rules and regulations must be carefully laid out. Supermarket systems and practices, household rewards and other mechanisms must be based on highly-principled ideals to strengthen the moral fabric of village society and motivate the masses to aim for lofty goals for everyone's benefit. **Fifth,** we should open the sales and circulation links of tourism products and innovate consumption docking, trade logistics, organization and processing.

海南琼中黎族苗族自治县红毛镇什寒村：
构建多方共建、融合发展的什寒模式

Zahan Village, Hongmao Town, Qiongzhong Li and Miao Autonomous County, Hainan Province:
Form a Zahan Model with Co-Construction and Integrated Development

摘要

海南省琼中黎族苗族自治县什寒村依靠天然生态环境、资源禀赋、民族风情等独特优势，通过农旅融合、文旅互动，推动形成“政府 + 公司 + 农民合作社 + 农户”多方共建、“产业发展 + 生态保护 + 文化传承 + 环境整治 + 休闲旅游 + 高效农业 + 品牌农业”融合发展的什寒模式，重点发展养蜂、益智、铁皮石斛、农家乐等一批有区域特色、有竞争优势的旅游业态，加快什寒从“有旅游、有产品”向“有旅游、有产品、有产业”升级，从乡村脱贫走向乡村振兴。

挑战与问题

海南省琼中黎族苗族自治县什寒村坐落于琼中黎母山和鹦哥岭之间的高山盆地中，海拔 800 多米，村庄交通不便，是琼中最偏远、最贫困的村庄之一。但什寒村天然在生态环境、资源禀赋、民族风情等方面具备独特优势，那么如何解决什寒村的交通问题、如何充分利用什寒村的现有资源开发适合其发展的旅游产业、如何解决旅游发展投入所需资金等问题便迫在眉睫。

措施

1. 紧扣农旅融合，促进产业实现转型升级。一是调整优化农业产业结构。根据什寒村的实际情况，因地制宜，引导农户大力发展“短、平、快”农业特色产业，种植益智 2600 多亩，发展养蜂 2000 多箱，采取“龙头企业、专业合作社、村集体经济、种养大户 + 基地 + 农户”四种产业扶贫模式，引导成立了群生养蜂专业合作社，推动农户抱团发展。二是加快发展体验型休闲农业。成立县旅游总公司，结合什寒村现有的农业特色产业，开发经营“蜂蜜采割”“割稻捞鱼”“蓝莓采摘”等农事体验项目，促进农业与旅游业融合发展。

2. 实施文旅互动，黎苗特色文化有效彰显。一是深入挖掘黎苗文化元素。什寒村黎苗文化底蕴深厚，在深入挖掘什寒黎苗婚俗、“三月三”黎苗节庆等黎苗生活习俗的基础上，不断融合外来文化精华，推动什寒形成具有地方特色、民族风格鲜明、兼具现代时尚感的独特黎苗文化。二是抓好旅游宣传策划包装工作。挖掘黎苗语言文化元素，打造什寒“奔格内”（“奔格内”是黎语“来这里”的意思）旅游文化品牌，使其成为琼中乡村旅游对外宣传的新名片。

3. 完善旅游要素，村民参与度不断提升。挖掘黎苗传统特色饮食，引导有条件的农户经营黎、

苗农家乐，打造什寒黎苗特色长桌宴，开发三色饭、竹筒饭、山鸡、野生芭蕉芯、白花菜、鱼茶等原生态特色美食。结合黎苗文化，将黎族的甘工鸟和苗族的牛角等黎苗图腾元素融入民宿建筑，并按公寓式酒店规格对民宿进行装饰，打造民族风情浓厚、简约舒适的“奔格内”民宿休憩场所。引导农户参与乡村游项目开发，大力发展户外探险游、自驾车游、骑行游、户外露营、森林科考等项目。支持农户开发“什寒山珍”系列旅游产品，对铁皮石斛、蜂蜜、灵芝、山兰米等农家特色农产品进行包装和推销。不定期举办篝火晚会表演原生态黎苗歌舞，引导村民创作水平高、品质精的民俗歌舞，使之成为来什寒游客必看节目。

4. 创新经营模式，完善旅游扶贫长效机制。积极探索产业帮扶方式，推动形成了“政府 + 公司 + 农民合作社 + 农户 + 品牌 + 基地”多方共建、“产业发展 + 生态保护 + 文化传承 + 环境整治 + 休闲旅游 + 高效农业 + 品牌农业”融合发展的经营管理新模式，重点发展养蜂、益智、铁皮石斛、农家乐等一批有区域特色、有竞争优势的旅游业态，加快什寒从“有旅游、有产品”向“有旅游、有产品、有产业”升级，不断增强“自我造血”功能。

5. 注重资金整合，加强旅游配套。以开展交通扶贫为契机，利用什寒山地坡缓、植被丰富、田园景观优美等自然条件，修建进山旅游观光公路和国家步道，配套完善自行车绿道、木栈道、乡村巴士、自驾车营地、指示标识等设施，构建“慢游”的旅游出行体系。坚持“政府主导、企业参与、金融支持、依靠群众”的共建原则，结合富美乡村建设，统筹整合专项扶贫资金，大力改善什寒村的环境卫生、村容村貌、村道户道、景观景点、文化广场、游客咨询中心等基础设施建设，为什寒乡村旅游奠定了良好基础。

成效

什寒村成功的产业转型升级，使村民的收入不再依靠单一的种植收入，而是可以通过合作社分红、土地分红、开农家乐、民宿务工等方式增加个人经济收入，提高村民生活水平。什寒曾经是琼中最偏远、最贫困的村庄之一，2009 年，农民人均纯收入仅为 946 元；2020 年，村民人均纯

收入达到18000元，较2009年增长了19倍。目前，村庄旅游从业人员已达436人，占全村人口的97.6%。

经验与启示

1. 生态保护是前提。“绿水青山就是金山银山”，保护生态环境是实现旅游扶贫的重要前提。什寒在旅游开发过程中，始终坚持以“居民零动迁、生态零破坏、环境零污染”为宗旨，以“村民不失业、不失地、不失居”为基础，不搞大拆大建，用原生态的自然环境、优美的田园风光吸引八方来客，实现“增资产、增就业、增收入”的目标。

2. 规划先行是基础。规划是行动的先导。坚持把什寒旅游扶贫摆在首要位置，高起点、高标准狠抓什寒发展规划编制和实施，先后出台《什寒村委会联手扶贫规划》《什寒村危房改造实施规划》《什寒村村庄建设规划》等文件，为什寒村建设和发展提供了全方位的支持和保障。

3. 改革创新是动力。改革是推进“三农”发展的强劲动力。在县委、县政府的领导下，村民积极利用集体或个人闲置土地、民房或劳务等资源入股企业、合作社，以参股的形式分享农村改革红利，建立了政府、企业、村民利益联结机制，不断增加自身收入。

4. 黎苗文化是依托。在什寒乡村旅游开发过程中，通过宣传引导，什寒村民逐渐认识到自身黎苗文化的价值，开始重新审视黎苗婚俗、原生态歌舞表演、传统手工艺等非物质文化遗产，并对其加以充分保护和利用，实现文化效益和经济效益双促进、双发展。

下一步计划

“什寒模式”开创了旅游扶贫新模式，琼中县将持续依托“旅游+”计划，从以下方面着手，不断加以完善。一是硬件提升。狠抓环境整治，继续完善基础设施，增设非物质遗产展示馆、会议厅、旅游商品展厅等服务功能区。深挖文化内涵，完善什寒村旅游娱乐设施建设，结合农业旅游、文化旅游开发趣味性强、参与性强的旅游产品。二是软件提升。加强乡村旅游人才培养，开展乡村旅游从业人员教育培训，切实提升村民素质及参与乡村旅游经营的能力，夯实旅游扶贫人才基础。依托当地黎苗文化，加强民族特色技艺培训，在实现非物质文化遗产保护的基础上增加旅游的情趣。强化乡村旅游的标准化管理，构建“食、住、行、游、购、娱”等方面的标准化管理和从业人员的日常规范化管理，为乡村旅游持续发展提供良好环境。三是市场资本化运作。抓好与旅游企业的合作，利用PPP模式，以农村资源变资产、资金变股金、农民变股民的“三变”改革试点为手段，发挥政府指导和企业市场化运作的双重优势，积极撬动社会资本，加大对什寒乡村旅游重点项目的开发和投入，增强什寒的旅游接待能力，提高什寒的旅游服务水平，实现乡村振兴。

Abstract

Endowed with the unique advantages of a natural ecological environment, rich resources and ethnic customs, Zahan Village, Qiongzhong Li and Miao Autonomous County, Hainan Province is a unique model created by a multi-party co-construction of "government + companies + farmers' cooperatives + peasant households" and integrated development of "industrial development + ecological protection + cultural inheritance + environmental improvement + leisure tourism + high-efficiency agriculture + brand agriculture" through the integration of agriculture and tourism and interaction between culture and tourism. It develops tourism industries with regional attributes and competitive advantages, such as beekeeping, alpinia oxyphylla, dendrobium officinale and agritainment, all of which have accelerated the progression from "tourism and products" stage to "tourism, products and industries" for Zahan Village.

Challenges and Problems

Located in the mountain basin between Limushan and Yinggeling of Qiongzhong County, Zahan Village, with an elevation of more than 800 meters, Qiongzhong Li and Miao Autonomous County, Hainan Province is inconvenient to transportation, and is one of the remotest and poorest villages in Qiongzhong. However, endowed with unique advantages of natural ecological environment, rich resources and ethnic customs, measures have to be taken to solve the problems in traffic, the means to use existing resources to develop tourism industries suitable for village development and obtaining the required investment fund for tourism development.

Measures

1. Integration of agriculture and tourism for industry transformation and upgrade. First, adjust and optimize agricultural industry structure. Based on the local conditions in Zahan Village, farmers are guided to develop agricultural industries with short maturation period and grow more than 2,600 *mu* of Alpinia oxyphylla and feed more than 2,000 boxes of bees. Also, it has to establish professional beekeeping cooperatives to promote the common development of farmers through the four models of poverty alleviation through industrial development of "leading enterprises, professional cooperatives, village collective economy, big specialized households of crop and animal productions + bases + peasant households." **Second,** accelerate the development of experience-based leisure agriculture. The County Tourism Co., Ltd. is established based on the existing attributes of Zahan's agricultural industries. It aims to develop projects such as "honey collecting," "rice harvesting and fishing" and "blueberry picking," and promote the integrated development of agriculture and tourism.

2. Integration of culture and tourism to promote the Li and Miao's folk traditions. First, utilize more Li and Miao cultural elements. Zahan Village enjoys a rich Li and Miao cultural heritage, including wedding traditions and the "March 3" lunar festival. Integrate

the ethnic elements of their traditional heritage with local customs and modern fashion to showcase the unique fusion of cultures. **Second,** scale up the tourism promotion, planning and marketing. The language and cultural elements of the Li and Miao groups should be explored to create the "Bengenei" (means "come here" in Li language) brand of Zahan Village. Such brand should be developed into a new marketing slogan to popularize rural tourism in Qiongzhong.

3. Enrich tourism products for more extensive participation of villagers. The traditional special diet of the Li and Miao ethnic groups should be explored to encourage more Miao and Li agritainment among peasant households, develop Tok Panjang (an exquisite banquet on long tables with Li and Miao elements), and create ecological specialties such as three-color rice, bamboo-tube-cooked rice, pheasant, wild banana stem, capparidaceae and fish tea (fermentative fish with steamed sticky rice, a cuisine similar to sushi). With respect to the Li and Miao culture elements, totems such as the Gangong Bird symbolizing the Li nationality and the horns symbolizing the Miao nationality are added into the building of B&Bs which are decorated according to the specifications of apartment-style hotels, in an effort to develop a simple and comfortable "Bengenei" B&B with strong ethnic characteristics. Farmers are encouraged to develop rural tourism projects, and conduct outdoor adventure tours, self-driving tours, cycling tours, outdoor camping, forest scientific survey and other projects. Great supports are provided for farmers to exploit the tourism products of "Zahan Mountain Treasures," to package and sell specific agricultural products such as dendrobium officinale, honey, ganoderma lucidum and Shanlan rice. Bonfire evening parties are held from time to time to stage original Li and Miao performances. Villagers are guided to create high-level and quality folk songs and dances, which have become a must-see program for tourists in Zahan Village.

4. Develop new business models and create a viable long-term poverty alleviation through tourism program. The ways and channels for effective industrial assistance have been explored along with new business models featuring multi-party co-construction of "government + companies + farmers' cooperatives + peasant households + brands + bases" and integrated development of "industrial development + ecological protection + cultural inheritancc + environmental improvement + leisure tourism + high-efficiency agriculture + brand agriculture," and tourism industries with regional characteristics and competitive advantages have been developed, such as beekeeping, alpinia oxyphylla, dendrobium officinale and agritainment. As a result, all these accelerate the progressions from the "tourism and products" stage to "tourism, products and industries" stage.

5. Highlight fund integration for advanced tourism supporting facilities. Based on the opportunity of poverty alleviation through transportation development, and the natural qualities such as gentle slopes, rich vegetation and beautiful pastoral landscapes, tourist roads and national trails are built and supporting facilities including bicycle greenways, wooden plank roads, rural buses, self-driving camps and signs are equipped to build a "slow travel" system. By adhering to the co-construction principle of "government leading, enterprise participation, financial support, and mass-oriented" concept and taking into account the construction of rich and beautiful villages, special poverty-alleviation funds are integrated to improve the construction of infrastructure such as sanitation, village appearance, roads, scenic spots, cultural squares and tourist information centers, thereby laying a sound foundation for tourism development.

Results

The successful industrial transformation and upgrading of Zahan Village has provided more channels to increase villagers' income and improve their living standards, including cooperative and land dividends, agritainment operation and working in B&Bs, eliminating the single income stream derived from agricultural planting.

Zahan Village, with its remotest location, was once one of the poorest villages in Qiongzhong. In 2009, the per capita net income of farmers was only RMB 946. In 2020, however, the per capita net income of villagers reached more than RMB 18,000, with an increase of nearly 18 times compared to 2009. A total of 436 villagers were engaged in the tourism business, accounting for 97.6% of the village's population.

Experience and Inspirations

1. Ecological protection is a prerequisite. "Lucid waters and lush mountains are invaluable assets," and protecting the ecological environment are important prerequisites for poverty alleviation through tourism. During the tourism development of Zahan Village, the tenet of "no resident resettlement, no ecological damage, and no environmental pollution" is strictly followed to guarantee that the jobs, lands and homes of the villagers are not damaged. Large-scale demolition and construction are not advocated, and original ecological environment and charming pastoral scenery are developed to attract visitors from all over the world, thereby increasing tourism assets, and job opportunities, expanding the

villagers revenue streams to reduce or eliminate their reliance on a single-source income.

2. Planning is the foundation. Planning drives the action. With poverty alleviation through tourism in Zahan Village as the priority, the preparation and implementation of its development plan involved top quality blueprints in documents such as the *Zahan Village Committee's Joint Poverty Alleviation Plan, Implementation Plan on Zahan Village Dilapidated House Reconstruction, and Zahan Village Construction Plan.* They were successively issued and provided comprehensive support throughout the entire process of planning and construction.

3. Reform and innovation are the engines of transformation. Reform drives the development of "agriculture, rural areas and farmers." Under the leadership of the county party committee and the county government, villagers used collective or individual idle land, private houses or labor services and other resources to invest in enterprises and cooperatives, and gain dividends from rural reform in the form of equity participation. The benefit of the coupling mechanism between government, enterprises and villagers is established, resulting in an increase in their income.

4. Li and Miao culture is the basis. During the tourism development of Zahan Village, villagers gradually realized the value of the Li and Miao culture through publicity and guidance. They were inspired to re-examine the intangible cultural heritage such as wedding customs, original ecological performances and traditional handicrafts. More importantly, they were motivated to protect and make full use of them, thereby advancing the development of cultural and economic benefits.

Next Steps

Since the Zahan Model has created a new model of poverty alleviation through tourism, the following aspects will be further improved based on the "Tourism +" plan in Qiongzhong County. **First,** upgrade the hardware. More emphasis should be put on environmental governance to improve infrastructure, and service function zones including intangible heritage exhibition halls, conference halls and tourist product exhibition halls should be added. Moreover, cultural connotations should be further utilized to improve the entertainment facilities in Zahan Village, and highly interesting and participatory tourism products should be developed based on both the agriculture-tourism integration and the culture-tourism interaction. **Second,** upgrade the software. The training of rural tourism talents should be strengthened. Education and training for rural tourism practitioners should be provided to improve the villagers' skills in rural tourism operation, nurturing the talents in poverty alleviation through tourism. More training on ethnic Li and Miao cultural skills should be offered. Tourism development should be premised on the protection of intangible cultural heritage. Moreover, the standardized management of rural tourism should be strengthened to develop a standardized management of "food, housing, transportation, travel, shopping and entertainment," including the daily standardized management of employees to ensure a sustainable development. **Third,** manage and operate market capitalization. Cooperation with tourism companies should be pursued and implemented. Pilot reforms to turn rural resources into assets, capital into equity, and farmers into stockholders should be conducted through the PPP model, to give full play to the dual advantages of government guidance and enterprise market operation, leading to more social capital to flow into the village. Development and investment in key rural tourism projects, reception capacity and tourism service level for rural revitalization will likewise improve.

江苏无锡市惠山区阳山镇：
田园综合体模式带动乡村脱贫

Yangshan Town, Huishan District, Wuxi City, Jiangsu Province:
Pastoral Complex Model Drives Rural Poverty Alleviation

摘 要

江苏省无锡市阳山镇是特色蜜桃小镇，既有“亿年火山、万亩桃林、千年古刹、百年书院”的资源禀赋，又有“特色农业、生态宜居、休闲度假、文化养生”的鲜明特征。近年来，阳山镇高举乡村振兴的大旗，以生态立镇为前提，以富民强村为目标，以产业融合为路径，走出了农村改革、美丽乡村建设、田园综合体的阳山高质量发展“三部曲”；先后获得全国改革试点镇、国家4A级旅游景区、全国美丽宜居小镇、全国特色小镇、江苏省旅游风情小镇、江苏省五星级乡村旅游区、江苏省首批特色田园乡村等诸多荣誉。

挑战与问题

江苏无锡市阳山镇是著名的水蜜桃之乡，离主城区距离较远，位置较偏僻。阳山镇总面积 44 平方公里，其中度假区面积 17.5 平方公里，常住人口 6 万人。随着城镇化建设的推进，村民逐渐外迁，一些自然村的民居空置率高达 80%，出现空心村。人口的外迁也导致年轻人不愿意种桃，从业者年龄大多在 50 岁以上，桃农断层，阳山水蜜桃的种植技术无法得到良好的推广，且无法注入新的活力。另外，阳山镇的旅游主要以桃花和水蜜桃为媒介展开，乡村旅游季节性强，旺季过旺，淡季过淡。加之乡镇财政薄弱，住宿、餐饮、厕所、停车场等配套设施在旅游旺季时难以满足游客的需求，淡季时又大量闲置。

措施

1. 推进乡村体制改革。农村改革奠定乡村振兴基础，所以要积极推进农村土地承包经营权与宅基地的流转，聚集土地要素，激发农村发展的内生动力。为了发展休闲农业和乡村旅游，2008 年，阳山在江苏省第一个提出并开始进行农场化改造、规模化经营，成为全国首批开展土地流转的村镇。

2. 推进乡村环境整治。环境整治绘就美丽乡村底色，阳山镇以宜居、宜业、宜游特色蜜桃镇为发展定位，编制总规、整合土地，搬离了度假区内 156 家低效企业、散乱污企业，疏减了 130 个过密的一般村庄，为美丽乡村建设腾出了发展空间。从创建最美村道、最美村庄、最美河道、最美赏花点起步，完成 18 条农村道路提档升级，以点带面完

成3个自然村144户农村住房改建工程，建成11个美丽村、20个宜居村、100个整洁村，实现了从“点上盆景”到“线上风景”的转变。

3. 推动乡村旅游发展。乡村旅游发展是乡村振兴的引擎。2012年，阳山镇在全国首个提出“田园综合体”并付诸实践，为小镇注入田园、风情、艺术、康养等内涵，实现了多业态融合，形成了集现代农业、文化旅游、田园社区为一体的综合发展模式。政府当好搭台人，落实好基础设施和公共服务配套，新建游客中心、生态停车场，新改建A级厕所，完善导览系统。鼓励社会资本参与乡村旅游建设，在招商引进大项目的同时探索农村宅基地三权分置改革，乘着“三块地”改革东风，积极推进闲置农房翻建工作，鼓励村民利用民居改建民宿，还把集约土地出租给品牌公司，打造精品民宿。

4. 打造节庆活动品牌。春有半程马拉松、桃花节、全国大学生写生节开幕式，夏有蜜桃节、音乐节，秋有丰收节，冬有年味节。在节庆活动中贯穿“春花、夏桃、秋娱、冬浴”四季主题。阳山度假区还在周末、节假日为民宿客人提供免费花艺课及烘焙课，以增加阳山度假区旅游业态的人气。

成效

目前阳山的住宿接待设施房间数超1000间，已对外营业的16家精品民宿和1家帐篷营地提升了阳山度假区的住宿品质；阳山精品酒店和民宿逢春节、五一等节假日入住率达85%，周末入住率达70%。2020年，阳山度假区全年接待游客逾200万人次，桃产业链总销售收入实现15亿元，入选“全国乡村特色产业十亿元镇”。2021年，阳山半程马拉松活动日接待游客量达10万人次，阳山影响力持续扩大。

阳山成功创建冯巷、前寺舍、朱村3个省级

特色田园乡村，将产业“植”入乡村，打造“乡购”“乡居”“乡游”等村庄主题，让“一村一主题、一村一产业”成为现实。阳山的村落，正逐渐从纯水蜜桃种植主产村，蜕变成兼具水蜜桃种植、销售、休闲观光旅游、乡村文化体验的美丽乡村。以桃源村和阳山村为例，桃源村村集体固定收入从初期的 50 万元增长到 2020 年的 489 万元，完成了从经济薄弱村到美丽乡村的蜕变。阳山村 2020 年村民人均收入 5.48 万元，同比增收 6%，村级经营性收入达到 394 万元，比 2017 年增加 178 万元，增幅 82.4%，7 个市级贫困村全部脱贫。

经验与启示

1. 立足特色，打造品牌。乡村振兴要立足于特色产业和本地特色，紧扣核心，打出打响品牌。因地制宜，依托当地自然和文化优势，聚集资源，集中打造和宣传。对于特色产业，政府要做好品牌规范管理来提升规模效应。

2. 立足人才，多方聚才。人才振兴是乡村振兴的关键和基石。加强乡村人才建设，不仅要盘活农村存量人力资本，实施就地取“才”，还要打通人才要素融入乡村振兴建设的渠道，实施多方聚才。一方面，培养政治素质优、群众认可度高、带富能力强的乡土人才；另一方面，制定优惠政策鼓励大学生回乡创业，吸引技术和经营人才来乡村发展。

3. 立足资源，村镇联动。振兴乡村，离不开资金和资源的投入。集体土地三权分置、允许经营权流转，让民间资本为乡村振兴发挥杠杆作用。乡村的闲置农房是宝贵资产，要进行盘活利用。可利用优质农房资源引进乡村新产业、新业态。做好“闲置农房激活”文章，既可带动百姓增收，又能丰富乡村旅游业态，通过产业振兴乡村。

下一步计划

深耕“田园度假”这块品牌，把握后疫情时代新消费、新经济增长点，推进文旅、农旅、体旅、养旅等的融合，打造一批兼具文化内涵、生态价值、科技品位、体验感受、分享乐趣的高溢价产品，让更多人愿意来、留得住、能消费，将“绿水青山”变为“金山银山”，推动“美丽风景”向“美丽经济”不断转化，打造“全时 + 全季 + 全域 + 全景”的大文旅格局。

Abstract

Yangshan Town, Wuxi City, Jiangsu Province is a characteristic peach town, endowed with "age-old extinct volcanoes." It is also known for its century-old "academies." Other local characteristics include agriculture, idyllic environment, leisure and vacation, and health culture. The town has relied on its ecological system. It is focused on enriching people and strengthening villages. It has held high the rural revitalization banner, blazing a trail of Yangshan high-quality development featuring rural reform, beautiful village construction and a pastoral complex that follows the integration path of industries. It has received successively many honors such as a national reform pilot town, a national 4A-level tourist attraction, a national beautiful and livable town, a national characteristic town, a tourist-styled town in Jiangsu Province, a five-star rural tourist area in Jiangsu Province and the first batch of characteristic pastoral villages in Jiangsu Province.

Challenges and Problems

Located far from central downtown, Yangshan Town is a remote place famous for its peaches. It covers a total area of 44 square kilometers, of which the holiday resort area is 17.5 square kilometers. It has a population of 60,000 people. Villagers are slowly moving out due to the advancement of urbanization, leading to a vacancy rate of dwellings in some natural villages as high as 80%. Even hollow villages have appeared. The population's out-migration has also made young people reluctant to grow peaches. Most of the those who do are over the age of 50, contributing to the scarcity of farmers. The planting technology of Yangshan's juicy peach cannot be promoted without a booster shot of new energy and vitality. As tourism in the town is mainly based on the appreciation of peach blossoms appreciating and tasting of honey peaches, it is easily affected by the rural tour seasons. Many people come during the peak season of peach blooming and harvesting. Very few come during off season. Accommodations facilities and services such as catering, toilets and parking lots can hardly meet the needs of tourists during the peak season. However, they lay idle during the off-season.

Measures

1. Advance reform of rural systems. The town promotes the transfer of rural land contract management rights and homestead use rights to stimulate an endogenous rural development. It has given priority to the land element because rural reform is the foundation for its revitalization. In 2008, to develop leisure agriculture and rural tourism the town initiated farm transformation and large-scale operation in Jiangsu Province. More importantly, the town was also among the first batch to transfer land use rights in the country.

2. Promote the improvement of rural environment. Since the town has abundant peaches, it is positioned as an ideal place for living, working and travelling. In fact,

it has become a cornerstone for beautiful villages. It has formulated a master plan, integrated the land, moved out of the holiday resort 156 inefficient enterprises or poorly managed and polluting-small enterprises. It also evacuated and reduced 130 over-dense general villages to make room for the construction of beautiful new villages. So far, it has upgraded 18 rural roads and completed 144 rural housing reconstruction projects in three natural villages in a holistic approach. Overall, 11 beautiful villages, 20 livable villages and 100 clean villages were built, accomplishing the transformation into a scenic tourism destination.

3. Boost rural tourism development. Rural tourism development is the driving force of rural revitalization. In 2012, for the first time in China, the town put forward the "pastoral complex" and put into practice by injecting pastoral, customs, art, and health concepts. The integration of multiple industries has created a comprehensive development model integrating modern agriculture, cultural tourism and a pastoral community. The government implements the construction of infrastructure and public service facilities by building new tourist centers and ecological parking lots, renovating A-level toilets, and improving the navigation system. While encouraging social capital to participate in the rural tourism construction and invest and introduce large projects, it explores the reform of the separation of rural homesteads' ownership, qualification and use right. Taking advantage of the reform of rural land acquisition, entry of rural collectively owned commercial construction land into the market, and housing land, it proactively promotes the renovation of idle farmhouses, encourages villagers to convert their homes into B&Bs and leases intensive land to brand companies for building boutique B&Bs.

4. Create brands for festival activities. Throughout every year, the town holds many festivals and other related fun activities infused with its local culture. Some of them are half marathons, Peach Blossom Festival and the opening ceremony of the National University Student

Sketch Festival in spring. The Peach Festival and Music Festival are held in the summer, while the Harvest Festival is held in autumn and the New Year's Eve Festival in winter. The four-season themes of spring flowers, summer peaches, autumn entertainment and winter bathing run through every festival activity. Every weekend and on holidays, the Yangshan Holiday Resort also provides free courses in horticulture and baking for B&B guests to increase the popularity of its tourism business.

Results

More than 1,000 rooms of accommodation facilities in the town, a total of 16 boutique B&Bs and one camping site have significantly enhanced the quality of accommodation in Yangshan Holiday Resort. During the Spring Festival, May Day and other holidays, the occupancy rate of boutique hotels and B&Bs typically reaches 85%, while its weekend occupancy peaks at 70%. In 2020, the resort received more than 2 million tourists. The total sales revenue from its peach industry was RMB 1.5 billion. In the same year, it was selected as a one-billion-yuan town for rural characteristic industries in China. In 2021, the Half Marathon in Yangshan Town attracted 100,000 tourists per day. The town's influence is expected to continue to expand.

The town has successfully created three provincial-level characteristic pastoral villages of Fengxiang, Qiansishe and Zhu. It has planted industries into rural areas to create themes such as "village purchase," "village dwelling," and "village travel." The town's slogan is "one theme and one industry for one village." Villagers hope this will become a reality. The villages of Yangshan Town are gradually evolving from their main production of purely growing peaches to idyllic ones characterized by the sales of peaches, leisure and

tourism, and rural cultural experience. Taking Taoyuan Village and Yangshan Village as examples, the collective fixed income of Taoyuan Village rose from RMB 500,000 in its initial stage to RMB 4.89 million in 2020. This completed the transformation from an economically weak village to a beautifully productive one. In 2020, the per capita annual income of Yangshan villagers reached RMB 54,800, a year-on-year increase of 6%. Its village-level operating income reached RMB 3.94 million, an increase of RMB 1.78 million, or 82.4% over 2017. To date, seven municipal poverty-stricken villages have been lifted out of poverty.

Experience and Inspirations

1. Build brands based on characteristics. On the basis of special industries and local features, we will make great efforts to develop the core industry for the purpose of establishing high reputation in the market. Once that is achieved, we then can pursue rural revitalization. Based upon local, natural, and cultural advantages we need to pool all resources to build and promote local brands according to local conditions. For characteristic industries, the government should make efforts in brand standardization and management.

2. Attract talents from various sides. Talent recruitment and retention is the key to rural revitalization as it revitalizes the human capital stock. Channels for the integration of talents into rural revitalization must be thoroughly explored. We can cultivate local talents with excellent political quality, high public recognition and strong ability to create wealth. Preferential policies should be formulated to encourage college students to start their own businesses in their hometowns. Technical and business talents in the countryside must be developed.

3. Promote village-town interaction based on resources. Without the investment of funds and resources, rural revitalization will be difficult to realize. The separation of rural collective land ownership, farmers' contracting right, and land management right for collective land, as well as the transfer of management rights, allows private capital to leverage the revitalization of rural areas. Idle farmhouses in the countryside are valuable assets and must be utilized. High-quality rural housing resources can be used to introduce new industries and emerging businesses into the countryside. Making good use of idle farmhouses can increase people's income and enrich the rural tourism industry. This is a proven path to rural revitalization through industries.

Next Steps

We will put in great efforts to cultivate an idyllic vacation brand. In the post-epidemic era, we need to identify and hold firmly to growth points in new consumption and new economy. Also, we must promote the integration of cultural, agricultural, sports and health tourism. This will then create a group of high premium products featuring cultural connotations, ecological values, technological tastes, experience and pleasure sharing. This will entice more and more people to come, extend their length of stay and increase their consumption. Thus "lucid waters and lush mountains" are turned into "invaluable assets." Overall, we will promote the continuous transformation from "beautiful scenery" to "beautiful economy" and create an expanded cultural tourism blueprint of "full time + full season + full domain + full view."

河南鹤壁市淇县凉水泉村：
“一条旅游主线，五种利益联结”产业扶贫新模式

Liangshuiquan Village, Qi County, Hebi City, Henan Province:
A New Mode of Poverty Alleviation by Developing Industries with “One Main Line of Tourism and Five Kinds of Linking Benefits”

摘 要

河南中旅集团在河南省鹤壁市凉水泉村以“高端民宿开发”为一条主线，将整体租赁民宅、流转土地林地、“三员三小”就业、群众投劳务工、农特产品销售五种利益相联结，助力凉水泉村全面脱贫，使该村成为中国传统古村落的保护典范、乡村旅游示范基地和旅游产业扶贫基地。

挑战与问题

河南省鹤壁市凉水泉村位于淇县西部太行山区，总人口 46 户 93 人，贫困人口 35 户 67 人，是省级贫困村。凉水泉村历史悠久，文化底蕴深厚，70 多座建于清末民初、灰瓦石墙的民居依山而建，是国家级传统古村落；凉水泉村旅游资源丰富，“不老泉”和“五龙泉”两股四季流淌不息的泉水凉爽甘甜、明目养颜。但这些人文和自然旅游资源没有被盘活，没有给凉水泉村带来发展的契机。

措施

1. 资产托管，统一旅游规划。河南中旅集团与凉水泉村签订战略合作协议，对凉水泉村实施资产托管，进行整村旅游开发。截至目前，已累计投入 5140 万元，其中整合财政各类资金 1640 万元，用于易地搬迁和基础设施提升；中旅集团投资 3500 万元，用于项目一期工程建设。中旅集团按照不同的房屋价格，对全村的石头房屋进行整体租赁，村集体每年增收 33 万元；并将贫困户的土地和林地全部进行流转，每年每户均获得收入 1.1 万元。

2. 高端民宿，盘活旅游资源。河南中旅集团计划总投资 1.8 亿元，引入台湾民宿设计理念，将凉水泉村的古村落民居打造成高端民宿度假区。区域内有石光院子、花田木屋、星空果岭、悬崖竹屋等风格的民宿酒店，并配有牛棚咖啡、羊圈西餐厅、猪舍茶吧、山里人家特色餐厅、古民居展示馆、医务室、养生堂、五谷磨坊、空中泳池、观景台、高尔夫果岭、妙音台文化广场、石光书画院、石光阁会议中心、甜蜜世界、采摘果园、野兔山、跑马场等服务设施，形成“食、住、行、游、购、娱”一体化的高端民宿酒店度假区。

3. 三员三小，提供旅游就业。河南中旅集团通过“三员三小”就业政策，聘用贫困村民成为服务员、公司雇员、群众演员，助其参与小客栈、小商铺、小餐饮的经营。通过民宿理念的传递和科学的培训，贫困村民逐渐转变角色意识，成为乡村民宿的参与者、经营者。

成效

自中旅集团开发建设以来，凉水泉村石头房屋整体租赁，村集体每年直接增收 33 万元；土地和林地流转，每年每户均能获得土地流转收入 1.1 万元；村民参与景区开发建设，日人均收入

120～200 元；村民通过经营山核桃、山小米、大红袍、花椒等农产品，户年均增收逾 1000 元；村民参与经营小客栈、小商铺、小餐饮，户年均增收 1.5 万余元。凉水泉村 2018 年户均增收 2.55 万元，2019 年户均增收 3.5 万余元。河南中旅集团对凉水泉村的开发建设，不仅有效保留了古村落的原始形态，更营造了良好的民宿文化氛围，使当地贫困村民获得了固定财产性收入，帮助山村实现了脱贫致富奔小康的目标。

经验与启示

1. 整体租赁。河南中旅集团结合当地实际情况，以村集体为对象，与当地街道办事处签订战略合作协议，通过土地流转、租赁房屋等方式获得基础土地资源。

2. 打造民宿。乡村让生活更美好，那么该如何记住乡愁，盯住即将消失的变化？“小民宿大世界”是一场深刻的大运动，乡村变革的主体。河南中旅集团深知，中国已全面进入休闲度假时代，民宿作为逆城市化的发展方向，其兴旺乃大势所趋。

3. 村民参与。人是文化得以传承的核心。在凉水泉村高端民宿酒店休闲度假区，曾经的贫困村民随处可见，如今他们是服务员、群众演员、菜园管理员甚至精品民宿管家，他们身上散发着当地朴素的文化气质，他们口口相传的故事就是当地文化的载体。

下一步计划

乡村民宿的打造，离不开种植、养殖体验。要想带给游客原汁原味的种养体验，就必须结合当地村民的农耕管理经验和特色种养殖技术，同时还要精细化包装、配套绩效管理。深入做好“旅游 + 种植”“旅游 + 养殖”，打造朴门农场，从种植体验、朴门理念、采摘体验到品尝体验，多角度形成闭环式的体验流程，带动山村种养殖产业升级，实现增收。河南中旅集团将继续对凉水泉村乡村民宿进行深耕细作，帮助山村脱贫致富奔小康，助力区域经济建设和乡村旅游发展，走出一条特色乡村振兴道路。

Abstract

The Henan China Travel Service Group has worked to eradicate poverty in Liangshuiquan Village. The village now serves as a model for the protection of ancient Chinese villages. What CTS has done is providing a base for rural tourism and a base for poverty alleviation using the tourism industry. Henan China Travel Service Group developed a "high-end homestay inn" that serves at the principal line. This development has been linked to five benefits including the overall rental of private houses, circulation of rural lands and forest lands, encouraging employment as attendants, company employees and figurants or working in inns, stores, and food stalls, encouraging local residents to do labour work, and sales of local agricultural products.

Challenges and Problems

Liangshuiquan Village is located in Hebi City, Henan Province, which is located in the West Qi County, west of the Taihang Mountains. The total population of the village is 93 people who come from 46 households. Out of the 93 people, 67 live in poverty. Liangshuiquan is one of the most national-level villages in China. It boasts a long and ancient history with rich cultural backgrounds. The hillside folk built their homes during the late Qing Dynasty and the early Republic of China. The village is known for its cool, sweet spring water which flows from both the Everlasting Youth Spring and Five Dragon Springs, which run all year round. However, tourists do not visit the Liangshuiquan Village that much, which fails to bring opportunities for the small village.

Measures

1. Liangshuiquan Village has signed a strategic cooperation agreement with Henan China Travel Service Group. This agreement places the assets of Liangshuiquan Village into a trust agreement with Henan China Travel Service Group. CTS will work to develop tourism for Liangshuiquan Village by investing into its development. So far, RMB 51.4 million has been invested, of which RMB 16.4 million has already been used on upgrading infrastructure and relocation expenses. CTS has already invested RMB 35 million in the first phase of construction. Also, during this phase, CTS has leased all the private stone houses in the village, a strategic move which generated RMB 333,000 for the whole village.

CTS has also circulated all the rural land and forest land of poor households, which gave households an average of RMB 11,000.

2. The Henan China Travel Service Group plans to invest RMB 180 million into Liangshuiquan Village. The design concept currently consists of high-end homestay inns in Taiwan Region and involves the transformation of homes in Liangshuiquan Village into holiday resorts. They will include Stone Ray Yards, Cabin in Blossoms, Fruity Mountain under Starry Sky, and bamboo House on the Cliff. Additionally, the resort will be well equipped with service facilities such as Cowshed Café, Sheepfold Resturant, Pigsty Teahouse, Specialty Restaurants in the Mountainous Houses, Exhibition Hall of Ancient Folk Houses, Medical Room, Regimen Hall, Grain Mill, Skyline Swimming Pool, Observation Deck, Golf Green, Cultural Plaza of Miaoyin Tower, Stone-ray Painting and Calligraphy Academy, Meeting Center of Stone-ray Pavilion, Sweet World, Orchard for Picking Fruits, Hare Hill, Racecourse and much more. With all the amenities, this holiday resort and high-end homestay inns have all the makings of a comfortable vacation.

3. The Henan China Travel Service Group has employed poor villagers to participate in the operation of the village. They will work at the inns, stores and food stalls throughout the resort. By working at the resort, the villagers will become more aware of the vital role they play and will become enthusiastic participants of the homestay inns.

Results

Since the development and construction by the China Travel Service Group, homes in Liangshuiquan village have generated an annual income of RMB 333,000. Also, the circulation of rural and forest lands creates an additional RMB 11,000 for each household annually. Villagers who participate in the development and construction of the scenic areas can earn a daily income of between RMB 120–200. In addition, the villagers have increased their annual income by selling walnuts, mountain millet, Dahongpao pepper, and other agricultural products. Those who participated in the operations of small inns and food stalls have seen an

increase of their annual income by more than RMB 15,000. These programs have resulted in an increase of the average household income of Liangshuquan residents. In 2018, the average household income for a villager was RMB 25,500, and in 2019 it reached RMB 35,000. New developments and construction in Liangshuiquan Village preserve the original form of the ancient village and create a good cultural environment of homestay inns. Because of this, the poor villagers have a fixed and stable income which helps their mountain village attain prosperity.

1. Overall rental. The Henan China Travel Service Group will sign a strategic agreement with the local sub-district office of the Liangshuiquan Village to obtain land resources through home leasing and land circulation from the village.

2. Building homestay inns. Life is better in rural areas. The homestay inn movement is significant as it drives the core transformation of rural areas. China has entered an era of leisure, vacation, and homestay inns, leading to the hotly trending counter-urbanization developments in the country.

3. Participation of villagers. People are the center of cultural heritage. In high-end vacation resort of homestay inns at Liangshuiquan Village, the once impoverished villagers can be seen everywhere. They are attendants, figurants, vegetable garden managers, and even boutique hotel butlers. Their cultural temperament is simple, and they pass on on their culture by word-of-mouth stories.

Next Steps

The homestay inns of the rural area must provide authentic experience of planting and feeding animals. Farm management and characteristic planning and feeding techniques of the local villagers must be combined to allow tourists who want to experience authentic rural life know and understand the reality of being a local villager. We should implement different systems of "tourism planting" and "tourism feeding." By adding these systems, we can form a permaculture farm in which a closed-loop experience is created with the multiple facets of planting, picking fruits and vegetables, including food tasting. This should generate income for mountain villages and increase the income of the local people. The Henan China Travel Service Group will continue to dedicate their efforts to develop the homestay inns in Liangshuiquan Village, help the mountain village to achieve prosperity, help improve the regional economy and rural tourism, to carve a local rural revitalization path with the village's distinct characteristics.

内蒙古锡林郭勒盟多伦县白音部落生态旅游度假区：“旅游+”融合发展模式

Baiyin Tribe Eco-tourism Resort in Duolun County, Xilin Gol League, Inner Mongolia Autonomous Region: “Tourism +” Integrated Development Model

摘要

内蒙古自治区锡林郭勒盟多伦县白音部落生态旅游度假区依靠“旅游+”的融合发展模式，将当地蒙元文化、马文化、体育资源等融入旅游，发展多元化、体验式旅游产业。当地政府积极践行“绿水青山就是金山银山”的发展理念，带领当地农牧民脱贫致富。

挑战与问题

白音部落生态旅游度假区位于内蒙古自治区锡林郭勒盟多伦县滦源镇多伦湖畔，当地的村民一直保持着半农半牧的生活方式，发展意识薄弱，且过度放牧导致当地生态退化严重，土壤沙化。由于土壤裸露于空气中容易受到大风的侵蚀，农耕用地减少，村民经济收入来源单一，发展水平滞后。

措施

1. 成立旅游企业。景区周边的农牧民以土地入股的形式成立了旅游公司，这种方法既让村民成为公司股东，提高闲置土地的利用率，又激发了村民发展的积极性；同时，通过招商引资 1.2 亿元发展旅游业，填补村民资金不足的短板。

2. 发展蒙元特色民宿。白音部落生态旅游发展有限公司对原有的 50 户村房进行装修改建，以 80 万元 / 户的标准，建设蒙元风格的房屋外立面、室内装饰，以及水电管网、家电等配套设施，总计投入 4000 万元。在乡土特色的基础上，打造高档舒适的居住环境，通过企业化管理、专业化的培训打造蒙古族特色民宿，实现了当地村民“家家有产业，人人有事业”的现代化新农村。

3. 凸显蒙元文化。白音部落生态旅游度假区投资 6000 万元用于充分挖掘当地特有的“马”文化，建设“马文化 + 蒙元文化 + 体育赛事”的产业布局，建设有多伦诺尔剧场演艺园区、草原野生动物园区、蒙古马文化展示园区，还有牧民家访体验园区、蒙元民俗博物馆、野马驯养园区、蒙古族生活服饰体验区、草原竞技场（骑马、射箭）、蒙古族婚礼广场，以及蒙古族工匠手工艺园区、蒙元主题 live house 现场演绎音乐酒吧、蒙古包主题酒店群及商业街区的主题旅游矩阵，堪称中国蒙元文化项目数量众多的、规模超大的综合性主题旅游度假区。

4. 举办大型活动。白音部落生态旅游发展有限公司承办和举办了内蒙古国际马术节、“映象多伦湖 · 镜美蒙古马”摄影大赛、白音部落杯国际冰上龙舟赛、多伦县过年七天乐冰上龙舟体验赛、COC 越野拉力冰上龙舟赛等多项赛事活动，以赛事拉动旅游业的发展。白音部落生态旅游度假区致力于成为“以环境打动游客、以文化迷住游客、以热情留住游客和以服务感动游客”的草原旅游服务标杆。

成效

白音部落生态旅游度假区现已建成国家 3A 级旅游景区，成为当地旅游服务集散中心，有效地整合了当地的旅游资源，丰富了当地的旅游项目，规范了当地的旅游市场。景区通过解决就业、疏散游客等方式，提高了当地村民的经济收入。2019 年，投入 300 多万元建设扶贫销售展厅，供村民销售当地土特产及民族工艺品；和前九号村签订建档立卡户帮扶合同 10 户，进行定向帮扶，设立扶贫商业岗 10 处，岗位出租所得利润全部归贫困家庭所有，直接帮扶贫困户 20 人；解决当地 100 余人就业，向当地农家乐输送游客 3000 人，直接带动周边农家乐收入 50 余万元；捐款近 40 万元，用于资助失学儿童及其他公益事业。

经验与启示

1. 转变观念。长期习惯于农牧生活的当地村民发展意识比较薄弱，要发展，首先要促使其转变观念，唤醒当地村民一起进行乡村振兴，让大家深刻意识到“绿水青山就是金山银山”的发展理念，进而引进新的发展思路。

2. 融合发展。白音部落生态旅游度假区依靠“旅游 +”的融合发展模式，将当地文化、体育、

互联网等融入旅游，发展多元化、体验式旅游产业。“旅游 + 文化”，将当地特有的农耕文化、蒙元文化、马文化等注入旅游发展中，为旅游发展注入了灵魂；“旅游 + 体育”，通过举办一系列冰上龙舟赛、越野拉力赛、环湖马拉松等经典赛事，将体育与旅游相结合，打造出群众参与性强的全民娱乐体验项目。

下一步计划

下一步，白音部落生态旅游度假区计划持续通过“旅游 +”的融合发展模式，着力打造自驾车营地、蒙元文化体验区、后九号民宿改造等项目，将当地村民的发展和旅游产业紧紧捆绑在一起。特别是对旅游产业结构进行调整，拉动消费，促进增长。按照计划，改造后的民宿是以马文化为主的马村，着力传播马的文化及蒙古马精神。马村的改造，主要保留村庄原有的乡村文化，使其在保留当地风土人情的基础上各有特色，让游客既能感受到当地的风土人情，又能体验到星级酒店的待遇。通过统一培训，当地村民在各自民宿用心经营，提高管理服务，进一步解决当地就业和提高当地村民经济收入，实现乡村振兴、共同富裕。

项目建成后，将会扩大多伦旅游的规模，提升旅游产业的竞争力，有力地促进区域经济发展，使各产业配套协调发展，促进经济发展，从而产生良好的经济效益和社会效益。

Abstract

The Baiyin Tribe Eco-Tourism Resort in Duolun County, Xilin Gol League, Inner Mongolia Autonomous Region has integrated the local Mongolian Yuan culture, horse culture and sports resources to develop a diversified and experiential tourism based on the "Tourism +" framework.The local government has implemented the "lucid waters and lush mountains are invaluable assets" development concept to move local farmers and herdsmen out of poverty and improve their standard of living.

Challenges and Problems

The resort is located on the banks of Duolun Lake, Luanyuan Town, Duolun County, Xilin Gol League, Inner Mongolia Autonomous Region. Local villagers have been leading a farming-pastoral lifestyle that has contributed to their low awareness for development. Adding to its disadvantageous position is excessive grazing which has caused serious ecological degradation and desertification. Exposed soil is eroded by strong winds, resulting in decreased land for farming, unitary channels for income generation and lagging development.

Measures

1. Establish tourism enterprises. Farmers and herdsmen around the scenic area have set up tourism companies by pooling land as shares to increase the utilization rate of idle land.This practice has turned villagers into company shareholders and has sparked their enthusiasm for development. Offsetting its financial constraints is the RMB 120 million tourism development investment fund the Baiyin Tribe Eco-Tourism Resort has received.

2. Develop characteristic B&Bs with Mongolian Yuan culture. The Baiyin Tribe Eco-Tourism Development Co., Ltd. has refurbished 50 original houses in the village.It has also built Mongolian-style house facade, water and electricity pipe network, initiated interior decoration and installed home appliances at an average of RMB 800,000 per household for a total investment of RMB 40 million. A high-end comfortable living environment with local characteristics has been developed and Mongolian-style B&Bs have been built through corporate management and professional training, resulting in a new modern countryside based on the "industry for each household and job for each person" principle.

3. Highlight the Mongolian Yuan culture. A total of RMB 60 million has been invested in the resort to explore the local unique "horse" culture, build an industrial layout of horse culture + Mongolian Yuan culture + sports events and establish Dolon Nor Theater Performance Park, Grassland Wildlife Park, Mongolian Horse Culture Exhibition Park, Herdsmen's Home Visiting Experience Park, Mongolian Yuan Folk Museum, Wild Horse Taming Park, Mongolian Costume Experience Area, Grassland Arena (horse riding, archery), Mongolian

Wedding Square, Mongolian Craftsmen's Handicraft Park, Mongolian Yuan Themed Live House Music Bar, yurt-themed hotel groups and tourism-themed matrix of commercial blocks. Consequently, the resort has turned into a comprehensive mega tourism resort infused with the rich Mongolian Yuan culture.

4. Organize large-scale events. The Baiyin Tribe Eco-Tourism Development Co., Ltd. has organized several events such as the Inner Mongolia International Equestrian Festival, "Duolun Lake · Mongolian Horse" Photography Contest, Baiyin Tribe Cup International Ice Dragon Boat Race, Duolun County New Year's Seven-Day Joy on Ice Dragon Boat Race and COC Cross-country Rally Ice Dragon Boat Race to drive its tourism development. The resort is committed to creating a tourism service benchmark that will impress tourists with the environment, fascinate them with culture, retain them with enthusiasm and move them with topnotch services.

Results

The resort has been transformed into a 3A-level tourist attraction. It has also become a distribution center for local tourism services. Its integration of local tourism resources has enriched and standardized the local tourism market.

The scenic area has solved the village's employment problem, helped increase the income of local villagers and the diversion of tourists to agritainment. In 2019, more than RMB 3 million was invested to build a poverty alleviation sales exhibitionhall for local villagers to sell local specialties and ethnic handicrafts. Agreements were also signed with ten archived impoverished households in Qianjiuhao Village for targeted assistance. Moreover, ten business posts for poverty alleviation were set up, with all the profits from rental jobs going to poor families. This has offered direct assistance to 20 impoverished households and helped more than 100 people find local jobs. The resort has also directed 3,000 tourists to local agritainment, further increasing the income of surrounding agritainment to more than RMB 500,000. It has also

donated nearly RMB 400,000 for children who have dropped out of school and other public undertakings.

Experience and Inspirations

1. Idea transformation. The long-term agricultural lifestyle has resulted in the local villagers' low awareness of and enthusiasm for development. To get them on board the rural revitalization wagon, their mindset has to be changed first before the concept of "lucid waters and lush mountains are invaluable assets" and other ideas for advancement can be successfully introduced.

2. Integrated development. With the development model of "Tourism +" as the foundation, the resort has integrated local Mongolian Yuan culture, horse culture and sports resources into a diversified and experiential tourism industry. The "tourism + culture" model has incorporated unique local farming culture, Mongolian Yuan culture, horse culture, etc. into tourism development. It has combined sports and tourism through classic events such as ice dragon boat races, cross-country rally races and lake-ring marathons—all of which have turned into popular entertainment experiences with mass participation.

Next Steps

The resort plans to continue to adopt the integrated development model of "Tourism +" for projects that include self-driving camps, Mongolian Yuan cultural centers and renovation of Houjiuhao B&Bs. Local villagers will also be assimilated into the tourism industry whose structure will be especially adjusted to stimulate consumption and promote growth. Since they are recognized as the means to disseminate the Mongolian horse spirit and culture, the B&Bs that are slated for transformation are mainly horse villages. During their reconstruction, the original rural culture of the village will be demonstrated through preserved indigenous customs. This ensures tourists can enjoy the service of star-rated hotels while experiencing local culture. Villagers will perform operation and management services in their respective B&Bs through standardized training, further solving the local employment problem and increasing the income of local villagers to achieve rural revitalization and common prosperity.

Once the project is completed, the scale of Duolun tourism will be expanded to enhance its competitiveness and promote regional economic development through the coordinated development of various industries for broad economic and social benefits.

黑龙江佳木斯市汤原县：
全域旅游助力乡村脱贫

Tangyuan County, Jiamusi City, Heilongjiang Province:
All-for-one Tourism Facilitates Rural Poverty Alleviation

摘 要

汤原县制订旅游发展总体规划和美丽乡村建设规划实施方案，深入融合红色文化、森林文化、朝鲜民俗文化，引入民营资本，打造精品民宿、乡村旅游点、乡村度假地等旅游项目，开发了集餐饮、住宿、采摘、休闲娱乐于一体的旅游产业链，发展乡村旅游，推动乡村美、村民富，促进产业融合，带动全域旅游发展。

挑战与问题

黑龙江佳木斯市汤原县全县共辖4镇6乡，共有137个行政村，全县总人口247631人，有朝鲜、满、回等20个少数民族。汤原县面积3420平方公里，森林覆盖率为33%。汤原县没有县内出发通往景区的公交线路；农户周围的环境状况较差，基础服务设施建设落后，交通、供电、供排水、绿化等配套不全，不能很好地满足游客“食、住、行、游、购、娱”等多方面的需求，甚至不能满足游客安全、卫生等基本需求。汤原县发展没有总体规划和专项规划，开发建设缺乏长期性、整体性和系统性。旅游服务功能缺少创新，开发档次低，游客参与性不强，产品雷同现象严重，特色不明显，发展活力严重不足。

措施

1. 打造乡村旅游“百里景观大道”。以沿线上的金星村、北向阳村、北靠山村、竹青村、香山村、腰营林场、大亮子河林场7个村为节点，打造乡村旅游“百里景观大道”（从大亮子河国家森林公园至汤旺金星村），开发了集餐饮、住宿、采摘、休闲娱乐于一体的旅游产业链，支撑带动全域旅游发展。

2. 发展民宿旅馆和农家乐餐饮。汤旺乡金星村突出朝鲜族民俗游特色建设，推进民宿经济发展。汤原镇北靠山村立足于红色文化旅游景观，建设靠山屯生态园、民居民宿、采摘园、抗联浮雕文化墙、红色抗联雕塑等。竹青村、香山村、亮子河林场、腰营林场突出森林文化景观的打造，建设民宿民居等。

3. 创新发展模式。汤原县引入民营资本——黑龙江方圆国际旅游开发有限公司（以下简称“方圆国旅”）助力乡村发展。在民宿旅馆和农家乐餐饮建设资金投入上，政府与企业共同出资建设：政府负责房盖、门窗、墙面、庭院建设，企业负责室内改造建设。目前，方圆国旅已投入建设资金3000余万元。在收入分配上，农民、企业、政府按不同比例分配。农民以房屋入股形式提供房屋

的，按 15% 参与利润分配；以房屋租赁形式提供房屋的，每年可得租赁费 5000 ～ 7000 元。

通过“旅游企业 + 农户”方式，与贫困户签订绿色蔬菜（白菜、辣椒）、家禽（鸡、鸭、鹅）饲养、山特产品、食用菌等订单，激励贫困户参与农家乐等旅游服务以增加其收入，让贫困户在旅游产业链、价值链的打造中切实受益，增加其收入。目前，已有 200 多户农户与公司签订合同，发展庭院经济和特色养殖。

成效

汤原县乡村旅游优先招录乡村旅游扶贫重点村建档立卡贫困户从事保安、保洁、餐饮服务等工作，从业人员年人均增加收入 1.6 万元。乡村旅游的发展，累计带动农户 1250 户发家致富；2019 年，乡村旅游产业直接带动 480 户农户增收，2020 年，乡村旅游产业直接带动 500 户农户增收。

经验与启示

1. 高站位、高起点编制发展规划。坚持规划先行，做到没有规划不能设计、没有规划不能施工。按照“因地制宜、突出特色、合理布局、和谐发展”的总体要求，编制乡村旅游专项规划，出台提升乡村旅游发展实施计划。将乡村旅游发展规划与国民经济和社会发展规划、脱贫攻坚规划、土地利用总体规划等规划有效衔接起来。推动乡村旅游规划与村镇规划、森林旅游发展规划、休闲农业发展规划等专项规划实现合并编制。

2. 高标准完善乡村旅游基础配套设施。将乡村旅游与现代观光农业发展相融合，将高标准农田建设、家庭农场、合作社建设、烤烟基地建设等植入乡村旅游，同时改善旅游道路、饮水用电等基础设施。与精准扶贫相结合，选取旅游公路沿线重点扶贫村（金星、北靠山、竹青等）推动示范带动升级，提升档次和竞争力，并确定对扶贫村贫困户、

贫困人口的帮扶路径、支持措施和收益安排。加强环境综合整治，重点做好乡村旅游节点房屋改造和环境绿化、美化、亮化。按照“一乡一品”“一村一品”的要求，因地制宜完善休闲广场、村办公所、文化墙、栅栏等设施，预留小庭院、小景观，立志做成精品、做出特色。按照服务质量等级评定标准，对“食、住、行、游、购、娱”配套服务设施和安全生产设施进行提档升级改造，以达到安全、卫生、便利要求。

下一步计划

按照汤原县乡村旅游布局，持续完善“百里景观大道及五点”建设：“百里景观”的范围，从大亮子河国家森林公园至汤旺金星村，包括沿线上的金星村、北向阳村、北靠山村、竹青村、香山村、腰营林场、大亮子河林场 7 个村屯和林场；“五点”则是指场县共建高效经济作物观光园、胜利乡高科技农业示范园、香兰镇双河村、香兰镇陶家村和大亮子河花海综合体。

Abstract

Tangyuan County, Jiamusi City, Heilongjiang Province has formulated a plan for cultural tourism. This plan seeks to improve the beauty of the village as well as integrate the red culture, forest culture and folk culture of Democratic People's Repubic of Korea into its design. In addition, there will be development projects that focus on industrial chain, accommodation, and entertainment venues. The goal is to highlight the beauty of the village and provide a comfortable life for the villagers.

Challenges and Problems

The county includes 137 administrative villages consisting of six townships in four towns with a total population of 247,631 from 20 ethnic minorities such as the Korean, Manchu, and Hui nationalities. It covers an area of 3,420 square kilometers, with a forest coverage rate of 33%. However, the area's existing infrastructure is very underdeveloped as it does not provide acceptable services. For example, the village does not have a bus that can take tourists to scenic areas. Nor does it have a solid supply of water, power or drainage. It also fails to meet basic demands for meals and dining, lodging and transportation. There is no overall planning that would focus on the long-term goals of the village due to tourism limitations, which include a shortage of service functions, low level of development and lack of participation.

Measures

1. Create a "Baili Landscape Avenue." There are seven villages on the route to the main village. They are Jinxing Village, Beixiangyang Village, Beikaoshan Village, Zhuqing Village, Xiangshan Village, Yaoying Forest Farm, and Liangzi River Forest Farm. This geographic cluster prompted the drafting of a rural tourism bill called "Baili Landscape Avenue" to promote a tourism industrial chain by accommodating the needs of tourists.

2. Develop catering for B&Bs and agritainment. One of the pillars of folklore tourism of Democratic People's Repubic of Korea has been established in Jinxing Village. The basis of this development was the red culture tourism and the promotion of the B&Bs. Beikaoshan Village in Tangyuan Town has also constructed the Kaoshantun Ecological Park, rural dwellings and B&Bs, gardens and anti-Japanese United Army cultural relief walls, anti-Japanese United Army sculptures and other similar projects. Xiangshan Village, Liangzi River Forest

Farm and Yaoying Forest Farm have all emphasized the development of forest culture, the construction of rural dwellings and B&Bs.

3. Innovate development models. The county has introduced the private capital Heilongjiang Fangyuan International Tourism Development Co., Ltd. (Fangyuan International Tourism) to drive rural development. The government entered into an agreement with private sector companies that will see both sides play similar roles in village development. Developments earmarked for government funding include B&B construction, hotels and agritainment. Projects that will be funded by the private sector are home construction, doors, windows, walls and courtyards. The private sector will also be responsible for interior renovation and construction. To date, the Fangyuan International Tourism has invested more than RMB 30 million for construction. In addition, the income is distributed by farmers, enterprises and the government in different proportions. Farmers who provide houses by pooling them as shares can participate in the profit distribution at 15%, and those who provide houses by house leasing can obtain the annual rental fee of RMB 5,000 to 7,000.

With the "tourism enterprises + peasant households" model as the framework, the Fangyuan International Tourism has cooperated with impoverished households on green vegetables (cabbage, chili), poultry (chicken, duck, goose) breeding, special mountain products, and edible fungi. This will benefit many people because these services can increase their household income. Overall, the villagers benefit the most from the construction and tourism services. More than 200 households have agreed to participate in the village development.

Results

Impoverished households are prioritized for job recruitment in security, cleaning, and catering services

throughout the county. As a result of this program, the annual per capita income of employees have increased by RMB 16,000. It has also helped a total of more than 1,250 rural households. The rural tourism industry has directly increased the income of 480 rural households in 2019. In 2020, it increased the income of 500 rural households.

Experience and Inspirations

1. Compile development plans with forward-looking concepts. Planning is the first step as construction cannot begin without it. More efforts should be made to create special plans for rural tourism and rural tourism development enhancements. It is also vital to link the planning of rural tourism development with the development of national economic and social development, poverty alleviation, and overall land use. Special planning for villages, towns and forest should also be combined for the greater interest of the nation.

2. Improve supporting infrastructure of rural tourism with high standards. It is necessary to ensure that rural tourism is developed in tandem with modern tourism advancement. Key villages along the tourist road (Jinxing Village, Beikaoshan Village, Zhuqing Village, etc.) are selected to demonstrate the role of rural tourism for poverty alleviation. More importantly, the environment should be improved by emphasizing the renovation of homes along the Baili Landscape Avenue. The product for one township and one product for one village should include facilities such as leisure centers, village offices, as well as cultural walls. In light of the service quality rating standards, the supporting service facilities for meals and dining, lodging, transportation, travel, shopping, entertainment and safety production facilities should likewise be upgraded for comfort and convenience and to meet safety and hygiene standards.

Next Steps

The construction of Baili Landscape Avenue and Five Stars should be prioritized and perfected. Baili Landscape Avenue refers to the route from Liangzi River National Forest Park to Jinxing Village of Tangwang Township, including seven villages and forest farms along the route such as Jinxing Village, Beixiangyang Village, Beikaoshan Village, Zhuqing Village, Xiangshan Village, Yaoying Forest Farm, and Liangzi River Forest Farm. And Five Sites refer to the High-Efficiency Economic Crop Sightseeing Park, Shengli Township High-Tech Agricultural Demonstration Park, Shuanghe Village of Xianglan Town, Taojia Village of Xianglan Town, and Liangzi River Flowers Sea Complex.

新疆和田市吉亚乡阔恰村：
大漠胡杨景区助力乡村脱贫

Kuoqia Village, Jiya Township, Hotan City, Xinjiang Uygur Autonomous Region:
Populus Euphratica Scenic Spot in Desert Helps Rural Poverty Alleviation

摘要

大漠胡杨景区位于新疆和田市吉亚乡阔恰村阿和公路沿线，距离和田市区 18 公里，与阿和沙漠公路相连，交通便利，由政府投资和企业招商引资共计 1.7 亿元，占地面积 6000 余亩，按照国家 4A 级旅游景区打造，现已成为和田旅游标杆。

挑战与问题

景区开发前原是一片垃圾场，自然资源禀赋不佳。景区建成后，公共服务配套设施较少，娱乐设施单一；村民汉语水平普遍不高，缺乏摊位交流沟通及经营能力，导致主体意识不强，等、靠、要，不主动创造条件提升服务水平，后续的经营管理发展面临人力、智力上的匮乏。由于旅游区设施不完善、游客素养不高，村民自身庭院环境卫生差、意识差，随着旅游活动规模的扩大，景点垃圾遗弃量日益增加，旅游区内大量垃圾被随意抛洒堆积，破坏了自然景观。

措施

1. 规划先行，完善基建。规划是保障旅游开发可持续发展的唯一有效办法。阔恰村首先编制旅游规划，坚持人与环境的和谐，贯穿生态理念，体现文化内涵，反映地域特色，并与土地利用总体规划、基本农田保护规划、城镇体系规划以及交通水利等规划相衔接，实现旅游长效发展、可持续发展。阔恰村现已建成面积 1500 平方米的游客中心、面积 100 平方米的旅游厕所、面积 3000 平方米的停车场等公共服务设施，还建有 200 米长美食餐饮摊位长廊、30 多个临时摊位、5 公里健身木栈道、22 个观光亭、1000 平方米赛马场、4000 平方米帐篷酒店，以及滑沙、骑骆驼等旅游项目设施。

2. 注册公司，创新模式。注册成立和田阔恰大漠旅游有限公司，代表村民处理旅游相关事务，最大化争取村集体的利益和收入。创新农户与新型经营主体的利益联结机制，采取“龙头企业 + 农户”方式，聘请经理人走专业化道路。采取专项资金折股量化返还的方式解决村民资金不足的问题。后期每年每户按照总投入的 8% 返还给村集体，作为村集体收入。这一经济行为，既免除了村民的后顾之忧，又可以让村民尽早享受到旅游业带来的实惠，有效地调动了村民的积极性。

3. 招商引资，借力节庆。通过项目落实招商引资，不断完善基础设施和旅游内容，并积极利用节庆日、环塔拉力赛、美食大赛等节庆赛事活动，形成良好、健康的旅游文化氛围，打造宜居、宜业、宜游的美丽和谐新景区。

为提升景区影响力，2019 年国际赛事环塔拉力赛的终点和闭幕站首次被引进和田并落户景区。环塔营地总投资3000万元，占地340亩，建成尼雅人家帐篷酒店及配套用房21间，赛事过后成为“大美南疆”第一站，带给游客全新的越野文化体验。2019年，在环塔赛事闭幕式的三天时间里，景区通过举办美食节、音乐节以及闭幕式隆重大型演出等吸引20万游客，村民通过摆摊设点收入300多万元。现在，和田市很多大型文化活动都会选在景区举办，如中国文化旅游节、重阳节、中秋节等节庆赛事活动，形成了良好、健康的乡村文化氛围。

成效

大漠胡杨景区成为市域旅游的重要景区之一，带动阔恰村当地贫困农民参与到了旅游经济活动当中来。景区建成后，和田市每年累计接待国内外游客450万人次，这其中，有35万人是奔大漠胡杨景区和阔恰村而来。2018年“十一”黄金周期间景区接待游客近10万人次，村民收入200多万元。目前，景区已解决阔恰村300人就业；辐射带动周边1000人在保安、保洁、导游、餐饮、服务等岗位就业；同时刺激并带动周边乃至全乡旅游相关产业快速发展。

经验与启示

1. 传承文化，弘扬传统。文化需要在生活中

体验、感受和领悟，这是阔恰人一直以来秉承的理念。因此，大漠胡杨景区建设项目更多考虑了将本地特有的文化元素自然地融入日常生活中去，让游客以参与的方式休闲，以休闲的方式感悟。如胡杨观赏木栈道及赛马场，经过统一的设计和打造，对传统文化和本村的风土人情进行了深度挖掘；规范观赏木栈道，对存活年代较久的胡杨进行标注及保护，让观赏的游客感受到大漠胡杨的精神。

2. 精准定位，乡村旅居。将居住和旅游融为一体，可以让人们找到生活和工作无间相融的状态。因此，一方面以和田市及周边县市的居民为长期客源定位，另一方面以被环塔文化IP吸引来的游客为高潮式客源定位，阔恰村的旅游开发总体定位为：乡村旅居，别来无恙。

下一步计划

1. 加强智慧乡村旅游建设。以乡村为整个景区场所，以乡野农村独特的自然景观、人文景观、民俗风情以及传统的手工艺品等旅游资源为依托，以乡村旅游产品为载体，与旅游电商、现代物流等相关企业建立合作关系，持续推进“乡村旅游后备厢工程”“一村一品”产业建设，促进“旅游＋农业＋互联网”融合发展，引导乡村旅游与互联网等现代信息技术结合，发展智慧乡村旅游。

2. 加强营销宣传攻势。采取统一营销、统一运作的模式，由专业机构帮助村民进行营销宣传。“制造网红”，与具有强大影响力的博主合作，邀请他们拍摄并体验阔恰的乡村旅游；邀请抖音、快手以及美拍等社交媒体上粉丝基数较大的大众意见领袖游玩景区，通过拍摄游玩重点项目小视频，吸引游客前来游玩。

3. 加强景区项目建设。积极招商引资，吸引众多实力很强的企业共同开发乡村旅游。阔恰村将陆续引进蔬菜采摘观光大棚项目、大漠胡杨景区提升项目、瀚海“渔”乐园、摘星营地项目、沙漠赛马场项目以及影视城项目，形成以景区为核心的闭环式旅游基地，有效促进旅游业飞速发展。

Abstract

The Euphratic Scenic Spot in the desert is one the most popular tourist destinations in Kuoqia Village, Jiya Township, Hotan City, Xinjiang Uygur Autonomous Region. It is 18 kilometers away from Hotan City and connects to Akesu-Hotan highway. The government as well as private enterprises have invested RMB 170 million here. It covers an area of more than 6,000 *mu* and it has been designated as a 4A-level tourist attraction and has become the benchmark for Hotan tourism.

Challenges and Problems

Before its development, the scenic spot was not a popular destination to visit as there were no natural resources. Once the project was completed, the spot lacked public service, infrastructure and entertainment options. Most villagers spoke only Chinese and were not able to communicate without translators. The villagers were waiting for government assistance rather than making changes on their own. Because of this, the project lacked direction and manpower. The villagers also lacked skills in maintaining the village. Consequently, tourist areas were substandard. As tourism numbers grew, so did the garbage in the area. Villagers did not bother to clean the area.

Measures

1. Plan first before improving infrastructure. Since planning is the only effective way to ensure sustainable development, the Kuoqia Village created a tourism plan based on harmony between people and the environment. This ecological concept was also focused on the region's culture, long-term sustainability, farmland protection, urban systems and water conservation. The village has made several infrastructure upgrades including a 1,500-square meter tourist center, a 100-square meter tourist toilet, a 3,000-square meter parking lot and other public service facilities. A 200-meter-long catering corridor, more than 30 temporary stalls, a 5-kilometer fitness wooden trestle, 22 sightseeing pavilions, a racetrack of 1,000 square meter, a tent hotel of 4,000 square meters and facilities for sand skiing and camel riding were also built.

2. Register a company and innovate model. The Hotan Kuoqia Desert Tourism Co., Ltd. was incorporated to handle tourism-related affairs on behalf of the villagers and maximize the collective interests and income of the village. The connection between the business and the peasants was done through the "leading enterprises + peasant households" concept. Hired managers were also tasked to offer specialized jobs to certain people. Sometimes the villagers had insufficient funds, but that was resolved by a quantitative return of special funds that were converted into shares. Each household held a part of 8% of the total investment in the village collective. This economic arrangement was beneficial to the villagers as they reaped the rewards brought by tourism.

3. Attract investment and capitalize on colorful traditional festivals. New initiatives were created for a sound and healthy tourism cultural atmosphere and a beautiful scenic area for the tourism industry. Some of these initiatives included the implementation of certain projects, expansion of investment opportunities, infrastructure improvements and public celebration of traditional festivals for certain events.

The terminal and closing stop of the Taklimakan Rally was introduced to persuade tourists to visit the village. The first of this project was introduced in Hotan for the first time in 2019 and was held in a scenic spot. A total of about RMB 30 million was invested on the rally camp, which covers an area of 340 *mu*. Niya family style tent hotels and 21 supporting rooms were built. After the event, it became the first stop of "South Xinjiang with Great Beauty," which brought a new cross-country cultural experience for tourists. The three-day closing ceremony of the 2019 Taklimakan Rally drew 200,000 tourists through a food festival, music gala and grand performances. The villagers earned more than RMB 3 million by helping with event staff functions. Since then, many large events have been held in this area such as the Chinese Cultural Tourism Festival, Double Ninth Festival and Mid-Autumn Festival.

Results

The Populus Euphratic Scenic Spot has become one of the most important scenic spots in the city. This tourist attraction has enabled the poor locals to make money. After the scenic spot was completed, 350,000 of the 4.5 million domestic and foreign tourists received by Hotan City each year visited this scenic spot and the village. During the Golden Week in October 2018, it received nearly 100,000 tourists, resulting in the villagers' income topping more than RMB 2 million. Today the scenic spot

offers 300 local posts. It has also led 1,000 people to find jobs in security, cleaning, tour guide, catering and service. This spot contributes to the rapid development of tourism related industries in the surrounding areas and even the whole township, which in turn will help stimulate the economic development of the surrounding areas.

Experience and Inspirations

1. Preserve, protect and pass on traditional culture. Culture must be experienced to be understood. This has always been the guiding philosophy of the Kuoqia people in this village. In building the scenic spots, more consideration has to be given to the implementation of the local customs and culture. The wooden trestle is an example of a unified design and construction that bears the imprint of the village's traditional customs and heritage. By standardizing the viewing wooden trestle and marking and protecting the Populus trees which have survived for a long time, the visitors can feel the spirit of Populus euphratica in the desert.

2. Accurate positioning and rural living. Villagers can bridge the gap between life and work by participating in village tourism. By targeting residents of Hotan City and surrounding counties, the village's overall tourism development positioning is anchored on safe and sound rural residences.

Next Steps

1. Strengthen smart rural tourism. The countryside is the whole scenic spot. It relies upon the natural rural landscape for tourism. The village, in turn, relies on culture, folk customs and traditional handmade crafts. The village is looking for ways to ensure that the goods produced by its locals are pushed out to as many people as possible. This is done through e-commerce, modern logistics and other relevant enterprises. This provides continuous support for rural tourism development, promote the industrial construction of "one product for one village." It is also important to advance the development of "tourism + agriculture + internet" and the combination of rural tourism and modern information technologies to develop a smart rural tourism program.

2. Strengthen marketing and publicity. The village will adopt a unified marketing and operation policy and invite professional institutions for more publicity. It will work to "create internet celebrity" through cooperation with influential bloggers by inviting them to experience and film Kuoqia's rural landscape. They will also be "making use of internet celebrity" by inviting KOLs with large social media fan base such as Tik Tok, Kuaishou and MP to visit the scenic spot and entice tourists by filming bucket videos here.

3. Further construct scenic spot projects. The village will attract investment and powerful enterprises for a joint rural tourism development. It will successively introduce vegetable picking and sightseeing greenhouses, Populus Euphratica Scenic Spot in Desert promotion, Hanhai "fishing" paradise, star collecting camp, desert racetrack and film and television city projects to form a closed-loop tourism base anchored on the scenic spot to promote tourism development.

云南丽江市玉龙纳西族自治县白沙镇玉湖村：

生态立村、旅游富村、文化兴村

Yuhu Village, Baisha Town, Yulong Naxi Autonomous County, Lijiang City, Yunnan Province:

Village Development through Ecology, Tourism and Culture

摘 要

云南省丽江市玉龙县玉湖村坚持以“实现共同富裕”为出发点和落脚点，以构建“小康玉湖、生态玉湖、魅力玉湖、和谐玉湖”为目标，实施“生态立村、旅游富村、文化兴村”三大战略，创新发展机制，通过盘活旅游业和发展养殖业，带领全体村民走上致富道路。

挑战与问题

云南省丽江市玉龙纳西族自治县白沙镇玉湖村下辖 9 个村民小组，农户 383 户，人口 1465 人，其中农业人口 1385 人，劳动力 732 人。全村面积 77.78 平方公里。乡村基础设施不完善，优质高产高效农业匮乏，2003 年，玉湖村经济总收入仅为 234 万元，旅游收入仅为 18 万元。农民年人均纯收入仅为 937 元，人均有粮 300 多公斤，吃粮靠返销、花钱靠贷款、生产靠救济，是丽江市典型的后进村。

措施

1. 创新发展机制。按照“依法、自愿、有偿”的原则，通过转让、出租、转包、入股、互换等方式，创新农村土地流转机制；鼓励农户以荒地入股、栽种时出力出肥，由村合作社投资苗木、管理经营，见效后农户按入股面积分红、合作社适当提成的方式，切实增加农民收入；通过成立旅游开发合作社，组织全体村民合作开发，共享旅游发展的成果。在收益分配上，把总收入按照适当比例划分为旅游促销费、个人所得、管理人员工资、办公经费、基础设施建设资金、教育基金、特困救济金和年底全员再次分配金，每家每户都参与旅游经营，全村形成“人人参与旅游，个个忙于做事，集中精力挣大钱，专心致志奔小康”的局面。

2. 盘活旅游业。玉湖村充分发挥自然景观、民族文化资源优势，着力发展极具纳西古村落与纳西民族文化特色的乡村旅游，已形成特色民居建筑群、洛克故居、黑白水古战场遗址、白沙细乐、东巴文化、民风民俗等文化旅游景点。辖区内乡村民宿发展较好，旅游产品体系日渐成熟，基础设施和公共服务不断完善，形成了以玉湖旅游合作社为主，以村民自发参与的旅游客栈、旅游餐饮、旅游购物为辅的旅游产业格局。

3. 发展养殖业。充分利用和整合3万多亩草地和草坡资源，通过品种改良、草场建设、扶持专业大户等措施，大力发展牛、羊等畜牧养殖业；进一步做好“水文章”，加强水源地保护和水源区水利设施建设，在建成玉湖水库、加紧建设文海水库的基础上，修建若干梯级小水库和小水塘坝、小围堰等，利用水质好、气候冷凉等特点，发展“虹鳟鱼”等高端水产养殖业，并培育成重点产业。

成效

玉湖村经济收入从2003年的234万元增加到2020年的1600万元，旅游总收入从2003年的18万元增加到2020年的逾1200万元，村民年人均纯收入从2003年的937元增加到2020年的10000多元。目前，全村参与旅游服务人员接近800人。玉湖村先后获得“中国传统村落名录”“中国少数民族特色村寨”“中国美丽休闲乡村”“中国宜居村庄”“全国乡村旅游重点村”等多项殊荣，成为丽江市“生态、文化、旅游、和谐”的示范村，吸引了众多的国内外游客。

经验与启示

玉湖村坚持以实现共同富裕为根本出发点和落脚点，实施“生态立村、旅游富村、文化兴村”三大战略。

1. 生态立村。玉湖村加强生态环境保护，以环保制度、旅游发展、项目建设、绿色产业、整治村容村貌“五个带动”为重点，使玉湖村从生态文明建设中受益和发展。玉湖村结合自身实际，优先

把改善乡村环境、提高群众生活质量作为建设重点，先后投入 300 多万元，完成了 2500 米柏油路建设、710 米村道硬化、3000 多米的兴玉渠建设；修建了停车场、管理房、环保厕所、景观水系；实施了全村人畜饮水工程，使村民都喝上了清洁甘甜的自来水；补助实施了 123 户庭院美化、厕所净化工程；新建了村卫生室，由村集体出资，让每个村民参加新型农村合作医疗；以教育基金为保障，加大教育投入，创办农民夜校，开办多期旅游服务技能及种养实用技术等培训讲座，提高群众的旅游服务意识，丰富其科技知识。

2. 旅游富村。玉湖村以全村共同致富为目标，走合作开发新模式。玉湖村能够正确处理好人与人、户与户之间的关系，通过成立旅游开发合作社，组织全体村民合作开发，共享旅游发展的成果。重点开发了“沿着洛克足迹，走进玉龙雪山”为主题的骑马徒步生态观光旅游，村民在合作社统一调度和安排下，以户为单位，轮流参与。在收益分配上，把总收入按照适当比例划分，每家每户都参与旅游经营，全村不分老幼均能参加年终分红。

3. 文化兴村。玉湖村梳理与重构纳西文化，从“生产生活、精神信仰、文化艺术”三大方面入手，打造“纳西文化 +”模式，推进文旅融合发展。用产业思维重塑特色、用目的地思维重塑吸引力，构建“1+ 1+ 4+ 10+ X”乡村旅游体系，即：1 特色马经济（骑马体验、场景演绎、马术培训）+ 1 创意旅拍（全球旅拍第一目的地）+ 4 大导流项目（好好生活雪山音乐节、小小骑士茶马古道基地、低空飞行基地、自然博物探索基地）+ 10 大非遗院落（白沙细乐院、纳西婚俗院、东巴纸艺院、东巴木雕院、纳西小吃街、网红游客中心、沉浸式街区演绎、高端主题民宿、纳西风情民宿、野奢营地）+ X 个旅游配套。

下一步计划

玉湖村将坚持“生态优先、绿色发展”理念，把农旅融合作为乡村全面振兴的关键抓手，以农促旅、以旅兴农。深入挖掘自然生态、历史文化、民俗民居等特色资源，以“旅游 +、+ 旅游”为突破点，完善旅游基础设施，创新旅游产品开发，助推经营主体不断做大做强；打造自然博物探索基地、小小骑士茶马古道基地、旅拍基地、东巴文字院、白沙细乐院、精品民宿等玉湖村乡村振兴项目，让游客“进得来、留得下、记得住”，让美丽乡村真正红火起来，推动乡村振兴，真正实现“生态美、产业兴、百姓富”的有机统一。

Abstract

In adherence to the pursuit of common prosperity and with the goal of building a well-off, ecological, glamourous and harmonious village, the Yuhu Village, Yulong County, Lijiang City, Yunnan Province, has implemented the strategies of village development through ecology, tourism and culture (underlying the village through ecology, enriching the village through tourism, and revitalizing the village through culture), developed new mechanism, and helped all the villagers become prosperous through the invigoration of the tourism industry and development of the breeding industry.

Challenges and Problems

There are nine village groups in Yuhu Village, Baisha Town, Yulong Naxi Autonomous County, Lijiang City, Yunnan Province, with a land area of 77.78 square kilometers and a population of 1,465 from 383 rural households, including an agricultural population of 1,385 and 732 people for labor force. The village lacks rural infrastructure and has limited high-quality, high-yield and high-efficiency agriculture. In 2003, the total economic income of the village was only RMB 2.34 million, of which RMB 180,000 was tourism income. The local farmers' per capita net income is only RMB 937, while the food per capita more than 300 kilograms.

It is an impoverished village, mainly due to its reliance on back selling for food, financial loans and government production relief.

Measures

1. Develop new mechanism. The new rural land transfer mechanism is developed on the basis of the "lawful, voluntary, and paid" principle through transfer, leasing, subcontracting, shareholding, and exchange. Farmers are encouraged to invest in shares through wasteland and contribute human labor and fertilizers for planting. Village cooperatives are responsible for the investment in nursery stocks and their operation. Farmers will then earn dividends according to their invested land area. Appropriate commissions are given to cooperatives, increasing the income of farmers. All villagers are organized to share in the outcome of tourism development through the establishment of tourism development cooperatives. Income and expenses are categorized into tourism promotion expenses, personal income, salaries of managerial staff, office expenses, funds on infrastructure construction, funds on education and relief funds on extreme poverty. Income distribution and year-end redistribution of funds for all staff are determined based on a fair and proportional calculation. This ensures the involvement of households in tourism operations, with each villager engaged in the work so he could earn money and enjoy a moderately prosperous life.

2. Invigorate the tourism industry. The Yuhu Village strives to develop rural tourism in conjunction with the ancient Naxi villages and Naxi ethnic culture. The latter's favorable natural landscape and ethnic cultural resources have led to the creation of cultural tourist attractions, including typical native residential buildings, the Former Residence of Rock, the Battlefield Site of Heibaishui in Lijiang City, Baisha Xiyue (ancient music of the Naxi Nationality), Dongba Culture, and folk tradition and customs. The village boasts a sound rural B&B development, gradually maturing tourism product system and constantly improving infrastructure and public services. It has developed a tourism industry framework with tourism cooperatives as the mainstay, supplemented by tourism inn, catering and spontaneous shopping by villagers.

3. Develop the breeding industry. More than 30,000 *mu* of grassland and grass slope resources are fully utilized and integrated. Cattle, sheep and other stockbreeding are developed through species improvement, grassland construction and support for large and specialized family operations. The protection of water source regions and construction of water conservancy facilities in source areas are reinforced. With the construction of Yuhu Reservoir and Wenhai Reservoir, a number of small cascade reservoirs, small dams, small cofferdams, etc., are also built. The high-end red trout aquaculture of the red trout is successfully developed into a key industry due to the area's excellent water quality and cold climate.

Results

The village income increased from RMB 2.34 million in 2003 to RMB 16 million in 2020. Total tourism income increased from RMB 180,000 in 2003 to over RMB 12 million in 2020, while the villagers' per capita net income increased from RMB 937 in 2003 to more than RMB 10,000 in 2020. Currently, nearly 800 villagers are engaged in tourism services. More admirably, the village has won many honors such as a traditional Chinese villages list, a village with Chinese ethnic minority styles, a beautiful leisure village in China, a livable village in China, and national key village in rural tourism. It has become a demonstration village for "ecology, culture, tourism and harmony" in Lijiang City, attracting many local and foreign tourists.

Experience and Inspirations

In adherence to the pursuit of common prosperity, the Yuhu Village has implemented development strategies through ecology, tourism and culture. Ecology underpins its sustainability, while tourism is enriching the village and culture is revitalizing it.

1. Ecology as the underpin for tourism development. The Yuhu Village has strengthened the ecological and environmental protection system to develop tourism, benefit the green industry and improve its look and style. Guided by its priority of boosting its rural environment and its villagers' quality of life, the Yuhu Village has invested more than RMB 3 million for the construction of 2,500 meters of asphalt roads, the hardening of 710 meters of village roads, and the construction of more than 3,000 meters of Xingyu Canal. Parking lots, management offices, environmentally friendly toilets and landscape water system have been built. The drinking water project for men and livestock is implemented, giving villagers the opportunity to drink clean and sweet tap water. A total of 123 projects that include courtyard beautification and toilet purification are launched from a subsidy. Village clinics are newly built with funds contributed by village collectives, thus making medical services accessible to villages and new rural cooperatives. Through an educational funding support, investment in education is reinforced. Farmers' night schools featuring multiple training seminars on tourism service skills and practical techniques for planting and breeding are established, increasing the villagers' awareness and knowledge of the tourism industry.

2. Enriching the village through tourism. With

its goal of achieving prosperity, the Yuhu Village has developed a new model of cooperative development. With the proper address of the relationship among people and through the establishment of tourism development cooperatives, villagers are organized to make a collective effort for development and the outcome of tourism development shared by everyone. The ecological sightseeing tour of horse-riding and hiking with the theme of "Into Yulong Snow Mountain by Following Rock's Footprint" is pinpointed for development. Under the unified arrangement for cooperatives, villagers take turns engaging in the project, with each household as a unit. The total income is proportionally divided for income distribution, thus ensuring the involvement and participation of each household engages in the tourism operation and allow all villagers, young and old, to obtain year-end dividends.

3. Revitalizing the village through culture. The reconstruction and understanding of the Naxi culture allows the Yuhu Village to promote integrated cultural development. It is dedicated to the development of a "Naxi culture +" derived from all aspects of "production and life, spiritual belief, culture and art." An industry mindset is adopted to reshape tourism products and their brand allure while staying true to their native characteristics and build a "1 + 1 + 4 + 10 + X" rural tourism system as follows: one characteristic horse-related economy (horse-riding experience, scene interpretation, equestrian training), one creative photo-shooting tour (Top 1 destination for travel photography worldwide), four diversion projects ("Enjoy

Life" Snow Mountain Music Festival, "Little Knights" Ancient Tea Horse Road Base, Low-altitude Flight Base, Natural Museum Exploration Base), 10 intangible heritage yards (Baisha Xiyue Yard, Naxi Wedding Customs Yard, Dongba Paper Art Yard, Dongba Wood Carving Yard, Naxi Snack Street, Internet Celebrity Visitor Center, Immersive Block Interpretation, High-end Themed B&Bs, Naxi Style B&Bs, Luxury Camps), and X supporting projects for tourism.

Next Steps

In compliance with the concept of ecological priority and green development, the village will take the integration of agriculture and tourism as the key to overall rural revitalization. Characteristic resources such as natural ecology, historical culture and folk customs and folk residences will be extensively utilized. Tourism infrastructure will be improved, and new tourism products will be developed with "tourism + , + tourism" as a breakthrough for the facilitation of a stronger and more sophisticated business entities. Rural revitalization projects such as the Natural Museum Exploration Base, "Little Knights" Ancient Tea Horse Road Base, Travel Photography Base, Dongba Characters Yard, Baisha Xiyue Yard and boutique B&Bs will be developed, providing convenient access to tourists and leaving them with enduring favorable impressions. A flourishing development can be achieved in this beautiful village, and rural revitalization can be advanced to attain the organic unity of "beautiful ecology, prosperous industry, and rich people."

西藏拉萨市尼木县卡如乡卡如村：
“核乡寻忆”沟域休闲项目模式

Karru Village, Karru Township, Nyêmo County, Lhasa City, Xizang Autonomous Region:
“Memory in Walnut Town” Leisure Valley Project Model

摘 要

西藏自治区拉萨市尼木县卡如村通过采取“公司+合作社+农户”的运营模式，形成了政府主导、企业运营、合作社参股、农牧民增收的“三位一体”产业扶贫模式，积极增加内生动力，挖掘旅游资源。“核乡寻忆”沟域休闲项目按照“完善配套、提升供给、产业融合、振兴乡村”的原则，夯实项目产业振兴基础，以文旅产业为抓手，更好地带动当地村民就业，促进产业、生态、组织、文化和人才的发展，实现精准扶贫。2018 年 10 月，全村实现脱贫，走上乡村振兴之路。

挑战与问题

西藏拉萨市尼木县卡如村地处雅鲁藏布江中游北岸的高山峡谷地带，是拉萨市的“西大门”，境内有 318 国道通过，是日喀则进入拉萨的必经之地，距离县政府 20 公里，平均海拔 3920 米。卡如村下辖 3 个自然组，2018 年全村共有 110 户 558 人，其中劳动力 264 人，残疾人 12 人，低保户 9 户 34 人。全村耕地面积为 299.6 亩，人均仅有 0.54 亩。全村草场面积为 69415.2 亩，林地面积为 134 亩，全村牲畜有 1300 头。当地农牧业不发达，收入渠道少，劳动力流失严重。

措施

1. 促进农旅融合。运用“自营 + 合作”方式，实现特色农产品销售，与卡如村建档立卡贫困户签订合作协议，打造藏家桃树茶园和老阿妈青稞酒坊，以引导客源的方式向外输出高原特色农副产品，推进农业现代化。充分挖掘当地文旅资源，积极保护森林、湿地等生态旅游资源，大力发展乡村旅游，开发精品旅游线路，以大力发展旅游业。建成以百亩桃园、游客接待中心、非遗展示中心、卡如温泉驿站和千年核桃树为内容的卡如村“核乡寻忆”沟域休闲区。

2. 创新项目建设。卡如村在北京援助资金的支持下，大力发展沟域经济，对传统农业、文化旅游产业进行融合发展。卡如村“核乡寻忆”沟域休闲区项目以集休闲农业、森林观光、民俗体验、文化旅游、天然温泉、餐饮住宿等功能于一体的沟域文旅生态休闲区，为游客提供“食、住、行、游、购、娱”的全方位配套服务。项目旨在增强对藏地原乡文化的保护、传承与发展，打造尼木县全域旅游的重要结点，发展文旅产业，以促进精准扶贫和当地农牧民的可持续发展。

3. 挖掘传统文化。尼木县作为“拉萨的作坊”，是传统手工艺人的栖息地，拥有藏靴、藏陶、藏鼓等 8 个非遗项目（其中，国家级三项、自治区级五项），其中尼木藏香、雪拉藏纸、普松雕刻合称“尼木三绝”。卡如村积极发展特色民族手工艺文化，引入尼木县国家级、自治区级非遗传承人及其代表性作品，在满足游客体验需求的同时培养非遗传承人，真正实现对西藏非遗文化的保护、传承、发扬和创新。

4. 加强设施建设。近年来，为适应尼木县全域旅游、乡村旅游发展的需要，尼木县不断完善交通、住宿、公共环境等各项基础设施。尼木县卡如村投资 2500 万元对村容村貌和基础设施进行完善，通过实施“厕所革命”、对污水进行集中处理、进行垃圾分类管理，整治村容村貌。卡如村目前已建设游客中心 1 个，并配有 1 个可同时容纳 40 辆自驾车的停车场，以及一定数量的旅游厕所，一切皆以服务游客为宗旨。

成效

卡如村“核乡寻忆”项目通过采取“公司 + 合作社 + 农户”的运营模式，形成了政府主导、企

业运营、合作社参股、促进农牧民增收的“三位一体”产业扶贫模式。2018 年，该项目为 59 户建档立卡贫困户和边缘户以及项目所在地的 24 户村民分红，共计分红 32 万余元。此次分红，以“真金白银”的方式增加了贫困户对脱贫致富的信心。一期、二期项目总体建成以来，不断为合作社提供分红收益，老阿妈青稞酒坊和格桑小院民宿每年各分红 2.4 万元，为当地群众提供就业岗位 26 个，其中卡如温泉驿站解决 13 人就业、卡如景区解决 13 人就业，每人每月平均工资 2800 元。卡如沟域经济项目运营以来，2018 年盈利收入中给当地贫困户年底分红资金 30 万元，2019 年分红 50 万元，2020 年分红 30 万元，帮助 11 户 51 人顺利实现脱贫。

经验与启示

1. 以村民为中心，打造宜居乡村。项目建设首先要以对村容村貌和基础配套设施水平的提升为基础。生态宜居是实现乡村振兴的关键，也是发展乡村旅游的根本。通过对项目地村民住房实行“三改一整”，实现对生活环境的改造提升，打造人与自然和谐共生的乡村发展新格局，最终实现百姓富、生态美的统一。

2. 以市场为导向，完善项目供给。项目定位为区域级旅游聚集点，以市场需求为导向，完善项目配套，形成了以“民俗接待区”为先导、以“森林度假区”为延展、以“驿站休闲区”为重心的多层次文旅产品。其中，“民俗接待区”以乡风乡貌民俗体验为基础；“森林度假区”依托尼木国家森林公园，突出体现高原独特的生态风貌；“驿站休闲区”在充分结合温室种植的基础上，挖掘天然温泉、本地特色餐饮，打造综合休闲服务区。

3. 以产业为抓手，巩固扶贫成效。项目建设通过文化旅游业融合农业发展的产业发展模式，有效改善了区域产业结构，形成了以“三产消化一产、带动二产，一产、二产反哺支撑三产发展”的产业闭合，夯实了区域“产业振兴”的基础。产业发展过程中，对本地村民因地制宜地开展职业技能、服务意识、服务规范等方面的培养，促进本地村民就业技能的提升和思想意识的改变，实现“扶贫、扶智和扶志”，进一步巩固了扶贫成果。

下一步计划

1. 大力提升综合配套水平。围绕“食、住、行、游、购、娱”六要素，建设卡如温泉驿站二期项目等，提升硬件设施水平。完善卡如村农旅功能要素，提升服务接待水平，做到“食有特色、住有条件、行有基础、游有内容、购有商品、娱有活动”。

2. 大力提升优质服务。紧紧围绕游客需求，持续完善卡如“核乡寻忆”景区和温泉驿站饮食、住宿、购物等生活服务，优化文明引导、紧急救护等志愿服务，在游客旅游全过程中提供无微不至、体贴周到的服务。

3. 大力提升宣传力度。依托“雅江河谷”“卡如温泉”“卡如千年核桃古树”“卡如桃林种植基地”“赤朗国家森林公园”等优质资源优势，邀请网络知名媒体加大旅游宣传、推广力度；与旅游景区加强合作，积极利用“两微一端”、抖音、快手等社交媒体加强线上、线下的宣传工作。

Abstract

Karru Village, Karru Township, Nyêmo County, Lhasa City, Xizang's Autonomous Region, has adopted the "companies + cooperatives + peasant households" framework to create a "trinity" of poverty alleviation model through industrial development with the government playing the dominant role. The project, however, is run by enterprises with the participation of cooperatives to increase the income of villagers and herdsmen. This setup is expected to enhance the endogenous influence of the villagers and motivate them to proactively explore tourism resources. The "Memory in Walnut Town" Leisure Valley Project adheres to the principle of "improving supporting facilities, upgrading supplies, integrating industries and achieving rural revitalization." It enhances the foundation for the revitalization industry, focuses on the cultural and tourism industry and powers the employment of local villagers. This project also promotes industrial, ecological, organizational, cultural and talents development for a targeted poverty alleviation. In October 2018, the whole village was lifted out of poverty and embarked on beginning its own journey to rural revitalization.

Challenges and Problems

Karru Village is located in the alpine and gorge region on the north bank of the middle reaches of the Yarlung Zangbo River and serves as the west gate of Lhasa City. It is the only way connecting Shigatse City and Lhasa City via the National Highway. It is 20 kilometers away from the county government and has an average altitude of 3,920 meters. In 2018, there were 558 people in 110 households, with 264 labor force, 12 disabled, 34 and 9 low-income individuals and households respectively. The arable land of the whole village is 299.6 *mu*, only 0.54 *mu* per capita. The grassland area is 69,415.2 *mu* and the forest area 134 *mu*. It has 1,300 livestock. The local agriculture and animal husbandry are underdeveloped, with limited income opportunities and severe labor shortage.

Measures

1. Promote the integration of agriculture and tourism. We use the "self-support plus cooperation" method to assess the sales of characteristic agricultural products. In addition, there was a Cooperation Agreement with the filed poor households in Karru Village to build the Xizang's peach tree & tea garden and Old Alma Highland Barley Distillery. This agreement also called for the exportation of the characteristic agricultural and other derivate products produced on the plateau as well as guiding customers for agricultural modernization. Tapping into local cultural and tourism resources, developing forest, wetland and other ecotourism projects will help with the rural tourism development. More importantly, the building of "Memory in Walnut Town" Leisure Valley Area on 100 *mu* of peach forest, tourist reception center, the intangible cultural heritage exhibition center, Kara hot spring station and 1000-year old walnut trees will greatly accelerate the development of the village's tourism economy.

2. Innovate projects. With Beijing's financial assistance, the village works hard to develop its valley economy and integrate the traditional agriculture and cultural tourism industries. "Memory in Walnut Town" Leisure Valley Project in Karru refers to a culture-tourism ecological leisure area that integrates leisure agriculture and contains the following: forest sightseeing, folk custom experience, cultural tourism, natural hot spring, catering and accommodation, a full range of tourist-supporting services of "meals + dining, living, traveling, tourism, entertainment, and shopping." It is designed to enhance the protection, preservation and development of Xizang's native culture by building an important node of the whole-region tourism in Nyêmo County. Also, it will develop the cultural tourism industry to promote targeted poverty alleviation and sustainable development for the benefit of local peasants and herdsmen.

3. Explore traditional culture. As the "workshop of Lhasa," Nyêmo County gathers traditional craftsmen and boasts intangible cultural heritage, three of which are on national level. Of these, five are on the autonomous region level, including Xizang's boots, Xizang's pottery and Xizang's drums. Among them, as well are the Nyêmo Xizang's incense, Shera Xizang's paper and Pu Song carving which are collectively known as "three wonders of Nyêmo." The village cultivates its characteristic national handicraft, representative work by nurturing successors from Nyêmo County to its cultural heritage. It also promotes the legacy, protection and innovation of Xizang's intangible cultural heritage.

4. Strengthen facility construction. To meet the development needs of the whole region and the county's rural tourism, the village worked in recent years to improve various infrastructure such as transportation, accommodation and public environment. The village has invested RMB 25 million to improve its appearance and infrastructure, implement the "toilet revolution" and conduct a centralized sewage treatment and classified garbage management. To serve tourists in the country, it has presently built a tourist center, a parking lot for 40 self-driving vehicles, and a number of tourist toilets.

Results

The project has adopted the operation mode of "companies + cooperatives + peasant households" to create a "trinity" of poverty alleviation model through industrial development with the government playing a leading role. This is operated by private enterprises with the participation of cooperatives, resulting in the increase of the income of peasants and herdsmen. In 2018, 59 recorded poor households, marginal households and 24 households in the project' site received dividends totaling more than RMB 320,000. The dividend is given in "genuine gold and silver," leading them to gain confidence in their ability to improve their standard of living. Since the overall completion of phase I and phase II, the project has provided dividend income for cooperatives. The highland barley distillery and Gesang Courtyard B&Bs have received a dividend of RMB 24,000 each year, provided 26 jobs for local people, including 13 in Karru hot springs station and 13 in Karru scenic spot, with an average monthly salary of RMB 2,800 per person. Since the project's operation, local impoverished households received profit-derived dividends of RMB 300,000 in

2018, RMB 500,000 in 2019 and RMB 300,000 in 2020. A total of 51 people from 11 households were successfully lifted out of poverty.

Experience and Inspirations

1. The first phase of the project is the building of a livable village for villagers. Since ecological livability is not only the key to rural revitalization but also the foundation of rural tourism, the improvement of village appearance and infrastructure is a priority. Through the implementation of "three changes and one renovation" for houses in the project area, the transformation and improvement of the living environment is expected to unify wealth and ecological beauty and create a new rural development framework of harmonious coexistence between man and nature.

2. The second phase will improve the market-oriented project supply. It is positioned as a regional tourism gathering point to meet market demand and improve project supporting facilities for a multi-level cultural and tourism product with a rural-style "folk reception area" as the guide, "forest resort" as extension and "hot spring leisure area" as the focus. With the Nyêmo National Forest Park as the centerpiece, "forest resort" highlights the unique ecological style of the plateau. "Hot spring leisure area" fully combines greenhouse planting, excavates natural hot springs and local characteristic catering to create a comprehensive leisure service area.

3. The third phase zeroes in on the industry as the starting point to consolidate the results of poverty alleviation. The construction of the project is based on the industrial development model of integrating cultural tourism with agricultural development. So far, this has improved the regional industrial structure, formed an industrial loop where the tertiary industry assimilates the primary industry and drives the secondary industry. The primary and secondary industries circles back to support the tertiary industry. This phase also consolidates the foundation of a regional "industrial revitalization." At an industrial development, local villagers were trained with vocational skills, service awareness and service norms according to local conditions. This helped scale

up their employment skills and elevate their ideological awareness. "Ambition and education support prior to poverty alleviation" was achieved to consolidate the achievements of poverty alleviation.

Next Steps

1. Improve comprehensive supporting facilities. We shall focus on the six elements of "meals + dining, living, traveling, tourism, entertainment, and shopping." In addition, we will build the hot springs station as Phase II of the project and upgrade facilities in the process. Meanwhile, we shall improve the functional elements of agricultural tourism in Karru Village, standardize its service and reception to fulfill the goal of "characteristic food, comfortable living conditions for all as well as transportation foundation, meaningful journey, abundant goods and colorful activities."

2. Enhance quality service. To keep the tourists' needs top of mind, we will continue to improve living services such as catering, accommodation and shopping in the scenic spots. Hot spring stations, voluntary services such as cordial guidance will provide tourists excellent all-around services.

3. Increase publicity. Based on excellent resources such as "Yajiang Valley," "Karru hot springs," "Karru walnut tree of thousands of years," "Karru peach planting base" and "Chi Lang National Forest Park," we shall invite KOLs of well-known internet media for publicity and promotion. Also, we will cooperate with tourist attractions for the proactive use of their public accounts on Weibo, WeChat, news client, Tik Tok and Kuaishou, etc.

2018—2020 旅游减贫案例回顾

2018—2020 Tourism Poverty Alleviation Practice

2018

01/ 安徽金寨小南京村：多措并举、融合发展旅游扶贫
Xiaonanjing Village, Jinzhai County, Anhui Province: Multiple Measures and Integrated Development of Pro-poor Tourism

02/ 重庆武隆区："旅游 +N" 多产业融合发展
Wulong District, Chongqing Municipality: "Tourism + N" Multiple Industries Integration Development

03/ 河北涞水野三坡："双带四起来" 旅游减贫新模式
Yesanpo, Laishui County, Hebei Province: Tourism Poverty Alleviation New Model "Double Drive Factors and Four Establishments"

04/ 河南栾川重渡沟："水 + 竹"——农家特色旅游扶贫
Chongdugou, Luanchuan County, Henan Province: "Water + Bamboo" — Rural Pro-poor Tourism

05/ 湖北大冶龙凤山："三产融合" 旅游扶贫
Longfeng Mountain, Daye City, Hubei Province: "Integration of Triple Industries" Poverty Alleviation

06/ 湖南花垣十八洞村：农旅一体 "以一带四"
Shibadong Village, Huayuan County, Hunan Province: "Four Mobilized by One" Poverty Alleviation through Agricultural and Tourism Integration

07/ 江西大余丫山：旅游扶贫 "三级受益"
Ya Mountain, Dayu County, Jiangxi Province: Tourism Poverty Alleviation "Three-level Benefit"

08/ 山东淄博中郝裕村：公司化运作乡村旅游扶贫
Zhonghaoyu Village, Zibo City, Shandong Province: Rural Pro-poor Tourism in Incorporate Operation Way

09/ 中青旅：践行企业社会责任、实施旅游精准扶贫
CYTS: Practice Corporate Social Responsibility and Implement Targeted Poverty Alleviation through Tourism

10/ 华侨城：三亚中廖村文化旅游 + 美丽乡村建设
Overseas Chinese Town Holdings Company: Culture Tourism + Beautiful Countryside Construction in Zhongliao Village of Sanya City

11/ 爱彼迎：分享住宿助力印度乡村妇女减贫
Airbnb: Empower Women through Home-sharing in Rural India

12/ 地中海俱乐部：全球化与支持小农户发展
Club Med: Globalization and Support Small Peasant Households' Development

13/ 福建寿宁下党村：红色旅游新地标
Xiadang Village, Shouning County, Fujian Province: Red Tourism New Landmark

14/ 甘肃甘南藏族自治州：旅游扶贫减贫
Gannan Xizang's Autonomous Prefecture, Gansu Province: Poverty Alleviation through Tourism

15/ 广西富川岔山村：古道繁华，旅游扶贫走出一片艳阳天
Chashan Village, Fuchuan County, Guangxi Province: Ancient Road Successfully Lifts Chashan Out of Poverty

16/ 贵州黔西南纳孔村：产业融合与民俗文化融合
Nakong Village, Qianxinan Buyei and Miao Autonomous Prefecture, Guizhou Province: Industry Convergence and Folk Culture Convergence

17/ 海南保亭槟榔谷：打造“富游 + 富农，景区 + 农户”共同体
Hainan Baoting Betel Nut Valley: Build "Rich Tourism + Rich Farmers, Scenic Area + Peasant Households" Community

18/ 鄂旅投减贫：开发一个景区，带活一方经济，致富一方百姓
ECOTIC Poverty Alleviation: Develop a Scenic Area to Bring Local Economy and Enrich Local People

19/ 江苏宜兴白塔村：乡贤白塔，乡村振兴的践行者
Baita Village, Yixing City, Jiangsu Province: Virtuous Baita Becomes an Practicer of Rural Revitalization

20/ 宁夏西吉龙王坝村：穷山村实现了华丽变身
Longwangba Village, Xiji County, Ningxia Hui Autonomous Region: Big Change for A Poor Mountain Village

21/ 陕西留坝：探索乡村旅游开发扶贫新路子
Liuba County, Shaanxi Province: Explore New Methods of Rural Tourism Development and Poverty Alleviation through All-for-one Tourism

22/ 四川稻城麻格同村：创新理念，激发乡村旅游内生动力
Magetong Village, Daocheng County, Sichuan Province: Stimulate Rural Tourism with Innovative Ideas

23/ 天津蓟州区郭家沟：休闲养生地，山水郭家沟
Guojiagou, Jizhou District, Tianjin Municipality: Place of Leisure and Health Preservation, Landscape of Mountain and River

24/ 新疆生产建设兵团第十师 185 团：特色旅游扶贫模式
The 185th Regiment of 10th Division of Xinjiang Production and Construction Corps: Characteristic Tourism Poverty Alleviation Model

25/ 中国国际航空股份有限公司：突出地方特色，量身定制旅游产业帮扶
Air China Limited: Highlight Local Features and Tailors Tourism Support Plan

26/ 中国铁旅：与新疆旅游互通的桥梁
CRTS: A Tourism Bridge Connecting with Xinjiang

27/ 同程旅游：助力“梵天净土、桃源铜仁”品牌升级
Tongcheng Travel: Help to Upgrade the Brand of “Heaven on Earth, Idyllic Tongren”

28/ 途牛：旅游扶贫，为爱前行
Tuniu.com: Tourism-based Poverty Alleviation for Love

29/ 携程：“美丽乡村”旅游专区打造，助力乡村振兴
Ctrip: Build “Beautiful Countryside” Tourism Zone to Boost Rural Revitalization

2019

01/ 贵州遵义花茂村：精准扶贫与环境治理并重，乡村振兴新范本
Huamao Village, Zunyi City, Guizhou Province: Precision Poverty Alleviation & Environmental Management — a New Model of Rural Revitalization

02/ 世界银行：保护甘肃文化遗产，惠及百姓生活
World Bank: Protect Gansu’s Cultural Heritage and Improving People’s Livelihood

03/ 杭州萧山：对口帮扶贵州从江，协作旅游扶贫
Xiaoshan City, Hangzhou Province: Pair-up with Congjiang, Guizhou Province in Tourism Assistance for Poverty Alleviation

04/ 保加利亚“与风之爱”城堡：保护与旅游开发共生之路
“In Love with the Wind” Castle, Bulgaria: Heritage Protection and Tourism Development Going Hand in Hand

05/ 江西婺源篁岭：共享经济领航与复兴“篁岭晒秋”
Huangling Village, Wuyuan County, Jiangxi Province: Revitalize the Scenery of “Autumn Harvest” through Sharing Economy

06/ 爱彼迎：探索共享经济和旅游结合的减贫新模式
Airbnb: Explore a New Model of Precision Poverty Alleviation Combining Shared Accommodation with Tourism

07/ PATA 基金会：越南沙坝实践，构建最富启发意义的负责任旅游
PATA Foundation: Offer New Inspiration on Responsible Tourism at Sa Pa, Vietnam

08/ 山东沂南：全域旅游助力革命老区扶贫亮丽开篇
Yinan County, Shandong Province: All-for-one Tourism Writes a Bright Opening for the Poverty Alleviation of the Old Revolutionary Base Area

09/ 域上和美：探索文旅扶贫的可持续发展模式
Usunhome: Explore a New Model of Poverty Alleviation by Cultural Tourism at Cijuelin Village, Lhasa, Xizang's

10/ 陕旅集团："山花工程•后备厢行动"打造旅游扶贫"陕旅样本"
Shaanxi Tourism Group: Build "Shanhua Project · Car Trunk Action" — a Model of Tourism Poverty Alleviation by Combining "Internet + Destinations"

11/ 世界银行：助推黎巴嫩文化遗产和城市发展项目实现减贫
World Bank: Lebanon Cultural Heritage and Urban Development Project for Poverty Alleviation

12/ 福建泰宁水际村："三大协会"助力库区移民村脱贫
Shuiji Village, Taining County, Fujian Province: "Three Associations" Supports Poverty Alleviation among Reservoir Immigrants

13/ 河北易县狼牙山：中凯集团打造多彩四季美丽经济
Langya Mountain, Yi County, Hebei Province: Zhongkai Group Cultivates New Model of Tourism Development—Colorful Seasons, Beautiful Economy

14/ 川旅集团：文旅融合助推四川稻城麻格同村提前脱贫
Sichuan Tourism Development Group: Assistance in Poverty Alleviation by Integrating Culture with Tourism at Magetong Village, Daocheng County, Sichuan Province

15/ 新疆乌什：全域旅游助力农牧民脱贫增收
Wushi County, Xinjiang Uygur Autonomous Regions: All-for-one Tourism Facilitates the Poverty Alleviation and Income Increase of Farmers and Ranchers

16/ 贵州安顺："塘约经验"新时代农村改革典范
Anshun City, Guizhou Province: "Tangyue Experience" Creates a Model of Rural Reform for the New Era

17/ 安徽霍山堆谷山村：形成"霍山堆谷山现象"乡村旅游实践，激发内生动力
Duigushan Village, Huoshan County, Anhui Province: the "Duigushan Phenomenon"— A Good Practice of Rural Tourism to Stimulate Inner Driving Force for Development

18/ 世界银行：助力孔孟遗产重现辉煌，老城区改造利商惠民
World Bank: Assistance in the Revival of Confucius-Mencius Heritage and Renewal of Old Towns to the Benefit of People and Commerce

19/ 世界银行：综合施策助力格鲁吉亚文化遗产地卡赫基实现振兴
World Bank: An Integrated Approach for the Regeneration of Kakheti, the Cultural Heritage Center of Georgia

20/ 山东枣庄兴隆庄村：欧亚集团助力"旅游＋扶贫"孕育新动能
Xinglongzhuang Village, Zaozhuang City, Shandong Province: Eurasia Group Promotes "Tourism + Poverty Alleviation" to Nurture New Momentum

21/ 河南卢氏县新坪村豫西百草园：景区带村创新“三金扶贫”模式
Yuxi Flower Park, Xinping Village, Lushi County, Henan Province: Create “Rent + Salary + Dividend” Model of Poverty Alleviation through Tourist Site Development

22/ 湖南怀化黄岩：“能人带村 + 村民众筹”的旅游扶贫新模式
Huangyan Township, Huaihua City, Hunan Province: A New Model of Tourism Poverty Alleviation of “Villages Led by Able Villagers + Villagers' Crowdfunding”

23/ 西藏林芝：旅游扶贫精准破解“美丽贫困”
Nyingchi City, Xizang's Autonomous Region: Tourism Poverty Alleviation Offers Precise Solution to “Beautiful Poverty”

24/ 湖南雪峰山：共享旅游经济共同体，构建共享共生共赢的减贫模式
The Xuefeng Mountain, Hunan Province: The Poverty Reduction Model of the Community of Shared Tourism Economy, Featuring Sharing, Joint Development and Win-Win Results

25/ 世界银行：保护传承贵州自然与文化遗产，促进脱贫致富
World Bank: Protect and Inherit the Natural and Cultural Heritage of Guizhou and Promoting Poverty Alleviation and Income Increase

26/ 湖北罗田燕儿谷：村企联建助推旅游精准扶贫
Yan'er Valley, Luotian County, Hubei Province: Village-Enterprise Collaboration Supporting Targeted Poverty Alleviation through Tourism

27/ 广西龙胜：森林旅游扶贫走出全域旅游发展新路子
Longsheng Ethnic Autonomous County, Guangxi Province: Forest Tourism Opens up a New Path of All-for-one Tourism Development

28/ 云南世博集团：推动哈尼梯田遗产保护与旅游减贫融合发展
Yunnan Expo Tourism Group: Explore New Ways to Promote Integrated Development of Heritage Protection and Tourism Poverty Alleviation at Yunnan Yuanyang Hani Rice Terraces

29/ 宁夏六盘山：隆德联社“文化旅游系列贷”助力精准扶贫
Liupanshan Region, Ningxia Hui Autonomous Region: Longde Cooperative Supports Precision Poverty Alleviation with “Cultural Tourism Series Loans”

30/ 字节跳动：山里 DOU 是好风光，抖音成为文旅扶贫新抓手
ByteDance: “Amazing Mountains on Douyin” — Culture Tourism for Poverty Alleviation

2020

01/ 广西河池市巴马瑶族自治县：充分发挥生态优势，打造特色旅游扶贫

Bama Yao Autonomous County, Hechi City, Guangxi Zhuang Autonomous Region: Give Full Play to Ecological Dominance and Create Featured Tour for Poverty Alleviation

02/ 世界银行约旦遗产投资项目：促进城市与文化遗产旅游的协同发展

World Bank Heritage Investment Project in Jordan: Promote Coordinated Development of Urban and Cultural Heritage Tourism

03/ 山东临沂市兰陵县压油沟村："企业 + 政府 + 合作社 + 农户"的组合模式

Yayougou Village, Lanling County, Linyi City, Shandong Province: A Combination Mode of "Enterprises + Government + Cooperatives + Peasant Households"

04/ 江西井冈山市茅坪镇神山村：多项扶贫措施相辅相成，让山区变成景区

Shenshan Village, Maoping Town, Jinggangshan City, Jiangxi Province: Complementary Help-the-poor Measures Turn the Mountainous Area into a Scenic Spot

05/ 中山大学：旅游脱贫的"阿者科计划"

Sun Yat-sen University: Tourism-based Poverty Alleviation Project "Azheke Plan"

06/ 爱彼迎：用"爱彼迎学院模式"助推南非减贫

Airbnb: Promote Poverty Alleviation in South Africa with the "Airbnb Academy Model"

07/ "三区三州"旅游大环线宣传推广联盟：用大 IP 开创地区文化旅游扶贫的新模式

Promotion Alliance for "A Priority in the National Poverty Alleviation Strategy" Circular Tour: Utilize Important IP to Create a New Model of Poverty Alleviation through Cultural Tourism

08/ 山西晋中市左权县：全域旅游走活"扶贫一盘棋"

Zuoquan County, Jinzhong City, Shanxi Province: Alleviate Poverty through All-for-one Tourism

09/ 中国旅行社协会铁道旅游分会：利用专列优势，实现"精准扶贫"

Railway Tourism Branch of China Association of Travel Services: Realize "Targeted Poverty Alleviation" Utilizing the Advantage of Special Trains

10/ 河南信阳市新县田铺乡大塆村：耳目一新的"文创小店 + 乡舍农家 + 特色商品"旅游扶贫模式

Dawan Village, Tianpu Township, Xin County, Xinyang City, Henan Province: Completely Innovative Tourism-Based Poverty Alleviation Mode of "Culture & Creative Shop + Farmhouse + Characteristic Commodities"

11/ 万达集团"包县"帮扶项目：企业通过全要素投入推动可持续脱贫

"Counterpart Support for Counties" Project of Wanda Group: Enterprises Promote Sustainable Poverty Alleviation through Total Factor Input

12/ 穷游网：以文创产品为抓手，推动“文创＋旅行”的多维扶贫实践
QYER: Multi-dimensional Poverty Alleviation Practices of “Cultural and Creative Industry Development + Tourism” Supported by Cultural and Creative Products

13/ 世界银行格鲁吉亚伊梅列季亚州项目：用旅游目的地营销管理组织（DMO）促进私人资本的融资
World Bank Project in Imereti, Georgia: To Promote Private Capital Financing with Destination Management Organization (DMO)

14/ 四川南充市仪陇县朱德故里景区：构建“三模式”，助推“景区带村”旅游扶贫
The Scenic Area of Zhu De's Former Residence in Yilong County, Nanchong City, Sichuan Province: Promote the Poverty Alleviation through Tourism Featuring “Tourism Areas Boosting Village Development” through “Three Models”

15/ 贵州六盘水市水城县海坪村：“六业并举”开创易地扶贫搬迁“海坪模式”
Haiping Village, Shuicheng County, Liupanshui City, Guizhou Province: Build the “Haiping Mode” of Relocation-Based Poverty Alleviation with Six Key Measures

16/ 浙江丽水市遂昌县龙洋乡茶园村：用“情境乡村”建设新路径破解乡村活化难题
Chayuan Village, Longyang Township, Suichang County, Lishui City, Zhejiang Province: Solve Rural Activation Problems through a New Path of “Situational Village” Construction

17/ 中邮传媒助力甘肃甘南藏族自治州舟曲县扶贫行动：立足本行业资源优势，开展旅游精准扶贫
China Post Advertising Co., Ltd. Assists Poverty Alleviation in Zhouqu County, Gannan Xizang's Autonomous Prefecture, Gansu Province: Conduct Targeted Poverty Alleviation through Tourism Based on Resource Advantages of the Industry

18/ 重庆巫山县：“五大措施”探索乡村旅游助推扶贫新模式
Wushan County, Chongqing Municipality: Explore a New Model for Promoting Poverty Alleviation through Village Tourism with “Five Measures”

19/ 西藏拉萨市达东村：“景区带村”模式打造乡村旅游扶贫标杆
Dadong Village, Lhasa City, Xizang's Autonomous Region: Set a Benchmark for Rural Poverty Alleviation through Tourism by the Model of “Driving the Development of Villages with Scenic Areas”

20/ 河北承德市“一号风景大道”：打造风景道品牌，推进“非遗＋扶贫”试点
“No.1 Scenic Avenue” in Chengde City, Hebei Province: Build a Brand of Scenic Avenue and Promote the Pilot of “Intangible Cultural Heritage + Poverty Alleviation”

21/ 贵州黔东南苗族侗族自治州雷山县：大力发展乡村旅游，助推民族村寨脱贫
Leishan County, Qiandongnan Miao and Dong Autonomous Prefecture, Guizhou Province: Strive to Develop Village Tourism to Help Ethnic Villages Get Rid of Poverty

22/ 中国旅游集团：对口帮扶香格里拉，打造标杆项目
China Tourism Group: Provide Counterpart Support to Shangri-La and Build a Benchmarking Project

23/ 湖北恩施土家族苗族自治州宣恩县：紧扣“融合”，全域旅游发展助力脱贫致富
Xuan'en County, Enshi Tujia and Miao Autonomous Prefecture, Hubei Province: Alleviate Poverty through Integration and All-for-one Tourism Development

24/ 四川达州市宣汉县巴山大峡谷景区：文旅扶贫与生态保护相结合，确保真正脱贫奔小康
Bashan Grand Canyon Scenic Area of Xuanhan County, Dazhou City, Sichuan Province: Get Rid of Poverty and Build a Well-off Society Based on a Combination of Poverty Alleviation through Cultural Tourism and Ecological Protection

25/ 甘肃甘南藏族自治州：构建旅游扶贫新模式，探索精准扶贫新路子
Gannan Xizang's Autonomous Prefecture, Gansu Province: Forge a New Mode of Poverty Alleviation through Tourism, Explore New Ways of Targeted Poverty Alleviation

26/ 世界银行埃塞俄比亚旅游业可持续发展项目：克服困难长期推进，PDO 级别成果显著
World Bank Sustainable Tourism Development Project in Ethiopia: Overcome Difficulties, Exert Long-term Efforts and Achieve Remarkable PDO Level Results

27/ 河北保定市阜平县顾家台村、骆驼湾村：有计划、按步骤助力全县脱贫攻坚事业
Gujiatai Village and Luotuowan Village, Fuping County, Baoding City, Hebei Province: Fuel the County's Poverty Alleviation Cause as Planned Step by Step

28/ 山东威海市西山后村：“农户 + 合作社 + 公司”生态旅游开发，助力贫瘠乡村脱贫致富
Xishanhou Village, Weihai City, Shandong Province: Develop Ecological Tourism through the “Peasant Households + Cooperatives + Companies” Mode for Poverty Alleviation

29/ 内蒙古鄂尔多斯市乌审旗：激发精准扶贫内生动力，为乡村振兴注入新活力
Wushen Banner, Erdos City, Inner Mongolia Autonomous Region: Stimulate the Inner Driving Force for Targeted Poverty Alleviation and Inject New Vitality into Rural Revitalization

30/ 福建宁德市屏南县龙潭村：用“文创 + 旅游”模式激发乡村减贫内生动力
Longtan Village, Pingnan County, Ningde City, Fujian Province: Stimulate the Inner Driving Force for Rural Poverty Reduction with the Mode of “Culture and Creative Industry + Tourism”

31/ 安徽六安市霍山县陡沙河村：从贫困乡村到高端生态旅游度假村的涅槃
Doushahe Village, Huoshan County, Lu'an City, Anhui Province: Nirvana from an Impoverished Village to a Hi-end Ecological Tourism Resort

32/ 浙江杭州市淳安县下姜村：打好脱贫攻坚战，旅游减贫成效明显
Xiajiang Village, Chun'an County, Hangzhou City, Zhejiang Province: Win the Battle Against Poverty, and Achieve Remarkable Progress in Poverty Alleviation through Tourism

33/ 四川甘孜藏族自治州稻城县：坚持“旅游 + 扶贫”思路，探索“定制服务”脱贫模式
Daocheng County, Garze Xizang's Autonomous Prefecture, Sichuan Province: Stick to the “Tourism + Poverty Alleviation” Idea, and Explore the Poverty Alleviation Mode through “Customized Services”

34/ 世界银行马其顿共和国斯科普里旧巴扎项目：对当地文化遗产的投资显著提振经济和社会的双重发展
World Bank Project in Old Bazaar, Skopje City, the Republic of Macedonia: Investment in Local Cultural Heritage Has Significantly Boosted both Economic and Social Development

35/ 陕西安康市石泉县后柳镇中坝村：凭借“作坊小镇项目”实现旅游减贫
Zhongba Village, Houliu Town, Shiquan County, Ankang City, Shaanxi Province: Realize Poverty Alleviation through Tourism Based on the “Workshop Town” Project

36/ 内蒙古赤峰市喀喇沁旗西桥镇雷营子村：精准定位乡村旅游，让大山里的美景带来财富
Leiyingzi Village, Xiqiao Town, Harqin Banner, Chifeng City, Inner Mongolia Autonomous Region: Turn Beautiful Sceneries in Mountains into Wealth through Precise Positioning of Village Tourism

37/ 北京城建集团北苑大酒店下栅子村“大城小苑”精品民宿群：全面发力打赢“一企一村”精准扶贫攻坚战
“Dacheng Xiaoyuan” Boutique Homestay Cluster in Xiazhazi Village Developed by Beiyuan Grand Hotel under Beijing Urban Construction Group Co., Ltd.: Make All-out Efforts to Win the Battle against Targeted Poverty Alleviation through “One Enterprise for One Village”

38/ 河北石家庄市平山县西柏坡镇梁家沟村：红色旅游助力老区脱贫致富
Liangjiagou Village, Xibaipo Town, Pingshan County, Shijiazhuang City, Hebei Province: “Red Tourism” Helps Old Areas Get Rid of Poverty and Increase Income

39/ 黑龙江双鸭山市饶河县小南河村：另辟“摄影旅游基地”蹊径，实现脱贫致富梦
Xiaonanhe Village, Raohe County, Shuangyashan City, Heilongjiang Province: Achieve Poverty Alleviation through Tourism with a Unique Method of Building a “Photographic Tourism Base”

40/ 河南济源市：农旅融合创新帮扶，精准施策兴村富民
Jiyuan City, Henan Province: Alleviate Poverty by Combining Agriculture and Tourism and Increasing the Income of Farmers with Targeted Measures

41/ 吉林延边朝鲜族自治州光东村：主打少数民族特色的“民俗观光游”，助力脱贫奔康
Guangdong Village, Yanbian Korean Autonomous Prefecture, Jilin Province: “Folk Customs Sightseeing” with Ethnic Minority Characteristics Boosts Poverty Alleviation

42/ 安徽六安市金寨县渔潭村：利用“五个着力”，绘制乡村旅游扶贫蓝图
Yutan Village, Jinzhai County, Lu’an City, Anhui Province: Draw the Rural Poverty Alleviation Blueprint through Tourism with “Five Underlying Points”

责任编辑：杨沛武
责任印制：冯冬青

图书在版编目（CIP）数据

2021世界旅游联盟－旅游助力乡村振兴案例：汉英对照/《2021世界旅游联盟－旅游助力乡村振兴案例》编写组编．-- 北京：中国旅游出版社，2021.12
ISBN 978-7-5032-6876-2

Ⅰ.①2… Ⅱ.①2… Ⅲ.①乡村旅游—旅游业发展—经济发展战略—研究—中国—汉、英 Ⅳ.①F592.3

中国版本图书馆CIP数据核字（2021）第263902号

书　　名：2021世界旅游联盟—旅游助力乡村振兴案例

作　　者：《2021世界旅游联盟－旅游助力乡村振兴案例》编写组　编
合作出版：中国旅游出版社　世界旅游联盟
（北京静安东里6号　邮编：100028）
http://www.cttp.net.cn　E-mail: cttp@mct.gov.cn
营销中心电话：010-57377108，010-57377109
读者服务部电话：010-57377151
排　　版：北京中文天地文化艺术有限公司
印　　刷：北京工商事务印刷有限公司
版　　次：2021年12月第1版　2021年12月第1次印刷
开　　本：787毫米×1092毫米　1/16
印　　张：24.75
字　　数：326千
定　　价：98.00元
I S B N　978-7-5032-6876-2